RADICAL DUKE

Also by

DANIELLE ALLEN

Cuz: The Life and Times of Michael A.

Our Declaration: A Reading of the Declaration of Independence in Defense of Equality

RADICAL DUKE

How One
ARISTOCRAT—
and the **AMERICAN**
REVOLUTION—
Transformed **BRITAIN**

DANIELLE ALLEN

Liveright Publishing Corporation
A Division of W. W. Norton & Company
Independent Publishers Since 1923

Printed in the United States of America
First Edition

For information about permission to reproduce selections from this book, write to Permissions, Liveright Publishing Corporation, a division of W. W. Norton & Company, Inc., 500 Fifth Avenue, New York, NY 10110

For information about special discounts for bulk purchases, please contact W. W. Norton Special Sales at specialsales@wwnorton.com or 800-233-4830

Manufacturing by Lakeside Book Company
Book design by Barbara M. Bachman
Production manager: Lauren Abbate

ISBN 978-1-631-49755-1

Liveright Publishing Corporation
500 Fifth Avenue, New York, NY 10110
www.wwnorton.com

W. W. Norton & Company Ltd.
15 Carlisle Street, London W1D 3BS

Authorized EU representative: EAS, Mustamäe tee 50, 10621 Tallinn, Estonia

10 9 8 7 6 5 4 3 2 1

To all democracy renovators,

past and present

Contents

PART III.
SPREADING REVOLUTION
1774–1780

PART IV.
GOD SAVE THE KING, GOD SAVE REFORM
1780–1806

FAMILY TREE

King Charles II
1630–1685
and LOUISE DE KEROUALLE, LATER
DUCHESS OF PORTSMOUTH AND AUBIGNY
1649–1734

Charles *(1st Duke)*
1672–1723
m. ANNE, DAUGHTER OF LORD BRUDENELL
1669–1722

Charles *(2nd Duke)*
1701–1750
m. SARAH, DAUGHTER OF
EARL CADOGN
1706–1751

Louisa
m. EARL OF
BERKELEY

Anne
m. EARL OF
ALBEMARLE

Charles *(3rd Duke)*
1735–1806
m. MARY, DAUGHTER
OF 3RD EARL OF ELGIN
& AILESBURY
1740–1795

George
m. LOUISA, DAUGHTER OF
MARQUESS OF LOTHIAN

Caroline
m. HENRY FOX, LATER
LORD HOLLAND

Charles *(4th Duke)*
1764–1819
m. CHARLOTTE,
DAUGHTER OF 4TH
DUKE OF GORDON
1768–1842

Maria

Emily
m. SIR G. C. BERKELEY

Emily
m. 1st JAMES, EARL OF KILDARE, LATER DUKE OF LEINSTER
2nd WILLIAM OGILVIE

Louisa
m. T. CONOLLY

Sarah
m. 1st SIR CHARLES BUNBURY BT
2nd HON. GEORGE NAPIER

Cecilia

Georgina
m. EARL BATHURST

PROLOGUE

IN 2026, AT THE 250TH ANNIVERSARY OF THE DECLARATION OF Independence and birth of the United States of America, nearly all the landmasses on earth are carved up into nation-states. There are now nearly two hundred of them, with central governments, police forces, and, typically, militaries. Since the end of European colonialism and the fall of the Soviet Union, analysts routinely divide the world into liberal democracies like France, Germany, and the United States; autocracies where dissent is suppressed and there are no national elections, like China and Saudia Arabia; and competitive authoritarian states like Hungary, Russia, and Iran where elections persist performatively but are meaningless or limited in their impact.

The map of the world showed more variation 250 years ago than it does today. Empires like Britain, Spain, and Austria-Hungary governed colonies, viceroyalties, audiencias, captaincies, estates, and diets. Switzerland consisted of a loosely allied set of cantons, some of which were more aristocratic in their governance and some more communal. Indigenous peoples in the Americas, Africa, and what is now Australia formed themselves into mosaics of kingdoms, empires, chiefdoms, and stateless societies.

The years of the transition from an organic chaos that had emerged over millennia to a global order of nation-states are also known as the Age of Revolution—roughly equivalent to the reign of King George III of Britain, from 1760 to his replacement by a prince regent in 1811, when he succumbed to the inescapable clutches of his mental illness. Those years saw revolution in America, France, Ireland, Haiti, Peru, Poland, the

Netherlands, and Switzerland; sequentially, in many places, long-standing monarchies gave way to independent republics.

This Age of Revolution is easily imagined as a fire that ignited at the margins of empire—in distant lands where oceans, time, and expense made it hard for central authorities to wield control. The American colonists, we've come to understand, learned how to govern themselves partly because the British government was so very far away. Then when the Crown and Parliament sought to assert more control over the colonies, as the story goes, the homegrown spirit of self-government rose up to resist. From there, the revolutionary fire that started in America spread globally.

This leaves out the first chapter of the Age of Revolution. Its original epicenter was not Boston, but London—where the memory of Charles I and the Glorious Revolution had staying power for aristocrats and commoners alike. The rights of man, the theory of revolution, and calls for popular sovereignty—all of these developed earlier in London than in the colonies—and the radical energies of London spread from the metropole across the Atlantic and the Channel, as rabble-rousing dissidents fled for fear of punishment for sedition, and as business and personal letters home from colonial representatives in London tied together conversations between the colonies and the mother country.

Every act that provided the drumbeat of the march to revolution in the colonies had been foreshadowed in Britain. In 1765, the Americans rioted against a new tax on paper called the Stamp Act. But in 1763 the British themselves had already rioted against a newly imposed tax—on cider. The tax hit especially hard on ordinary people who were more likely to drink cider than the claret-quaffing elite. William Pitt the Elder, a leading Whig politician, who was often at odds with the Crown and the government, railed against the tax bill in words that have taught generations that a person's home is their castle: "The poorest man may in his cottage bid defiance to all the forces of the Crown. It may be frail; its roof may shake; the wind may blow through it; the storm may enter; the rain may enter; but the King of England cannot enter—all his force dares not cross the threshold of the ruined tenement!" The Crown's attempts at taxation reached too far into people's private lives, eroding the freedom to down a pint of cider (or two or three) within the walls of their own homes after a hard day's work.

Or take the Boston Massacre. In 1770, British soldiers shot into gathered crowds outside the modest but elegant brick Statehouse topped by a gilt lion and rearing unicorn. The building was home to the royal administration in Massachusetts Bay Colony. The soldiers killed five and further inspired anti-British sentiment in the colonies. Two years earlier, in 1768, British troops in South London had shot into crowds gathered on the grasslands at St. George's Fields, just south of the King's Bench Prison, and killed six. Protesters had gathered to resist the imprisonment of an inspiring radical member of Parliament. The killings on St. George's Fields roused England's radicals to more strenuous efforts, just as the Boston Massacre would fire up the Americans.

Or consider the iconic Boston Tea Party of 1773 when the fiercely self-reliant colonists were protesting economic policies—this time taxes on tea. This came after years of London riots by weavers, known as the Spitalfield Riots. From 1765 to 1769, just at the early onset of the Industrial Revolution, weavers frequently left their looms idle and took to the streets to protest government policies that eroded their earnings, to the benefit of the upper classes.

The French Revolution, too, was foreshadowed in Britain. In 1789, that revolution was launched when the ancient limestone prison, the Bastille, fell to revolutionaries. But in London in 1780, another old limestone prison, Newgate, had already fallen. During the five days of the incredibly shocking Gordon Riots, some fourteen thousand people stormed the British Parliament. Looting was widespread. Rioters assaulted members of the House of Lords. There was a narrowly averted attack on the Bank of England. Large swaths of London burned. More than three hundred people were killed before the Crown was able to suppress the violence. The iron gates of Newgate Prison were thrown open, and rioters flamboyantly scrawled on the walls, "By order of King Mob."

London was a hotbed of radical organizing in the 1760s and 1770s. Some of the first modern labor activism anywhere in the world emerged there during these years. Grassroots organizing against the government spread through the whole country and swept up everyone from farmers to civil servants to the working poor. The King became a target of seditious writing and assassination attempts. The right to revolution was asserted in newspaper articles in London in the 1760s before it was formulated in America in the Declaration of Independence. Yet this turbulent history is little acknowledged, so little acknowledged in fact that most popular histories completely ignore it.

At Madame Tussauds waxworks exhibition center in twenty-first-century London, an attraction called "The Spirit of London" offers tourists a historical ride through the ages of England's history. The ride starts in Tudor England, and passes through Plague scenes, the Great Fire of London, and the construction of Christopher Wren's St. Paul's Cathedral in the late seventeenth century. Then it jumps to the nineteenth century and Nelson's victory over Napoleon's navy at Trafalgar. It skips eighteenth-century Britain entirely.

This act of omission is startling to any visitor attuned to the great changes wrought in Britain's fortunes by the eighteenth century. But surely it has a straightforward explanation. The eighteenth century was a chaos of collapsing governments and political and military conflicts. It also included one of Britain's most regretted moments: the loss of the American colonies. What is there to memorialize in all that? In addition, eighteenth-century England came much closer to a revolution at home than official histories felt comfortable acknowledging. Not telling that story was probably one way the monarchy and the establishment stabilized themselves in the long nineteenth century. But the Age of Revolution included England at its center, and arguably the very first revolution of the era took place there.

OF COURSE, THERE HAD already been revolutions in the seventeenth century. Most vividly, there were the overthrow and horrifying execution of Charles I during the English Civil Wars. Oliver Cromwell's Commonwealth and then oppressive Protectorate were a radical departure from the monarchy. Only a few decades after the restoration of Charles II to the throne came the Glorious Revolution of 1688 when aristocratic families deposed King James II because of his Catholicism and replaced him with the Dutch stadtholder, William of Orange, who was married to James's sister. Both revolutionary moments—neither of them bloodless—set the stage for what would happen in the eighteenth century. The Cromwellian period introduced, but failed to realize, ideas of popular sovereignty and the leveling of social classes. The Glorious Revolution established the monarch as constitutional, serving at the pleasure of the leading aristocratic families, in its own way also a form of popular check on the Crown. By the dawn of the eighteenth century, the British monarchy would have looked very weak indeed compared to its muscular European counterparts.

Nor did the new century immediately improve the fortunes of the Crown. When in 1714 Queen Anne died and with her the House of Stuart ended its time on the English throne, there was a crisis. In 1701 Parliament had passed the Act of Settlement barring Catholics— including the descendants of James—from becoming king or queen of England. Anne had no heirs, despite her heroic efforts to produce one. She had seventeen pregnancies, but only one of her children survived beyond the age of ten. When she died, the country had to look far for a new monarch. No one in England qualified.

The nearest eligible Protestant relation was in the northwestern German principality of Hanover. The new king, George I, was a distant relative of Charles I. Hardly anyone in England knew him—he had never visited the country previously—and he spoke only German and French. He was immediately challenged by the descendants of James II, and a long-festering revolt broke out—the Jacobite rebellion. It would last more than four years. On George's coronation in 1714, protests erupted in twenty cities across the country.

Within six years of the new king's accession, his government was caught up in a colossal financial scandal—the South Sea Bubble—that bankrupted many of the aristocracy and made George hugely unpopular again. One of his leading ministers collapsed and died from a stroke. Anyone looking at the nations of Europe in 1720 and speculating which monarchy was likely to fall would have put their money—and it was such a great era of gambling—on England. The whole edifice of the Crown seemed to be teetering. Compared to the majestic rule of Louis XIV and Louis XV in France, the new Hanoverian kings of England seemed very frail indeed.

Yet by the end of the eighteenth century, the grandson of the first Hanover king, George III, sat securely on the throne in London, even though revolution had liberated America and overthrown the kings of France. In fact, the Hanoverian dynasty would peak only in the nineteenth century with the unparalleled success—and bombast—of Victorian Britain. Somehow the kings of England survived the revolutionary age. But their survival was hardly an indication that nothing had changed.

Superficially, the monarchy was the same; in fact, it went through a century of reinvention, driven by a brilliant and innovative reform movement that allowed its survival but at the same time put in place all the vital counterbalances that made modern democracy possible. Full revolution never reached England, but only because George III presided over what might be called a soft revolution—with considerable movements of the people but relatively little bloodshed, followed by institutional transformation. The political enlightenment that produced revolutions in other countries during the eighteenth century created in Britain the possibility for a new constitutional arrangement that limited the powers of the Crown and set the terms for a radical new popular sovereignty.

THREE, AND ONLY THREE, leading British political figures lived through and shaped this dynamic era of revolutionary experimentation and invention from start to finish. One was King George III himself; the second, a brilliant parliamentarian and theorist of modern conservatism, was Edmund Burke; and the third was an activist, visionary, and strategist who has not until now, I hope to demonstrate, received the recognition he deserves for his fundamental role in this most raucous of eras. He was Charles Lennox, the 3rd Duke of Richmond. Richmond was the first member of the House of Lords to propose recognizing American independence, and in 1780 he became the first person to introduce a bill in Parliament to extend the franchise to all adult men in Britain over the age of twenty-one. With his bill, he laid the foundation for a century of reform to come.

These three British figures, even when allied, as they sometimes were, were also in constant competition with one another for influence. The dynamics of their struggles—always driven by both ego and principle—did nothing less than shape modern British constitutionalism. Yet while the King's and Burke's stories are well known, Richmond's is not. He was tall, rich, and beautiful. Joshua Reynolds, who painted the Duke in his youth, remarked about his "superb eyes": "The great beauty of the Duke of Richmond's eye proceeded from its fine and uncommon colour, [a] dark blue, which would be totally lost on the stage, the light being constantly either too high or too low." He was, in other words, a blooming flower of nobility. As a senior peer of the realm, coming immediately after the royal family in the ranks of the aristocracy, Richmond's turn to radicalism could not have been predicted. His social standing gave the radicals a legitimacy they would not otherwise have had, so his support ensured their influence on the politics of the day. The Duke took his boundary-breaking work with the radicals far enough to strike fear in the heart of the King and his leading generals that, as the leader of a militia from Sussex, he had the means to attempt an armed attack on the government. In the end, Richmond was loyal—utterly loyal—to the British Crown, but he was equally loyal to the people. Those twin commitments laid the foundation for marrying monarchy and popular sovereignty in the form of modern British constitutional monarchy. In his own person, Richmond would fuse these loyalties and gift them to the Crown and the Crown's ministers as a stable basis for governance. Richmond was a defining figure of the revolutionary age.

RICHMOND DID NOT WORK alone. The King, Burke, and Richmond were matched in their longevity and influence by a fourth man, someone from outside the elite. This was Thomas Paine, son of a Quaker corset-maker from Thetford. Paine might reasonably be called a British, American, and French citizen—born in one country and adopted by two others. Or better still, as he would have preferred, a citizen of the world. In January 1776, a mere thirteen months after he had arrived in America, Paine published *Common Sense*, the first essay to argue that the Americans should seize their independence from the Crown. Historians estimate that it sold between 120,000 and 150,000 copies in the colonies in its first year, in a population of about 2 million free people. This is equivalent to selling millions of copies upon release today. It was the best-selling political pamphlet of the eighteenth century and is broadly recognized as the spark that lit the fuse of the American Revolution. It would also give Paine a new name. He would long be known simply as "Common-sense."

Before departing for America, Thomas Paine was also—for six world-changing years from 1768 to 1774—a citizen of Lewes, a market town in the county of Sussex in Southern England. There he was an obscure tax collector, working under the jurisdiction of the 3rd Duke of Richmond. As we shall see, Paine was not in Sussex by accident. Securing him this stable employment also permitted the Duke to engage him as one of a group of pamphleteers for the most influential and radical newspaper opinion pieces of the age, *The Letters of Junius*, which rocked Britain, took down the King's ministry, spawned numerous sedition trials, defined the rights of man for the Age of Revolution, and inspired the Americans. A copycat, Arthur Lee, published as "Junius Americanus."

The fact that the 3rd Duke of Richmond was Paine's first political patron has not previously been known. The work of their small circle of radicals—a duke, commoners, lawyers, soldiers, and at least one spy all united in the cause of liberty—was so heterodox, impactful, and dangerous that it was conducted in deep secrecy. The archives have long hidden a breathtaking, covert alliance: The Duke of Richmond and Thomas Paine were at the center of the Junius writings that announced the Age of Revolution.

RICHMOND GAVE THE FAMILY member to whom he left his papers careful instructions to destroy them. In addition, he appears himself to have comprehensively destroyed records from the period of the Junius years. His account books are missing from 1766, when his pamphleteers began publishing in the newspapers, to 1775, when he seems to have ceased that activity. Few of his letters from this period remain. His sister Sarah, too, destroyed her letters from June 1768 to June 1775. The humiliation of an adulterous pregnancy is generally understood to be the explanation. But was that the only thing the family wanted to erase from the record? Brother and sister were very close during those Junius years, and Sarah knew her brother well. She may have had more to hide than regrets or recriminations about her affair. Two other sisters' letters are also missing from this period. Emily's letters have a gap from 1769 to 1774; Louisa's from 1769 to 1773. Someone destroyed almost all the letters of their eldest sister, Caroline. Thanks to the generosity of the current Duke of Richmond and his father, I have been able to fill some of those gaps through research in the Duke's still-intact library, a collection that exceeds Thomas Jefferson's. His book purchases, underlining, and marginal notes make it possible to trace his intellectual development from the age of six to his death at seventy-one. Scholars have not previously had access to this material.

In addition, digitization dissolves privacy for all of us, even the long dead. Letters from Richmond that are in the archives of others and broadly dispersed are now much easier to find. This is also true for small mentions of him in the personal memoirs of a wide array of figures of the age. His associates have similarly become more visible in the archival record. Finally, the power of natural language processing in new technologies makes it at long last possible to attribute authorship for anonymous newspaper publications. Thanks to the diligent work of scholars over the past decade, voluminous new material has been identified as being by Thomas Paine, and recently published in the new six-volume 2026 edition of Paine's collected writings. When I found pseudonymous writings in the Duke's library and suspected from various shards of evidence that they had been authored by Paine, colleagues in the field were able to confirm those identifications. Telling the full story of the Duke of Richmond's radicalism, and of his partnership with Thomas Paine, would not have been possible without these new tools and the work of many other scholars.

WHY DID I PULL on the thread of the Duke of Richmond's life and the possibility of a connection to Thomas Paine to begin with? In the summer of 2016, my husband, Jimmy, and children, Nora and William, flew ahead of me to England for summer vacation. Their cab driver from the airport to London was characteristically chatty. He and Jimmy struck up a conversation about music; the cabbie had previously been a music producer. Somehow that story led to the cab driver sharing that he was from Lewes, in East Sussex, and that led in turn to his sharing a detail about the town that he thought would be of interest to visitors from America: Thomas Paine had lived there for six years. When Jimmy relayed that to me that evening, I sat bolt upright. I had never known that detail of Paine's biography, and I was at that moment trying to figure out what kinds of connections there might be between Sussex and the American Revolution.

The research team I directed at Harvard had recently made an exciting discovery. As part of a project to find all copies of the Declaration of Independence produced between 1776 and 1826, we had stumbled in 2015 on something special in the West Sussex Record Office, a small, nondescript county archival office in Southern England that is also the place where you go for your birth, marriage, and death certificates. Yet the West Sussex Record Office, we had learned, also housed a large-scale ceremonial parchment of the Declaration of Independence. Until we found this Declaration, the world had thought there was only one large-scale parchment—the one encased in preservative gases in the National

Archives in Washington, DC. While the Sussex Declaration, as we now call it, is on sheepskin instead of calfskin and has a list of names of signatories written out by a single clerk's hand, rather than the fifty-six distinct signatures of the men who committed their lives, fortunes, and sacred honor to one another; it is otherwise as grand and impressive as the parchment in DC. How on earth had such a memento found its way to Sussex?

Our research led to the conclusion that it had belonged to the 3rd Duke of Richmond and had entered his papers at some early point, relatively proximate to the American Revolution. It appears to have been commissioned by the Scottish American James Wilson, a lawyer, who signed both the Declaration of Independence and the Constitution, having served as a delegate in both contexts. He also became one of the first Supreme Court justices of the new United States. Wilson read out a copy of the Declaration during the Constitutional Convention in Philadelphia in June 1787 and would have needed to produce a reading text to do so. The trail of manuscripts and copies reveals that the Sussex Declaration was one of a set of two or three identical copies, and it was produced in America, as close scrutiny of its mode of production makes clear. Thomas Paine was with Wilson and Benjamin Franklin in Philadelphia when the two men were preparing for the Convention. Paine sailed for France—returning to Europe after an absence of thirteen years—just weeks before the Convention started and soon made his way to England. What better souvenir could he have taken along? It seems likely that Paine brought the parchment with him and paid a visit to his earliest patron to deliver it to him as a gift.

Paine was a courier of revolutionary talismans. When the already renowned revolutionary visited Paris in late 1789, the Marquis de Lafayette gave him the key to the Bastille, with a request that he pass it on to President Washington. Paine brought the key back to England where he passed it to John Rutledge Jr. to transport to Washington. Rutledge's father was a former governor of South Carolina who had also recently served as a delegate to the Constitutional Convention. In sending the key, Lafayette was returning a favor. Benjamin Franklin had sent him a copy of the Declaration of Independence from Philadelphia in 1783. It is probable that the parchment Declaration now in the West Sussex Record Office reached Richmond through Paine and that, just as he had passed the key to the Bastille to Washington, Paine is likely to have couriered a talisman of the American Revolution from America to one of its greatest defenders in England.

In every country in which he lived, Paine found a way to secure protection from one of the most distinguished members of that country's political elite: George Washington in America; the Marquis de Lafayette in France. And when he was in Sussex, he depended on the protection of the Duke of Richmond.

The investigation into the ties between Paine and Richmond led me into the captivating details of the Duke's life. There I found a fascinating man—a bibliophilic politician known as the most beautiful man in England; whose commitment to the political empowerment of ordinary people was unmatched by any other member of the aristocracy; who recognized that his reform vision lay well beyond the horizons of imagination for many of his contemporaries; and yet who persisted in this commitment to reform throughout his life. I found a kindred spirit.

My own investigations of the Declaration of Independence and its context and philosophical meaning have never been purely academic. I have sought to understand the era that gave birth to modern forms of self-government and to bring self-government to life again for citizens of mass democracies, who are now woefully trapped in the complexities of technology and globalized economies and sinking beneath a sense of disempowerment. That pursuit has led me to name as my life's cause the work of democracy renovation—reconnecting people to their civic experience, power, and responsibility, and redesigning our political institutions so that they are actually responsive to the people. I argue, for instance, that we need to renovate the US House of Representatives by expanding it to align with population growth. As I dug and dug into the archives, excavating Richmond's life, I was stunned to discover that he had himself already discovered that same metaphor of renovation. In a letter explaining his commitment to universal manhood suffrage, he explained that:

> the experience of 26 years, . . . whether in or out of Government, has equally convinced me that the Restoration of a genuine House of Commons by a Renovation of the Rights of the People is the only effectual Remedy against that system of corruption which has brought the Nation to Disgrace and Poverty and threatens it with the Loss of Liberty.

Here was someone, like me, with a radical imagination for future possibilities—stymied by his present. What was that like for him? What was the story of where his reform efforts succeeded and where and why they failed? Britain did eventually get universal suffrage. Had the Duke's work paved the way for that? How would I know? What lessons could I take for my efforts to bring self-government back to life in modern America? And had he in fact known and worked with Thomas Paine?

After years of archival spelunking, I found it—proof of the relationship between Richmond and Paine, not merely circumstantial evidence, which is legion, but hard evidence of their relationship. I found this evidence in the Duke's library.

THE SEAT OF THE dukes of Richmond is called Goodwood. It's an exceptionally beautiful 11,500-acre estate in the Sussex hills, with easy access to good hunting grounds and the wildflower-filled Downs of Southern England. At the end of the 3rd Duke's life, it encompassed seventeen thousand acres. The great house that anchors the property consists of three wings, angled as if forming three sides of an octagon. They have copper-domed towers at their ends and together form an imposing, elegant edifice in creamy limestone and grey flint. The interiors are lushly decorated with paintings, sculptures, porcelain, gilt ceilings, and fine eighteenth-century furniture. The southern-facing wing and its adjoining tower contain two libraries, one large and one small. The Large Library leads to the Small Library, via a jib door designed to look like a bookcase and obscure the passage. At 24 × 19 feet, the Small Library is small in name only. It is a dreamy reading nook, with two floors of books, ottoman, armchair, desk, and Napoleon's campaign chair for the desk chair. In the eighteenth century, the walls were hung with scarlet paper, while the windows were framed by black velvet drapes, with a gold silk fringe. In the neighboring Large Library, the lower cabinets, beneath towering shelves of books, are decorated with ivory paintings of mythic images copied from antique vases and set against a red background. Richmond's sister Louisa called it "one of the prettiest rooms I ever saw." That statement is as true in the twenty-first century as it was at the time.

After the 3rd Duke's death, the library held nine thousand books. It is a treasure trove of classics—from first editions of Hobbes's *Leviathan* and the works of Voltaire and Rousseau to both volumes of the original 1775 and 1776 *Journals of the Continental Congress*. As I worked in the library over several summers, the butler, Monty, in shirtsleeves, tie, waistcoat, and pinstripe trousers, brought me sparkling water, tea, and cookies.

The thousands of volumes housed at Goodwood include bound collections of political pamphlets, with the word "Tracts" stamped in gold on the spine. Those pamphlets include one called *The Juryman's Touchstone*, a ninety-five-page essay published pseudonymously in 1771. The pamphlet offers a stirring if minutely technical defense of the rights of jurors. A few of the pamphlet's pages include small corrections in the hand of the Duke. On the flyleaf of the pamphlet there is also a dedication from the author: "To the Duke of Richmond as A Tribute due to him for His Strenuous Efforts & unwearied perseverance in the Defence of Constitutional Liberty this Pamphlet is presented by the Author."

This pamphlet was previously unknown. No copy is held in the British Library. There are only three other known copies, one at Yale, one in the New York Public Library, and one in the Library Company of Philadelphia that was cataloged as authored by Junius. I was several years into my work before it occurred to me that the firm, plain handwriting of the anonymous dedication might be that of Thomas Paine. Because he had supposedly not published any books until 1776, I had not considered him. But as I kept working, I came to see that the pamphlet addressed two matters of great concern to him—the Junius trials and the rights of jurors. In Lewes, Paine was an avid juryman, serving more often than any of his peers during his years in the town. I reexamined the inscription and checked it against other known instances of Paine's handwriting. To my eye, it looked like a match—especially the capital *T*s and capital *P*s. I turned to the editors of *The Collected Works of Thomas Paine* for review. They confirmed it as his hand. They also tested the text of the pamphlet via computer-assisted author identification software. That too came up as a match. The two main authors of *The Juryman's Touchstone* were Thomas Paine and Benjamin Franklin; the Duke of Richmond pitched in on two paragraphs, including the last which is about the House of Lords. I had found Thomas Paine's first book, and it put him squarely at the center of the Junius affair and clearly in relationship to the Duke.

THERE ARE OTHER TRACES of the relationship between Richmond and Paine in the Library at Goodwood. They reveal that the tight connection and warm mutual regard communicated in Paine's dedication of the pamphlet to the Duke did not last. Twenty-five years after the publication of *The Juryman's Touchstone*, the Duke sat in his library reading a very different kind of book. He had recently retired from serving for more than a decade as a British cabinet minister, and from three decades of involvement in British politics at the highest level. No longer tall and slender, he was now a portly, balding sixty-one. He tended to start his days—after a visit to his fields—with reading. Paine had recently completed the two volumes of *The Age of Reason*. Published from Paris, *The Age of Reason* carried the subtitle "Being an investigation of True and Fabulous Theology." Across 172 rhetorically brisk pages, Paine challenged institutional religion and the Bible. He argued for deism, an alternative to Christianity. For deists, some divine force has ordered nature, but there is no Christ, no crucifixion, no everlasting life, no God to whom to pray, only nature's laws to follow. Paine's book inflamed readers on both sides of the Atlantic and provoked many critical responses.

Now Richmond sat in his library reading one of those responses, entitled *Apology for the Bible, in a Series of Letters, Addressed to Thomas Paine.* The word "Apology" here carries the classical meaning of "Defense." This best-selling book of political polemic was published in 1796 and is structured as letters from the author, Richard Watson, an Anglican bishop and fellow member of the House of Lords, to a hated adversary. The tone of the letters addressed to Paine is personal. Righteous anger courses through the pages. The *Apology* traveled far and wide. In Massachusetts every Harvard student received a copy. Richmond left notes on 138 of the treatise's 385 hotly argued pages, including on the final page. This means he read the arguments against Paine from start to finish. It is one of the most annotated books in his collection.

No longer a friend to Paine, Richmond sided with Watson's bitter critiques. Watson wrote about Paine: "I hope that there is no want of charity in saying, that it would have been fortunate for the Christian world, had your life been terminated before you had fulfilled your intention." After reading this cruel wish, Richmond put a vigorous check mark of agreement in the margin. In the passion of the Duke's response flowed the rage of a once deep friendship betrayed. He and Paine had been fast friends and mutual admirers, locked in secret work to pursue universal manhood suffrage as two of England's most daring radicals until, in the 1780s, their politics parted ways. When that occurred, Paine turned on the

Duke in his public writings. Now Richmond wished Paine dead. Their history together—and their bitter break—has been hidden from view for over 250 years. In the story of first their friendship and then their break lies also an untold tale of the origins of modern popular sovereignty and constitutionalism.

Radical Duke seeks to set the historical record straight. It tells the story of how close Britain came to revolution in the very years when the Americans irrevocably crossed that line. In Britain, the Age of Revolution lacked the full bloody drama of America, France, or Ireland, but was quite as consequential. The tumults of the age produced a unique constitutional settlement in Britain that would endure far better than any other European monarchy, and arguably better than several of the republics that displaced monarchies. At the heart of the invention of this unique new arrangement was the complicated friendship and rivalry between a brilliant reforming aristocrat and a passionate, uncompromising polemicist, the 3rd Duke of Richmond and Thomas Paine. Each sharpened the case for popular sovereignty and fomented grassroots political movements. Each supported the emergence of republics onto the world stage for the first time in the modern era, and so together they laid the foundation for our own age. Each was in his way an architect of Britain's modern constitutional monarchy. Yet the central tale here is about the Duke—how a man with all the privilege of his times chose as his life's work the project of liberty for his fellow men. In this book, King George III and Edmund Burke are supporting characters, and so too, ultimately, is Thomas Paine. Richmond's story reveals a fascinating backstory for Thomas Paine—and fills long-standing gaps in our understanding of Paine's life. Yet the story in these pages belongs to the 3rd Duke of Richmond, one of history's great but unheralded reformers.

Duke in his political writings. Now Richmond without Paine dead. Their history together—and their intellectual links—has been hidden from view for over 200 years. In the story of first the [illegible] and [illegible] lies also a [illegible] tale of the origins of modern popular sovereignty and constitutionalism.

Radical Duke seeks to set the historical record straight. It tells the story of how and why Britain came to grow uneasy in the years when the Americans [illegible] that the [illegible] the Age of Revolution lacked the bloody drama of America, France, or [illegible] but [illegible] as consequential. The [illegible] of the age produced a unique constitutional settlement in Britain that would endure [illegible] better than any other European monarchy and arguably better than [illegible] of the republics that displaced monarchies. At the heart of the [illegible] the new [illegible] between a [illegible] of the [illegible] and [illegible] the 3rd Duke of Richmond and Thomas Paine. Each sharpened the case for popular sovereignty and [illegible] political [illegible]. Each supported the [illegible] of republics on the world stage for the first time in the modern era, and so together they laid the foundations for our own age. [illegible] this way an [illegible] of Britain's [illegible] constitutional [illegible] about the [illegible] how [illegible] In this book *Radical Duke* [illegible] characters [illegible] Thomas Paine [illegible] ways in our understanding of Paine. [illegible] the [illegible] belongs to the 3rd Duke of Richmond, one of history's great but unheralded reformers.

PART I

THE UNLIKELY MAKING OF A RADICAL

1735–1763

CHAPTER

I

YOUTH

1735–1748

A considerable young Nobleman of Sussex.

—THE DUKE OF NEWCASTLE, WRITING ABOUT THE YOUNG EARL OF MARCH

THE LIFE OF THE 3RD DUKE OF RICHMOND IS A SERIES OF MYSteries, the first among them being how a person of such lofty origins could have become a champion for the common man. Birth is not everything, of course, and Richmond was not the first, nor will he be the last, to choose his own mentors and influences. To see the significance of his choices—for a military life, for art, for radicalism, for the Americans, for constitutionalism, and finally, belatedly, for the King, we will have to see the background against which he chose, starting with a most privileged youth. Against a backdrop of luxury and indulgence, we will see irrepressible boundary-breaking, a taste for conspiratorial confidences, and the early flickers of political ambition. What came first, though, in the early years, was preparation to assume the responsibilities of aristocratic leadership.

Charles Lennox, (3rd) Duke of Richmond, Earl of March and Baron Settrington in England; Duke of Lennox, Earl of Darnley and Lord of Torboultoun in Scotland; and duc d'Aubigny in France—to list all his titles—was born on February 11, 1735, by the old Julian calendar.* The

* Pope Gregory had replaced the ancient Julian calendar with a new one in 1582 to correct for misalignment with the sun. By the middle of the eighteenth century, Britain's calendar was eleven days behind that in use on the Catholic Continent, which was causing problems for trade, diplomacy, navigation, and scientific correspondence. Britain finally converted in 1752. The transition included adding eleven days, shifting the Duke's recorded birthday from February 11 to February 22.

French philosopher Montesquieu (or, in full, Charles-Louis de Secondat, baron de La Brède et de Montesquieu) had spent eighteen months in England, just a few years earlier, working closely with the Duke's father and studying British constitutionalism. The German composer George Frideric Handel, who had followed his Hanoverian monarch, George I, to London and become the leading light of the British musical scene, was naturalized as a British subject in 1727. And a few months before the birth of Charles Lennox, in the colonies, the German-born publisher of *The New-York Weekly Journal*, John Peter Zenger, was acquitted by a jury in a trial for seditious libel for having published criticism of the royal governor, William Cosby, for corruption and incompetence. His case was a landmark for press freedom. At this early moment, when the first hints of rifts between King and colonies were starting to emerge, Charles Lennox was born into one of the most distinguished aristocratic families in the land, with topflight intellectual connections and maximal proximity to the royal family. The family supported the throne.

Charles Lennox was probably born in London, though this is hard to know for sure. At birth, his courtesy title was Earl of March, the title always used by the heir to the dukedom, much as the heir to the English throne is always known as the Prince of Wales. Not only were titles complicated but so were names. The little Earl of March was never addressed by his parents and siblings as Charles, but simply as "March." Household staff called him Lord March. He signed his letters "March," and he will be March in this narrative as well. His status as heir was always front and center.

In addition to March's family seat, Goodwood, the family had a home in London called Richmond House, a fine residence built within the grounds of Whitehall Palace, where their ancestor, King Charles I, was executed in 1649. This they occupied primarily during the fall and spring when Parliament was in session. The elegant residence overlooked the Thames, the busy mercantile highway of the era, with boats bustling up and down, and was just a five-minute walk from the Houses of Parliament. The family also owned, and often visited, a fine woodland hunting chateau just outside of Aubigny, France; there was also a second chateau in the town. Summer and early fall could often find them there. Finally, baby March's parents served frequent stints at the royal residence, St. James's Palace, half a mile from Westminster. They were courtiers with formal roles in the households of King George II and Queen Caroline. The dukes of Richmond had strategically embraced the new kings of Hanover and England, despite the Richmond family's connection with the deposed Stuarts.

The 2nd Duke of Richmond was Master of the Horse for King George II. He was proudly responsible for the stables and cavalry. March's mother, Duchess Sarah, was a Lady of the Bedchamber to the Queen. The infant Earl of March was the third son born to the Duke and Duchess "Taw," as her husband called her, but the first to survive infancy. "Taw" was pregnant twenty-seven times before her death at forty-six in 1751, a not unheard of number of pregnancies for the times though at the high end. Of these many pregnancies, only seven children survived to adulthood. Little March joined two older sisters, brilliant, strong-willed, twelve-year-old Caroline and four-year-old Emily, who would in her teens be described as "the loveliest lady of the English court." March was followed two years later by a cheerful, good-hearted playmate, George, as well as by the much younger Louisa, Sarah, and Cecilia. Cecilia died young. But the other six siblings—Caroline, Emily, March, George, Louisa, and Sarah—remained intensely close throughout their lives—despite much scandal and many dramatic turns of fortune.

Like any other leading aristocratic family, the Richmonds were well-supported by servants numbering in the dozens, without counting farm, stable, and hunting staff. The Earl of March's arrival was surely celebrated with barrels of ale sent to the servants above and below stairs both at Richmond House and at Goodwood. Ale had been ordered when the 2nd Duke was born. Now a duke and father himself, the 2nd Duke always enjoyed celebrations, and the birth of an heir would have merited one. Five months on, little Lord March was "grown so noisy," his father reported to a friend—a harbinger of the future 3rd Duke's strong and disruptive opinions.

March's unspoken first name, Charles, carried weight. He was named after his great-grandfather, Charles II, King of England, who reigned from 1660 to 1685. In the 1670s, little March's great-grandmother, Louise de Kéroualle, a handsome, doe-eyed French woman, served as a diplomatic bridge between the French and British courts. Sex and politics were fully entangled in that era. She became mistress to Charles II, a man notorious for his many lovers and known as the Merry Monarch for his wit and sociability. Charles's numerous mistresses bore him six illegitimate sons who survived to adulthood. He brought all of them under the protection of royal prerogative by creating dukedoms for five of them. Not only the Duke of Richmond, but also the dukes of Southampton, Grafton, Northumberland, and St. Albans, all owed their senior status in the British peerage to Charles II's voracious sexual appetite. The second title, the Duchy of Aubigny, was provided to Louise by the French Crown in recognition of her diplomatic services. Also attached to Richmond's British dukedom was a right to the duty paid on coal from Newcastle. This served as the family's primary source of income for more than a century. Despite his many illegitimate children, Charles II died without a legitimate heir, so the throne passed to his Catholic brother James, triggering the Glorious Revolution. For the next sixty-five years, the remaining supporters of the Stuart claim to the throne would be known as "Jacobites," after James's Latin name, Iacobus, and would periodically stage revolts against the sitting monarch.

Because of his royal lineage, the little Earl of March was what was called "a prince of the blood," or at least he was so called by the society literary figure Horace Walpole, son of Britain's first and longest-serving prime minister, Robert Walpole. This put him at the top of the aristocratic pecking order, coming immediately below the royal family. Yet as a descendant of one of the last Stuarts, prior to the Glorious Revolution, that inheritance was also inevitably somewhat suspect and conveyed a whiff of conspiratorial resistance. Named Charles after his father, grandfather, and great-grandfather King Charles II, the association was unmistakable. Writing letters as a child, although the young lord typically signed his letters "March," in two extant letters he signed, "C. March." That initial alluded to his royal blood, his sense of independence and prerogative, and his felt connection to his great-grandfather, Charles II. One of his greatest political rivals would be another prince of the blood, Augustus FitzRoy, the 3rd Duke of Grafton. Grafton was another great-grandson of Charles II, and just five months older than March.

In highly performative contrast to the Jacobites, the 2nd Duke of Richmond, little March's father, threw himself wholeheartedly into support for the Hanoverians. He dedicated his life to service to his king as a member of the Whig oligarchy. These were the aristocratic families who had recruited Prince William of Orange to take the throne during the

Glorious Revolution and then maintained close ties to the Crown, securing privilege and wealth through the arrangement.

Aside from serving as Master of the Horse and lord lieutenant for Sussex, bringing smugglers to justice, the 2nd Duke of Richmond also had local political responsibilities. In 1735, the year of his son's birth, he served for the year as mayor of Chichester, the West Sussex city nearest to Goodwood. The grey masonry spire of the Chichester Cathedral—fourth tallest in England, and the only cathedral spire in England to be visible from the sea—is at the center of many carefully designed prospects from Goodwood's gardens.

Even more important, Richmond was the West Sussex ally to Thomas Pelham-Holles, 1st Duke of Newcastle, whose seat was in East Sussex. Newcastle was one of the leading politicians of the day. He served continuously as a cabinet minister from 1724 to 1762, including as prime minister for the last five years. His brother, Henry Pelham, served as prime minister from 1743 to 1754, holding his seat in Parliament from Chichester, where the Duke of Richmond was responsible for the political machine. The Pelham brothers were a force to be reckoned with, and the 2nd Duke was very close to them as well as to the royal family. Yet the 2nd Duke was not himself especially political. His roles as Lord of the Bedchamber and then Master of the Horse required him to be studiously neutral on political issues, and just as he served his king ably, he also served Newcastle reliably, holding down a structure of alliances in West Sussex that aided and abetted Newcastle's hold on power. The two were close friends: Their published correspondence includes 462 letters between them or sent by an assistant on behalf of one of them.

A DISTINCTIVE FEATURE OF service to the Hanoverian kings for the Whig aristocrats in their close employ was entanglement in royal family quarrels. And the Richmonds were very close to King George II and Queen Caroline. The Richmond children played at St. James's Palace. In 1732, nine-year-old Caroline and her friends performed John Dryden's *The Indian Emperor, or the Conquest of Mexico by the Spaniards* at the Palace in front of the King and Queen. The boys may even have played indoor "base-ball, a play all who are or who have been schoolboys are well acquainted with," with other royal children. At some point in the late 1740s, the then-youngest child, Sarah, interrupted the King's walk in Kensington Gardens by toddling up to him and saying, "Comment portez-vous, Monsieur le Roi? Vous avez une grande et belle maison ici, n'est-ce pas?" "How are you, Mr. King? You have a very big and beautiful house here, don't you?"

French was, for Sarah and all the other Richmond children, equivalent to their native tongue. The siblings spent their early nursery years with silver cutlery and French-speaking governesses. March's earliest letters are in French. The King was so charmed by Sarah's French conversation that she became a regular playmate for the King himself. One story has it that, during one of their romps, he placed her inside a gigantic Chinese jar to see what she would do. Rather than panicking, she sat down and started belting out patriotic songs.

Yet despite this intimacy with the King and Queen, the young Earl of March is unlikely to have played with the King's grandson, George, who as a child held the title of the Duke of Edinburgh. George, Duke of Edinburgh, was born a little more than two years after the Earl of March, on June 4, 1738. He was born just six months after March's younger brother George. Both boys were loyally named after the King. But while they were age-mates, and name-mates, they were not playmates. The King and his son Frederick, Prince of Wales, George's father, were estranged.

March's father, the 2nd Duke of Richmond, periodically had to serve the role of shuttle diplomat carrying messages from the monarch to his son. Many from the King were filled with testy complaints about the lack of deference shown to him by the Prince of Wales. The Earl of March and his siblings would have felt the icy distance between their world in the King's protective shadow, and the banished Prince of Wales and his own courtiers, who looked askance at them. The 2nd Duke of Richmond was aware that the Prince of Wales's conflict with his father held the seeds of danger for his family. They could be caught on the wrong side of a royal power struggle when the King died. He sought to ward off antipathy through alliances. When March's sister Louisa was born in 1743, the Duke secured the Prince of Wales as her godfather. In the end, though, the Prince of Wales's opinions of the Richmonds would not matter because Frederick died before his father. His son George, just shy of his thirteenth birthday, became Prince of Wales and heir. The 2nd Duke had laid in no insurance with him. Little could he know that the rivalry between his own son and Frederick's son would come to define the politics of the age.

NOT ONLY DISPUTES AMONG ADULTS but also starkly different daily routines kept the future duke and future king apart in their youth. The education of the future George III was intense. His day started at 7 a.m. Instruction ran from 8 a.m. to 12:30 p.m., followed by recess, then more school, dinner at 3, and then more instruction, till supper at 8. Bedtime was between 9 and 10.

In contrast, the Earl of March and his brother George grew up in their early years largely in the British countryside. They had a good deal more outdoors time and less discipline for their early lessons. Their father was devoted to dogs, horses, and hunting, and soon so too were they. Not far from Goodwood, their father ran the Charlton Hunt—a foxhunting club for the aristocracy. The family had a small abode there, where the 2nd Duke slept during hunting season and where the children, too, overnighted on occasion. On the estate itself, their father also ran the first private menagerie in England. Over time its residents included wolves, raccoons, ostriches, baboons, monkeys, wild boar, a lioness, civet cats, and a Canadian moose, and hundreds of visitors arrived at the estate on weekends in the 1730s to take in these exotic sights. The children embraced this love of animals and kept numerous dogs, birds, and even a pet fox. And their father's global connections populated their imagination. Friends posted abroad sent the Richmonds shipments of shells, rum, civet cats, and at least one monkey.

The Duchess and her daughters took the shells and designed a gorgeous shell grotto. The family was also sent a young servant of African descent, whom the Duke named Thomas Robinson after the governor of Barbados who had dispatched him. He was dressed in exceptionally fine livery, and given a classical education. The Earl of March's cousin, Augustus Keppel, eventually to be a famed admiral, sailed around the world in 1740 in the HMS *Centurion,* and sent ornate columns from the ship that were installed in the massive kitchen at Goodwood during a redecoration. Peter Collinson, the famed Quaker botanist from London with strong ties to Pennsylvania colonists, sourced countless American plants for the Duke for cultivation on his grounds. Fruits of the great age of exploration regularly found their way to Goodwood to intrigue the children. In the 1740s, amid a craze for all things Egyptian, Richmond even staged the unwrapping of a mummy—an event which may have inspired the ornate Egyptian dining room designed at Goodwood. The colonial world was a joyful source of treasure and adventure for their accepting, youthful imaginations. There were no hints of the realities of conflict and oppression, nor intuitions about future colonial wars.

THE YOUNG EARL OF March was first sent to school at Westminster School in the autumn of 1743, at the age of seven, or possibly the spring of 1744. It must have been a hard transition. He was the first child to go to school in the history of his family. His father had been educated exclusively by a private tutor. By the 1740s the norm within the Whig aristocracy had shifted toward sending boys to Westminster, Winchester, or Eton, and then university at Oxford or Cambridge.

The headmaster, when March arrived, was Dr. John Nicoll. He himself was a Westminster alumnus, and had taken a degree at Christ Church, Oxford. The boys read from a range of classical texts—Martial, Ovid, Justin, Virgil. There was time for prayers and for sport. Cricket arrived at Westminster during these years, thanks to a family friend of the Richmonds, Sir John Sackville, who periodically paid the Earl of March a visit.

Nicoll was famous for easing up on the tough discipline of earlier years at the school. Of the Nicoll era it is said, "Throughout all the history of the School there has been no period, save one, when less knowledge was imparted, and few when more was acquired." Private studies were encouraged, in which students would work with specific tutors on subjects that interested them. Discipline at the school was lax enough that one older student, Charles Churchill (a distant ancestor of Winston Churchill), though still a teen, was able to take a wife and install her in his quarters. A family friend from these years, John Penn, future governor of Pennsylvania, did the same at Eton.

Little suggests that the Earl of March took his studies at Westminster terribly seriously. His mother wanted him to write home on a weekly basis, but he begged off, seeking a dispensation to write only every other week. "Dear Mama, I received your letter, and would have wrote to you on Thursday as you desired, but what whithe business and masters I could nott."* His real interests lay not in the world of letters, but in the world.

* Throughout I have left spellings as in the original unless they impede comprehension.

He added in his note to his mother, "I have heard some time ago, that Jamaica was taken by the French, but it is no more talk'd of."

The only story recorded about his time at Westminster concerns a prank perpetrated by March on the fifth-form Latin master Vincent Bourne. According to another student, Bourne didn't care at all what sort of verses his students turned in to him for their own work, as he was mainly focused on being the best Latin poet from Westminster School (he was also to be the last, since the vernacular use of Latin was in decline). This aspiration does not seem to have earned Bourne his students' respect. As the tale goes, Bourne was unkempt, and his hair greasy enough to tempt more than one boy to set it on fire. Among these was Lord March, who is said to have "set fire to his master's greasy locks and then boxed his ears to put it out."

An outdoorsman like his father; a prankster like both parents; curious about the far-flung reaches of Britain's empire; an undistinguished scholar; and devoted to his brother and their pet animals. This is who the Earl of March was at seven. In these same years in the American colonies, Thomas Jefferson had just been born. John Adams was studying at a town school in Quincy, Massachusetts, to prepare for entrance exams at Harvard College, and fifteen-year-old George Washington, who had been in local Virginia schools, had just abandoned formal schooling on account of financial difficulties stemming from his father's death.

DESPITE THE LAXITY OF discipline under Dr. Nicoll, Westminster turned out some of the most important political figures of the age, including Warren Hastings, who would become the first governor-general of India; the future prime minister Charles Watson-Wentworth, 2nd Marquess of Rockingham; another future prime minister, the 3rd Duke of Grafton; future chancellor of the exchequer William Dowdeswell; George Granville Leveson-Gower, future Marquess of Stafford; future admiral Augustus Keppel, cousin of March; and yet another future prime minister, William Cavendish-Bentinck, future 3rd Duke of Portland, also another relation. The Earl of March would serve much later in life in the cabinet of one of these former school fellows and vigorously oppose the administrations of two others while sparring in parliamentary debate with a fourth.

Already as schoolboys, the Westminster boys lived together through some of the most astounding military events of the period—from Frederick II of Prussia's lightning invasion of Bohemia in 1744, which shocked Europe with its speed, coordination, and ambition and established him as a rising power, to the 1747 capture of the well-fortified Dutch city, Bergen op Zoom, by the French, despite the city's having been considered impregnable. The Earl of March's years in school were central years in the War of the Austrian Succession. When the Holy Roman Emperor, Charles VI, died in 1740, he had left no male heir. Anticipating that this would occur, he had secured legislation to permit passing the throne to a female heir. His twenty-three-year-old daughter Maria Theresa succeeded him. Though she was doubted because of her youth and sex, she was resolute and politically creative. As it became clear that other rulers saw in her ostensible weakness a chance to advantage themselves, she rallied the Hapsburg nobility to military service with a speech given to her Parliament while cradling her infant child. All the crowns of Europe lined up either for or against Maria Theresa. Austria, Hungary, Britain (with its ties to Hanover), the Dutch Republic, and Sardinia fought for the Empress. Prussia, France, Spain, and Bavaria fought against her. The conflict extended to the colonies as well, and British and French troops engaged against each other in the farthermost theaters of war. War would eventually come to England too, with the invasion of Charles Edward Stuart, grandson of King James II, and better known as Bonnie Prince Charlie. His attempt on the throne would give even schoolboys at Westminster the chance to inherit the mantle of Whig leadership.

Before that, in the summer of 1743, the sixty-year-old King George II joined the war in person. He was the last British monarch to lead his own troops in battle. The 2nd Duke of Richmond, as Master of the Horse, was by his side at the Battle of Dettingen, not far from Frankfurt in Germany. The French ambushed the British but failed to encircle them fully. The King's horse bolted, but he famously kept his calm and rallied his men to a victory. Handel wrote a *Te Deum* to celebrate the victory, and the Duke ordered up a celebration, sending home instructions for expenditure on a victory celebration for Chichester. George II had, though, made a symbolic mistake of wearing a yellow Hanoverian sash into battle instead of British red. The Duke of Richmond soothed angry public opinion at home, writing letters testifying to the valor of the King at the head of his British troops.

—

FOR THE RICHMOND FAMILY the season of celebration soon gave way to a period of family strife. Their household was dramatically disrupted in the spring of 1744 when eldest daughter Caroline eloped with the commoner politician Henry Fox. Witty and intelligent, Fox had actively courted Caroline. She was his intellectual equal, an aristocratic woman without formal education but with rich and broad exposure to the most talented writers, thinkers, and scholars of the day and an appetite to appreciate their work. The celebrated Bluestockings, who advocated for women's intellectual advancement, were often wealthy but not aristocrats themselves. Without actively participating in Bluestocking salons, Caroline and her sisters had nonetheless been raised in a heady intellectual milieu, and their letters reveal them to have read widely and deeply. Caroline notoriously spent vacations reading philosophy, history, political pamphlets, and newspapers while taking the waters at Bath. She and Fox enjoyed hashing through the day's political problems together. In March, Fox asked Caroline for her hand at the theater, possibly *Hamlet, Macbeth,* or *Othello*, all playing early that month. She gave neither a yes nor no, but encouraged him to speak to her father, a de facto acceptance of Fox's proposal. But when Fox sought permission from her father to marry her, the Duke of Richmond turned him down. Fox was not the aristocrat the Duke and Duchess hoped for as their son-in-law. A fixed rule among aristocrats was always to marry within the peerage.

Fox, though, was determined that people should be permitted to marry for love—a highly progressive notion at the time—so he directly asked Caroline again for her hand. This time she gave it. On Saturday, May 2, 1744, Caroline's younger sister Emily walked her the anxious quarter mile from their stately Richmond House to the cupola by the Horse Guards—a baroque clock turret marking the ceremonial entrance to Whitehall and the threshold between court and government, between her family, so close to the Crown, and her future with a commoner husband. From there Caroline went alone to the home of a friend of her father's where she and Fox were secretly married. Her parents were enraged. They had planned a great ball for the following Friday, May 8. Even the Prince of Wales was expected to attend. They canceled it immediately. They required everyone in London society to choose sides, and they did not speak to their daughter or son-in-law for four years. The Earl of March for these years had lost his big sister, whom he much admired. Like her, he would prove to be intelligent, anxious, reckless, and drawn to wit and ambition.

While the illicit romance was playing out, the Continental War continued to rage and now spread to the colonies. France declared war on Britain in America, and the two great powers engaged in conflict in India. Despite the roiling political events, the demoralized 2nd Duke stayed away from London that fall and devoted considerable time to his world in Sussex. His close friend Martin Folkes, president of the Royal Society, joined him at Goodwood. The Duke began construction of an extension on his home that would later contain the very elegant Large Library. He invited Peter Collinson, the well-connected Quaker who routinely supplied the Duke with plants and seeds from the Americas for his estates, to visit. Collinson was not able to come, choosing instead to vacation on the Isle of Wight, due south of Goodwood, in the English Channel. He wrote the Duke to say that on clear days he could see Goodwood from the island.

James FitzGerald, Earl of Kildare, heir to the most senior peerage in Ireland, also visited Goodwood, to court Emily. His proposal in June 1745 was put off, with the requirement that he wait a year until Emily was fifteen. In the end he would have to wait eighteen months. During this period, the Duke turned his attention from the prospects of his two older daughters to those of his first son. He toyed with getting into a colonial venture to Nova Scotia in order to improve his son's financial prospects. He took up golf for the first time; and sent his cricket protégé, Lord John Sackville, to Westminster to teach the boys there the new game.

THEN WAR CAME TO England, and the Duke could not remain aloof. In 1745, the instability in Europe from the War of the Austrian Succession led to a rebellion at home. "Bonnie Prince Charlie" had long maintained a Jacobite court in Paris, gathering around him those who were ready to restore a Catholic monarch to Britain. In their antagonism to the British, the French government considered Bonnie Prince Charlie an asset to be deployed as part of the War of the Austrian Succession. Now France provided him with just enough financial resources to launch an attack on Britain.

The British government knew that Charles Stuart was plotting to reclaim the throne. Among the men the Duke had hosted at Goodwood in the summer and early fall of 1744 was Sussex native Colonel Edmund Martin, who served in the regiment of Captain James Wolfe (later the famous general who took Quebec from the French for the British in 1759). By late fall, Martin was serving in Scotland—where the bitter weather had kept the corn still green all the way into autumn and where the hills were already topped by snow. Constant rain kept Martin indoors, and he used the time to write to the Duke at length about the quality of the roads, forts, and geography. The Duke's questions must have emanated from a desire to understand what the state of military preparedness was, in the event of a landing by Bonnie Prince Charlie in Scotland. The young Earl of March must have had opportunity to listen in on his father's conversations with Colonel Martin, because this link to the regiment of Captain James Wolfe would soon become very important to him.

THE FAMILY'S IDYLLIC SEASON of romance at Goodwood came to a terrifying halt when news arrived that, on July 23, 1745, Bonnie Prince Charlie had landed in the Outer Hebrides with a plan to seize the British throne. War's distant Continental rumble had now reached sheltered British shores. The Pretender, as his enemies called him, had traveled from Nantes in a French privateer ship, the *Du Teillay*, accompanied by a French warship. The warship, though, was peeled away by an engagement with the British Navy, so Bonnie Prince Charlie landed without any army at all. Yet this inauspicious beginning turned quickly into the most aggressive internal conflict in England in several generations. By August 19, Charles Stuart had raised an army from the Scottish Highlanders. He tapped into long-standing loyalty to the Stuarts, long-simmering resentment at Scottish subjection to the British Crown, and hopes for Scottish independence. He gathered his rough, weather-worn Highlander troops under his flag at Glenfinnan and launched what came to be known as the Jacobite rebellion.

The Richmond family's Whig loyalties were tested. Charles I was their great-great-grandfather too. The Earl of March and Bonnie Prince Charlie were second cousins once removed, and March's sisters called the Pretender "our cousin." Even at Westminster the boys felt the reach of Charles Stuart's recruitment drive. The prince wrote personally to members of the nobility inviting them into his court and offering a reward for "the Elector of Hanover's head." He used the King's German title, Elector of Hanover, in his letters because of course he refused to acknowledge George II as King of England. The question of which families might in fact choose to join the Stuart cause agitated the school. There were boys enrolled whose relatives did enlist in Bonnie Prince Charlie's army, but the Head of School, Dr. Nicoll, "expressed a wish that their limbs and feelings should be left unhurt." He forbade the verbal abuse that Londoners were otherwise hurling at those who supported the Pretender, and despite strong feelings on both sides, he kept his boys in check. March knew where his family stood. Against the Richmond family's ties of blood to the Pretender, the long and dedicated service of March's father to King George II had been intended to insulate the family from any association between them and the Jacobites.

Even as alliances were being tested and shifting, events quickly accelerated. The Pretender was driving forward with alarming speed. On September 21, 1745, the Jacobites made a surprise attack on government troops at Prestonpans, about eleven miles east of Edinburgh on the Firth of Forth. Though greatly outnumbered, the Jacobite fighting forces were locals, and their familiarity with the terrain was decisive. They won within an hour and took roughly 1,500 government troops prisoner. This boosted Jacobite morale significantly and increased the power of the Jacobite army, which began a drive toward London. Fear spread in the South.

The King's second son, the Duke of Cumberland, was put at the head of the military to assemble a contingent to stop the Pretender. The Duke of Richmond found himself suddenly promoted to lieutenant general and placed alongside the Duke of Cumberland. On November 8, he was promoted to full general, with command of the cavalry, with orders to proceed to Lichfield, about 120 miles north of London. His task: stop the Jacobite advance.

Meanwhile, both his Duchess, "Dear Taw," and all of London were panicking. By December 1, the government began to assemble its armies around London, anticipating that the Pretender would reach the city. They sent for Hessian troops from Hanover. By December 3, rumors had begun to circulate that the French were going to sail from Dunkirk, cross the Channel, and land troops on the South Coast. Rebels were said to be marching to Wales. Terror spread among aristocrats that "the country people" were helping the rebels, and dread curled through the gloomy, wintry capital like a cold fog. Westminster School was breaking up for the holidays, but it wasn't to be a normal December with thoughts of hunting and holiday parties. March's father would not be home for Christmas, and his fifteen-year-old schoolfellow, Charles Watson-Wentworth, later the 2nd Marquess of Rockingham, and future prime minister, ran off to the army to join the regiments mustering around London. March surely felt the frenzy—and excitement—of war.

Despite the widespread anxiety, the British troops, with Richmond at their head, turned the tide in December. The Pretender made it as far as Derby, twenty-four miles north of Lichfield, where March's father had been stationed, and about 120 miles north of London. Here Richmond's troops held the line. They stopped the rebels' advance and then started driving the Jacobite army back north. Alongside other generals, Richmond chased the Pretender to Carlisle, ten miles south of the border with Scotland. There the British treated the Jacobites to a sound defeat. The battle's decisive result meant discharge from duty for Richmond and others. The 2nd Duke headed home and was there when his daughter Sarah Lennox was born two months later. Rockingham, who also fought valiantly at Carlisle, returned to school after the Christmas holidays. Even without Richmond and Rockingham, the British troops maintained their footing and continued to drive Bonnie Prince Charlie and his Scottish Highlanders ever farther north until their decisive defeat and surrender in April at Culloden, near the Moray Firth, an inlet of the North Sea. As for Rockingham, once back at school, the history of Westminster School reports, "He was too modest to boast of his adventure, and too earnest to repent of it."

Rockingham may not have directly reported on his exploits, but tales of martial glory had clearly captured March's imagination. He was now the son of a hero who had saved the British crown. Also, his uncle, Willem van Keppel, 2nd Earl of Albemarle, was promoted at the end of the war to commander in chief for Scotland. His cousin, George Keppel, had fought at Culloden with the Duke of Cumberland, second son of the King, and carried the victory message back to London. His other cousin, Augustus Keppel, who began his naval career at the age of ten, had recently spent four years circumnavigating the globe from 1740 to 1744, and served the British Navy dutifully throughout the War of the Austrian Succession, commanding his own ships. His father's service against the Pretender brought other military men into the family circle—Colonel Martin and Captain Wolfe in particular, as well as a naval officer John Fletcher, whose sailing days stretched back to the late seventeenth century and whom March met. Although the 2nd Duke owned a couple of books on fortifications, such books began appearing regularly in the family library only when the little boy would have been first old enough to start reading and appreciating them. The first shows up in 1741, then another in 1742, and the third and fourth in 1746 and 1747. They proliferate from that point on. How to defend England was the driving question of March's early school days. It would be one of the reigning passions of his life.

WHILE THE BRITISH AND Highlanders clashed with broadswords and muskets across the fields of Northern England, back in the South the Earl of Kildare had waged his own battle for Emily's hand with patience and gentle correspondence. By December 1746, this suitably aristocratic suitor had won. The affianced couple took their first walks together on Christmas Day at a newly built picnic pavilion on a high elevation at Goodwood, called Carné's Seat, with a view across the Channel waters to the Isle of Wight. They were married not even two months later, on February 7, and would soon make their life in Ireland. There Emily would travel an unusual path, developing radical sympathies quite different from her husband's politics. These emerge in quiet ways in her letters and developed through intellectual companionship with her children's tutor. It would, though, be many years before brother and sister came to recognize their shared political commitments.

March's movement toward radicalism lay years in the future still. For now, military valor had caught his eye. Surprisingly, his future military connections would eventually open up a wholly independent pathway into radicalism for the future duke. But for the time being in the late years of the War of the Austrian Succession, March continued to develop along his expected trajectory and in accord with the plans of his courtier father. Those plans involved the expectation of political leadership as a member of the Whig aristocracy.

The 2nd Duke discussed the question of how best to educate his son with his good friends, Folkes and Montesquieu. Just at the point March had been sent to school, Montesquieu reminded the two men of a generous offer he had made earlier to receive their sons in France when they were ready, where he would tutor them and provide mentorship. The philosopher wrote in a letter:

> Remember that you promised us, monsieur, your son for a year in Bourdeaux; we will put him in good company and we will do everything so one day he is just like his father. Perhaps one of the great provincial towns, for a young man who finds good company with honest people and friends, is better than Paris itself. I reply to you that I will have my eyes on him and that he will be a libertine only as a gallant man should be, and I will be his mentor.

Thanks to Montesquieu's promise, the young 3rd Duke would indeed stop to visit the philosopher and inventor of separation of powers and checks and balances during his Grand Tour. He would soon have a front row seat for the publication of Montesquieu's magnum opus, *The Spirit of the Laws*. First published anonymously in 1748, the book entered into English translations in 1750 and spread rapidly. In the book, Montesquieu contrasts monarchies, aristocracies, and republics. Each form of government turns around a defining principle: for monarchies, honor; for aristocracies, moderation; and for republics, virtue. The monarch uses the hierarchies and ranks of an honor society to direct ambition toward the interests of the state. Aristocrats, in contrast, recognize that their authority depends also on the well-being of the people and the assent of the people to their leadership. This leads aristocrats to moderate their power and to accept law and tradition, to keep their society in equilibrium. Finally, in a republic the governing principle is virtue—the idea that citizens must embody a commitment to lawfulness, self-sacrifice, and the public good for society to thrive. In offering to host the sons of Folkes and Richmond in his dull, provincial town, Montesquieu was offering to educate their sons into the moderation necessary for aristocratic leadership. Distance from the libertine indulgences of the capital would keep the young aristocrats better connected to good and honest people.

Yet the time had not yet arrived for March to go abroad. Sussex itself still provided plenty of its own opportunities for learning and leadership in provincial towns. Aristocrats interacted most freely with commoners during election season, and in the summer of 1747 conflict on the battlefield gave way to contests at the polls.

The shrewd prime minister, Henry Pelham, had called an election, one year before the scheduled end of the seven-year parliamentary session. The War of the Austrian Succession was at a stalemate: None of the central competing powers (Austria, Bohemia, Flanders, and Italy) had been able to achieve decisive dominance. The French routinely failed to hold their conquests, but neither could the British-Dutch alliance fully reclaim key territories. The stalemate was putting pressure on domestic British politics. The war was expensive and straining finances. The Jacobite rebellion had led to public criticism of whether the government was adequately handling national security. Pelham wanted to end the war, but he was cautious and valued stability above all else. He knew that he would need popular support to steer this policy change through. He saw the victory over Bonnie Prince Charlie as an opportunity to marshal anti-Jacobite, anti-Tory sentiment and to win a larger majority in the House of Commons so that he could achieve that. Hence his decision to call an election.

Because Pelham held his own parliamentary seat in Chichester and, along with his brother the Duke of Newcastle, drew much of his political power from Sussex, he was looking to the 2nd Duke of Richmond to help them lock down as many parliamentary seats in the county as possible during the 1747 elections. Richmond typically conducted his political business at the annual summer races in Lewes and at cricket matches in August, as well as at the annual assizes—or court sessions—held just before or after the races. He would routinely host dinners for local townsmen as a way of seeking to win their votes for his preferred candidate. Particularly influential townspeople would be asked to lend their support by canvassing further votes. In 1741 "Dear Taw" was sent out to win the support of an influential local parson. She attended long sermons in the summer heat to do so and suffered a miscarriage in the process.

Now, in 1747, at the age of eleven, the Earl of March was also called into service. He was tasked with taking to the stump during debates taking place at the local races and assizes to argue against a candidate from the party of the Prince of Wales, William Hall Gage. After Gage was defeated, the Duke of Newcastle wrote to March's father, on August 29, "I fully intended last week to write a letter of thanks to Lord March for having done the honors so well at Lewes, . . . & made Lord Gage appear as insignificant as He is." Newcastle continued by offering his respects to the Duchess and compliments to March, whom he now classed "as a considerable young Nobleman of Sussex."

Pelham's snap election paid off. He won the Parliament he sought and was able to lead the country to peace. The Treaty of Aix-la-Chapelle was signed in August 1748. In this joyful period, the Richmonds reconciled with Caroline, and after four years the integrity of the family was restored. Caroline, Henry, and their children were able to participate when the 2nd Duke ordered up a celebration for the victory in the war—fireworks over Richmond House fired from the Thames the following February. The Duke of Richmond was also proud of his sons, and on a day with the deepest snow he could remember, wrote to a former mistress: "My eldest boy, Lord March (a name not unknown to you!) is just 13, he is handsome, and lively to a degree; he is at college [i.e., Westminster]. His younger brother, Lord George, is still handsomer than he; he is 10 years old and is also at college. He is not so lively as his brother, but he is the best hearted lad in the world, and has as much wit and common sense as I could possibly desire."

Already as an adolescent, March was being trained to take the lead for the government's party, the establishment Whigs. He could not have been further from radicalism than this—awed by the victories of his father and friend Rockingham against the Jacobite rebels, deeply intrigued by questions of military strategy and the best approach to fortifying England, and ready to test his prowess at moderate aristocratic leadership by rubbing shoulders with grocers, printers, and parsons while fending off threats to stability from the political party of the Prince of Wales, a man disdained by his own father, the King. Nurture was forming him into a considerable young nobleman of a conventional cast. Yet nature was about to show its own force.

Chapter
2

PURPOSE

1749–1759

To be of some service to my country and
for an occupation and amusement for myself.

—3RD DUKE OF RICHMOND, TO HIS BROTHER GEORGE LENNOX, FEBRUARY 2, 1758

THE YOUNG EARL OF MARCH WAS BEING RAISED FOR A LIFE of measured, aristocratic leadership—groomed to become one of the "great oaks" of England, as Edmund Burke would later describe the role. Yet his nature would lead him in another direction. Once war in Europe gave way to peace, and cultural pressure to duty briefly subsided, in years that coincided with March's adolescence and young adulthood, his rebellious instincts began to show themselves.

With the conclusion of the Treaty of Aix-la-Chapelle in 1748, eight long years of war were finally over. Prussia now held Silesia permanently and had established itself as a great power. The Bourbons in Spain had taken and were confirmed in holding duchies in northern Italy. In the colonies, France and Britain swapped territory—Madras went to the British in India; Louisbourg in Nova Scotia to the French. The peace was not perfect. In the American colonies, France and Britain continued to vie for superiority, particularly in the Ohio River Valley, where Native American tribes were caught between the two European powers. The British colonists increasingly required defense.

Culture was shifting too. In London in 1749 Henry Fielding published *The History of Tom Jones*, the first novel in English literature with fully plotted unity of action. Soon most novelists would be probing questions of character and its development over time rather than loosely linking a series of episodes to show different features of a consistent character, like Don Quixote, who was the subject of luxurious tapestries that hung in a room created for them at Goodwood—the Tapestry Drawing Room.

March's father had described him as "lively to a degree," by which he meant, intelligent but also undaunted by rules and irrepressible. Adolescence heightened these features, as is visible in letters to his parents during their absences. In the summer of 1749, the 2nd Duke, ever faithful to his King, traveled to the Continent with a plan to take up the British ambassadorship in Paris. Peace had permitted resumption of diplomatic relations between Britain and France. The Duke did not actually want the ambassadorship, though, because of the immense personal expense involved in provisioning an equipage and ceremonially appropriate home. In the end he would avoid the appointment and not be long absent from Britain, but even in that small interim, hints of trouble with March began to emerge.

March and his brother had been left in the hands of a tutor, Mr. Gibberd, who was expected to support their study at Westminster and then, for March, matriculation at either Oxford or Cambridge, at the age of seventeen or eighteen. George, the second son, was also by now at Westminster but would then be directed toward training in the military, in line with the common convention among aristocratic families to send one younger son into the armed forces. March's father educated and admonished him by letter with lessons for which March dutifully thanked his father: "I am very obliged to you for your kind letter which I hope will have a proper effect upon me." In another letter, though, he wryly thumbed his nose at the efforts of his tutor and father to manage him through correspondence. "Dear Papa, I have just received your kind and obliging letter which brought me the welcome news of your all being in perfect health. I am very sensible that Mr. Gibberd is very desirous of my good behaviour, by his being so ready to acquaint you with it!" This he uncharacteristically signed "C. March," the "C" for Charles a reminder that he was descended from his pleasure-seeking great-grandfather. His signature had attitude—he was asserting his independence, his self-sovereignty. This use of his first initial would return later in his life, again to signal his independence.

March's resistance to rule was clearly a habit. In early fall, just before the opening of Westminster, Gibberd took the boys to Oxford for a tour. For March this was the visit of a prospective student. Gibberd reported that the faculty members who had toured the campus with them were impressed by March's curiosity, but March himself claimed to have been interested only in pretty horses that he saw on the road—and in dogs. On the road home he was bitten in the face by one of them. He wrote to let his father know about the incident, once again acknowledging admonishments: "At my return from Oxford, I received your letter and was very sorry I gave you occasion to caution me about my writing well, which was in some measure owing to my not having good pens, but chiefly to my own negligence concerning which I shall take greater care in the future." He then reported that a large dog had flown at his face, "after I had been giving him some meat." Mr. Gibberd's cover note, though, provided the full picture. "The Pinch Lord March received from the Dog, was I believe, owing to his teasing, or playing too roughly with him, tho' frequently caution'd against it."

March was a boisterous, sometime reckless adolescent with very little parental supervision and plenty of self-confidence. He was often described as having an active mind. This brought with it an impulsive, frenetic energy that led him to push the bounds of propriety and safety. Unsurprisingly, he got into his share of trouble, to his mother's apparent distress. He was smart enough to try to pacify her so that she didn't share the news of all his escapades with his less tolerant father: "Dear Mama, I have reflected with great concern upon the uneasiness I gave you at dinner, by a behaviour which I am extremely ashamed of, and sorry for. I scarce know with what face to ask your pardon, after having had occasion to desire it so often, but shall esteem it as a particular favour if you would so far oblige me as nott to mention my ill behaviour to Papa, but forgive, Your most Penitent, dutiful & obedient Son, March."

He did not stay penitent, dutiful, and obedient for long, though, especially around young women, who seem to have captured his attention around this time. In June 1750, after his father had returned from his aborted tour of duty, and sitting in his father's office right under the nose of his father's secretary, March wrote a long, spicy, confessional letter to his brother-in-law, Henry "Harry" Fox, to report on his attempted seductions. This letter, too, he signed C. March, invoking the Merry Monarch. The letter caused Henry Fox enough concern that, without sharing its details, he advised the Duke that March should not remain at school where he had a great deal of freedom to come and go as he pleased, perhaps too much freedom. The worry was that, like other schoolboys, Charles Churchill and John Penn, he would surreptitiously take a wife.

The Duke decided that March should be removed from the temptations of London and, instead of continuing at Westminster, should be sent on a tour of the Continent. He reached out to the natural scientist Abraham Trembley, from Geneva, famous for discovering that polyps are animals, not plants, and asked him to serve as his son's chaperone, or "bear-leader," as the role was dubbed at the time.

Before the plans could be enacted, however, the 2nd Duke of Richmond fell ill. He had been struggling with a stomach ailment for some time, and in July 1750 he took a turn for the worse. Although he was able to join the Duke of Cumberland at a dinner party on July 27, four days later he was desperately sick. His secretary, Sedgwick, summoned the family doctor for advice, but there was nothing to be done. On his deathbed, the Duke of Richmond reiterated his request to Trembley that he serve as tutor for his sons. By August 8, 1750, he was dead of bladder cancer, at the age of forty-nine.

CHARLES LENNOX, FORMERLY KNOWN as the Earl of March, was now, at fourteen and a half, the 3rd Duke of Richmond. He was not the only young aristocrat to lose a father that year. Frederick, Prince of Wales, died after being caught in the rain in the garden and falling ill. His son, George, three years younger than Charles, became the heir presumptive to the throne and gained the title Prince of Wales. Both young men lost their fathers during a brief interregnum of peace—between the end of the War of the Austrian Succession and the onset of the Seven Years' War. They would have just a few years to find their own sense of purpose as adults before events would summon them. The tectonic plates of global politics were starting to shift. The early stages of industrialization were transforming their domestic situation, and political philosophy changed the horizons of politics.

Britain's empire already stretched far enough that world events affected it domestically. The Seven Years' War would begin first in America in 1754 as the French and Indian War, after years of skirmishes culminated in George Washington's ill-fated expedition to Fort Duquesne. It would come to embrace the globe. In India the Mughal Empire was fracturing. Regional powers like the Marathas, the Nizam of Hyderabad, and the Nawabs of Bengal had been independent for decades and others were joining them. The British East India Company and French East India Company squared off against each other in the contest for alliances, pulling their nations into another theater of war.

As to the economy, Europe was rapidly urbanizing. In London, Westminster Bridge, a ten-minute walk from Richmond House, opened in 1750 after eleven years of construction, and pointed toward expanding suburbanization. The largest cities—London and Paris—now had populations of 700,000 and 500,000, respectively, and were growing rapidly. Water and waste management systems were introduced as well as lighting and paving for roads. As artisans and rural migrants joined the throngs filling the cities, wealth and poverty increasingly jostled up against each other. Suburbs like Spitalfields expanded rapidly. Home to a long-standing Huguenot community famed not only for silk-weaving but also the capture and sale of songbirds like linnets, goldfinches, and chaffinches, the neighborhood was afflicted by poverty and crime because of the economic precarity of the cloth industry. More than its fair share of residents were hanged in the eighteenth century. In these years, London's nightwatchmen were established, and Paris introduced a police force.

The cultural revolution of the Enlightenment was also well underway. The year the 2nd Duke died, Jean-Jacques Rousseau published his *First Discourse*, the *Discourse on the Sciences and Arts*, in answer to a prize competition question: "Has the restoration of the sciences and arts contributed to the purification of morals?" Rousseau's answer was no. He argued that the sciences and arts cultivated vanity, which degrades virtue and corrupts society from its healthy natural state. The advancement of the arts and sciences allowed the wealthy to indulge in luxury while the poor became more dependent and degraded. These themes of corruption, wealth and poverty, true virtue, and the natural equality of humankind would become defining issues in the adult political lives of both young men, the Prince of Wales and the 3rd Duke of Richmond, and each would play a role in leading his country—George of necessity, Richmond by choice.

FOLLOWING HIS FATHER'S WISHES, the newly minted Duke of Richmond withdrew from Westminster School to travel with Trembley, who first took him not to luxurious and busy Paris but to Calvinist Geneva. Again moderation was the theme. Years later, Richmond would recall that it was Geneva where he had first begun to read seriously. Boredom drove him to it.

In addition to his tutor, young Richmond was also now equipped with a set of extraordinarily well-connected and influential guardians whose job was to guide him and oversee his finances until he came of age at twenty-one. They included an uncle—the Earl of Albemarle, who was at the time ambassador to France; two brothers-in-law—Henry Fox, Caroline's husband, and Lord Kildare, Emily's husband; and a political mentor, the Duke of Newcastle. Newcastle was still secretary of state, a post he had held for twenty-six years. His brother, Henry Pelham, was still prime minister. They were the two most powerful men in England, after the King. Lastly, Richmond's father had bequeathed him a fortune that annually produced an income of seventeen thousand pounds, equivalent to more than four million dollars in 2024 dollars. Richmond was being sent abroad, under the supervision of these men, to complete the education that would allow him to inherit his father's mantle as a pillar of tradition and stability for the monarchy. Instead, his time abroad would introduce him to the philosophy and personalities that would turn him into a radical.

As the Grand Tour proceeded, there was a constant struggle between what Richmond was expected to do and what he wanted to do. During their journey to Switzerland, Trembley and Richmond collected the books that would support the young Duke's course of study: a history of Geneva, purchased in Leiden; a history of ancient and modern Rome, complete with illustrations; a natural history of the Adriatic Sea. There were also texts focused on the practical, economic, and political. A treatise on agriculture, a history of the Roman Senate, memoirs of the House of Brunswick, one of the great royal families of Europe; a map of the Netherlands; a catalog of the collections of Florentine museums; the battle plans and journals from the siege of Flanders in Belgium; and a book providing instruction in the exercise of small arms and great guns. The young Duke's imagination was intended to be nourished by Virgil's

Aeneid, Diderot's plays, and *Azor, ou le prince enchanté*, a novel about an island populated by mutes and a parrot that changes the lives of the mutes. But when Trembley reported to the Duke's guardians about how things were going, he mentioned none of these books. Instead, he noted that "the Duke loves dogs prodigiously and also the human race and the feminine race."

The liberal arts education and social playfulness of this first year abroad were interrupted the following summer when the Duke's mother died just shy of her forty-sixth birthday. Whatever the impact on his young heart, his already buoyant finances were boosted further by his mother's passing. He inherited the family homes—both Richmond House in London and Goodwood in Sussex. All the riches of the coal duty now came to him fully. His brother George joined him on the Continent under Trembley's care, and except for brief visits back to England, the two young men would stay abroad with Trembley until 1756, when Richmond came of age and returned to London to enter the House of Lords and take charge of his own financial affairs. George was all playfulness and good humor, and possessed little to no ambition. The two boys had always been different in temperament and interests, but also always close.

After George's arrival, the divergence between what the tutor hoped the Duke would learn and what he was really interested in only grew. Alongside dogs and women, Richmond had a third overarching passion: military affairs. After the Duchess's passing and George's arrival in Geneva, the young duke began to educate himself for a military career. His first step was to secure a commission as ensign in the 2nd Foot Guards, also known as the Coldstream Regiment of Foot Guards, the oldest regiment in the British Army. This regiment has the special responsibility of protecting the monarchy. His fifty-year-old uncle and guardian, the Earl of Albemarle, was the regiment's lieutenant colonel. Within a year, without having served at all, Richmond managed to secure the promise of a promotion to captain in his uncle's regiment, to be awarded sometime the following year. He also wrote to his guardians asking to come home.

Permission to return was denied. Presumably, given Trembley's reports, his guardians continued to worry about Richmond's amorous nature and preferred that he spend down its fires abroad. Trembley's solution was to determine that he and the two young men would travel for a period in France and take up Montesquieu's offer to be a mentor to Richmond.

Trembley, Richmond, and George traveled through Lyon, Marseille, and Montpellier on their way to Bordeaux to stay with the philosophical Baron, who was at the height of his fame. Montesquieu had published *The Spirit of the Laws* anonymously in French in 1748. The first English translation came out in 1750. In 1751 the Catholic Church added the book to its list of banned books. Montesquieu's theories of separation of powers and checks and balances threatened the authority of any established church. Trembley and Richmond prepared for this trip by reading Montesquieu's original French edition, in a two-volume edition published in Geneva, bound in red leather. Richmond would become a lifelong reader of Montesquieu. He later acquired a book of maxims extracted from *The Spirit of the Laws* in 1758, and a complete six-volume set of Montesquieu's works in 1764. Montesquieu's vocabulary for constitutionalism and the rule of law would find its way into Richmond's letters and writings for the rest of his life. Finally, something had made an intellectual impression on the young duke.

AFTER THREE MONTHS OF travel, and life-changing conversations about constitutionalism with Montesquieu, Richmond, George, and Tremblay arrived in damp, wintry Paris, a city of grandeur and inequality, in time for Christmas of 1752. The Louvre was still a royal residence. Imposing private townhouses with private gardens lined elegant avenues in areas like Faubourg Saint-Honoré while the working poor crowded into tenements in noisy, stinky neighborhoods like Faubourg Saint-Antoine, the Marais, and the Île de la Cité, where there were open gutters and waste was thrown into the street. Richmond's fifty-year-old uncle and guardian, the Earl of Albemarle, had accepted the ambassadorship in place of Richmond's father when the 2nd Duke declined the office. He welcomed them into the glittering universe of French *ducs*, *marquis*, *comtes*, *vicomtes*, *barons*, and *chevaliers* who circulated around the French court.

There the young British duke met a man who would change his life and give him his sense of purpose. James Wolfe was a twenty-five-year-old lieutenant colonel for the 20th Regiment of Foot. He was tall with light blue eyes and already battle-hardened. He had served at Dettingen, Laufield, Falkirk, and Culloden—famous battles all. He was self-educated but well read, a volatile military genius. As a boy, he had roamed the countryside around his home with a friend mapping out battle plans and strategy.

In a letter to his father from December 4, 1752, Wolfe reported meeting Richmond at Lord Albemarle's home. There the two young men, one aged twenty-five and the other just shy of eighteen, discussed organization, discipline, and training of the various armies of the Continent. The letter confirms that the young duke made a strong and positive impression on the soldier. Wolfe wrote: "As far as my discernment goes, he promises to make a considerable figure in our way, to which his genius seems to lead him." Wolfe was especially impressed by Richmond's seriousness about soldiery. He added, "What is uncommon at eighteen he is not entirely taken up with the outward appearances and gildings of soldiership, but aims at the higher and more solid branches of military knowledge."

On New Year's Day 1753, thanks to Albemarle, both Wolfe and Richmond found themselves at Versailles, the largest palace in the world, set amid two thousand acres of meticulous gardens, where the forty-three-year-old king, Louis XV, was holding court. Slender and graceful, with pale skin, fine features and light brown hair, the shy but witty King was still popular, and even nicknamed, "The Well Loved." Only later would his reclusiveness, indecision, and disengagement from governance lead to a decisive withdrawal of popular support. In the King's court at Versailles, the scene was "splendour and magnificence," Wolfe reported, but it left him "cold." He derided the fawning excesses, in which "a multitude of men and women were assembled to bow and pay their compliments in the most submissive manner to a creature of their own species." Wolfe was a thoroughgoing egalitarian.

Richmond offered Wolfe a ride home in his coach that evening and that coach ride was the beginning of an intense friendship. They must have found themselves aligned in their reaction to the court. As they rumbled back into Paris, Richmond sought the seasoned soldier's advice. He confided that he had secured a promotion to captain in his uncle's regiment and offered Wolfe a paid role if he would be his tutor in military affairs and his guide "through the fortified towns of the Low Countries and into the Lorraine." Though the proposed compensation was considerable, Wolfe declined. He suggested instead his friend and fellow soldier, Guy Carleton, also twenty-eight. At the time, Carleton was, like Richmond, a captain, though with several years of experience under his belt. He would eventually rise to being the governor-general of British North America. Carleton accepted the job. By the time Richmond received his promised next commission, in June 1753, it was no longer in his uncle's regiment, but now in Wolfe's: the 20th Regiment of Foot.

Wolfe was an inspiring leader. Another of his soldiers said, "He made me read not only military books, but philosophy; he gave me liberal notions of every kind." This is clearly the kind of influence Wolfe had on Richmond. In the 20th Foot Richmond also met another young man equally influenced by Wolfe and his intellectual tastes who would be important to his political journey, William Petty Fitzmaurice. In 1761 Petty Fitzmaurice would become the 2nd Earl of Shelburne, thanks to a surprise inheritance through his mother's side of the family. He would be a distinguished politician, supporter of the Americans, and eventually the prime minister responsible for bringing the American Revolution and war with France to their conclusion.

IN FEBRUARY 1753, WHEN Richmond turned eighteen, he, Trembley, and George returned to London for a brief visit. It was the first time he had been home in two and a half years. He arrived in a city trying to grapple with rising religious pluralism. Methodism was beginning to spread and dissenting Presbyterian and Baptist chapels were quietly adopting more rationalist, proto-Unitarian theology—even though denial of the Trinity remained illegal. Parliament was preparing to debate the Jewish Naturalisation Act, which would allow Jews to become naturalized British citizens without having to profess allegiance to Christianity. It would pass in April—one of England's first major steps toward modern religious toleration—but then be repealed a year later after a wave of anti-Semitic backlash.

This 1753 visit was Richmond's first appearance in London society as his father's heir. At Holland House, the home of his sister, Caroline, and brother-in-law Henry Fox, he danced at his first ball. Several of his military companions were in attendance as well, including Carleton. His late father's friends were eager to see him and to report to their networks on how he was doing. Among these was the botanist and lover of America, Peter Collinson, a good friend of the famous American scientist Benjamin Franklin, who had just the previous month been awarded the Copley Medal by the Royal Society, Britain's most prestigious scientific honor, "on account of his curious Experiments and Observations on Electricity." The award was made in absentia because Franklin was at that time still in Philadelphia. Collinson had been very close to the 2nd Duke of Richmond because of their shared love of botany and natural history. Collinson wrote to Franklin about "the young duke of Richmond," reporting that the young man had asked that his regards be sent to John Penn. The American network was keeping tabs on young Richmond.

The London visit was brief. George stayed back in London, but Trembley and Richmond were soon on their way again to continue the Duke's education. Trembley thought a university education was necessary in some form and, in the fall of 1753, Richmond enrolled at Leiden for roughly six months. George rejoined them in early 1754 and by the spring, Richmond, George, and Trembley went mobile once more: to Berlin, to meet Frederick the Great, an austere man with rigid military bearing, then at the height of his intellectual and administrative energy. Then on to Bohemia and Moravia, and after stops in Brussels and Brunswick, to Vienna, where they spent fifty mornings in the new Museum of the Imperial Court (the Kaiserliches Hofmuseum), also known as the Cabinet of Natural History. They made stops in Venice—where they were held up when the whole Venetian Lagoon froze over in the Great Frost of January 1755—as well as Rome, Naples, Florence, Pisa, Turin, Bern, and the Rhineland, before they wound up back at The Hague. Near Strasbourg they encountered troops drilling and training; Richmond insisted on pitching his tent to observe from close at hand.

The trio met, in one place after the next, many leading intellectuals of the day. The physician and expert in anatomy, Antonio Cocchi, and Paolo Frisi, a mathematician, in Pisa. The botany professor and architect responsible for repairing St. Peter's Basilica, Vitaliano Donati, in Turin. Albrecht von Haller, a poet and natural scientist, in Bern. Charles Marie de La Condamine, explorer of Peru, in Paris. After the end of the War of the Austrian Succession, a Grand Tour had once again become the norm for heirs of aristocratic families, but the typical length was two years, followed by time at Oxford or Cambridge. Richmond was unusual in staying abroad for five years and for meeting such a wide array of the Continent's intellectuals.

Throughout, Richmond continued his correspondence with Wolfe. They exchanged frequent letters for the six years following their meeting and discussed a variety of military matters. Richmond sent proposed exercises for troops to Wolfe for feedback. Wolfe shared words of affirmation. He had shared Richmond's proposal with his superior officer who, Wolfe wrote, "received 'em with a smile & foretold your future Fortune in Arms." Wolfe also wrote to Richmond with an extensive critique of the state of the British military preparedness to defend its south coast, the coastline of Lennox's home county of Sussex. They exchanged observations about the growing signs of movement toward war in Europe. Frederick and Maria Theresa were both working on troop readiness with new exercises and reviews. Wolfe urged Richmond to be observant of the European methods.

To understand the military build-up he was seeing, Richmond requested pamphlets and maps from his tutor. Whereas most of the older male mentors in Richmond's life—and his guardians in particular—all insisted that the young duke resist his urges for active duty and concentrate on his cultural and historical education, Wolfe fanned the flame of his interest and gave him reason to think a call for service might soon come.

Also of special importance for Richmond during this time were the stops in Italy, where he visited all the galleries, picked up the usual aristocratic souvenirs such as signet rings with ancient engravings, and met a cluster of impressive young artists. He could be loutish and callow: From Florence, he reported to his brother-in-law that he had particularly appreciated the *Venus de' Medici*; "I am in love with the Venus and take great pleasure to stroke her bum and thighs," he wrote. In Rome, though, his engagement with the arts grew more serious. He discovered that since 1751 an Irish aristocrat, the Earl of Charlemont, who later founded the Royal Irish Academy in Dublin, had sponsored an English art school, "The Academy of English Professors of the Liberal Arts." The academy provoked concern in the Roman political authorities and the Vatican about the cultural impact of a Protestant school at Rome, and they had recently closed it down. Richmond got to know the circle of artists connected to it and became a patron and ultimately an advocate, seeking to help the artists find space free from the interference of authorities. He began to commission artists, starting with two portraits of himself—each

While on the Grand Tour, the young Duke of Richmond traveled with his dogs, which would become a lifelong practice.

BY PERMISSION OF THE TRUSTEES OF THE GOODWOOD COLLECTION.

reflecting in some way his earliest passions: dogs, women, and military strategy, in order of discovery.

In the first painting, by Pompeo Batoni, Richmond stands with his hands gently cradling the head of one of his beloved spaniels. (We can assume he traveled with them throughout his Grand Tour; traveling with his hunting hounds and pet dogs was a lifelong practice.)

In the second painting, by Anton Raphael Mengs, young Richmond wears Van Dyke dress: clothes from the era of his great-grandfather, Charles II. The portrait signals his connection to his amorous ancestor

The young Duke of Richmond dressed in seventeenth-century garb from the era of his great-great-grandfather Charles I.

BY PERMISSION OF THE TRUSTEES OF THE GOODWOOD COLLECTION.

and communicates his own rakishness, but then there's a visual joke in the picture. The bust behind him is not Venus but Minerva, the highly rational, asexual goddess of war. She symbolized strategy, rather than the chaotic aspects of combat. He might lead his guardians to believe his attention was all on Venus's bum, but his own iconography claimed Minerva as his presiding spirit.

From conversation with artists like the architect William Chambers, the sculptor Joseph Wilton, and the painter and designer Giovanni Battista Cipriani—who must have voiced frustrations with patronage in

England and Italy—Richmond concocted a plan. England had no great patron of the arts for public purpose. Those aristocrats who did collect art kept their acquisitions private, just like the Medici in Florence. The expatriate artists living in Rome, though, had begun to conjure up a national cultural project whereby the aesthetic power of Greece and Rome could infuse and strengthen British cultural life—if only there were a school where striving young British artists could learn from great works of art. Here was a role for an ambitious young duke.

Richmond decided to commission William Chambers to build an addition to Richmond House to house a sculpture gallery. He would fill the gallery with casts of all the great sculptures in Italy. He would throw open the doors to anyone over the age of twelve who wanted to learn and who could exhibit some basic skills (this may have included girls as well as boys since women were among those who won prizes through the allied Society of Arts). It would be the first public arts school in England. Joseph Wilton and Giovanni Battista Cipriani would come to London to direct the school on Richmond's behalf. He would give out prizes to cultivate the best of British creativity. It was a bold idea. In an undated letter from Wolfe to the young duke, Wolfe seems to allude to it: "I hope your Grace will have it in your power to execute your favourite Plan—& every future great project of yours tending to the Public good."

Richmond's father had sent him on the Grand Tour to rein him in and teach him moderation. Instead, Richmond used the journey to widen his horizons, take inspiration from the progressive vision of the Enlightenment, and forge a sense of personal purpose. He started to imagine a new England—one that would reverse the decay of corruption. His ambition met the moment because the world of his guardians was on the verge of crumbling.

ON THE NIGHT OF December 2, 1754, Mount Vesuvius split open with a thunderous roar, spewing fire from its summit and a new gaping fissure on its eastern flank. Molten lava surged toward the villages of Ottaviano and Mauro, devouring vineyards and lighting the winter sky with an eerie, blood-red glow. From Naples to the Bay, terrified spectators watched in awe as the mountain raged, its glowing cone growing higher, casting the shadow of ancient Pompeii, which had been discovered only in 1748, into the imagination of Enlightenment Europe. While the worst of the eruption had ceased by the time Richmond, Trembley, and George reached Southern Italy, some minor flows resumed in January 1755, and they had the chance to observe these fearsome molten rivers as the trio traveled from Rome to Naples.

At home all their friends and family had been living through volcanic eruptions of their own, political earthquakes that had begun in the spring of 1754 when the prime minister, Henry Pelham, suddenly died. He had held the role since 1743 by virtue of being the head of the House of Commons (a role formalized as leader of the House of Commons only in the nineteenth century). His death destabilized not only the King's administration, conducted through the prime minister, but also the lower house of Parliament.

Two of Richmond's politically crafty guardians—the Duke of Newcastle and Henry Fox—vied to succeed Pelham. Ten days after his brother's death, Newcastle became prime minister, but the sharp-elbowed jockeying for power and position continued. The domestic political turbulence was especially ill-timed since conflict was starting to intensify between Britain and France. There were clashes in the Ohio River Valley and naval skirmishes, too. These disputes were expensive and soon the British government put pressure on the royal governors in the colonies to raise funds to support the military action. Complaints about taxation began to increase. Parliament was increasingly divided over whether it should legislate on behalf of the colonies. Benjamin Franklin, now postmaster general for the colonies, played a key role in the formation of the Albany Congress, and proposed the Albany Plan of Union, the first effort of the colonies, still acting as Britons, to form themselves into a league for mutual defense and coordination.

In London, factions began to align around questions of foreign policy. By May 1755, Henry Fox had been elevated to secretary of state in Newcastle's administration. In the House of Commons, William Pitt the elder, the Paymaster-General of His Majesty's Forces and most powerful popular politician of his day, was beloved by the general public and established himself in opposition to Newcastle. Newcastle wanted to contain the conflict with France through diplomatic alliances. Pitt, on the other hand, wanted to strengthen the British military and directly respond to French aggression, prioritizing engagement in the colonies. For him, the best defense was a strong offense. It was a classic hawks-versus-doves debate. Pitt continually resisted the policies of the prime minister until he was dismissed from the office of paymaster general of the forces in November 1755, and replaced by Henry Fox, as the pendulum swung again.

Wolfe wrote to Richmond shortly before the young duke returned home in January 1756 to encourage him to come to Canterbury where Wolfe's regiment was headquartered to pay both himself and the troops a visit. Wolfe explained the lesson he wanted Richmond to learn: "You will find a wide difference between the Troops of some other Nations & our own: however when you have seen their Faults, it may, some time or other, be in your power to correct them + I believe your Grace will think it an object worth your care & attention here after." Wolfe was encouraging him to see his native land with a critical eye and to carry a sense of responsibility for its improvement.

Richmond crossed the Channel back to London in January 1756, arriving in a world destabilized by colonial entanglements and domestic political jockeying. His two London-based guardians, Fox and Newcastle, were utterly consumed with intense political strife. At the same time, the old Whig oligarchy was starting to fracture, the military was degrading, and pressures were building within a population with growing literacy but shrinking access to the franchise. The percentage of the people with the vote in eighteenth-century England had always been small, but it had grown even smaller over the course of the century because of practices used by the elite to control elections. The country as a whole was also sliding inexorably toward war with France. On February 22, 1756, with his birthday now measured by the new Gregorian calendar, Richmond turned twenty-one. Now of age, Richmond could finally direct his fortune as he saw fit. He rewarded Trembley so generously for his services over five and a half years on the Grand Tour that Trembley never had to work again. Richmond now believed his nation needed his services. He had come home with a purpose and a plan—to help his country achieve progress in the military and fine arts. Before he could act on it, though, there was one more thing to attend to: He also needed a wife.

BY 1756 RICHMOND WAS a single man in possession of a significant fortune and a senior peerage in the British aristocracy. He was not, however, the only eligible bachelor that season. Another was his Westminster classmate, Augustus FitzRoy, Earl of Euston, soon to be Duke of Grafton. The two courted in parallel. In Richmond's case, his eye fell on Lady Mary Bruce, the daughter of an earl, technically two rungs below him on the aristocratic hierarchy, but in practice of the same social station.

Lady Mary was a flirtatious, brown-eyed beauty, given to chatter, relatively unlettered, and more likely to spend her time embroidering than reading a book. She gave little attention to her dress. She would come in from riding and wear her riding clothes to dinner. Four days after Richmond had turned twenty-one, he danced with Mary and "rested his gaze" upon her at the opera to such an extent that rumors of their engagement sprouted at once. Richmond wrote in early January 1757 to his brother George, who was serving with a regiment in Scotland, about the situation.

> I was told tother day that I had propose[d] myself *en mariage* to lady Mary Bruce and that on my account she had refused Lord Bruce [a cousin]. But I cannot flatter myself with that unless it was, *mes beaux yeux*, for I had never spoke to her [to offer my hand] at the time she refused him. But since I have had the honor of dancing with her at Norfolk's house and look'd at her at the opera and that you know is foundation enough for being sure of a man's marriage.

Richmond, in other words, had been made to consider whether Mary was the one he should marry by virtue of her having started a rumor to that effect. She, it would seem, knew what she wanted, even if he did not. At least not yet.

Richmond was not exactly infatuated. He continued to weigh the merits to George in language that jars twenty-first-century ears with its misogyny:

> I do not see why I should not seriously marry? But there is the great if. Without knowing her tis ten to one upon everie woman that she has something of the Bitch in her. And if I should find the least of it, from that moment tis all over. If I find her as I could wish, then so good an opportunity is not to be lost. But to be sat-

> isfied whether it is so, or not, I will try to get acquainted with her and see how it is.

Wolfe must have heard the rumors because when he wrote to Richmond on January 19, he had very clear advice. Richmond would be better off with "country diversions," the "becoming recreations of a soldier." He worried that Richmond might succumb to "Gaming . . . eating & the Pox, . . . the Vices of the effeminate & those that loosen'd the morals and ruin'd the constitutions of half of our Country-men." Wolfe's efforts to restore Richmond's attention to matters of sport and war were in vain. Richmond asked Mary's stepfather, General Henry Conway, to make a marriage proposal on his behalf. That received Conway's and Mary's assent, and soon Richmond was able to write to his brother about his fiancée, comparing her memorably to a piece of furniture that he would soon be moving into Goodwood.

In the same letter in which he reported to George on the success of his proposal, Richmond shared news of his latest military promotion: He was to train two battalions throughout the summer. It seemed that perhaps an opportunity to serve was beginning to emerge.

After two celebratory balls and a bill approving his marriage was read in the House of Lords (since approval by both houses of Parliament and the King was required for aristocratic unions), on April 1, Richmond and Lady Mary were married. The omnipresent socialite and diarist Horace Walpole wrote that it was "the perfectest match in the world; youth, beauty, riches, alliances, and all the blood of all the kings from Robert Bruce to Charles II. They are the prettiest couple in England." And while they may have been the prettiest, their social set included other glamorous couples, like the recently married Duke of Grafton and his own new Duchess, Anne.

Richmond and Duchess Mary were apparently besotted. In the summer of 1757 Lady Mary traveled with Richmond to join him and his troops. She captivated his attention throughout. He wrote to his brother to apologize for writing infrequently because "whenever I have any leisure I employ it so agreeably with the Lovely Dutchess that I have not the heart to set to anything else." Back in London, too, Mary remained a distraction. Guests found that breakfast would be as late as 11 a.m., "their Graces not being up" any earlier than that. Nieces and nephews played all day at being the Duke and Duchess of Richmond by "kissing eternally." Richmond's sister Caroline wrote to Emily, "She does love him vastly." Evidently, the Duke and new Duchess of Richmond were young, infatuated, and quite often in bed.

The bachelor general Wolfe was not impressed. He didn't visit to pay his respects on the marriage. His apology a few weeks later was shot through with ironic undertones: "My not having been to wait upon your Grace will leave no suspicion, I hope, of incivility, because my hearty wishes for your happiness are I persuade myself, fully known to you." And he concluded his note with a pointed warning: "I would have you fill all the offices and duties of Life with equal worth and honour; with comfort and satisfaction to yourselves & service to Mankind; a good Husband & a Father seldom fail to make a good subject & occasionally a useful Soldier."

Alongside his marriage, the 3rd Duke of Richmond embarked in 1756 and 1757 on the full exercise of his prerogatives, powers, and responsibilities—which included the renovation and aggrandizement of both of his estates, the ceremonial taking of his place in the House of Lords, and getting elected to the Royal Society, the leading scholarly association of England. Members of the society attended meetings to learn about breakthrough scientific discoveries. The highlight of Richmond's first year of membership was a set of lectures given by another new member, Benjamin Franklin, who had recently arrived in London. Franklin presented papers on electricity, including his experiments with kites. Richmond and Franklin were also soon both new members of the new Society for the Encouragement of Arts, Manufactures, and Commerce. It blended an interest in fine arts and practical inventions—from new methods of spinning wool to techniques for mass producing replicas of the carnelian, agate, and jasper signet rings that aristocrats brought home with them from the Grand Tour. Franklin joined from America as a corresponding member in 1756 and then joined in person when he came to London the following year. Officially, Franklin was in London to represent the Pennsylvania Assembly in negotiations between the colony and Britain. Seeking to improve communication and coordination between the government and the colonies, Franklin quickly embedded himself among the Duke of Newcastle's supporters, who favored a gentler touch over colonial affairs. Richmond's growing public role was at last bringing him into direct contact with what would become the most challenging issue of his age: the question of America.

EVEN WHILE RICHMOND WAS learning to live as a married man, an active member of the House of Lords, a frequent participant in the cultural societies of London, and a friend to at least one American, he also continued his correspondence about his professional future with Wolfe. A few days before his installation as a member of the House of Lords, Wolfe wrote to him encouraging him to seize his new role with vigor:

> To an active mind like yours my Lord, the great business of the Nation (at this most critical and interesting juncture) must afford fresh matter of entertainment & improvement. I am glad your Age allows you to be present at the debates; & I hope you will live to see the good effects of the spirit and resolution that appears universally & which there will remain unshaken.

A global convulsion was about to break out that would make the great business of the nation even more all-consuming for the Duke of Richmond. After months of mounting tensions between Britain and France—naval skirmishes and colonial clashes—Britain formally declared war on May 17, 1756, transforming a series of regional conflicts into a global war that would engulf Europe, the Americas, Africa, and Asia. Eventually it would be known as the Seven Years' War.

The early exchanges did not go well for England. On May 20, in the first battle, the French Navy defeated the British and seized the island of Minorca. Newcastle and Fox were both obliged to resign from the government. Pitt, who had been arguing for more investment in defense, took over. Richmond was quickly promoted—again without ever having seen active duty or even much formal training—to lieutenant colonel of the 33rd Foot, and in the summer of 1756, prior to his marriage, he was with his troops in Holland and Germany.

The pressures of war accelerated the destabilization of domestic politics, and the turbulence sparked new thinking among activist newspaper writers and an increasingly literate public. The idea that governments were legitimate only with the consent of the governed began to appear in the popular press. One periodical, *The Monitor: Or British Freeholder*, especially in 1756 and 1757, argued hotly for the British constitution, for which Montesquieu had renewed the world's appreciation. The British constitution was, they wrote, "the most perfect form of government, that ever was instituted," "better . . . than that of any other nation now existing." The idea of the divine right of kings was "absolutely worn out of the minds of men" and "entirely exploded." *The Monitor* argued adamantly that the only basis for legitimate government was a social contract with the people and that the natural process of degeneration evident in the recent upheavals demanded that British institutions now be " 'furbished up,' revised to bring them back to first principles."

In a constant stream of letters, Wolfe continued to sound the alarm about decay and corruption. Over the course of the summer, as the dispiriting war wore on, Wolfe turned up the pressure on Richmond to find a way to contribute. Lamenting the "disjointed State" of affairs in Britain, he exhorted Richmond to give up everything to fight for his country and constitution: "Every honest Man in the Kingdom should take arms, dismiss his superfluous servants & Equipage; keep his Family in the Country; & give some help of his Estate into the Exchequer." He urged Richmond to defend the constitution, and to embrace "self-denial, courage, temperance & Magnanimity." Wolfe distrusted an aristocracy wasting its time "siding at Horse Races or shooting Grouse, when all the rest of the World are in Arms." Wolfe must have known that in addition to investing his energies in Mary, Richmond was absolutely guilty of "siding at Horse races" and other aristocratic pursuits. Wolfe's pen thrust deep, and he turned the blade as he continued his effort to turn Richmond's attention back to military questions. He also tutored him on the specifics of defense for the South Coast.

Richmond could not indefinitely ignore Wolfe's bleak view of Britain's affairs and he internalized Wolfe's exhortation to lead. He wrote to his brother in dark terms echoing Wolfe's: "England is on its decline, nothing rigorous is done, our Government is weak, and always open to any bold Popular man to seize, fickle and unsteady and never pursuing one vigorous plan." His difficulty was that although much was expected of him and he also hoped for much for himself, he was finding no path to fulfill those expectations. He had battalions to train, but he was not being sent to war. He was frustrated, he told George, that he had been overlooked for active service. "Tis hard they will not let me learn my business," he confided.

September 1757 marked a low point for Richmond. The world was on fire. His country needed him, or so he believed. He felt himself possessed by an intense commitment to service to a degree unusual for those coming from his high rank. Yet no one had called him to serve. This was, though, about to change.

BY THE DAWN OF 1758, the Seven Years' War had spread to five continents. In Britain, Pitt was planning major offensives—including an attack on Louisbourg (in Canada) and increased operations in India and West Africa. France felt the mounting pressure and was defending its colonies under increasing economic strain. Richmond took actions early in the year that revealed a new clarity of purpose about how he would advance a career of public service. He enrolled for duty as a justice of the peace; he began to study political philosophy. He annotated Emmerich de Vattel's *The Law of Nations: Or, Principles of the Law of Nature Applied to the Conduct and Affairs of Nations and Sovereigns* and closely studied Vattel's arguments about taxation, the rights of commerce, and the equality of poor and rich. The self-pity of the previous year's letters to his brother has dissipated. He had entered the army "to be of some service to my country and for an occupation and amusement for myself." He acknowledged that—thanks to Duchess Mary—he no longer needed occupation or amusement. Yet the aspiration to serve still fired his soul. Indeed, he hoped it would "ever subsist." And in the absence of an immediate opportunity for military leadership, he chose to lead instead in the arts.

In February 1758, Richmond and the artists he had befriended in Rome opened their sculpture gallery at Richmond House. The school was an immediate triumph. It was covered in the papers. The Society for the Encouragement of Arts, Manufactures and Commerce reached out to ask if their members could train there. The most talented artists of the day flocked to it—painters Joshua Reynolds, George Stubbs, and George Romney; the miniaturist Richard Cosway, the medalist Lewis Pingo, and seal-engravers Nathaniel Marchant and Edward Burch. Ready for a new portrait of himself, the Duke commissioned Reynolds. Reynolds's 1758 portrait defines Richmond as he had come to understand himself. Gone is the aristocratic finery. Now he presents himself in his simple soldier's redcoat. He had a military career, if not on the field, at least on canvas.

Richmond's shining success quickly caught a rival's eye. In an ominous harbinger of things to come, the Prince of Wales countered the opening of Richmond's sculpture gallery by offering contracts to Wilton, Chambers, and Cipriani. He would steal Richmond's protégés, and his anticipated cultural influence, right out from under him.

JUST AS RICHMOND BEGAN to experience some professional success, so too Britain's military fortunes began to rally. Pitt was blowing new life into the armed forces, turning the tide of the war and transforming morale at home. In 1759, he delivered what the British called the "annus mirabilis," the year of miracles: a series of significant military victories during which Richmond was finally invited to join Prince Ferdinand of Brunswick on the Continent as an aide-de-camp.

As day broke on August 1, 1759, in the small town of Minden in the Electorate of Hanover, allied British, Prussian, and Hanoverian forces under Prince Ferdinand's command prepared to confront the powerful French Army directly. The French outnumbered the British and their allies and thought that a frontal cavalry charge would settle the contest quickly. Six courageous red-coated British infantry regiments stood their ground, though, bayonets fixed and muskets ready. They would bear the brunt of the battle. One survivor wrote, "It is astonishing, that this victory was gained by six English regiments of foot, without their grenadiers, unsupported by cavalry or cannon, not even their own battalion guns, in the face of a dreadful battery so near as to tear them with grapeshot, against forty battalions and thirty-six squadrons, which is directly the quantity of the enemy which fell to their share." This British victory ended the French threat to Hanover and was the first big win of the annus mirabilis. Richmond came home a hero.

Far greater heroism, though, was waiting for Wolfe in North America the following month. In the early hours of September 13, he led a bold and perilous assault against the French at the Battle of Quebec, striking at the heart of New France. Quebec City, perched high on a cliff above the St. Lawrence River, was thought nearly impregnable—its steep elevation offering natural defenses no army had yet breached. Despite being weakened by dysentery, Wolfe defied convention and led his troops in a silent, treacherous climb up the cliffside under cover of darkness, seizing the heights before dawn and stunning the French. The precision and daring of the operation won the day for Britain. Wolfe himself led from

Here, in a 1758 portrait, the Duke of Richmond presents himself as a soldier; as ever, his dog is with him.

BY PERMISSION OF THE TRUSTEES OF THE GOODWOOD COLLECTION.

The Duchess of Richmond often wore her riding habit, as in this painting, when others would have changed into finer clothes.

BY PERMISSION OF THE TRUSTEES OF THE GOODWOOD COLLECTION.

This grand monument to General Wolfe in Westminster Abbey was installed thanks to the efforts of the Duke of Richmond.

IMAGE © 2025 DEAN AND CHAPTER OF WESTMINSTER.

the front, but was struck multiple times during the battle. Finally, he collapsed after a musket ball tore through his chest. He died moments after hearing that the French were in retreat—and that victory was his.

The British Navy ferried Wolfe's body back to England where it arrived at Portsmouth, just twenty-five miles southwest of Goodwood. Richmond sent Joseph Wilton to meet the ship and take a death mask from Wolfe's face. After a long sea journey, Wolfe's corpse left Wilton little to work with. Richmond, though, was undeterred. He was determined to memorialize Wolfe and advocated in Parliament for the creation of a monument. Wilton was commissioned by the government to sculpt a memorial depicting his death, and it stands to this day in Westminster Abbey, a stirring tribute from a young man to his mentor. No British aristocrat or politician worked as consistently, publicly, and personally to celebrate General James Wolfe as did Richmond. He is the reason Wolfe remains iconically inscribed in history books. Richmond also memorialized Wolfe internally—the general's politics of reforming egalitarianism would stay with the Duke for the rest of his life. The first seeds of Richmond's radicalism lay in the lessons about corruption that he learned from Wolfe.

A quarrel with his King would bring his radicalism to full bloom.

Chapter 3

A NEW KING AND A QUARREL

1760–1763

In short, his behaviour is that of a man who has neither sense, good nature, nor honesty.

—THE DUKE OF RICHMOND'S SISTER, SARAH LENNOX, ABOUT KING GEORGE III, 1761

JUST AFTER BREAKFAST, ON SATURDAY, OCTOBER 25, 1760, King George II had a fatal heart attack while sitting on his "close-stool," which is to say, his toilet. His valet heard "a noise louder than the royal wind" and then the thud of the King's body hitting the floor. In the war with France, Britain was in the ascendant, having nearly conquered all of Canada and gained mastery on the seas. Prussia was under intense pressure but, with Hanoverian help, holding the line. Yet the King's death would cause an avalanche of political change. His heir, George, Prince of Wales, was out riding when he received the news. He had disdained his grandfather's court, viewing it as morally decayed and politically unprincipled. He was set on change. The moves he would make in the early years of his reign would drive many talented young men, among them Richmond, to seek associations and avenues of influence outside the reach of the King. Richmond was pushed farther than the rest—all the way to radicalism.

THE NEW KING, GEORGE III—young, tall, broad-shouldered, fair-skinned, and blue-eyed with powdered hair—was the first Hanoverian monarch to be born in Britain and speak English as his native tongue. He was also one of the best-educated men in Britain. When he died sixty years later in 1820, he left behind 79,910 books. During his childhood and youth, his strenuous school day started at 8 a.m. and ended at 8 p.m. From his teens, it was filled with everything from political philosophy to art and architecture by his Scottish tutor, John Stuart, the 3rd Earl of Bute, or "Bute" as everyone knew him. Before he was twenty-one, the Prince of Wales had written a two-hundred-page paraphrase of Montesquieu's *Spirit of the Laws*, tracing as he went its arguments about British constitutionalism and the need to preserve its de facto system of checks and balances. He had completed essays asserting the wrongness of slavery and examining economic issues like mercantilism, agriculture, and early industrial policy. Together Bute and the Prince studied the arguments of Henry St John, 1st Viscount Bolingbroke, in his essay, "The Idea of a Patriot King." A patriot king would serve as a unifying force for the country, transcending party. They discussed the last testament of the Prince's father, Frederick, who had also advocated that the monarch should stand apart from and above party. Frederick had drafted this text specifically to support his son's education.

King George III's education taught him to see himself as being at odds with his grandfather's loyalists—the Old Whigs, who had held all the posts in the Old Man's government. Their preponderance led to accusations of corruption—incredible wealth and employment opportunities flowed to Whigs through their political power. By 1760, between a fifth and a quarter of members of Parliament, and half of the peers in the House of Lords, received income from offices or pensions that were on paper the gift of the sovereign. But in reality George II had let the Whigs guide the allocation of these roles.

George III acceded to the throne with the view that the Whig leadership had subordinated the needs of the nation beneath the personal interests of a few great families. He was determined to break Whig power and, for that matter, party power. He wrested control of posts from the Whigs, invited Tories into his government and, for the first time in generations, included them in the royal grants of jobs or "places," as they were called. The first decade of his reign would be a continuous battle to put the Whig families in their place—to make them servants of the King and of Britain's interests, not arbiters of national direction. He wanted the politicians to fall into line behind the Crown.

—

THE RELATIONSHIP BETWEEN KING George III and Charles Lennox, 3rd Duke of Richmond, would have been complicated regardless of any clash of political ideologies. Personal feelings played a big role. A year earlier Richmond's fifteen-year-old sister, Sarah, had been sent from her sister Emily's home in Ireland, where she had lived since their mother's death eight years earlier, to London. There she lived with their eldest sister, Caroline, and Henry Fox, and her cousins, including Charles James Fox. By 1759 the Foxes were wealthy thanks to Henry Fox's appointment by the Whig administration to the role of paymaster general, which had made him the equivalent of a multimillionaire. The Foxes had leased Holland House, a grand Jacobean mansion with extensive formal gardens and sprawling parkland. They would eventually own the two-hundred-acre property, then the largest private residence in London, bigger even than Buckingham Palace. They ran their home as a lively center for Whig social and intellectual life—with political guests and children mingling freely over meals. Sarah was sent to them to be introduced to society and find a husband.

As a toddler, Sarah had been a playmate for King George II. The old man was fonder of her than of his own grandson. After her arrival in London in November 1759, she went quickly to court to resume her close relationship with the royal family. She possessed a vivacious nature that drew people to her company, and was considered beautiful, though few could say precisely why. As her uncle Henry Fox put it, "Her beauty is not easily described, otherwise than by saying she had the finest complexion, most beautiful hair, & prettyest person that ever was seen." He added, "but this is not describing her, for her great beauty was a peculiarity of countenance, that made her at the same time different from & prettyer than any other girl I ever saw." She was the toast of the season. The future George III was smitten.

On Thursdays and Sundays, the royal family held "mixed-company drawing rooms," where both men and women affiliated with the politicians in office, and their guests, could call on the royal family at St. James's Palace in the crimson and gold presence chamber. Guests would gather in small groups around the edges of the room, and the royals would circulate among them. These "drawing rooms" were interspersed with "levees," which were held on Wednesdays and Fridays (also on Mondays during sessions of Parliament) and conducted the same way but were men-only, and therefore focused more on political than social business. Sarah was frequently at court for the drawing room. Soon, George was confiding to Bute: "What I now lay before you I never intend to communicate to any-one; the truth is the D. of Richmond's sister arriv'd from Ireland towards the middle of Novr; I was struck with her first appearance at St. James's, my passion has been encreas'd every time I have since beheld her. She is everything I can form to myself lovely."

Sarah's family set to work trying to elicit a marriage proposal. The Prince himself had the same idea. His confession to Bute continued: "I am daily grown unhappy, sleep has left me, which never was before interrupted by any reverse of fortune, I protest before God I never have had any improper thought with regard to her; I don't deny having often flattered myself with hopes that one day or other you would consent to my raising her to a throne."

Richmond doesn't appear to have been involved in the day-to-day management of Sarah's interactions with the Prince, but the question of his sister's relationship to the future king certainly fell within his duties as head of the family, something he took quite seriously.

While Fox plotted doggedly—and would later repeat the effort by trying to install another niece as the King's mistress—Richmond probably had a more mixed view. A marriage between his sister and the Prince of Wales would bring an end to any prospect of a political career. Such a union would immediately cast him into a role more like his father's—a close member of the royal household obliged to remain strictly neutral on political questions. He would be obliged to suppress his already well-developed and strong opinions about decay in the British military and society, as well as his concerns about a British economy that fostered smuggling and exposed the poor to harsh criminal law, and his sense of personal commitment to correcting these problems. Joining the royal household might seem like an elevation but would clip his wings.

Just as the family could not entirely know how besotted the Prince of Wales was with Sarah, neither could they know how violently opposed to such a union were both the Prince's mother, Augusta, and his tutor, Bute. Augusta and Bute recognized that a marriage to any young woman from one of England's leading aristocratic families would plunge the future king into the alliances and entanglements of party politics. They insisted he seek the safe neutrality of a German princess.

The decision could be postponed only until his grandfather died, whereupon the newly risen King George III accepted the direction of his mother and Bute. He looked to his Hanoverian network. He confidentially charged the ambassador from Hanover resident in London to draw up a list of eligible German princesses. All the while, throughout the first half of 1760, cheerfully unaware of the marriage brokering underway on the Continent, Fox continued to coach Sarah on how to entice the young King.

WHILE THE KING QUIETLY sought a bride, and Fox connived for Sarah's future, Richmond was busy negotiating places for male family members within a much recast British state. In November and December of 1760, the new king gave appointments and promotions to members of his own circle over the heads of Richmond and his family. This offended the Duke, who was sensitive to slights. He sought an audience to seek redress for his grievances.

Once he had paid his respects, the audience with the King proceeded smoothly. The King asked the Duke how it was that he had never considered any line of work other than the military. Richmond explained that he had avoided politics because he had not wanted to be subjected to the authority of his guardians. He told the King: "I had not chose to put myself under an obligation to the Duke of Newcastle, or even to my brother-in-law Mr. Fox, being unwilling to connect myself with any Minister." In contrast to most other ambitious young men at the time, he had chosen to avoid "faction," attachment to any particular party, in favor of preserving his personal independence. The King very much approved. Each of them had read and absorbed Montesquieu and believed it might be possible to steer toward a politics where the spirit of the laws—constitutionalism directed toward the public interest—would triumph over the petty squabbles of personal favor-giving and backstabbing.

That shared sympathy was enough to inspire George to ask Lord Bute to "sound out" Richmond as to whether he would take an appointment as Lord of the Bedchamber. Bute obliged at the next levee day. It was an important invitation: Lords of the Bedchamber were among the closest personal associates of the royal family. They accompanied the King throughout the day. Other rising political talents had filled the position previously. Two of Richmond's schoolmates served as Lord of the Bedchamber—the Marquess of Rockingham from 1751 and the Duke of Grafton from 1756 to 1758. Both would go on to be prime ministers.

Richmond requested twenty-four hours to consider the opportunity. Accepting the appointment would limit his ambition, but perhaps the anticipation of a union between Sarah and the King led him to think this loss of independence would soon be necessary anyway. Whatever the case, Richmond quickly decided to make a formal application for the role. The King confirmed his choice, and shortly Richmond visited the King again to "kiss hands." In this ritual, appointees literally knelt and kissed the King's hands to signal acceptance of their responsibilities.

THE PARTNERSHIP BETWEEN THE young, moralizing King and his equally young but irreverent senior peer lasted for exactly three days. What happened between Richmond and George to bring about a rapid reversal was a scandal. Richmond was still writing letters to explain himself twenty-five years later.

Immediately after Richmond kissed George's hands, news had come from the front in Germany. In the most recent battle, Richmond's brother George Lennox had performed heroically alongside Ferdinand, Prince of Brunswick. On October 15, amid the oaks, beeches, and pines in the German woods, when "all [Ferdinand's] people were either killed or driven off," George and another soldier carried the injured Ferdinand off the field in their arms. Despite George's heroism, two more junior officers were promoted over his head into the rank of colonel and aide-de-camp to the King. This infuriated Richmond. He charged up from Goodwood to London to protest.

He was not the only aggrieved nobleman. The Duke of Grafton's younger brother, Lord Charles FitzRoy, another aristocratic second son expecting a military career, had also been passed over. Both dukes sought audiences with the King to ask that the decisions be reversed and that their younger brothers receive the appointments they had earned. The Duke of Grafton was the first to be received. He politely asked for consideration of his brother, found himself refused, and departed after three minutes. Richmond, in contrast, came in with a prepared speech, stayed for twenty minutes, enraged the King, resigned the new appointment to the Bedchamber, and left in a fury. As he passed through the antechamber and shared the news of his resignation, he was asked whether he had also resigned his appointment as colonel over a regiment, to which he brusquely declared, "No." Courtiers were left guessing at what had transpired. The King indicated he would never publicly report on the meeting: "It is too bad to be repeated."

The news that Richmond had resigned his appointment as Lord of the Bedchamber but not his regiment made the rounds in the city's political chatter. This choice to abandon one post but keep another was interpreted by his peers as undercutting any claim to injustice he might have had. If he and his family's honor had truly been affronted, he should have resigned both. Evidently, Richmond held on to what mattered most to him—not the tedious, politically neutered appointment in the royal household, but his military career. Later in life he said explicitly that he considered military service and public office different matters, to be handled differently.

Legendary gossip Horace Walpole also reported on the incident, recording that even years afterward, Richmond found it "had never been forgotten or forgiven." Walpole thought what mattered in the story was the contrast between the behavior of the two young dukes. They were so similar on the one hand—former schoolmates, both twenty-five years old, both "princes of the blood" as descendants of Charles II, two of the youngest and wealthiest members in the House of Lords, and society friends whose wives were close. Yet in temperament they were as far apart as the two poles: "The Duke of Richmond's figure was noble, and his countenance singularly handsome. The Duke of Grafton was low, but manly, and with much grace in his address. The passions of both were strong, but of the first, ardent; of the latter, slow and inflexible." Walpole recognized that the event augured a lasting rivalry between them.

A stark contrast between the dukes of Richmond and Grafton had now been drawn for the King and for the public. The impetuosity of one had sent him to the Continent and the military for his education; the second had dutifully gone to Cambridge and acquired the greater polish. Grafton was willing to be put in his place by the King; Richmond was not. Within the decade, Grafton would serve as prime minister; Richmond never would. Their once warm relationship would become utterly distant.

Richmond never acknowledged that he had made a mistake. He recollected the audience with the King twenty years later: "I thought it my duty to represent to his Majesty how great a mortification this must be to my brother, after having much distinguished himself during the whole war, to be not only neglected, but even to see his juniors rewarded, by being put over his head, for their services in this battle, where his behaviour had been so remarkable." Richmond suggested that he calmly and justly pressed his claim.

The King confidentially told a different story to Bute:

> I don't doubt but my Dearest Friend [as George called Bute] is anxious to hear what has passed between D. of R. and me; I have spoke very firmly to him, and he has on it resign'd the Bed Chamber, with expressions of the greatest duty, but he you know never speaks truth; I think this is the first time in my life that I have been thoroughly in a passion. I thank Heaven for being rid of him.

Within days, Richmond had yet another change of heart. He regretted his intemperate behavior and sought advice from, first, Bute, and then the King's uncle, the Duke of Cumberland, to see if he could remedy the situation. Cumberland told him that "he was sorry the Duke of Richmond, at twenty-[five], had quarrelled with the King, at twenty-two; and advised him to retire into the country." Cumberland understood that this early quarrel would set the tone of their relationship for many years to come. Richmond followed Cumberland's advice and chose an informal exile. He retired to his country house and withdrew from state business in London.

George Lennox seems not to have been much bothered by the whole business of his missed promotion. His attention was elsewhere. On Christmas Day, after all the hullabaloo, he eloped in Scotland, and then brought his bride, Louisa, to Goodwood. The newlyweds moved in with Richmond and his Duchess Mary.

THROUGHOUT THE SPRING OF 1761, London was abuzz with George III's coming coronation, scheduled for the fall. Aristocratic women wrote astonishingly long letters about what they would wear while the broader public followed newspapers that carried a mixture of imperial triumph and war fatigue. Anxiety was beginning to grow about the long-term costs of empire, and in America, the colonists were beginning quietly to chafe at the impositions of the British military. Through it all, George continued to dally with Sarah.

The King was sincere in his affection but weak-willed in his self-management. He and Sarah saw each other frequently at drawing rooms, at the theater, at church. He would call her over to his couch and converse with her for an hour at a time in front of all assembled society. On Thursday June 18, he said to her, loudly enough to be overheard, "Believe that I have the strongest attachment." But on July 1, King George III sent a summons to his Privy Council to meet the following week "upon urgent & important business." When the counsellors gathered—Henry Fox was in attendance—King George declared his intention to marry Princess Charlotte of Mecklenburg-Strelitz, a minor German royal and entirely unknown quantity to everyone in the room. Fox was aghast. After the news reached Sarah, she wrote to her best friend, Lady Susan Fox Strangways, another niece of Henry Fox, about the King: "In short, his behaviour is that of a man who has neither sense, good nature, nor honesty." She added: "The thing I am most angry at, is looking so like a fool, as I shall for having gone so often [to court] for nothing." Her romance was at an abrupt and humiliating end.

RICHMOND WAS NOT IN London that spring and summer to help Sarah with her hurt. His soft banishment to the countryside following his December 1760 audience with the King was real. Despite preparations for the upcoming coronation, he attended Parliament only four times in 1761. But his absence from London politics and royal levees did not mean he was altogether out of politics. He used the time in Sussex to experiment with building a local political operation and to explore his political options. During the March 1761 parliamentary elections, Richmond focused on controlling both seats elected to Parliament from Chichester. His cousin, Augustus Keppel, ceded one seat to George Lennox. This was compensation of a kind to his younger brother for his having lost out on the military promotion a few months earlier. The second seat was occupied by a sixty-five-year-old country gentleman named John Page, who had no interest in stepping aside so that Richmond could control the seat. He was, though, persuaded to serve only one more term, in exchange for Richmond's ceasing his efforts to displace him. Yet the three or four seats that Richmond controlled contrasted to the ten Newcastle typically dominated throughout his political career, and the fifty in the pocket of the Crown. In the end, Richmond never made gaining control of parliamentary seats a major priority. It required too much corruption.

During the summer, while Sarah was reckoning with her humiliation in London, Richmond used July to make the one and only trip he ever made to visit the family's ruined Richmond Castle, a gloomy, dilapidated eleventh-century medieval fortress in North Yorkshire. Along the way he stopped at many great houses to learn from his aristocratic peers about their investments in their estates—from agriculture to the arts—and to test out potential political alliances. His most significant visit took place when he arrived at the home of the Marquess of Rockingham, his former schoolmate, Lord of the Bedchamber for King George III since 1751, and the wealthiest man in England.

Rockingham was the heir apparent to succeed the Duke of Newcastle in leadership of the Whigs. He had every chance of one day becoming prime minister. Any opportunities for Richmond to serve in the cabinet would most likely depend on Rockingham. Ultimately, Richmond would indeed join the Rockingham Whigs and develop immense affection, if not unqualified respect, for the Marquess.

For the moment, however, Richmond steered away from party politics in favor of building ties to the community of artists, innovators, dissenters, and political radicals, including Benjamin Franklin, at the Society of Arts. He sought to replace his ties to the opportunistic Sir William Chambers, Joseph Wilton, and Giovanni Battista Cipriani. Among artists, the ranks of his protégés next included George Stubbs, whom Richmond invited to Goodwood to paint his horses and, eventually, the several moose that Guy Carleton, Richmond's former military tutor, would later send from Canada after his appointment as governor there in 1766, an appointment that resulted from Richmond's advocacy. In 1763, another then-unknown painter, George Romney, also began using the Duke's London gallery. Richmond was starting over, building a new circle outside of the King's influence. Among political figures, his protégés also now included the lawyer, philosopher, and politician, Edmund Burke, a tall, brown-haired, double-chinned Irishman born in Dublin, who had joined the Society of Arts in 1758.

—

THE REST OF LONDON, throughout the summer, was awaiting the arrival of Princess Charlotte from Germany. She arrived—a petite, dark-eyed, and talented harpsichord player devoted to Bach and Mozart—on September 7. At 3 p.m. on September 8, she met the King, and their wedding took place a mere six hours later. Lady Sarah's humiliation was compounded: As the most eligible aristocratic young woman in the country, she was compelled to serve as the first bridesmaid. Then, on September 22, two weeks after the royal wedding, George and Charlotte were crowned King and Queen at Westminster Abbey. For that ceremony, the Duke of Richmond served as Lord High Constable of England. He led the procession and fulfilled other duties during the six-hour service. He was able to secure an invitation for his friend Peter Collinson, whose own good friend, Benjamin Franklin, also attended. But that small ability to dispense patronage did not hide the central fact: Richmond and his sister had been put firmly in their places. They were supporting acts to the main event.

One further gesture from the King made Richmond's marginalization unmistakable—and deeply personal. For the coronation, George had ordered up a new coach, eventually dubbed the Gold State Coach, because its exterior is made entirely of giltwood, or wood covered with a thin layer of gold leaf. To craft the coach, the King commissioned Chambers, Wilton, and Cipriani, the three founding directors of Richmond's sculpture gallery. The gallery, launched in 1758 in Richmond House with such brio, had fallen on financially hard times during the Duke's absence abroad for military service. When he had returned from war in 1759, he had found notices hammered to the doors complaining that prizes had not been awarded. Chambers, Wilton, and Cipriani claimed they had gone unpaid. Once they received the commission for the King's coach, the artists resigned their roles with Richmond. They also left the very democratic Society of Arts (the nickname for the Society for the Encouragement of Arts, Manufactures, and Commerce) and, in 1761, formed a competitor, rather confusingly named the Society of Artists, more exclusively focused on the fine arts. Four years later, in 1765, the King officially gave their new society a royal charter. Richmond, even with his income of 17,000 pounds a year, could not pretend to compete for influence with the King, who controlled an annual income of 800,000 pounds a year.

In the eighteen months after King George II expired, Richmond saw his place in London society and politics utterly transformed—from ascendant leader in war and the arts to spurned subject.

RICHMOND WAS NOT ALONE in turning a critical eye on his assertive new monarch. The first decade of the reign of George III gave political contrarians much to rail against, and a new politics of opposition began to emerge. George's first decade of rule ultimately included seven different prime ministers, continuous riots and mob gatherings, and published dissent. The appetite of the general public for political news, opinion, and debate became voracious. By 1760, London had four daily newspapers and five that came out three times a week. The largest daily, *The Public Advertiser*, sold two thousand copies a day, and it would hit five thousand a day at a high point at the end of the decade thanks to the shock and anger at King George III's realignments of British politics. The efforts of the King's administration to suppress dissent only increased the dissenters' force and momentum.

All the elements of a decade of political conflict had been foreshadowed in the King's maiden speech to open Parliament the previous November, in 1760. The King tried to navigate between the hawks and the doves without offending either completely. He congratulated the country's war leaders on "very considerable victories" and declared the war not "bloody and expensive" as he had written in his first draft, but "just and necessary," a revision his cabinet had insisted on. He further vowed that, with Parliament's assistance, he was "determined . . . to prosecute this war with vigour, in order to [achieve] that desirable object, a safe and honourable peace." He also promised "a regular and becoming economy," that is, one that wasn't debt-laden. Peace, taxes, and austerity were in the offing, he indicated. The speech revealed a clear policy gap between the King and his Whig ministers. More, it showed George's desire to set policy, an intervention he considered not an intrusion on the constitutional balance between monarch and Parliament but a fulfillment of his constitutional duty to preserve the balance of a stable constitution and to address the problems of an economy bloated by many years of war.

George had moved the first chess piece when in March 1761—even before his coronation—he had made his "Dear Friend," Lord Bute, secretary of state for the northern department, which had formal responsibility for Continental Europe. Pitt, however, had entirely led policy in this arena for many years. Bute's appointment was an attempt to rein him in, and Pitt knew his position was untenable. In October 1761, just after the coronation and before the opening of Parliament, he resigned. He had been in office since 1746. He was the first major pillar of Old Whig power to fall.

Then, just after he had been crowned, the King initiated secret peace negotiations with France, against the policy of his government and behind his prime minister's back. This was a clear indication that he wanted to have Bute replace Newcastle as well. Newcastle, neither fully aligned with the King nor able to manage his former allies, hung on for half a year longer before he, too, resigned on May 7, 1762. He had held high office since 1724. The King immediately appointed Bute in his place. With Newcastle's resignation and Bute's appointment, the age of the Old Whigs came to an end. George could now freely pursue the peace treaty he desired to end the Seven Years' War, which he did truly consider "bloody and expensive," even if he had deferred to his ministers for his speech.

The younger generation of Richmond and his peers now faced a moment of choice. Would they follow the Old Whigs out of office and into opposition, including opposition to peace? For Richmond this choice came with a personal complication. Would he loyally follow Newcastle, his father's closest political friend, and his own former guardian, into an even more complete political exile than he already found himself inhabiting? Or would he break with the traditions that had shaped him and abandon traditional Whig alliances to seek his own path politically? His brother-in-law, Henry Fox, had now replaced Pitt as leader of the House of Commons; his stepfather-in-law, Henry Conway, was still an official in the Royal Household and had just been appointed southern secretary of state. Richmond's political network—consisting like everyone else's at that time of a set of family relationships—had split, with each half now stationed on opposite sides of a hotly engaged battle about the extent of the King's authority, the course of the war with France, and whether to embrace peace. Which side should he choose?

Richmond's immediate response was to try to avoid choosing. He watched from the sidelines over the course of 1762 as Newcastle joined with the Duke of Devonshire and the Duke of Cumberland (the latter was the King's uncle) to begin discussions about forming an Opposition—establishing a formal arrangement among a set of allies to challenge the

King's administration with routine opposition speeches in Parliament and a pre-planned agenda. A court spy wrote to Bute to alert him of a ducal "association" forming against him and named Richmond as a member of the "league of Dukes." In fact Richmond did not participate. He was, though, proximate: His friends the Marquess of Rockingham and Pitt did join the conversations among the Old Whigs.

The King took the warnings about the ducal association seriously. He wrote to Bute: "The league of the Dukes is a most contemptible one." Richmond's wider universe of age-mates were just as frustrated with George, with Bute, and with their overcautious elders. They began dining together in their homes and at an eating establishment called Wildman's, on Albemarle Street, in Picadilly, down the street from Bute's residence. Over meals they worked to formulate a plan of opposition and officially establish a "club." Newcastle kept his distance from the "zealous young men" and instead concentrated on organizing the older Whigs. Richmond held himself apart from both groups.

IN THE FLUID AND factional politics of George III's early reign, when most young aristocrats were rushing to define their loyalties, Richmond held back. His seemingly idiosyncratic restraint revealed a deeper, more careful, and independent recalibration. He was socializing closely with the Duke of Grafton, a leading figure at Wildman's, but he avoided political association with him and the rest of his age-mates. While he had resumed attendance at Parliament, he prioritized his personal life over political entanglements. When he was in London, he played tennis almost daily; now he also had tennis courts built at Goodwood. His sister Caroline complained in a letter about the Richmonds, the Graftons, and the rest of their set: "They play [cards] and sit up at one of their houses every night till four or five in the morning; then instead of their own equipages, they come home, six or seven together, in hackney coaches." The Duchess of Grafton was a "painted doll," and both the Graftons were already quite public in their taking of lovers.

Beneath this socialite persona, though, Richmond was becoming a political intellectual. He became a more serious reader and, during this time, his tastes began to shift from military affairs to law, politics, and philosophy. He was also quietly but persistently trying to recover the ground he had lost from his quarrel with the King. In the fall of 1762, after

Newcastle's resignation, Richmond stubbornly began to seek a return for himself to royal favor by working through his brother-in-law, Henry Fox. He asked Fox to explore potential roles that might be granted to him by the King. Fox was also busy working on behalf of the King to deliver votes for George's peace plan, which would eventually be the Treaty of Paris. For this Fox had to fend off the opposition from Pitt and the "zealous" young men. In Parliament, Pitt filibustered against the proposed peace terms in a speech that lasted more than three hours. Passions ran hot outside of Parliament too. The public—still very much committed to Pitt and his imperial policy—violently abused Bute when he traveled through the streets in his carriage, leaving him fearful for his life. On December 9, the fight came to a head. Parliament voted, and Fox delivered for the King by 319 to 65. The terms needed for the Treaty of Paris had been approved. In the Lords, the majority was also strong. Richmond voted with his sovereign for peace, and against the Opposition. He chose Fox and Conway, brother-in-law and father-in-law, not Newcastle, his father's best friend. This vote—this alliance—was how he would repair his standing, and soon he would get his reward.

BEFORE GEORGE III WOULD give out rewards, though, he took scalps. He demanded that all Opposition Whigs who had voted against the peace terms be removed from any offices they held. Newcastle, who had already given up the premiership, was now dismissed from the lord lieutenancy of Sussex. The Duke of Grafton was dismissed from the lord lieutenancy of Suffolk. The Duke of Devonshire resigned the lord lieutenancy of Derbyshire out of solidarity. Rockingham, who had already resigned his post as Lord of the Bedchamber in November, now also resigned his lord lieutenancy. Of course, dismissals for some created openings for others. This is how realignments played out in a world of immense patronage. Richmond seized the opportunity to put himself forward for a position. Privately, Fox underscored for the King Richmond's ongoing independence and warning that if the King failed to promote him, Richmond might "dine a fifth Duke at Devonshire House," that is, join the Opposition party being formed by the dukes of Newcastle, Cumberland, Portland, and Devonshire, who met at Devonshire's home.

Richmond also publicly communicated support for the King after the

Treaty of 1763 was formally ratified on February 10. Just as his father had launched fireworks over the Thames to celebrate George II's victory after the Treaty of Aix-la-Chapelle, Richmond and Duchess Mary threw a grand masked ball in early June on the terrace and in the gardens at Richmond House, with fireworks over the Thames. Six hundred people turned out and celebrated till 6 a.m. The Duchess of Richmond dressed as a Persian sultana; the Duchess of Grafton was Cleopatra. Walpole wore a sober hooded purple cloak. The royal dukes—York and Cumberland, respectively brother and uncle to the King—attended, and some ten thousand people watched the fireworks along the banks of the river, as newspapers reported. The lavish affair served as a message to the King: In this period of instability, Richmond would help restore the confidence of the people in the King's government.

By the fall it was clear that the Opposition would advance without Richmond. Newcastle and the "the zealous young men" had finally united, and Newcastle gathered around himself a set of "heads of business," to drive the work of opposition forward. Those "heads" included: the Duke of Grafton, Duke of Devonshire, Duke of Bolton, Duke of Portland, Marquess of Rockingham, Earl of Hardwicke, Earl Temple, William Pitt, William Legge, Charles Townshend, Charles Yorke, and James Grenville. Richmond was conspicuously absent.

In October 1763, Richmond's fence-mending paid off. The King awarded him an appointment as lord lieutenant of Sussex. In this role he was now "responsible for law and order and the execution of justice, including the collection of local taxes," throughout his home county. He now also stood at the head of a county militia and "had the right to call in troops to enforce his will." It was his first meaningful political appointment. Of course, the role was available only because his former guardian, his father's best friend, Newcastle, had been stripped of it by the King the previous December. Richmond's willingness to accept the role produced a rupture in his relationship with Newcastle that lasted for several years.

WHILE HE WAS TRYING to regain the favor of King George III, Richmond behaved placidly in public. He supported the King and his effort to steer the British constitution away from aristocratic leadership and decisively toward a constitutional monarchy. He had become a recognized "courtier," as letters of the time attest, meaning someone who could be counted on to do the King's business.

Yet being a "courtier" was not the whole of his story. Richmond's accommodating public countenance hid more complicated churnings beneath. In 1763, he read Rousseau's *Emile* and Plato's *Republic.* He also took up Henry Neville's *Plato Redivivus: Or, a Dialogue Concerning Government.* Neville was a critic of absolute monarchy, who believed that the power of the King should be limited and that governance should be conducted with the consent of the governed. He imitated the style of Platonic dialogue to argue for republican principles and the virtues of a mixed government that balances the powers of monarchy, aristocracy, and the common people. As well as reading into the history of Parliament, Richmond was also absorbing Algernon Sydney's *Discourses Concerning Government,* another important republican text that criticized absolute monarchy and argued both for the consent of the governed and their right to resist absolutism. Richmond was clearly beginning to rethink the very foundations of government.

His membership in the Society of Arts accelerated his intellectual experimentation. The society was one of London's most democratic civic associations, if not the most democratic. Decisions were made on a one-person, one-vote model, and women were admitted with voting rights. The society sought to advance not only art but also industry and trade and to knit colonies and mother country together. They gave out prizes for cocoons sent from Georgia and raw silk sent from Connecticut to enhance the silk industry and they tried to inspire viticulture in Virginia. Their interests were as much in the applied arts and sciences as in the fine arts—they sought to advance industrialization to support social progress. Like others in the Society of Arts, including Edmund Burke, Richmond asked searching questions about the legitimacy of the King's agenda, and indeed the limits of the Crown's power. Starting in 1761, Franklin was chair of the Committee of British Colonies and Trade; and beginning in 1763 the Duke of Richmond was a vice president of the society. This was his earliest commitment to a democratic organization.

Franklin, too, seems to have poured significant intellectual energy into the Society of Arts. Here men and women whose "natural bent of mind" was to science found each other, drawn by their forward-looking intellectual vitality. Other members included Thomas Hollis (nephew of the older Thomas Hollis who made the founding donation of books to Harvard's library); Hollis's good friend and eventual heir Thomas Brand Hollis (who took the second surname Hollis along with his inheritance to honor his friend); and, eventually, in the 1780s, John Adams, later America's second president. Thomas Brand Hollis would become one of England's greatest devotees of Thomas Paine. The radical currents in the society are unmistakable. Richmond didn't need to join the political Opposition. He didn't need to dine at Wildman's. The Society of Arts offered a base for increasingly radical conversations. It was also the context in which Richmond had his most stable and reliable opportunity to socialize outside the confines of the aristocracy.

The cast of inventive characters participating in the Society of Arts also included the Scottish astronomer and tinkerer, James Ferguson, who sometimes submitted his creations, from flour mills to orreries (mechanical models of the solar system), for prize consideration. Benjamin Martin, a maker of globes and spectacles, was also in Franklin's orbit, and in 1757 through 1759 Franklin attended lectures by both men. So too did another developing radical: Thomas Paine. The Society of Arts appears to be the context in which Paine met Franklin, and Richmond met Paine.

THOMAS PAINE, THE CORSET-MAKER who would become the eighteenth century's most important radical writer, was born January 29, 1736, one year after Richmond, ninety miles north of London, in Thetford in Norfolk, to a Quaker father and Anglican mother, who had him baptized in the Church of England. Until the age of twelve, he studied at Thetford Grammar School. Then he apprenticed to his father to learn the trade of making corsets and sails. When Paine came of age in 1757, one year after Richmond and two years before George III, he left his apprenticeship with his father to make his fortune at sea. After some months aboard the privateer *King of Prussia*, the tall, slim young man, his dark brown hair pulled into his signature ponytail, entered London's intellectual universe with prize money from the capture of enemy ships, self-confidence, and a Norfolk accent. He spent his money working on scientific projects, attending lectures in natural philosophy, and beginning to dabble in writing for the newspapers, including for *The Monitor*, which was making the case for constitutionalism. Through shared scientific passion, he connected to men like Franklin, Ferguson, and Martin, and through them, in all likelihood, to the broader network of members in the Society of Arts: not only Richmond but also Edmund Burke and Oliver Goldsmith.

By 1759, though, Paine was broke. He was no aristocrat. He was obliged to return to his trade as a corset-maker. He moved to Sandwich in Kent, near Dover on the coast across from France, and opened a shop. On September 27, he married Mary Lambert, a local serving woman, but tragedy soon struck. Mary died in childbirth in 1760, and their child with her.

In response to this personal loss, Paine left Sandwich and began a long journey through a professional wilderness. He was trying to climb England's political and social structures in the same years that Richmond too was seeking a new footing. Both men had to navigate an England changed by George III's aspiration to serve as a patriot king. For both, marriage marked their transition from youth to adult independence. Close in age, the rhythms of their lives harmonized, despite their social distance.

Leaving corset-making behind, Paine now sought a career in the excise, the civil service operation that policed smugglers and collected duties on internally produced goods. Excise officers, alongside customs officers, were responsible for collecting the revenue of the kingdom. The path to the excise was laborious and required, like every other professional opportunity in England, patronage. Paine pursued the office through officials in his hometown of Thetford, who turned to their member of Parliament for help. Their MP was General Henry Conway, Richmond's father-in-law, who held his seat at the pleasure of the Duke of Grafton. Conway passed the nomination to Frederick Frankland, commissioner of the excise, who was based in Sussex and whose nephew, William Frankland, was a member, like the Duke of Richmond, of the Society of Arts. William Frankland was also the sheriff of Sussex, and part of Richmond's political network. Whether aristocrat or worker, ambitious young men had to "pay court" to advance. King George III may have changed who might enter into the pathways of advancement, but he had not changed the nature of the pathway. Civil service exams were still well in the future. Purchase of "places" and patronage ruled the day. In his own way, Paine, like Richmond, was a courtier. In a society structured by patronage, people's lives depended on who was connected to whom. These webs of relationship held everyone's future, and they are what reveal their histories. Scholars have long been mystified by how Paine came to be appointed to the excise in Lewes. These networks explain his path.

But Paine did not end up in Lewes on his first assignment. Upon Paine's first application, through Conway, to the excise, Frederick Frankland appointed him to Grantham, in Lincolnshire, forty miles north of Thetford. In December 1762, Paine began service on an initial probationary appointment. Conway's patronage got him a job as an excise collector and no more. His literary talents must not yet have been fully in evidence; he clearly had not yet garnered Richmond's full attention. At least the excise post in Grantham was a job with the promise of advancement and stability. Paine could take a breath.

WITH THE SIGNING OF the 1763 Treaty of Paris and the end of the Seven Years' War, Europe could also take a breath. Britain emerged as the dominant global naval and colonial power, with its empire more than doubled—especially in North America and India. It had gained Canada and all territory east of the Mississippi from the French and Florida from Spain. France was exhausted and resentful, but matters weren't all rosy for Britain. Its massive war debt cast a shadow on its triumph, and in the summer of 1763 native nations across the Great Lakes and Ohio Valley rose in rebellion as Pontiac's War began. That great movement of Indigenous peoples would set in motion the dynamics that would provoke the American Revolution. The next era of British politics would durably remake the world order, in contrast to the temporary resting points that had followed the earlier wars.

Richmond approached these consequential years with an increasingly gloomy view of King George III as willful and arbitrary and of British governance as corrupt. He also felt growing comfort with nascent democratic practices, affection for the Americans, and a pleasurable sense of having achieved a hard-won political and social independence. Paine had by now had his first heady taste of a literary life at the intersection of politics. These ingredients held the makings of the radical each would become.

PART II

SEDITION AND SECRECY

1763–1774

Chapter
4

THE WILKES AFFAIR AND THE ORIGINS OF RADICALISM

1763–1765

Wilkes and Liberty!

—COMMON SLOGAN IN POPULAR UPRISINGS IN THE 1760S

BOTH RICHMOND AND PAINE WERE CAPTIVATED BY THE intellectual ferment of Enlightenment science and political philosophy. Their shared social universe rang with ennobling hopes for the progress of mankind. Both were men of pride and ambition; they chafed at how patronage shaped the sinews of power in Britain and decried the gap between merit and opportunity. The name they had for that gap was corruption.

Yet many intellectuals reserve their opinions for after-dinner debates, their utopias for the comfort of an armchair. Why did these men seek to convert ideas into action? Neither was particularly motivated by the prospect of personal gain—Richmond was born into wealth; Paine never seemed to care for it very much. Instead, each had a deep and intense feeling about what he was personally due, and what too was owed to all mankind. Both strained after professional opportunity, believing that a meritocracy would advance them. Each was to suffer repeated and seemingly arbitrary blows to personal ambition and find himself thwarted in his efforts to serve the public—alienating them from the establishment. That distance gave them a perch as observers of the decade's constitutional maelstrom—kicked off by efforts of the Crown to suppress dissent.

A tightly interlocking dynamic between taxation, dissent, suppression, and further dissent pushed to the surface the question of how the governing powers of a state should relate to the people. Richmond and Paine thought the answer lay in a truly independent legislature that might check the executive.

Ultimately it was the stings—the personal blows from the arbitrariness of the patronage system and the resulting bitter sense of exclusion from opportunity—that led them to take matters into their own hands, seeking to limit the executive and protect the legislature. Their full transformation into radicals progressed over a six-year period. The first stage was their coming to recognize that the blows they were suffering reflected not just their idiosyncratic personal situations but a broken system. That recognition began for them, as for so many other people at that time, including the colonists in America, with the affair of John Wilkes—which dramatized in real time the stakes of the rights of man and the fragility of the British constitution.

ALTHOUGH THE 1763 TREATY of Paris had brought the Seven Years' War to an end, all was not well in Britain. The economy was moribund. Droughts ruined several harvests; food prices spiraled. In London's Spitalfields neighborhood, the economic precariousness of the cloth industry worsened year after year. By the early 1760s, more than seven thousand looms were "out of employment." Throughout the 1760s, the Spitalfields silkweavers were continually striking and rising up in violent protests. When their advocacy for price controls to protect their industry failed in 1762, two thousand weavers assembled, broke up looms, and destroyed materials. Suffering further disappointment in 1763, thousands of weavers "in riotous manner broke open the house of one of their masters, destroyed his looms, and cut a great quantity of silk to pieces, after which they placed his effigy in a cart, with a halter about his neck, an executioner on one side, and a coffin on the other; and after drawing it through the streets they hanged it on a gibbet, then burnt it to ashes and afterwards dispersed," according to the November issue of *The Gentleman's Magazine*. Then in 1764, weavers marched to the House of Commons "with drums beating and banners flying," to demand bans on the importation of foreign silk. Britain was also still carrying huge debt from the Seven Years' War, and the government tried to address this by laying on additional taxes both in England and in the colonies: cider and paper in England; sugar, glass, lead, paint, paper, and tea in the colonies. The effect was the same in both places—rising dissent and unrest.

Topping off the instability, the King, in the midst of this great unrest, suffered the first episode of what historians now believe was bipolar affective disorder known since the early twentieth century as manic depression. This was the illness that would dramatically affect the later years of his rule, and earn him the moniker "mad King George." The "madness of George III" first revealed itself in the political whirlwind of a very contentious decade. The King disappeared from public view, though the Palace was able to hide his symptoms from public knowledge. Amid this chaos two rabble-rousers for the ages, one on each side of the Atlantic, kicked off political movements.

John Wilkes was a member of Parliament who, in 1762, had begun publishing an incendiary paper, *The North Briton*, to attack the then prime minister, Lord Bute. The government fought back with criminal charges. Wilkes was not a terribly sympathetic defendant. He was witty but also famously ugly, cross-eyed with a pockmarked face, and he was a reputed libertine. His finances were never sound, and his politics seemed to many to be driven largely by a desire for self-promotion. Yet in England his continuous battles with the Crown and government became the decade's most important cause for rights and liberty. "Wilkes and Liberty!" became a standing slogan for radical activists on both sides of the Atlantic. Many supported his cause despite actively disliking the man.

On the western side of the Atlantic, a Boston tax collector named Samuel Adams was also stirring up radical resistance to the Crown. A Puritan of middling height known for his plain dress, he had inherited a malthouse, which produced the ingredients necessary for brewing beer. He had no head for business, though, and his venture failed. His interests lay elsewhere—in politics and the question of the rights of colonial Americans. He was elected to the Boston Town Meeting and to the Massachusetts General Court, as the colonial assembly was called. Adams crafted the first objection of the Massachusetts representatives to the idea of being taxed by the legislature in England, instead of by themselves. Through newspaper writing and advocacy, he stirred up resistance to the many British taxes. Nor did he stop at words. By 1768, his advocacy would inspire mob action, building on several years of rising violence.

—

THE AIM OF WILKES'S paper, *The North Briton*, which achieved a circulation ten times greater than a rival published by the prime minister's allies, was to drive Bute from power. At this, he succeeded, for Bute resigned within a year of the launch of the paper. A few weeks later, in April 1763, the forty-fifth issue of *The North Briton*, which became famously and simply known as "No. 45," included an anonymous essay attacking King George III for selling out British interests in the peace talks with France and for failing the nation through the corruption and incompetence in his administration. It provoked a furious reaction.

A week after publication of No. 45, on April 30, 1763, Wilkes was arrested and charged with libel and sedition under a "general warrant," a legal instrument that did not specifically name the individuals to be arrested but permitted broad arrests. This set off an intense political fight over the rights of the press and the personal liberties of those subject to arrest. On May 6, the chief justice freed Wilkes on the grounds that he had parliamentary privilege—a long-standing rule that members of Parliament could not be arrested during parliamentary sessions and a certain period before and after. Wilkes immediately sued the government for false arrest and demanded one thousand pounds in damages.

The new prime minister, George Grenville, foolishly chose this febrile moment to impose a new cider tax, which the Duke of Grafton said, perhaps punningly, "raised a ferment in the country." Arbitrary arrest and burdensome taxation fused in the public imagination as evidence of growing tyranny from King George and his government and led to further protests and riots.

Richmond was actively tracking the radical currents newly rippling and spreading in London, on account of Wilkes's publication. He bought and bound all the issues of *The North Briton*, including the infamous No. 45. Yet he was also still keeping his opinions to himself. He did not join the set of aristocrats who had been flirting with forming a formal Opposition to the Crown and government and who now saw in Wilkes's arrest a way to accelerate their efforts.

By October 1763, not only the British people but also the American colonists were beginning to coalesce against the King. Early in that month, the King's administration proclaimed there would be no more western settlement by the colonists. The measure was introduced in response to advocacy from the Cherokees who sought protection and an end to depredations. The King's declaration also meant, though, that property values for land between the Allegheny and Mississippi plummeted. Among those who had been speculating on these lands and lost out were Patrick Henry, George Washington, and Benjamin Franklin. The British military in the colonies, no longer fighting the French after the end of the Seven Years' War, was now deployed to enforce the thirteen colonies' western boundary, known as the Proclamation Line. Taxes raised to fund the British military had turned into an investment in limiting the fortunes of politically prominent colonial leaders. Also, a wartime fighting force had morphed into a so-called standing army, which Whig philosophy said was anathema. Franklin routinely carried the complaints of the Americans into Whig circles as the Americans began to lay foundations for resistance.

Still, Richmond kept his peace. This is when he found himself rewarded for his silence with the appointment as lord lieutenant for Sussex. Paine, too, was quiet for the moment. Before he received his job in Grantham, Paine had been actively writing for *The North Briton*, with pieces in five of its issues in 1762. But for the first six months of 1763 he laid his pen down.

IN NOVEMBER, THE GOVERNMENT went after John Wilkes again and charged him with obscenity and blasphemy for a lewd poem. This time, to prevent Wilkes from using the defense of parliamentary privilege, a bill was proposed in Parliament to strip him of it. On Wednesday, November 23, the House of Commons passed resolutions that parliamentary privilege would no longer "extend to the Case of writing and publishing seditious Libels; nor ought to be allowed to obstruct the ordinary Course of the Laws, in the speedy and effectual Prosecution of so heinous and dangerous an Offence." The House also passed resolutions that the public hangman should burn an edition of *The North Briton*, No. 45, that had directly attacked the King. It was "a false, scandalous, and seditious Libel; containing Expressions of the most unexampled Insolence and Contumely towards His Majesty" and was likely to incite "traitorous Insurrections."

Both the Duke of Richmond and the Duke of Grafton were assigned to the House of Lords committee charged with considering the resolutions against Wilkes passed on to them by the House of Commons. The Commons wished to push through a vote in the Lords on the same day, but Richmond objected. His objection was procedural, not substantive.

Few lords were in attendance when the House of Commons introduced the matter to the Lords. Richmond's view was that all the peers should be duly informed in advance of any vote. At his urging, the vote in the House of Lords was postponed until the following Tuesday. After "decency [was] thus satisfied," Richmond and 113 other peers voted with the King to reduce the scope of parliamentary privilege and burn No. 45. With a hawk-eyed constitutionalism—highly attuned to the separation of powers thanks to his tutelage from Montesquieu, Richmond had defended the legislative prerogatives of the Lords. King and Commons wanted to override those in the heat of the moment. Richmond successfully defended the Lords' privileges and did so without breaking from the King.

In contrast to Richmond, thirty-four members of the House of Lords voted no. Seventeen of these, including the Duke of Grafton, not only voted against the King but also read into the record a stirring statement of dissent. Launching a new era of conflict over fundamental rights, they passionately defended press freedom, a matter that they thought implicated "the Personal Liberty of every common Subject." The ministry's decision to empower the secretary of state to designate a publication libelous and the vote to strip Wilkes of his parliamentary privilege "tore up" the "Independence of Parliament," and left it "buried under the Ruins" of established rights, they charged. They warned that the House of Lords was being asked to vote away "the Spirit of our Ancestors" and lamented that "a Parliament under perpetual Terror of Imprisonment can neither be free, nor bold, nor honest."

With this proud and fiery dissent, opposition had at last broken into the open. For the first time in the reign of King George III, a subset of aristocrats was establishing a formal platform to counter the King's administration from within the House of Lords. The statement of the dissent crystallized opposition and gave it stated goals and principles. Their rousing words did not affect the vote on burning the journal nor on reducing the scope of parliamentary privilege, but they did make clear that the time had come to choose sides.

Once again, Richmond chose to remain on the sidelines, this time to protect his newly awarded place as lord lieutenant. In contrast, not only Grafton but also the people chose Wilkes. Crowds broke the sheriff's coach glass and assaulted officials with dung, as the government representatives made their way to the ceremonial burning of No. 45. At the site, furious crowds wrested the kindling away from the hangman so that the paper could not be burned.

The courts, too, were on Wilkes's side. He won his lawsuit for false arrest and was awarded one thousand pounds in damages. When the verdict was delivered in his favor, crowds turned out in the streets chanting "Wilkes and Liberty!" In Parliament, buoyant Opposition members now turned immediately from defense of Wilkes to resistance to taxes and made their first effort to overturn the cider tax.

In the face of popular resistance, the King and government hardened their resolve. In January the government next moved to strip Wilkes, specifically, of his privileges. Ahead of this vote, the King and his ministers, through both bribes and threats, began to pressure people to vote with them. Richmond witnessed firsthand as his father-in-law, Henry Conway, who believed that votes on questions of basic rights should be a matter of conscience, not party program, became the target of the government's bullying approach in a late-night meeting that didn't even start until 10 p.m. The agitated government representative expounded on "the general matter of the propriety and possibility of keeping officers and military in place when they were in direct systematic opposition to the King's measures."

The eventual vote on the question of stripping Wilkes of his privileges was dramatic. He had been summoned to appear before a joint session of both houses of Parliament on January 19, 1764. In a startling turn of events, he did not appear. He had fled to Paris, where intellectual dissent from absolutism was simmering and where he would live in exile for several years. The vote was taken with Wilkes in absentia. Conway stuck to his principles and voted against the measure, despite the bullying. Richmond stuck with the King. Paine must have been watching attentively, but he stayed out of the press. The measure passed.

FOLLOWING WILKES'S SELF-EXILE TO France, the pressure on politicians to choose sides between Wilkes and the King, between British liberty and royal authority, grew only more intense. The first formal lists of members of "Wildman's Club," the main base for the Opposition, were published in 1764. All told, three clubs were formed in 1764. Not only Wildman's but also the Turk's Head Club, for intellectuals, and Brooks's, for the Whig elite, men like Richmond who were associated with the Old Whig elite but who had fallen out of favor with the King and now no longer attended court. This habit of associating outside the penumbra of royal authority was growing stronger for many who, until that point, had understood their universe to revolve around St. James's Palace. Among the clubs, Wildman's was the most politically aggressive, focused explicitly on developing an agenda to counter the King and his ministers. That agenda focused on elevating the issues of free speech and taxes that Wilkes had brought to the fore. These themes gained a head of steam in London even before they did in the colonies.

Even as lively new clubs sprang up, energized by distance from the Crown, Conway resisted calls to migrate to the formal Opposition. He kept his word. His name was absent from the list of members of Wildman's. So too was Richmond's. Like his father-in-law, Richmond continued to try to maintain relationships on both sides of a now clearly defined political divide. Yet Conway's careful effort to thread a needle—to vote his conscience but choose associations on the right side of the King—was for nought. Although Conway had supported the King and his ministers in all things other than the matter of Wilkes, the king dismissed him from office and removed him from all his privileges, on which he depended for his livelihood; he was not an independently wealthy man. As the acerbic society wit Horace Walpole, son of Britain's first prime minister, Robert Walpole, put it, "the boldness of the step was almost unprecedented."

Conway's April 1764 dismissal affected his friends and near relations deeply. Many rushed to his aid, including offering financial assistance. Walpole was also Conway's first cousin. To defend his cousin, he anonymously published a pamphlet condemning Conway's dismissal. Richmond also appears to have entered the pamphlet wars now, probably for the first time. Conway's treatment raised the very concerns that Richmond's mentor, James Wolfe, had taught him to take seriously. Here was proof that the high quality of the military was being undermined for political reasons. Here was evidence that the self-indulgent arbitrariness of a monarch might compromise national security. Here were ministers who sought to force English subjects, whether in England or the colonies, to submit to misguided policies against the dictates of conscience.

The direct blow to a family member, coupled with the violation of principle, pushed Richmond to break his silence—not yet, though, in his own voice. Instead, he hired a pamphleteer. Richmond had long watched his mentor and brother-in-law, Henry Fox, work with the scholar and divine Philip Francis Sr. to publish pamphlets and place pieces in the newspaper. Now, evidence in his library suggests, he appears to have contracted for the first time with his own pamphleteer, a twenty-one-year-old lawyer, James Adair, who wrote an anonymous pamphlet on the subject, "Thoughts on the Dismission of Officers, Civil or Military for Their Conduct in Parliament." Adair would remain one of Richmond's closest political aides for the coming decade, often writing parliamentary materials for Richmond and also anonymous newspaper pieces.

Richmond had perhaps not adequately covered his tracks in contributing to the Opposition discourse. In July, the prime minister called him in to determine whether Richmond had been badmouthing the government on account of the late-night bullying sessions with Conway in December. Richmond insisted that he had no part in spreading a narrative about what had occurred. The conversation was plainly tense and a cause of anxiety for Richmond. He took great pains to record the whole exchange in a lengthy memorandum in his journal. He seems to have been documenting the conversation to protect himself, fearful that the King's ministers might move against him in due course.

AS THE WILKES AFFAIR continued to rumble through 1764, Richmond attended Parliament more frequently, but he kept his head down and his focus on the mundane work of governing: He served on a naturalization committee, a beer duty committee, a guardianship committee, two enclosure bill committees, and two roads committees. He also spent considerable time that summer reviewing the troops in his role as a major general with responsibility for review of seven regiments. He would have been keenly aware that budget cuts had reduced the army from 120,000 service members to 48,000, with the Royal Navy seeing equally deep cuts. In his personal life, he had parted ways with Grafton socially and now modeled the kind of frugality that the King was urging on the debt-ridden nation. His midsummer account books now also record him forbidding that money be left in the house for servants, while he increased their wages in lieu of tips. This was an effort to root out corruption. Richmond saw tips as a form of bribe.

His reading in this time had led him back to Montesquieu but also to works of political economy. In 1764 he acquired a six-volume set of the philosopher's works. The spines are now well worn. These volumes were clearly among the most read books in his library. It's impossible to know whether he was drawn back to Montesquieu because the French philosopher's reputation was growing among radicals on both sides of the Atlantic or because the issues of the day brought questions of British constitutionalism so dramatically to the fore. Was the King overreaching his prerogative? What were the rights of the House of Commons and the House of Lords? And how did those rights relate to the basic liberties everyone had by nature? These were the questions raised by the Wilkes affair. They were also Montesquieu's questions, as Richmond was not alone in noticing.

Also well-enough worn to require rebacking was a two-volume book from 1764 on the "historical and chronological deduction of the origin of commerce." Richmond also read up on the British empire, studying the history of Scotland, Irish parliamentary history, a three-volume treatment of transactions in Bengal, and an account of excursions in North America. He bought books about the rights and prerogatives of the King and the public law of Europe. Soon he would also dive into the work of the physiocrats, such as the Abbé Baudeau, who had developed a vision of political economy that involved drawing on a land tax to relieve the sufferings of the poor. The desire to criticize the Crown, which had led to suppression of dissent, and which was triggering constitutional crisis, flowed from popular resentment of the state of the economy.

Solving the constitutional crisis clearly required thinking not only about how to find the right balance among the different parts of the British government and the rights of ordinary people, but also about how to secure a flourishing economy that would adequately provision the populace. Richmond was sympathetic, in other words, to the need for sound economy for the nation, and he was distressed by the ravages of poverty and burdensome taxes that lured too many into smuggling. He was unsure that the government's plan to layer on ever more taxes was the solution.

The Americans agreed with him. When the Sugar Act for the colonies, also known as the American Revenue Act of 1764 or the American Duties Act, was approved by Parliament, it provoked protest petitions from the colonial assemblies of Massachusetts, Rhode Island, Connecticut, New York, Pennsylvania, Virginia, North Carolina, and South Carolina. A Boston lawyer named James Otis Jr., would write an influential pamphlet that for the first time in the colonies made the case that there should be "no taxation without representation."

The government did not heed the colonists' increasingly rebellious mood. Among other reasons, they were distracted. Mid-January of 1765 was when the King began his first descent into a bipolar episode. He was visited by his physician and bled, while the court hid his true symptoms and allowed the rumor to spread that he was suffering from consumption. On March 1, 1765, even with the King essentially out of commission, the prime minister, George Grenville, who was a competent technocrat but with little political sense, launched a parliamentary salvo to pass the Stamp Act. This law would require American colonists to pay a tax on every piece of printed paper they used, including legal documents, licenses, newspapers, other publications, and even playing cards. It was another foolish mistake. In Boston, malthouse owner Sam Adams, merchant John Hancock, and lawyer James Otis Jr. formed the Sons of Liberty to protest the new law. Even if the Stamp Act had been enforceable in the colonies, the maximum revenue it might have earned was estimated at 45,000–65,000 pounds, or a fraction of the cost to Britain of keeping soldiers in America. In the end, the Stamp Tax earned precisely forty-five pounds. Richmond attended the central debates on the Stamp Tax, but when the vote was taken, he absented himself in an act of political calculation, as he also had done when the Sugar Act was passed. His willingness to vote loyally on the side of the King was faltering.

In America, the new law led immediately to "tumults and insurrections," from New England to the valuable Caribbean possessions. Loyalty was fraying across the Atlantic as well.

THE KING FINALLY EMERGED from his illness in April. When he did, his mind was on two things: ensuring that the monarchy would not be endangered by his own unpredictable health and swapping out the prime minister, Grenville, who was not only politically foolish but also peremptory, and whom George did not like as much as the uncritically loyal Bute. He turned to the succession problem first and asked Parliament to pass a regency bill that would establish a governance structure, or "regency," to be activated if he should become incapacitated while his son was still a child. He explained to Parliament that his "late Indisposition" had brought him the need to plan for his own death while his son was still "of tender years." Out of equally "tender concern" for his "faithful subjects" he wanted to provide for "their future Happiness or Security." George proposed that either his wife, Queen Charlotte, or anyone else from his royal family usually residing in Great Britain, should be the guardian for the Prince of Wales and Regent for the Kingdoms.

The royal family residing in Britain included a very large group of people, and this open-ended proposal concerned Richmond. He felt the terms of the bill gave the monarch too much discretion—and could permit an arbitrary and divisive choice by the King. Richmond was motivated by his low trust of George specifically, but also by the idea that the power of the executive should flow only through tightly constrained channels. Again, he was giving voice to Montesquieu. He made his arguments in Parliament vigorously enough to force furious negotiations between the Palace and Parliament. At last a compromise was reached: The regent would be Queen Charlotte, but if she were to predecease George, then the role would pass to the Princess Dowager.

After several years of biting his tongue, Richmond had broken his silence in a most dramatic way, crossing the King in a painfully intimate matter. Unsurprisingly, George took it as yet another affront from the Duke. What tenuous new connection Richmond had established with the sovereign vanished instantly, and immediately he felt the fresh sting of the King's resentment. The time had come for a new ministry, but Richmond would receive no distinguished place.

Once the issue of the regency was resolved in early May, the King turned immediately to ridding himself of his overbearing prime minister. He forced Grenville to resign and Henry Fox along with him. The administration collapsed. Independently, on May 14, at the very same moment, the silk weavers started to riot. The cavalry was called out and read the Riot Act to the crowd, requiring the gathering mob to disperse within the hour, under the threat of death. The weavers did disperse but attacked aristocratic houses as they left. Soon Wilkes's supporters joined in the fracas and the capital descended into six days of riots. Passions ran hot, and some politicians thought they might be facing an uprising as significant as the rebellion led by Bonnie Prince Charlie in 1745. They began to wrangle over calling in one or another military figure to lead a response. Richmond was proposed by some. The moment seemed in danger of tipping into armed conflict among different factions of the aristocracy.

Luckily, the King's uncle, the Duke of Cumberland, kept a cool head and talked everyone down. Finally, by the end of May, the riots were relatively easily suppressed, and the King got a new ministry in place. The

Marquess of Rockingham, aged thirty-five, accepted the premiership and brought in as his private secretary Edmund Burke, who was already famous as the author in 1757 of *A Philosophical Enquiry into the Origin of Our Ideas of the Sublime and Beautiful.* Rockingham was the first prime minister without prior cabinet experience. As ballast, Henry Conway was appointed as northern secretary of state, just a year after his dismissal from his earlier roles.

Because Richmond had not been a part of the active Opposition, he was not boosted by Rockingham's promotion. Nor did the King hold him in high enough regard to insist on his participation in the ministry. Richmond responded once more with doggedness. Depending on Albemarle and Conway to advocate for him, he was offered the ambassadorship to Paris or, more specifically, the role of Ambassador Extraordinary and Minister Plenipotentiary to the Court of Louis XV at Versailles. This appointment, which was to all appearances a step forward, stung. It was a relatively minor reward for someone who had voted loyally for the King over three years despite intense peer pressure. Richmond so believed in the rightness of his views on the regency question that he did not understand how he could have wronged the King in any way. As a matter of principle, he had not; his proposal for the regency was perfectly reasonable. As a matter of honor, though, he had failed to defer to his sovereign.

THOMAS PAINE, TOO, WAS living through a budding career that alternated between satisfying highs and stinging disappointment. In August 1764 he moved out of his probationary status at the excise and became a full officer in Grantham. He was honest and hard-working in the role, at least in those early days in 1764. He was responsible for riding out by horse from Grantham to Alford on the eastern coast, halfway between Norwich and York, collecting duties as he went. With a coastal "ride" such as this, hindering smugglers would have been among his most important responsibilities. He was surely observing much that was broken in the British economy.

Like Richmond, Paine was also under Conway's protection. He too experienced a setback in his career in the summer of 1765 as Britain was shaking off the cloud of Grenville's wretched leadership and coming to know Rockingham. The excise service was notoriously corrupt, and

Paine had had the misfortune to be assigned a post under the supervision of a particularly problematic senior officer named Swallow, who doctored Paine's books, creating fraudulent entries for assessments that were never done. In August 1765, a whistleblower alerted the higher-ups to the fraudulent accounts.

Improbably enough, Swallow's superior in office was named Birdsworth. Swallow had many more years in the service than Birdsworth, despite Birdsworth's having the higher rank. Birdsworth consequently found it too challenging to address Swallow's corruption directly. Intimidated by Swallow, Birdsworth fired Paine, on the principle that the last in is the first out. Just as Richmond was seething at how corruption was hollowing out the military, Paine bore the brunt of how it hollowed out the civil service. Corruption had thwarted his path. He had now been cast back into the world to seek a living from scratch.

Paine headed straight to London. Just before he was fired, he had resumed writing, this time for *The Public Advertiser.* He had also by now developed enough intellectual standing to soon secure a place as a teacher at Noble's Academy at Goodman Fields in London. Back in the capital, he found the city abuzz with news that nine of the thirteen American colonies had presumptuously formed themselves into a Congress—now known as the Stamp Act Congress—and had met in New York to prepare petitions to Parliament for repeal of the act. The leading intellectual light of the Stamp Act Congress was Bostonian James Otis Jr. His message, "No taxation without representation," had crossed the Atlantic, complete with a Declaration of Rights and Grievances. In this early declaration, the Americans professed loyalty to the Crown but insisted that they should be taxed only by their own elected representatives and not by Parliament where they, like most Englishmen, had no direct representation.

Their arguments chimed with all those burdened by tax in Britain who played no role in electing Parliament. Richmond and Paine both registered the point. In the fall of 1765, Paine picked up the pace of his political writing. One more stint at the excise awaited him, but that next time he would seek to merge the role with advocacy. He had made the transition to radicalism. Richmond would still make one more effort at conventional professional success—via his ambassadorship—before he too would fully join the cause.

Chapter

5

RICHMOND FINDS HIS VOICE

1765–1766

I think the Duke of Richmond will become a considerable man.

—EDMUND BURKE

IN THE LATE 1750S, AS THE SEVEN YEARS' WAR WAS UNFOLDING, Richmond had stewed in London, desperate to be dispatched to the European front. He had waited years, studying military strategy and tactics in books, before he got his opportunity for heroism in the field at Minden. Now, in 1765, he was just beginning to develop his parliamentary and rhetorical skills. Right when a major battle was brewing in the House of Lords over whether to repeal the Stamp Act, a top-priority policy goal of the new Rockingham ministry, Richmond found himself dispatched abroad, away from the action. It wasn't what he wanted at all. Although Paris carried a reputation as the "Centre of Taste, Magnificence, Beauty & every Thing that is polite," as one travel journal put it, Richmond thought it a backwater. For him London was the place to be.

When the Richmonds arrived, Paris was full of English travelers seeking to escape Britain's "exorbitant taxes" and to indulge in "Eatables and Drinkables"—hares, partridges, woodcocks, pheasants, and turkeys—while enjoying a "mild & more moderate Air" than in England. A sluggish, muddy Seine, lined by houseboats where washerwomen did their best to wring cleanliness from filth, rolled through a city of stone-fronted buildings and narrow streets. "All the foreigners of distinction," the travelogue said, lodged in the elegant neighborhood of Faubourg Saint-Germain, whose enclosed, manicured gardens contrasted to narrow and dimly lit streets throughout the rest of the city where street corners were mobbed by beggars. Surrounding suburbs were afflicted with broken-down poverty. British visitors missed their country's "fine & stately Parcel of Oaks, Elms or Ash" and mocked France's ubiquitous pollarded trees as "trees cut into fire-shovels and stuck into pedestals of chalk." But there were also signs of progress. The hackney coaches may have been "squalid and forlorn," but they rumbled along paved roads. Gone were the "uneasy Joltings of London streets." Freethinkers debated Rousseau's irreligion after dinner in salons hosted by famous women in deshabille, and even the dissident Wilkes managed to live in the Faubourg Saint-Germain, exchanging house calls with aristocrats.

In this Paris of rich and poor, satiated and grasping, visual wonders and reeking sewers, Richmond found his voice. He uncovered practical and political opportunities that transformed him from a lonely advocate insisting on minor points of constitutional procedure into a leading architect of British policy, foreign and domestic. While Paine taught and wrote in the thick of London's political conflicts, Richmond developed a wholly independent policy vision and offered it up as a service to the Crown, eagerly, sincerely, and repeatedly. Although he would be rebuffed, and rebuffed again, he would eventually find paths to influence outside the court, via radical, secret strategies.

RICHMOND WOULD NOT STAY long in the French capital—ultimately only three months—and he arrived late. In Paris gossips had begun to wonder when the Duke of Richmond would arrive until in early October a Parisian diarist recorded hearing one evening "that, as the Duke of Richmond's Pack of Dogs were come over this Day from England to Paris, it was not to be reasonably expected that his Grace would be long behind." In fact, that diarist would still have weeks to wait. The Duke was moving far more slowly than his hounds.

Delayed in England by the death of a nephew, the Duke finally disembarked in the port city Calais on October 30, with the Duchess and, as secretary, his brother George. They were met by a thirteen-gun salute, the commandant, mayor, and other town officials. He quizzed Calais merchants on the local economy, finding that they sent brandy and tea to London but got only money back. Britain, he learned, was running a trade deficit. He fended off questions from French officials, who were very skeptical of his assertion that "nothing could be more settled than" the new administration of the Marquess of Rockingham. To the contrary, everyone understood that the King had appointed the youthful, inexperienced Rockingham, who had been active in the Opposition for the previous two years, only as a choice of last resort. All expected that when the King could change his prime minister, he would. Good soldier that he was, though, Richmond carried the message that the government was strong.

Richmond did not travel directly to Paris. He went first to Dunkirk and got to work on what was to become a lifelong obsession: ensuring that the French coast was not fortified in ways that could threaten Britain. The 1763 Treaty of Paris, which had been ratified two years earlier, had included the provision that the French should dismantle fortifications at Dunkirk and close the harbor to warships. This they had not done. France did not actually want to give up Dunkirk's strategic utility and consistently tried to reinterpret or minimize the treaty's requirements. Richmond's government instructed him to overlook the situation, but he chose not to. His Sussex estate had views of the English Channel. Potential for a French attack via the South Coast consumed him throughout his life.

He took with him to Dunkirk a military colleague from Minden, Colonel Roy, for whom his father-in-law General Conway, now secretary of state for the southern department, had recently secured an appointment as surveyor general of the coasts and engineer for making and directing military surveys in Great Britain. Roy's charge was to find an engineering solution by which the fortification breakwaters could be destroyed without flooding the surrounding farms. It was no longer primarily artists whom Richmond was pulling into his circle of innovation and policy. Now it was also military men. By this point he had not only Roy in his circle but also his former lieutenant from the 33rd Regiment of Foot, now Captain Thomas Jones, who would become his most trusted and confidential personal aide.

WHEN THE DUKE AND Duchess at last arrived in Paris on November 6, still without their luggage, which had been marooned by low rivers, they found an immediate escort and mentor in Horace Walpole, who was an habitué of the salons. A slight man possessed of "one of the most puny, thin, delicate and meagre Constitutions & Frame of Body this Day in England," Walpole was suffering from gout and had moved to Paris for the winter in the hopes that the more moderate climate would relieve his pain. Well-connected to the city's showy aristocracy, he immediately busied himself orienting the Duke and Duchess. He introduced the couple to the key political and social figures and accompanied them to the theater and opera. The Richmonds' residence was the Hôtel de Brancas, an elegant neoclassical mansion, also in Faubourg Saint-Germain. It had recently been rescued from use as a riding school. To equip their lodgings, Walpole and the Richmonds traveled to Sèvres, near Versailles, to visit a porcelain factory. There they spent 500 pounds, or $300,000 in today's dollars, just on tableware. This made Richmond, then and still to this day, the greatest English patron of Sèvres porcelain. He took advantage of Parisian artistry and ordered porcelain painted with images from George Edwards's *A Natural History of Birds* (1743–51) and his *Gleanings of Natural History* (1747–64). The Duke owned and lent these books to the factory so that their engravings could be copied, making his the first pieces of Sèvres porcelain to bear the iconic birds.

As a newly arrived ambassador, Richmond found a full portfolio awaiting him. Dismantling the harbor fortifications at Dunkirk was his pet priority, but there was also other unfinished business from the 1763 Treaty of Paris, including challenges around fishing rights in Nova Scotia and the problem of English merchants who had been left holding now worthless French paper money when France relinquished Canada to the British. The treaty had included a commitment to their compensation by the French, but it had stalled.

The French capital was also filled with English dissidents, with an unusually porous social boundary between them and the aristocrats. Richmond's predecessor as ambassador had ignored Wilkes and declined to return his calls, but Richmond visited him. A second radical activist, John Horne, later to be called John Horne Tooke, was also in the French capital. The three would before long become comrades in arms for radical causes of parliamentary reform.

The political controversies of the day were much on Richmond's mind as he followed the parliamentary debates that raged back home about American taxes and the Stamp Act. The new Rockingham administration had decided to try to repeal the Stamp Tax, and took a more conciliatory policy toward America. Through his time in the Society of Arts, Richmond had developed the view that the best relationship between mother country and colonies would be one that facilitated the easiest and most productive possible trade relations. He wanted America and Britain each to be the other's first market. For this, he considered repeal of the ill-conceived tax indispensable. Already in a letter to Conway on November 30, less than a month after his arrival in Paris, desperate to get back to parliamentary debate in London, he let Conway know—and Conway was now not only his father-in-law but also his superior in office—that he planned to request leave to return home. He was, he added, preparing his brother to step in for him as ambassador by including him in meetings with the leading French politicians.

Yet even with a distracted mind, Richmond got an incredible amount done in his first two months in Paris. His fifteen-page letter to Conway also detailed his thinking about the reparations issue and Dunkirk. He managed to deliver a deal to the British merchants that brought them 120,000 pounds more than they had understood themselves to have claim to. His success depended on exceptional mathematical abilities. On January 28, 1766, he was triumphantly able to deliver an order for Dunkirk signed at Versailles by the very haughty duc de Choiseul, the French foreign minister, "to putt the jetties at the level of [the beach] [and] to be done in front of the Engineer of the British king."

THEN, ON FEBRUARY 20, having been granted leave and moving in great haste to make it back to Parliament for the debates on repeal of the Stamp Act, Richmond left the Duchess in Paris and, traveling with Roy, made his way back to London on the first available fishing boat. The seas were rough that month. Another ship sailing from London to Dunkirk went down within days of when Richmond traveled. Landing at Dover probably required him to disembark through rough chop at the shore, leaving him wet and cold. Still, he had arrived just in time to join debates about the Stamp Act that began on February 24.

The government was defending the act on the grounds that the Americans were "children planted" by the government's "care" and "nourished up by our indulgence," but were now refusing to contribute to their own protection. They had to take up their share of the burden. The Opposition in Parliament instead saw the tax on the colonists as of a piece with the assaults on British liberty in the Wilkes affair and ever-increasing taxation. Another protégé of General Wolfe, Colonel Isaac Barré, argued in the House of Commons that, far from having been planted in the colonies by the government's care, the colonists had in fact traveled across the Atlantic to escape injustice. It was "oppressions [that] planted them in America," he retorted. What was problematic to Rockingham, Richmond, and the others was that the arbitrary imposition of a tax on the Americans both undermined good relations with an economically valuable community of fellow Englishmen and entrenched practices of domination on the part of the Crown. The Americans violently agreed with their friends in Parliament. Riots were unfolding in the colonies from Massachusetts to Barbados. Repeal of the Stamp Act was the single greatest priority of the Rockingham administration, and Richmond endorsed repeal wholeheartedly.

Richmond was present in the House of Lords on March 5, 6, and 7 to hear the petitions from the merchants of London, Bristol, and Glasgow in support of the repeal, as well as the petition of the Virginia agent, and the views Benjamin Franklin presented in person. By early March, the Duchess had caught up with her husband and was back in London. On March 8, during a break in parliamentary business, they hosted his sister Sarah, now wife of Charles Bunbury, at Richmond House for dinner. Richmond must have been exhausted. After the meal, his wife went to hear Maria Teresa Agnesi's opera, *La Sofonisba*, at the King's Theatre, but Richmond fell asleep on the couch, leaving his sister to write letters. Before Sarah finished writing to her friend Susan, though, she was able to add a timely piece of information: "My brother is just awake, & bids me tell you that the repeal of the Act is passed in the House of Commons and will be a very near thing in the H. of Lds very soon he is viollent for it." Although there is no transcript of Richmond's remarks in the House of Lords, he was clearly influential in arguing against the act. Afterward Edmund Burke wrote, "I think the Duke of Richmond will become a considerable man." Richmond had clearly found his voice.

After an orgy of fiery rhetoric, the repeal of the Stamp Act passed in the House of Commons by 250 to 122. On March 17, it won in the House of Lords by a majority of over 30. As news of repeal of the Stamp Tax spread through London, "bells rang in every part of the city" and "[a]t night many coffee houses and other houses in the city were finely illuminated," as *The London Chronicle* reported. On April 11, the cider tax was scrapped as well. The bells pealed again. Festive parades were organized. Sheep, ox, and lamb were sacrificed and roasted, and shared throughout whole towns. Hogsheads of cider were liberally dispensed. The liberation of the colonists from a burdensome tax was of a piece with relief to the British themselves from their burdensome tax. On both sides of the ocean, ordinary people had reason to celebrate that popular opinion had brought the King's ministry to heel. As Rockingham's memoirs report, "On the 23rd of April a grand dinner was given at Drapers' Hall in celebration of the repeal of the Stamp Act. It was among the most brilliant ever seen in the City, and the *Chronicle* "duly record[ed] that nine dukes were amongst the company." The Duke of Richmond was surely among them.

THE CELEBRATIONS OF THE Stamp Act repeal were as boisterous in America as in England. But underneath the glee there was division. The British had wanted the act repealed because they thought it was a bad tax. The Americans had wanted it repealed because they didn't think the British legislature, where they weren't represented, had the right to tax them at all. Their own colonial legislatures were taxing them, and that seemed to the colonists sufficient.

Aware of this disagreement, and its potential long-term consequences, the Rockingham administration moved quickly to reassert the right to tax the colonies. The same men who were the heroes of the Stamp Act repeal—including Rockingham and Richmond—on the same day also passed the brief and much-resented Declaratory Act. This pronounced, in two short paragraphs, that the Parliament, the supreme authority in the colonies, had the power to tax them "in all cases whatsoever." Taking back with the second hand what the repeal had given with the first, the Declaratory Act put front and center for the Americans the question of whether they owed their allegiance to the King or to Parliament. While the Americans hadn't, to that point, questioned the King's authority over them, they did question whether they owed deference to an English legislative assembly. After all, did they not have their own colonial assemblies? Should it not be their own assemblies that advised the King on his policy toward them? As Benjamin Franklin put it succinctly, "The sovereignty of the Crown I understand. The sovereignty of the British legislature out[side] of Britain I do not understand." The Americans imagined a universe where, under the broad protection of the British empire, different sovereign entities all functioned with legislatures working independently from one another and in collaboration with the King. The members of Parliament, though, considered their combined authority to be on par with that of the King—a separate but equal branch of government—and could not entertain as reasonable that they would be considered as but one of many legislatures all working with, and in subordination, to the King.

Although repeal was a victory for Rockingham's administration, the victory was shaky. More lords had argued against repeal than for it, and the King gave them cover. Instead of punishing them for voting against the government, as he had done in the Wilkes affair, he let it be known that he would look the other way. Then, when the Rockingham administration tried to correct the abusive use of general warrants that had led to Wilkes's arrest two years earlier, some of their own Opposition allies—William Pitt and the Duke of Grafton—outflanked them by proposing an even more comprehensive rejection of warrants. The Rockingham administration was neither bringing the King's friends to their side, nor holding together the forces that had been united in opposition in the previous year. Onlooking foreign governments began to assume the government would collapse. By late April 1766, in the House of Lords, Grafton described the administration in which he served as northern secretary of state as lacking "authority, dignity, and extension." He resigned on May 14. There would be two months of bitter infighting before the Rockingham administration finally collapsed, during which time all the alliances and agendas of the future decade were shaped.

WHEN RICHMOND HAD LANDED in Calais, the French who greeted him had doubted that the administration in which he served had staying power. Richmond had insisted on the strength of the Rockingham administration. Now, as the administration was incontrovertibly, embarrassingly collapsing around him, Richmond nonetheless thought that at least he would have staying power. He knew he had done important work in Paris, on Canada and Dunkirk. In fact, he thought he deserved a promotion. To replace Grafton, Rockingham moved Conway to northern secretary of state, and Richmond put his hand up for southern secretary of state, a leading role in the cabinet.

Richmond's powerful enemies were, however, still implacable. His former mentor, Newcastle, whom he had succeeded as lord lieutenant of

Sussex, opposed him and so did the King, of course. Each time Richmond's name was put forward, the King offered counterproposals. By now George III's negative view of Richmond was fixed. He wrote, "that Duke had neither the abilities, temper, or experience requisite" for the role.

Richmond's focus on constitutionalism à la Montesquieu—where law triumphs over men—left him averse to parties and factions, much as the drafters of the US Constitution would also be, thanks to the influence of Montesquieu. He sought to balance all the orders of government and worked for unity and stability across party lines. Rather than working through a faction—that is, a specific set of men connected by patronage networks—to advance his policy goals, he typically tried to bring members of all the political networks on board with his view, putting pressure on whomever he considered to hold the key lever of power that might bring change, often doing so tactlessly, as he had done with the duc de Choiseul in Paris. This meant he belonged ultimately to no faction and so was without the alliances and relationships he needed for securing promotions. Only once Rockingham and the King had scraped the bottom of the proverbial barrel and found no alternative to Richmond did George authorize his prime minister to appoint Richmond as secretary of state for the southern department, with responsibility for the American colonies.

Despite the clear resistance to his appointment, Richmond shook off any negativity and got right to work. He truly was born to serve. He immediately picked up implementation of the Stamp Act repeal and continued the work he had been doing on Canada from his ambassadorship. He recommended toleration for Catholics in Canada in a first for colonial policy. He also began to address the question of how residents of a colony might be connected to the English government—directly through the King, assisted by a local assembly. With remarkable acuity, he was beginning to design what would eventually become the Quebec Act—an act passed in 1774 that finally did grant freedom of religion to Catholics in Canada and restore French civil law in the colony. While the act alienated the American colonists—who viewed its tolerance of Catholicism and restoration of French civil law as threats to their British liberties—it paved the way for the British Empire's emerging strategy of governance through accommodation of local customs within imperial administration. To entrench his policy approach, Richmond secured the appointment of Guy Carleton, his former military tutor, as governor of Quebec.

Even more important, in the brief two months that he served as secretary of state before the Rockingham ministry collapsed, he asked the question of what factions or political parties should be like in Britain, and how they should operate. In this work his closest intellectual collaborator, Edmund Burke, was now Rockingham's secretary. Burke was coming to see parties—principled associations formed to uphold the national interest through consistent policy—as distinct from factions driven by personal ambition. Defined this way, parties were also necessary for good governance. In the cauldron of that summer's fierce negotiations for roles and places, Burke, Richmond, and their allies conceived the modern party system.

British politics had turned for a long time around a debate between "men and measures": Should politics be pursued for the sake of bringing patronage appointments to one's network (*men*) or to advance specific policy ideas (*measures*)? Historically, eighteenth-century party leaders like Newcastle had focused mainly on men, using office to advance themselves and their cronies. Pitt, in the late 1750s, offered a dramatic alternative, adhering to specific policies such as advocating a strong military, and disregarding any obligation to keep a specific set of elite cronies happy. His slogan was "Measures, not men." He careened through different political alliances, including sometimes being at odds even with his own brothers-in-law. The best orator of his generation, Pitt earned the support of the people, and this allowed him to keep his eye on his policy goals. As a populist, he didn't need a faction.

Rockingham now pursued yet another new style of politics. His slogan was "Men *and* measures" (emphasis added). He sought to build strong bonds of loyalty and affection within his party, but he also asked those bound together to commit to a single stable policy agenda. Burke was the intellectual architect of that agenda, the foundation for modern party politics. Yet as Rockingham tried to achieve this, Richmond pushed him, throughout the summer's negotiations, toward something even more ambitious. In addition to Rockingham's alliance, three other factions were operating in British politics at the time: a faction led by the Duke of Bedford, which relied on the old style of politics focused on men; a faction led by Pitt, which focused on measures; and a small faction led by the much hated Bute and known as "the King's friends."

Richmond wanted Rockingham to take all three factions into his own alliance to forge a modern party—despite how much they had been previously opposed to one another, and despite how much the Rockinghamites considered the Bute faction in particular corrupt. He believed that Rockingham would be able to stabilize his government only by pursuing this kind of unity party. Richmond's earnest proposal of this unconventional idea at a party meeting provoked a sharp reaction, nearly bringing the meeting to an early end. As he recorded in a memo to himself, "Ld. Rockingham bounced off his seat and the D. of Newcastle put on his Hat to go away, both exclaiming 'Good God, would you have us joyn My Lord Bute! No, lett us keep our fingers clean.'" Richmond wanted to take the commitment to measures all the way, overlooking animosities among men to form the biggest possible tent. Rockingham was not willing to go that far.

Richmond was, like Pitt, an absolutist for measures, willing to tear through the cobwebs of favors and ledgers of insults—eager to disregard personal concerns—in forging the party agenda. This is why the two men—over the course of the two decades they shared in British political life—ultimately found themselves sometimes bitter adversaries and sometimes vigorous allies. When they agreed on measures, they could easily ally; and when they did not, they would not. In British politics of the day, it was not at all obvious that one would break with a political ally because of a policy disagreement. Often politicians chose to overlook substantive disagreements to preserve access to the trade in favors. This explains Conway, who moved from one administration to another, across quite opposed policy regimes. Richmond helped the Rockingham party stay resolutely focused on policy—instead of favor trading—and worked extensively with Burke on the party's agenda: favorable relations with America, taxation, and basic constitutional liberties.

In other ways, Richmond differed from Pitt. He sought to build strength not by speaking directly to the people but by uniting all factions of the elite. Another difference was in style. In the House of Commons, Pitt could rely on vehement oratory to gain power through the affection of the people. As a member of the House of Lords, Richmond operated in a world driven almost entirely by loyalty and patronage, and dominated by a culture of indirect speech. Frank speech, which might destabilize relationships, was more costly in the House of Lords than in the House of Commons. Richmond's bluntness was a liability. He had found his voice, but in Parliament his vehemence and certainty did not always produce the desired results.

The politicking among a clutch of proud, obstinate, opinionated men yielded no stable government for Rockingham. On July 11, 1766, the Rockingham ministry fell. The members of the cabinet all attended the day's levee with the royal family and then resigned at its close. While they insisted on their continued willingness to serve "their King and Country to the best of their Abilities," they said they had chosen to resign because "they were not thought sufficient." The King replaced Rockingham with Pitt, to whom he also awarded an earldom, elevating him to the House of Lords as the Earl of Chatham. From that point on, he would simply be known as Chatham. Letters to the editor of *The Public Advertiser* applauded the change, which "greatly raised the Expectations of all true friends of Great Britain and its Colonies." Readers eagerly hoped that they would once again have a government marked by "harmony," and that from this would flow increased trade and improved constitutionalism, both things Richmond also wanted.

Consistent with his focus on measures rather than men, Richmond offered Pitt his continued service as secretary of state but was rebuffed. His role was given to the Earl of Shelburne, William Petty Fitzmaurice, another former protégé of Wolfe's and a veteran of the Battle of Minden. Richmond's former schoolmate, the Duke of Grafton, was brought back into office as first lord of the treasury. Richmond had been in office for roughly nine months as ambassador (and only three actually in post) and barely two as secretary of state. He had been diligent. He had been creative. He had been dutiful. And yet he was offered nothing in the King's new government. Richmond's anger must have been immense. What was he to do with the vision and voice he had by now so clearly developed?

THOMAS PAINE HAD ALREADY found his way to influence the day's political questions. He too had found his fortunes cycling quickly up and down during this period. He also suffered short employments and underestimation. Having been dismissed from his role as a new excise officer in 1765, now in the summer of 1766 he sought to recover a place. On July 3, he petitioned the national Excise Office, writing, "The time I enjoyed my former commission was short and unfortunate—an officer for only a single year. No complaint of the least dishonesty or intemperance ever appeared against me." The fact that the previous dismissal had been ill-founded must have been apparent to everyone because on the very next day, July 4, his petition for readmission was granted. Regrettably, though, there was no post available for him. Paine remained adrift professionally. He continued his teaching in Goodman's Fields, Aldgate, and then Kensington. There is also some evidence that during this period he spent time preaching, possibly in Dover.

In addition to teaching and preaching, by now Paine was also writing regularly for the London political papers, either anonymously or under a pseudonym. On February 22, 1766, during the middle of the Stamp Act debates, Paine published a letter to the printer of *The Public Advertiser* under the pseudonym Philanthropos, in which he mused on the question of whether British subjects born abroad carried the same Magna Carta rights as Englishmen at home. Maybe was his answer. In September, in *The Gazetteer*, the subject was policy measures taken by the new Pitt administration to address a terrible crisis in grain prices. Paine's contributions were infrequent—three pieces in 1766 and four in 1767—but the pace would soon pick up. Like Richmond, Paine had found his voice and also a network of collaborators. That network included two other young men whom Richmond came to know during his summer of despondency: Philip Francis Jr. and James Burgh. Paine's burgeoning activity on this front may well explain why—when at last another excise post was offered to him in Cornwall—he turned it down. Cornwall was too distant from London for him to pursue collaborations with his growing network of activist friends.

AFTER RICHMOND WAS DISMISSED from office, he soon headed for Paris with the Duchess to nurse his wounded pride. As would become his pattern, he used summer travel to Paris for extensive reading, once again about war, politics, and philosophy. Before he left for the Continent, he carried out some unfinished business from his time as secretary of state. He formed connections with two ambitious young men, who shared his sense of grievance and who were making a name for themselves as political writers for the papers.

Philip Francis Jr., son of Henry Fox's pamphleteer, was principal clerk in the War Office. A dark-eyed, slender-nosed, ruddy man, he had served as secretary to the ambassador to Portugal in 1760. He was also a prolific writer of anonymous political pieces for papers. He and Richmond knew each other distantly—through the relationship between Fox and Francis Sr.; because Richmond himself also subscribed to Francis Sr.'s publications; and because Francis Jr. was the civil servant sent to meetings of the House of Lords to report on military promotions as they were made.

In May, just after Richmond was appointed secretary of state, Francis had sent him a thirty-three-page private letter on the political and commercial relations of England and Portugal. Evidently frustrated that he had not heard anything back from Richmond, Francis published a pseudonymous note in *The Public Advertiser* on August 1, complaining about the "constant dissolutions of cabinets" and "cabals of the great families." He carped at "many of no talent or desert being placed over the heads of others better entitled to advancement." Francis compared Portugal to England favorably because Portuguese ministers acknowledged the letters and adopted the ideas of more junior men and gave them appropriate credit. Francis's newspaper piece echoed the themes and concerns that had motivated Richmond already for more than a decade—of merit overlooked, of establishments willfully blind to good ideas rising from new quarters. Presumably needled by Francis's public letter, Richmond finally answered the private one. He let Francis know that he was headed to France but promised they would meet when he returned. Richmond had long collected protégés in the arts and from the military. Francis was an early addition to a new category of "particular friends," as he called them: political pamphleteers.

Two years earlier, in 1764, Richmond had in all likelihood hired James Adair as a pamphleteer to protest Conway's dismissal. Now, in addition to preparing to strike up a connection with Francis, Richmond appears to have engaged a second radical writer, James Burgh, to advocate for his own cause in the papers. Raised in Scotland as a Presbyterian, Burgh was a dissenter; he rejected the Church of England and embraced religious toleration. From the early 1760s Burgh participated in coffee-house meetings with a group called the Honest Whigs, whose members included Benjamin Franklin, and other radical thinkers who were soon in Richmond's circle, including Richard Price, a dissenting moral philosopher. Burgh was the earliest theoretician of universal male suffrage, an argument he would put forward in 1774 in his three-volume work, *Political Disquisitions*.*

But for the moment he took up a far more modest writing task. In September, under the pen name "Atticus," Burgh criticized the dismissal of the Duke of Richmond and the appointment of Shelburne in his place. It's possible that he wrote in order to attract Richmond's attention and earn a commission. It's more likely, though, that Richmond simply engaged him as a way of carrying his arguments forward while out of office. Burgh, writing about Richmond, under the guise of Atticus, complained: "That a young English D—, of the First Distinction should be turned out for [Shelburne], after having the Seals in his Custody but three Weeks. It seems as if his G— — had been called in merely to be affronted."

Richmond had planted his voice in the papers, and there it would continue to resound. Ultimately, Richmond would support a whole series of Atticus pieces. In all likelihood, Richmond engaged Burgh for this piece of writing at about the time he wrote to Francis and before he headed to Paris. In Paris, he kept up with his political and philosophical education. His brother, George, and sister-in-law, Louisa, were there too. While they kept late hours playing cards, Richmond focused on his reading: books like *Historical Essays about Paris*, *The Elements of Fortification*, and *A Succinct Exposition of the Controversy between Hume and Rousseau*. Despite the setbacks, his seriousness of purpose and taste for Enlightenment thought were undimmed. Now at last—as in his engagement of Burgh—he was also ready to throw his lot in with the dissenters and radicals, pamphleteers and polemicists. As summer gave way to fall, he must have felt a sense of building excitement, the kind that comes with a new project.

* It had an astonishingly long subtitle: *An Enquiry into Public Errors, Defects, and Abuses. Illustrated by, and Established upon Facts and Remarks, Extracted from a Variety of Authors, Ancient and Modern. Calculated to Draw the Timely Attention of Government and People to a Due Consideration of the Necessity, and the Means, of Reforming Those Errors, Defects, and Abuses; of Restoring the Constitution, and Saving the State.*

Chapter
6

THE INVENTION OF JUNIUS

1766–1768

A Man so injured has no Redress or Consolation, but what he finds in the Resentment and generous Sympathy of Mankind.

—JUNIUS, NOVEMBER 21, 1768

NEWS TOOK ABOUT ONE MONTH EASTBOUND AND TWO WESTbound to travel back and forth across the Atlantic between England and the colonies. The repeal of the Stamp Act in London in March was boisterously celebrated in Boston in May, while the bleaker news about the Declaratory Act took longer to sink in. This temporal lag from event to reaction to subsequent event is deeply unfamiliar to a twenty-first-century reader. Accustomed as we are to a world where every day brings breaking news from the whole world over, where alliances and positions shift weekly, and where decisions can appear to be taken instantly, the slow looping timescales in which events unfolded in the eighteenth century leave us hungry for action when one can only faintly glimpse whorls, eddies, and disturbances deep below the surface as the river of ordinary life—farming, marketing, trading—rolls on.

OR BETTER, PERHAPS, THE dynamic in the first two years following repeal of the Stamp Act was like a murmuration of starlings at dusk—a restless, whirling mass, each element twisting through the air, uncertain of where it was headed, yet somehow tethered to an invisible center of gravity. That center of gravity was a conception of ancient British liberties that had to be protected, with constitutionalism as the shield. But then came disagreements over how to define those liberties and how to organize that constitutionalism. Anonymous newspaper writers on both sides of the Atlantic weighed in, trying to define the terrain. Philanthropos, Sejanus, Anti-Sejanus, An Englishman, An Officer, A Hater of Impositions, Palladio, A Constitutionalist, An Observator. Their pen names hinted at the range of political tribes and conflicting points of view.

THE TWO YEARS FOLLOWING the repeal of the Stamp Act through the fall of 1768 were a time of continuous adjustment of opinion, policy, and alliances for everyone involved in Anglo-American politics—nothing moving fast. The King and his government still needed to solve their debt and revenue problems. They had lost decisively on the Stamp Act but were not willing to walk away from their pursuit of a "becoming economy." The Rockingham ministry was now returned to Opposition. The Rockinghamites, which now included Richmond, searched for paths to check the Crown and support the Americans but also wished to insist on parliamentary supremacy in relation to both Crown and colonies. How all these goals were to be met simultaneously was unclear; who was political friend or foe, equally obscure. As Richmond put it in a letter to a political ally, "We have now I think no prospect but confusion for some years at least!"

In the debate over the Stamp Act, the case for repeal had rested on a distinction between internal and external taxes. Internal taxes were imposed on goods and services produced and used within the colonies. External taxes were duties on traded goods. Another word for them was tariffs. British politicians uniformly regarded tariffs as legitimate across the imperial holdings, even if some thought that internal taxes should be imposed on them only by the colonies' local legislative assemblies. Based on this understanding, the brilliant, provocative, and relentless chancellor of the exchequer, Charles Townshend, who was brought into the ministry by the now gout-ridden, largely absent Pitt in the summer of 1766, proposed a new set of duties in the summer of 1767 on glass, lead, paint, paper, and tea. He also passed legislation to create new customs commissioners to be based in Boston. The impact of the Townshend Acts spiraled outward, subtle at first, but disruptive—stirring the starlings into flights of jostling opinion and counter-opinion on both sides of the Atlantic.

The British had expected the Americans to accept the Townshend duties, since they were external, not internal, taxes, but the position of the colonists was growing firmer. They would come to oppose the duties aggressively with boycotts. It took time for these dynamics to come clear. In the colonies, reaction to the Townshend duties fluttered and turned, hesitant. In Boston, tempers crackled just beneath the surface. In Philadelphia, merchants paused mid-contract. And then, like a sudden ripple through the flock, John Dickinson's *Letters from a Farmer in Pennsylvania* swept through the colonies—cool, clear, and precise. He contended that Parliament had no right to tax the colonies at all—not for internal taxes and not for external duties or tariffs either.

So confounding were the politics of the time that the implications of different policy positions were often obscure. Anticipating where public opinion would land required a prophetic capacity few had. No single voice commanded a movement on either side of the Atlantic, and no one could yet say where things were heading. Something was changing, though. As argument and counterargument unspooled in the papers, a direction emerged. Fragments of protest, resentment, and principle began to fold into formation—not yet revolution, but no longer disarray. The question was which voices would lead. After Dickinson's clarion call, the next voice to bring shape and direction to the rising revolutionary politics would emerge in London. It would be the voice of Junius.

After two years of sorting through confusion, experimenting with points of view, settling on allies, and seeking to shape opinion through newspaper writing, Richmond and a network of radical writers would, through the biting, philosophically rich invective of the Junius letters, at last pull the starlings on both sides of the Atlantic into settled flight. Like *The Federalist Papers*, the Junius letters were a set of newspaper opinion essays that defined the politics of the age. Also like *The Federalist Papers*, they were written by many hands. There was no single person who was "Junius," just as there was no single person who was "Publius," the pseudonym under which Hamilton, Madison, and Jay published *The Federalist Papers*. Unlike *The Federalist Papers*, the Junius letters have never received their due in analyses of the political innovations of the age. The mystery of "who" Junius was has kept scholars from seeing "what" Junius accomplished with the series of letters that exposed and denounced government corruption, incompetence, and domination under the ministries of

George III—while advocating for constitutional liberty, accountability, and the rights of the British people. These letters toppled a ministry and clarified the choices of the age. Like *The Federalist Papers* two decades later, they were the most impactful political writings of their age and set the stage for the debates about basic rights and constitutionalism to come. They asserted the principle that government must be accountable to the people and constrained by law and provided the intellectual framework for revolution. Before Junius took flight, shaping the politics of the age, the starlings needed to whirl, twist, and find each other, and fall into formation. That is what occurred in the years between the fall of 1766 and 1768.

THIS STORY OF JUNIUS as the creation of a group of writers linked to the Duke of Richmond has not previously been told. Two centuries of hoping to solve the mystery of Junius as a single individual led to sixty-one candidates. This was a fundamental mistake, and a strange one to have made. The sixty-two Junius letters are written in more than one voice. If Junius had been one person, he would have been an individual of Shakespearean gifts. Although the style varies across the letters, the political agenda is unitary.

Scholars have occasionally observed that the letters pursue a consistent policy, that they reflected aristocratic experience and perspective as well as insider knowledge of cabinet-level affairs, and that the agenda of the letters aligned with that of the Duke of Richmond. Scholars had also noticed that there was a link between Junius and three other pseudonyms used by political pamphleteers: Atticus, Lucius, and "C." What they hadn't noticed was that Atticus first appeared on the scene to defend the Duke of Richmond and repeatedly defended his obsessive agenda of achieving the demolition of the fortifications at Dunkirk, a policy that no other politician advocated.

Alongside the clear connection between Atticus and the Duke of Richmond, the use of the pseudonym "C" carries new weight. Like the letters labeled "Atticus" and "Junius," the political letters of the 1760s labeled "C" align with the policy positions that Richmond also advocated publicly in his own name. This detail is suggestive. After all, in his teens, Richmond had sparingly used his initial "C" in signing letters. In the two surviving juvenile instances, the letters relate to boundary-breaking or clandestine behavior—indication of a certain self-conception. Also, both the "C" letters and the Junius letters reference and display a social network that also aligned with Richmond's network.

Two other details support the case that Junius's voice flowed from a network of writers closely affiliated with Richmond. First, there are the author identifications for the essays themselves. Scholars have recently been able to identify the authors of pseudonymous political essays published in eighteenth-century newspapers through computer-assisted author identification methodologies. They have identified a coherent network of authors who worked together across the body of letters published under the pseudonyms "C," Atticus, Lucius, and Junius. These are primarily Philip Francis, Thomas Paine, Edmund Burke, and James Burgh, as well as a few others who contributed less frequently, such as the rabble-rousing John Wilkes. All had a close intellectual and political engagement with Richmond. Second, there is *The Juryman's Touchstone*, an essay written in 1771 by Paine, Benjamin Franklin, and Richmond, to advance Junius's cause and defend his publishers, and dedicated by Paine to Richmond for his "Strenuous Efforts & unwearied perseverance in the Defence of Constitutional Liberty." That Richmond and Paine were allies and collaborators in these years is indisputable.

Junius did not spring up fully formed as a political voice in January 1769. He had to be invented first and honed. This was a process that took two years, as Richmond learned how to orchestrate public political efforts in Parliament alongside clandestine political operations in the papers. Such coordination would become one of his main means of influencing politics for the coming decade and a half, at least until he started writing under his own name in 1780. Until then, he depended on the pens of others.

By the fall of 1768, three writers were routinely advancing Richmond's agenda in the press, all using the pen names "Atticus" and "Lucius": Edmund Burke, Philip Francis, and Thomas Paine. Their essays advanced Richmond's major preoccupations—that the talented should be promoted, in place of the current system of corruption; and that the different branches of government should be protected in their prerogatives in relation to each other. How this group formed makes its own tale.

FIRST CAME THE VISION. Aged thirty-one, Richmond entered the fall of 1766 already a disappointed and frustrated man, despite his success in aiding the Stamp Act repeal. The politics of the preceding three years had taught him that frank speech was dangerous. He had acted on his conscience—on the matter of the King's regency—and for that he had paid a penalty. His work and talents had been passed over repeatedly. Yet he had a strong sense of duty, and a powerful feeling that the eddies and whorls that he observed within British politics—of royal dominance, corruption, and weakening parliamentary independence—meant the country was on the wrong track. He had begun to make a name for himself as a speaker in the House of Lords. He had attracted some admirers, including Edmund Burke; befriended some who had felt the sharp end of the suppression of speech, John Wilkes and John Horne Tooke; and taken the time to get to know talented young intellectuals and writers. He had noticed how effectively some older politicians worked with ghostwriters and pamphleteers to drive the public agenda.

Richmond spent two years of the Chatham ministry, from the fall of 1766 through 1768, trying to drive forward a vision of a government united across lines of party division, one that would pursue a healthy constitutionalism where the prerogatives of each order—King, Lords, and Commons—were duly respected and protected; where public policy was motivated by a concept of the public good, not the prospect of personal financial benefit; and where efficiency and energy could be achieved in the administration of government by ensuring that the most talented could rise to the top. He had a universe of people ready to assist him in this work—from members of the Society for the Encouragement of the Arts, Manufactures, and Commerce (where he had been vice president since 1761), to his political network in Sussex, to the talented young men in the military and cultural spheres who also subscribed to his vision. Yet he had only an imperfect means of advancing his goals in national politics—participation in the now relatively weak, oppositional Rockingham party. Coordinating letter writers for the newspapers gave him another outlet. Newspaper readership was growing rapidly and brought new political opportunity. Richmond seized it.

VISION WAS NOTHING, THOUGH, without partners. From his wider network of associates, Richmond settled on a smaller set of "particular friends," with whom he worked closely. First among them was Burke. Richmond and Burke—the one "reckoned warm and hot" by contemporaries; the other, more cautious—had known each other since the late 1750s when each became involved in the Society of Arts alongside Benjamin Franklin. After the dismissal of the Rockingham ministry, they began to coordinate more consistently. From their letters, we can tell that at least by the summer of 1767 they were routinely meeting and swapping notes about the Rockingham party agenda.

They turned to the papers as early as the fall of 1766 to take on Chatham. Burke, Burgh, Francis, Paine, and others wrote; Richmond gave speeches in the House of Lords. One member of the network, publishing as "A.Z.," reminded readers that Britain had won its wealth through "the Arts of Peace, Manufactures, and Commerce" and inveighed against the war debt that had now led to "grievous and unparalleled taxes upon every necessary of life." These taxes were causing tumults among the people, and courting revolution, emigration, and the erosion of Britian's commercial success. In October, Paine, still without regular employment and writing independently under the name "Simplex," joined the conversation to draw attention to how the poor—whether in smoky cities or sodden villages—were scraping by on shrinking wages but faced rising bread prices, after a year of hard, harvest-ruining weather and the subsequent grain crisis. Paine wanted to make clear that he was not motivated by any kind of personal interest. He wrote, "I am in no business, nor can party have aught to do here." He wrote, instead, "as a citizen of the world, and a brother of the whole." He found he could no longer stay silent in face of the facts he could see around him, and had grown impatient and frustrated waiting with "the expectation of some abler pens attempting the common cause."

As Atticus, the group praised the "just and patriotic Reflextion" on the Stamp Act of a "late great Commoner," but in calling Chatham "a late great Commoner," they were also attacking him for having abandoned the House of Commons in favor of a peerage offered by the King. The confrontation with Chatham was provoked by the grain crisis. Several consecutive poor harvests in England and on the European Continent had sent food prices skyrocketing. Merchants were selling to the highest bidder, including when that bidder was in a foreign country. This left England with food shortages, and hunger was on the rise. At Newbury, Exeter, Oxford, Birmingham, Nottingham, and on and on, crowds broke into bakeries, mills, and butcher shops and turned all the wares out into the streets for the taking, a traditional form of politics in the street. When the crisis worsened, Chatham's administration, as an emergency measure, removed duties from foreign imports of grain without seeking an act of Parliament. This plainly unconstitutional maneuver left officials who carried it out open to prosecution. Arguments arose over whether Chatham could and should have achieved that with an act of Parliament, or had legitimately deployed emergency powers. Proponents argued that the government had no choice but to act swiftly to prevent starvation, while opponents contended that proper legal channels could and should have been followed.

In letters and at party meetings throughout 1766, Richmond urged Rockingham to oppose Chatham publicly, in Parliament. When Rockingham hesitated, Richmond took matters into his own hands. In a debate on the grain crisis on December 6, 1766, he unleashed himself vehemently against Chatham. The newly minted earl was sensitive to his status as a recent arrival in the House of Lords and defiantly proclaimed that he would "set his face against the proudest connection in the country." Richmond, ever the ferocious guardian of prerogative and privilege, superciliously exclaimed: "Nobility will not be browbeaten by an insolent minister." Tempers ran so hot that proceedings in the House of Lords had to be suspended until order was restored. The two men were required to pledge on their honor that they would not pursue their conflict any further, nor seek satisfaction for the words exchanged. Only this way was a duel fended off, and Richmond was chastened for a time into a more measured presence in the House of Lords.

AFTER VISION AND PARTNERSHIP, the next element required for the invention of Junius was a motivating context. This came in the form of Richmond's frustration with acting solely through his party. Because Rockingham hated public speaking, he began to rely on Richmond more and more to carry debates, and so throughout the spring of 1767 Richmond for the first time became the principal speaker for the Opposition in the House of Lords. The Opposition had one early victory when Richmond led his colleagues and they defeated the administration's effort to lower land taxes, the one kind of tax they approved, because they considered it a sound basis for stabilizing the economy and addressing the needs of the poor. A string of parliamentary losses followed over how much control the ministry could assert over the East India Company, a British colonial trading concern that was now ten years into its seven-decade process of taking possession of India; over opposition to annuity payments for the King's brothers; over their failure to block the chancellor of the exchequer's new duties on the Americans—the Townshend Acts. The Rockinghamites also sought to advance the Canada Bills that Richmond had worked on while in office. When the government stalled on these, Richmond moved a resolution censuring the administration for having failed to develop a governance plan for Quebec. The motion was defeated in the House of Lords 73–61, despite the several branches of Opposition Whigs having come together. Even with all of Richmond's energetic engagement, the Rockingham Opposition had not by late spring gathered enough political force to dominate Parliament.

Yet despite the frustration of the spring of 1767, Richmond was not yet ready to give up on conventional politics. He, Burke, and Rockingham spent the summer plotting their next attempt to overturn Chatham's ministry and strategizing over how to fight their way back into government. They passed essays and notes back and forth and paid each other visits, with Burke visiting Richmond at Goodwood three times that summer and fall—at Richmond's insistent urging—and Rockingham joining him twice. Richmond's cousin, Admiral Keppel, by now famous for naval victories over the French, also joined Burke for one of the visits. This was the only summer of his political career when Richmond's lush Sussex estate, always golden and glorious in August and with commanding views of the sea, served as an anchoring point for his party while Parliament was out of session.

Pitt's promotion from "Great Commoner," as he had earlier been known, to Earl had undermined his standing with the broad public. His gout disabled him from attending to business; he had largely handed over the reins to Grafton, who was in turn driven primarily by the razor-sharp but mercurial Townshend, who was riling the Americans. The government was weak, but what alliance could cohere to overturn Pitt's leadership of the government and restore Rockingham to the premiership remained elusive. Once again Richmond argued for a unity government that would cut across the various factional lines. He advocated working with the Bedfordite George Grenville and even for incorporating Chatham within any ministry Rockingham might head. Neither Rockingham, nor other party members such as Conway, could accept these proposals, however. Once again Rockingham found it hard to shift from his loyalty to the specific "men" who had joined him in his program of "measures and men," in order to embrace politicians from other factions. Richmond recognized the distance between himself and Rockingham and confessed to Newcastle that he was beginning to think the others "all in extremes" of opinion.

Burke feared that growing differences between Richmond and Rockingham might cause Richmond to break with the party. He saw in him "many signs of uneasiness." He advocated to Rockingham that Richmond be given a party project to keep him on board. He wrote to Rockingham: "He has an anxious, busy mind. Work must be cut out for him, or he will not be satisfied easily." He was sure that if a meaningful mission could be found, Richmond would be "faithful and resolute," and prove "an essential part of the strength" of the party.

This was not to be. Rockingham wasn't ultimately able to satisfy Richmond's appetite. The Duke's anxious, busy mind drove him to send the Marquess long, hectoring letters in favor of his unity plan. Rockingham, out of frustration, stopped inviting Richmond to party meetings that he held to plan for the winter parliamentary session.

By the end of December 1767, all negotiations that might have brought the Rockingham Whigs back into government had failed. It was now clear that they would have to learn how to live in opposition. The men all pointed fingers at each other. Many blamed Richmond for attempting impossible forms of alliance. Richmond blamed Rockingham for a lack of ambition, energy, and flexibility. He was fed up and ready to try a different path.

Meanwhile, in Boston, the Sons of Liberty were also fed up and gaining strength. Nonetheless, conflict was still contained. Protests were constantly threatening to emerge but being quashed by political leaders like Sam Adams and James Otis Jr., who sought to channel the energy into legal, peaceable responses. The Americans reacted to the Townshend Acts—and the many new duties they imposed—with boycotts on the importation of British goods. Women spun flax on town greens, publicizing their commitment to local manufacturers. In the shadow of Faneuil Hall, merchants gathered in uneasy clusters, debating whether to sign the nonimportation agreement, while dockworkers stood idle at the wharves. Across the colonies, newspaper writers urged colonists to wear homespun and drink

Painted here before her marriage to Charles Bunbury, Sarah Lennox was famously charming and attractive.

ART INSTITUTE OF CHICAGO, MR. AND MRS. W. W. KIMBALL COLLECTION. PUBLIC DOMAIN VIA ART INSTITUTE OF CHICAGO.

sassafras tea instead of imported British blends. In taverns, artisans and apprentices spoke of Parliament's arrogance and vowed to resist. A distracted British government—squabbling over positions and roles—was by no means ready to meet the moment, still unaware that across the ocean its measures had stirred a new kind of political energy.

RICHMOND'S OWN CHARACTERISTIC DISTRACTION led him also to miss storm clouds gathering on his own doorstep. His sister Sarah's marriage was in trouble. Sarah had married Sir Charles Bunbury, a member of the House of Commons whose home was in Suffolk. Charles Bunbury notoriously cared more for horses than anything else; he was no match for the lively and literary Sarah. But thanks to the King's misplaced attentions, Sarah had lost two years of her eligible maidenhood. Bunbury—unsuitable in terms of both station and temperament—was all that was left.

As a substitute for any kind of rewarding companionship with her husband, Sarah had recently been spending a great deal of time in Paris salons, amid men and women bedecked in lace cravats, dazzling embroidered silks, and floral brocades. There she had become attached to circles of French radicals, whose sexual mores were as advanced as their politics. Back in London, she whiled away the hours at Richmond House, coming for dinner, cards, and chats with the Duchess, and soon found herself the object of attention of another frequent guest, William Gordon, a handsome, restless redhead from one of the largest landholding families in Scotland.

RICHMOND WAS NOT ALONE in being fed up with party politics. The Rockinghamites' political defeats and their general sense of impotence reduced their participation in Parliament in the late winter and early spring of 1768. Richmond and Rockingham kept clear of Parliament in early 1768 and were surely among those that Benjamin Franklin reported on in a letter that communicated his concern that all the friends of the Americans were leaving the government.

Out of government, with no road to power, stewing in frustration, Richmond began to collaborate more intensely with his secretive network of pamphleteers. In the New Year, he maintained a campaign to bring the different factions together into a unity government, but now through private letters sent directly to Chatham and Grenville, encouraging them to take up the project of uniting the several Whig factions. When he was young, Richmond had signed his most confidential letters "C. March." Now, it appears that he engaged Burgh and Burke to draft private letters advancing his agenda, first anonymously and then over the signature "C."

As the New Year dawned, *The Merchant of Venice* was playing at Covent Garden—with Portia pursuing justice in disguise. Real life, too, had its secrets and dark messages. On January 2, Chatham received a letter signed only "C" and endorsed "private & secret to be opened by Lord Chatham only." It had been drafted by Richmond's pamphleteer Burgh with some help from Burke, and its purpose was to warn Chatham of a factional coup about to be attempted against him by the Duke of Grafton. Flattering Chatham that only his spirit and abilities could save the country, the letter ended by urging him to incorporate the Rockinghamites and Grenvillites in his political network." "C" was trying to push Chatham toward the same unity arrangements that Richmond had tried and failed to sell to Rockingham.

On February 6, "C" wrote to George Grenville. Grenville had been prime minister immediately before Rockingham and had infamously passed the Stamp Act. He headed the Bedfordite faction. "C" flattered Grenville too, claiming to esteem his "spirit and understanding," and again emphasized the importance of secrecy: "It is not, Sir," he wrote, "either necessary or proper to make myself known to you at present." "C" went even farther and exhorted Grenville not to show the letter to anyone, nor even to mention receiving it. Enclosed with the letter was a highly critical essay on the domestic taxation policies proposed by the new chancellor of the exchequer, Lord North. As in the letter to Chatham, "C" was trying to rouse Grenville to resist Grafton and North, the real leaders of the Chatham ministry given the near total absence of the ailing Chatham.

WHAT HAPPENED NEXT IS shrouded in mystery. The network of pamphleteers who had written the occasional Atticus letter advancing Richmond's agenda concocted a plan to prosecute a more comprehensive campaign in the newspapers—and against the leading ministers who were governing under the authority of the largely absent Chatham, in particular the Duke of Grafton and the chancellor of the exchequer, Lord North. The first steps of this plan involved getting precisely the right network of writers in place for a more aggressive and time-consuming effort. Philip Francis had a good position at the War Office and did not need a full-time job. He could moonlight to advance Richmond's agenda, for instance, but he didn't have enough time to mount a concerted pamphlet war. Thomas Paine was, however, available. Richmond had a solution.

On February 29, 1768, Paine finally received his next assignment as an excise rider for Sussex, based in Lewes. Paine would work under the authority of the local lord lieutenant, the Duke of Richmond. As one of two hundred voters in Lewes, Paine would have a role to play, too, in local politics, alongside the Duke. He was also ripe for recruitment into the Headstrong Club, the local Lewes association of literati and radicals who published anonymous pieces in the local paper and held their meetings at the White Hart tavern, where all political meetings in Lewes occurred, including those attended by the Duke. Paine's job as an excise officer in Lewes allowed him to remain near enough to London to be fully embedded in its radical intellectual network, and close enough to Goodwood to work for the Duke of Richmond. It was a perfect opportunity for both men. Ambitious and supremely confident in his own abilities, Paine was about to embark on six years of surreptitious writing and strenuous grassroots organizing that would perfectly prepare him to become the voice of revolution.

IN MARCH 1768, AS inseparable from his horse and saddlebags as from his pen and paper, the excise officer Thomas Paine rode into Lewes in the middle of one of the most dramatic election seasons in British history. Parliament had been sitting since 1761, the date of the elections that had immediately followed George III's accession to the throne. It had now completed a full seven-year term. Richmond was managing only his second election, and he moved to assert control over the MPs in Lewes and Chichester, the town and city anchoring respectively the east and west halves of Sussex, the county of his lord lieutenancy.

Far more exciting than what was unfolding in Sussex was what was happening in north and northwest London. These geographies fell in what was at the time Middlesex, the "principal county" in the country, as Benjamin Franklin called it. The Middlesex elections that year outstripped any others in the country for drama because John Wilkes had returned from his exile in Paris to run for office despite being an outlaw. He had written to the King to ask for pardon, stood for election without having received that pardon, and won. Benjamin Franklin wrote, "It is really an extraordinary event to see an outlaw and an exile of bad personal character, not worth a farthing . . . carrying [i.e., winning the election] for the principal county."

The government, though, refused to accept Wilkes as the election victor. His original sanction had included expulsion from Parliament, and the government judged this meant Wilkes could not be seated despite his win. Despite Wilkes's popular support, the government continued to pursue him. On April 20, after his victory, Wilkes surrendered to the Court of the King's Bench and waived parliamentary immunity. He was fined and thrown in prison at St. George's Fields in Southwark, an expansive meadow on the south bank of the Thames. Ordinarily used for cricket games, grazing, and strolling, St. George's Fields now turned into a protest staging ground. A volatile crowd estimated at fifteen thousand strong gathered outside the prison shouting "Wilkes and Liberty!", "No

Liberty, No King!", and "Damn the King! Damn the Government!" On May 10, the Riot Act was read, and one bystander was shot by accident. The crowds began pelting the troops with stones, and the troops opened fire. Seven or eight people were killed, and further dozens injured, in what is now known as the Massacre of St. George's Fields. London's equivalent to the Boston Massacre came two years earlier than the American event. The crowd of artisans, laborers, and radicals surged over the Westminster Bridge toward the city and moved on St. James's Park. They considered tearing down Buckingham Palace and seemed ready to threaten the King himself.

Sticking to its guns, the government called a fresh election for the Middlesex seat. Unbowed, Wilkes ran again from prison, won again, and was expelled again, with fresh waves of outrage ensuing. The whole cycle would be repeated several times, before the government insisted in 1769 on seating Wilkes's opponent. Wilkes became a cause célèbre that fueled the growth of popular radicalism. The interest in the Middlesex election drove the readership of the flourishing newspapers. By 1770 daily newspaper sales hit an astonishing twenty-five thousand, and, with readership in coffeehouses, 500,000 people may have been consuming political news on a daily basis, in a country with a population of around 7 million. In Lewes, where Richmond carried out most of his election work, *The Sussex Advertiser*, in existence since the 1750s, became an anchor for a network of local radicals and wholeheartedly supported Wilkes.

During that electrifying spring of 1768 election season, Richmond for the first time went public with his own support for Wilkes. In a letter to the Duke of Newcastle, written after the St. George's Fields Massacre, he confessed that he hated "a mob that rises against law and acts by force," but was glad that the people were showing the government "a spirit of liberty" by defending their right to elect whom they wanted to govern them. The endorsement caused a schism for him with his brother-in-law, Henry Fox, and also put him at odds with his father-in-law, Henry Conway. It set him apart, too, from the Duke of Grafton, who had supported Wilkes in 1763 but was now spearheading the government effort to keep him out of office. In May Conway attacked those who were affiliated with Wilkes as fostering "factitious connections." Burke answered him in the House by arguing that "connections among persons of principle were right." Richmond would have agreed completely. The point of politics, as he saw it, was precisely to forge connections of people around the right set of principles, not the other way around. And if Richmond was finding connections among persons of principle to be in short supply in his parliamentary life, they were now abundantly available in Lewes.

PAINE LIVED A DOUBLE political life in Lewes—one public, one private. Paine's Sussex landlord, Samuel Ollive, the local sheriff, had the job of presiding over the election. Paine would have been pulled directly into the electioneering and the mania around Wilkes upon his arrival. He was certainly pulled into the political and literary life of Lewes. William Lee, publisher of *The Sussex Advertiser*, published two of Paine's letters under the pseudonym "Humanus," one on the innovation of fire escapes and one castigating the Poor Laws. In Lewes, Paine participated in politics publicly.

His secret hours—and Richmond's too—were just as full. Shortly after Paine reached Lewes, in the spring of 1768, four affiliated authors all wrote for *The Public Advertiser* under the pseudonym "C": Philip Francis, William Moore (who eventually founded *The Crisis*, a radical magazine), Thomas Paine, and John Horne Tooke (who played a leading role in several radical societies from this point through his death in 1812). Richmond's network of radicals appears to have been testing what it would be like to wage a more concerted campaign in the papers. Five letters by "C" appeared between April and July of 1768, covering a range of political themes all aligned with Richmond's parliamentary agenda—the government's response to Wilkes, criticisms of the government's use of the *nullum tempus* legal doctrine to reclaim property, and the commission of trade.

The spring letters have the look and feel of an audition process. Moore and Horne Tooke delivered performances as "C" with tones of deference to the King. Paine and Francis, in contrast, brilliantly realized the character of a blistering critic. This was clearly what the director sought, because Paine and Francis won the part. They became the chief pamphleteers for the Junius letters—Richmond's lead voices in his writing regiment. Working closely with Paine and Francis, Richmond would advance his agenda through letters to the papers. He would eschew "connection," stated commitments of loyalty to a specific party, and strike out on his own to lay out a distinctive policy vision. With the choice of Paine and Francis over Moore and Horne Tooke, Richmond pivoted in a more radical direction. In Britain, the jostling of the starlings had come to an end; the murmuration had at last fallen into formation and was ready to maintain a single direction.

In America, the murmuration of starlings had also—after two years of restless surging, looping, and crisscrossing—fallen into formation, led there by the voice of Sam Adams. Support for Wilkes ran strong not only in Middlesex and the City of London, in Lewes and other towns all across England, but also in America. It was of a piece with the objections to the Townshend Acts. Sam Adams finally crystallized these in the so-called Circular Letter for which he secured passage from the Massachusetts Assembly in February 1768. He then sought adoption of the statement in other colonies before dispatching it to Britain to convey the message that while the Americans accepted the supremacy of British law, they would not accept taxation without representation. On May 9, British customs officials in Boston seized John Hancock's ship, *Liberty*, for smuggling. The mood in Boston was febrile, and crowds reacted by seizing and burning the sloop of the customs officer. Embers of rebellion had now burst into sparks of violence. In June, Sam Adam's cousin, John Adams, led the Boston Sons of Liberty in drafting a letter of praise and encouragement to the "Illustrious Patriot," John Wilkes.

Then, when the British ministry demanded that the Massachusetts Assembly rescind the Circular Letter, the Bostonians refused. Escalating further, the royally appointed governor formally dissolved the Massachusetts assembly on July 1. Instability was bursting out into political conflagration. This was true in Britain also. In June, there was another government reshuffle and by the autumn, the government tumbled in free fall yet again. On October 12, 1768, Chatham resigned and handed the premiership over to the Duke of Grafton. That same month British troops landed in Boston carrying instructions to restore order. On both sides of the Atlantic, political fires had ignited that would no longer be easily extinguished.

RICHMOND AND HIS ALLIES were quick to go on the attack. September and October brought additional private letters from "C" to Grenville, drafted by Francis. Then they accelerated their public efforts. They abandoned "C," for public usage, and revived their original pseudonym, "Atticus." They also introduced two more ancient Roman avatars, first

"Lucius," and then finally "Junius," the persona they would inhabit for the ensuing three years. "Atticus" probably referred to Titus Pomponius Atticus, a Roman plutocrat renowned for his wealth, literary patronage, and close friendship with the political orator Cicero. Atticus was also known for his philosophical detachment and avoidance of public office, embodying the ideal of a cultured, impartial observer. The other two names probably alluded to Lucius Junius Brutus, the founder of the Roman Republic who led the revolt against the last Roman king. Lucius Junius Brutus was a byword for liberty and republicanism.

Richmond's writing regiment—Paine, Francis, and Burke—delivered five Atticus letters and eight Lucius letters into the combustible political environment of the fall of 1768. All the letters advanced themes that had grown central to Richmond's work. The essays tackle issues of political economy and the problems of trade and debt. They lament the status of Richmond's pet project: The fact that "Dunkirk remains undemolished." They harp on the "weakness and decay" of England, and "the alarming differences which threaten a rupture with our colonies." They anatomize in fine detail the shortcomings of the ministers then in office.

Atticus also warned of threats from France, another perennial theme for Richmond, and the vulnerability to France that was created by the disturbances in America. As he saw it, the hostile temper of the colonies toward Britain, the huge national debt and weak economy, and the country's internal political squabbles gave France a clear opening. Atticus warned: "Our enemies [France] now have, or in a very little time will have the fairest opportunity they can wish for to force us into a war." Then Atticus turned to the economy, dwelling on the high price of labor, the decay of trade, and "the ruinous system on which it is conducted." And just as Richmond celebrated the spirit that British supporters of Wilkes showed in defending him, Atticus acknowledged "the spirit which has gone abroad through the colonies." This was Montesquieu's vocabulary. He saw in the spirit of a people the force that gives human events their shape. Just as Richmond regularly channeled Montesquieu, Atticus also did. In considering the American spirit, Atticus was clear "what consequences that spirit must and will produce." If the conflict between mother country and colonies could not be averted, "from that moment they become an independent people." The consequences for Britain would be ruinous. An independent America would "open their trade with the rest of the world, and England is undone."

Hoping to preempt critics, Atticus offered a justification for laying out so much bad news so bluntly and forcefully. He aspired to be "a good subject," and it was a good subject's job to rouse the attention of his country, to give the alarm, to point out the danger to be addressed. He unabashedly laid out a policy vision that he hoped a great minister might pursue, while also lamenting the unlikelihood that the current weak and distracted ministry would be able to do so. First, he argued, the government needed to provide a fund to prepare for war with France. By preparing for the worst, the country might reasonably hope for the best, he asserted. The second step would be to come to terms with the colonies. Britain should yield some ground in exchange for a promise that the Americans would cease to claim more rights, privileges, or prerogatives than Britons at home. Such policies, he argued, could unite Britain and also "the reasonable part of the Americans" in shared dedication to British liberty, ever the flock's center of gravity.

This was Richmond's vision and the agenda he would pursue for the coming fifteen years. He had long expressed worries about Britain's decay and fears of the loss of colonial trade, and he had grown only increasingly certain of the solution. First, Britain must check France. Next the government should accommodate the context-specific needs of the colonies to stabilize agreements with them. This was precisely the agenda he had pursued while in France as ambassador. What was different now for Richmond was that he no longer believed he could advance this agenda through office or Parliament alone. He needed a pamphlet war.

IN LONDON SPECULATION ON the source of the Atticus letters grew rapidly. They were assumed to come from the Rockingham Whigs. This was partly right. Intellectually, Richmond had formed his views in close collaboration with Burke, and the two men had defined the intellectual agenda of the Rockingham Whig party. In another sense, though, the attribution to the Rockingham party was wrong. Richmond was no longer a man of the party. By the spring of 1768, after several seasons of fractious engagement with his party colleagues, he began to remove himself from parliamentary participation. Out of frustration with Rockingham's lack of assertiveness and creativity, he seems to have withdrawn completely by the summer. The feeling was mutual. His colleagues did not invite him to the meetings to prepare for the 1768–69 parliamentary session. Like Paine, Richmond was turning himself, for a season, into a "man without connections."

In fact, Richmond was so thoroughly fed up with conventional politics that he did not participate in Parliament for the whole of 1769. He wrote to Rockingham, "I trust I shall be forgiven staying away." He explained that he found himself needing to indulge "in [his] present disposition which I will give no name to." He hoped that time would wear it out. Historians have wrongly thought Richmond was here alluding to depression. Yet there is no evidence across Richmond's life for general introversion and no evidence in this period for depression other than his absence from Parliament. He gave plentifully of himself throughout his life to social occasions—from balls to theatricals, and from local politics to an extensive network of male social associates. In the same period as he was absent from Parliament, Richmond attended yet another glittering ball, this one thrown in London for 2,500 guests by the King of Denmark. The Duke dressed as a farmer, and his Duchess "as the beautiful Fatima, wife of the deputy to the Grand Vizier." Richmond's withdrawal from Parliament in 1769 was a matter of choice, not health. He had become consumed with waging political war through the newspapers. He no longer needed Parliament because he had found other political weapons.

THE PERSONA OF JUNIUS was introduced in November 1768, probably in order to throw hunters off the scent. Compared to the Atticus and Lucius letters, the sixty-two Junius essays are much more ambitious in their exposition of constitutional theory, more scathing in their criticisms of leading politicians, and more unrelenting in their attacks. They communicate a far higher degree of strategy and intentionality.

Most importantly, they defined what people have a right to expect of their King, namely that the King himself recognize that his own authority rested upon the consent of the governed. In the broader arc of constitutional history, Junius stands as a precursor to later democratic reformers—linking eighteenth-century English radicalism to transatlantic movements for representative government and civil rights. The Junius letters also toppled a government. The agenda that Richmond could not advance through the Rockinghamites—the ouster of the current ministry, now with Grafton at its head—Richmond instead prosecuted and delivered through Junius.

ON NOVEMBER 21, 1768, with Paine as the lead drafter, the network introduced Junius to the world with a letter that returned to the subject of Wilkes. Justice, law, and the liberty of the constitution had all been violated by the government's treatment of Wilkes. Junius promised to come to Wilkes's defense, proclaiming: "A Man so injured has no Redress or Consolation, but what he finds in the Resentment and generous Sympathy of Mankind." The purpose of the letters would be to further rouse that resentment and sympathy, a potent brew to marshal against a monarchy obviously losing control.

The British political world had been turned upside down over a five-year period. In 1763, Richmond had studiously avoided the Opposition, trying to climb back into the King's good graces. His erstwhile friend and now competitor, the Duke of Grafton, had, in contrast, rallied the "zealous young men" to Wilkes's cause and into formal opposition at that time. Now, having inherited a tottering ministry from Chatham, the Duke of Grafton sought to keep Wilkes imprisoned. Famous for his very public relationship with the courtesan Nan Parsons, Grafton abandoned his own professions of principle as easily as he had betrayed his wife.

Richmond, in contrast, had found his voice to defend parliamentary privilege during the first round of the Wilkes affair, felt it grow stronger when he tackled the King's overreach in the regency case, and then came fully into his own as ambassador to France when he began to develop his own policy vision—even against the express commands of his superior. As confident in his own abilities and vision as Paine was in his, Richmond refused any longer to defer—to Rockingham, to Grafton, to the King. Through the Junius letters, he was declaring his own independence. Simply choosing independence, in a world of patronage and place, was radical. It was surely not Wilkes's injuries only that motivated the letters.

When the first Junius essay pledges to defend a man needing to find redress through the generous sympathy of mankind, Junius might also have been speaking about Richmond. The Duke had been injured repeatedly over several years with regard to "ties of honor, professions of friendship, and obligations of party," exactly the same injuries attributed to Wilkes. Neither Paine nor Francis could directly claim such a complete set of injuries. Only Richmond could. Redress for Wilkes through these essays would also be redress for him.

THE ONE THOUSAND BRITISH troops who landed in Boston in October brought home to the Americans the realities of the power of the British monarchy. The city entered into a period of growing confrontation and radicalization. *The Boston Gazette*, a newspaper aligned with the resistance movement, castigated the troops. The Boston Town Meeting passed palpably angry resolutions decrying imperial overreach.

November and December 1768 equally brought home to Richmond just how much the King's exercise of power offended him—on political, cultural, and personal fronts. Richmond chose not to attend the opening of Parliament on November 8 and so he missed the King's hardline speech setting out his policy on America, where the King disavowed any basis for conciliation. The King opened with a condemnation of the behavior of his "misled" subjects in the colonies. He had thought that they "were returning to a just Sense of their Duty." Now he had recognized that "the Spirit of Faction" had broken out again. He condemned Boston's passage of "measures subversive of the Constitution" that manifested a clear disposition for independence. Where Richmond proposed a path of negotiated settlement, the King had hardened his resolve for pure conflict. All the writing Richmond and his colleagues had done thus far had softened the King not one bit. By the middle of December two more British regiments, another five hundred troops, would be dispatched to Boston, not a gesture of deterrence but a performative assertion of imperial will. The machinery of war, once theoretical, was now plainly in motion for all to see.

The King then matched his display of hard power with an equally aggressive use of soft power. On Monday November 28, 1768, four artists had an audience with the King to seek his patronage for a new "professional society for the arts of design." They sought to create an academy that would focus on "the moral and didactic purpose" of art, not on artisanship and technological innovation to strengthen the economy. They saw the nation's interests served by an academy for fine arts, without the attachment to the practical arts. On December 10, George approved the Instrument of Foundation of the Royal Academy. The Instrument sought to centralize and concentrate cultural power. The new academy would have no more than forty members, and the King would personally approve the appointments. Contrary to the Society of Arts, so dear to Richmond, this new Royal Academy would have no democratic mechanisms of decision-making. The founding artists of the new academy were led by Joshua Reynolds and included Sir William Chambers, Joseph Wilton, and Giovanni Battista Cipriani, the very men who had helped Richmond set up his sculpture gallery and memorialize Wolfe a decade before. The meaning of George's cultural move was clear for all to see. As one newspaper writer put it, "You disdain sir, to mingle your royal favour with the vulgar, the honest, ardent wishes of the people . . . and therefore instituted the Royal Academy, so that the plumes of prerogative might wave in triumph over the cap of liberty."

Royal triumph, and the humiliation of Richmond, reached even into the personal realm. During the spring of 1768, the feckless William Gordon had made his way to the country home of Richmond's sister Sarah Bunbury. Her husband was away, and Gordon stayed for several months. When he left, Sarah was pregnant. At the end of May, when Sarah wrote to her sister Louisa to let her know that news, she allowed her sister to think that the baby, who would be named Louisa after her sister, was her husband's. Then in December, Sarah gave birth in London, and shortly after, crushed by the weight of deception and remorse, she confessed to Charles Bunbury that baby Louisa's father was in fact William Gordon. The revelation plunged the family into crisis, and matters only worsened in the spring, when Sarah eloped with Gordon in a desperate bid to steer by her own lights—only for him to discard her shortly after, leaving her disgraced and utterly alone. The ill-considered marriage to Bunbury, always a misalliance for Sarah, had been the byproduct of the King's protracted flirtation with her, and her ruin now stood as a painful emblem of his long pattern of humiliating the family.

Blow after blow had landed upon Wilkes. Blow after blow had landed upon Richmond. These royal insults seem to have shredded any further hesitations he may have had about charging his regiment of writers to take on the King's ministers, and ultimately the King himself. In the coming year, Junius would ignite a political firestorm in Britain, and America would learn his name.

Chapter 7

JUNIUS ROCKS THE MONARCHY AND AMERICA TAKES NOTICE

1769

The name of Stuart, of itself, is only contemptible;—armed with Sovereign authority, their principles are formidable. The Prince, who imitates their conduct, should be warned by their example; and while he plumes himself upon the security of his title to the crown, should remember, that as it was acquired by one revolution, it may be lost by another.

—JUNIUS, LETTER TO THE KING, DECEMBER 1769

AS THE NEW YEAR DAWNED IN 1769—WITH THE SHORT, dark days of English winter—so too did the strangest and most dramatic period in the 3rd Duke of Richmond's life and career. His political arguments were carried to the British public by his newspaper regiment, writing in the persona of Junius. The end of the first year of letters built to the peak of an extraordinarily direct attack on the King. Everyone involved was in danger of being tried for seditious libel. This year brought the early phase of the reign of George III to its shakiest point—and to the stunningly speedy collapse of another administration in January 1770 within days of the opening of Parliament. Radical forces had arrayed themselves and were hammering at—and eroding—the fortified authority of the Crown. Junius was their most powerful voice.

Philip Francis handled the business correspondence with the printer of *The Public Advertiser*, Henry Woodfall, his former schoolmate; he signed the private letters addressed to the publisher, "C." His handwriting gave no clue as to his or his group's identity, disguised as it was by the dropping of all capitalization, so it could not easily be used to make an identification. The printed public letters were signed "Junius" or "Philo-Junius" and, with their consistently vituperative, patriotic, and vehement voice, they captivated political and literary London. Of sixty-two letters plus a preface and dedication, computer analysis reveals that Paine had a hand in thirty-four, Burgh seventeen, Burke fifteen, Francis eleven, and Wilkes ten.

Francis did more than write. He also researched material for the letters. Slender and with finely drawn features, he was born in Dublin, like his friend Edmund Burke. His scholarly father, Philip Francis Sr., more or less lived at Holland House, the home of Richmond's oldest sister, Caroline, and her husband, Henry Fox. Francis Sr. also ran a school where he taught Edward Gibbon, the author of *The History of the Decline and Fall of the Roman Empire*. Francis Jr. himself was educated at St. Paul's, where his classmates included Woodfall. Because of his job in the War Office, he often attended meetings of the House of Lords. He had an extraordinary memory and was able to create transcripts of the speeches he heard there. He was one of the people who helped bring transparency to parliamentary debates by passing verbatim accounts to newspapers, a practice the Junius letters advocated. He also had a habit of tracking political debates and sending memos to key political figures. These men would incorporate his writing into their own speeches and essays. Francis, in his memoirs, tells a story of hearing Chatham regurgitate one of his memos "verbatim" as if it were his own. His memoirs make clear that he held himself in very high regard, albeit with good reason.

The historian and double agent Thomas Mante, who spied for both the British and the French, is also likely to have been involved in the Junius circle. The French Secret Service recorded an eyewitness account of seeing him at work on the famous letter to the King. He was based in the French Channel port of Dieppe, where his cover was sheep-breeding. One reporter of his movements wrote: "You know His under-taking to introduce English Sheep on a tract of land given to him near Dieppe, & this gives pretexts for going along the Coast where His Sheep plan is known even to the Smuglers. The Keeper of the Ship at Brighthelmstone [i.e., Brighton] manages his correspondence." Mante considered Richmond enough of an ally that when he found himself in prison in France in 1776, he wrote to Richmond seeking assistance (he also wrote to Benjamin Franklin for help, in 1779). He clearly expected that Richmond would provide for him. In the postscript to his letter, he also suggested to the Duke that he might try to communicate with him via invisible ink: "If you receive a letter without a signature, hold it to the fire." The two men were collaborators well-versed in the arts of secret communication.

Richmond must have provided the requested assistance. A year later, Mante and his wife hosted two of Richmond's nephews, Edward Fitzgerald and Charles Lennox, for dinner in Dieppe, where, as Edward reported to his mother, Mante's wife made a "most excellent dish" called *compôte de cure.* "First, you must take and slice some pears, apples and oranges very thin. Then put some sugar and a tablespoonful of brandy. Then squeeze an orange into it, and then eat it." The extended Richmond clan was attached to the radical networks Richmond had grown connected to in France.

Another writer, Thomas Northcote, author of *Observations on the Natural and Civil Rights of Mankind, the Prerogatives of Princes, and the Powers of Government*, may also have been involved in the Junius circle. He was certainly an active pamphleteer in subsequent years for the Society for Constitutional Information. He too was paid by the Duke for newspaper writings. When Northcote fell on hard times, he, like Mante, felt that Richmond owed him assistance. In 1786, he wrote to all and sundry seeking support, including John Adams, then the United States ambassador in Britain, to whom he complained that the Duke had deserted him.

Finally, James Adair was also involved, though probably not as a writer of the letters. Adair had been Richmond's first hire as a writer, and he was a long-standing supporter of the cause of John Wilkes. He served as a lawyer for the publishers of the Junius letters and for the Middlesex Freeholders trying to protect the election of Wilkes. Many years later, after Richmond and Burke had parted ways, Burke would describe Adair as "that low, intriguing and perfidious tool." Adair would remain for many years one of Richmond's fixers.

All these men constituted the corps of intellectual, political, and legal talents that Richmond engaged to advance his political agenda through the power of the pen. Richmond and his men used special paper for the correspondence of the Junius letters: folio-size sheets with the Pro Patria watermark. This paper, sometimes called foolscap, was a favorite for republicans, including Benjamin Franklin. The watermark represented the Maid of Dort, an allegorical female figure seated within a garden or walled enclosure, holding a lance topped with a liberty cap and a shield bearing the arms of Dordrecht, a symbol of the Dutch Republic's defense of freedom. Woodfall also used Pro Patria paper when he printed the collected edition of the Junius letters. In one letter after another, Richmond's regiment destroyed the prime minister, the chancellor of the exchequer, and even the King. Cumulatively their letters set the political universe ablaze.

The Junius letters were not the only writings Richmond encouraged or commissioned in this period. In 1769, Burke published his first major political essay, "Observations on a Late State of the Nation." This was followed in 1770 by his anonymous publication of "Thoughts on the Cause of the Present Discontents." Richmond had pressed Burke to write the latter, as Burke explained in a letter. The Duke praised the pamphlet in the House of Lords as containing his "Creed." Similarly, when Richmond was working with James Adair on matters related to the East India Company in 1773, he also encouraged him to write for the papers to advance their agenda. Richmond's routine sponsorship of a network of talented writers to advance his arguments was employed to its greatest effect in the Junius letters.

The Junius letters were bestsellers. When they first began to appear, the daily circulation of *The Public Advertiser* was three thousand. The Junius letters drove it to a consistent number of nearly four thousand, and even to five thousand for the December 1769 issue, in which Junius took on the King directly. Nothing since Wilkes's diatribes in *The North Briton* had so engaged the public and provoked the Crown and government. The quest to discover Junius's identity became a metropolitan parlor game. Even the great Shakespearean actor David Garrick tried to sniff out the man behind the mask by pressing Woodfall for information, but the Richmond network went undiscovered.

THE NOVEMBER 1768 ESSAY had just been a trial balloon. Ultimately, the group did not include that piece when they published a collected version of the essays in a single volume. The official Junius series launched on January 21, 1769, in *The Public Advertiser*. Junius took up the themes of the laws and liberties of the English people and the preservation of their constitution. The letters channeled all the great political philosophy that Richmond, and the others too, had been reading: Montesquieu and Locke, l'abbé Baudeau and Emmerich de Vattel, Cesare Beccaria on punishment, and Plato's *Laws*, all books in Richmond's library. In the first essay, in a lofty flight of philosophical principle, Junius conjured up a right of revolution. When free people submit to executive authority, they do so only because they are complying with laws which they have themselves enacted, the letter argued. When that free people's rights "have been invaded," questions must be asked about when it would be "treachery to themselves not to . . . resist."

At the start of the Junius project, Richmond's regiment of writers adhered to the convention that the King was never at fault, only his ministers. Junius's argument was simple: The shadows gathering over the bright sun of British freedom came from the corrupt and incompetent policies of the prime minister, the Duke of Grafton. "The finances of a nation, sinking under its debt and expences, are committed to a young nobleman already ruined by play." Grafton had become "minister by accident" and had demonstrated no accomplishment "unless a wayward, wavering inconsistency be a mark of genius." The "spirit" of British liberty was likely to rise up.

While the Duke of Grafton took more fire from Junius than any other public figure, the writers did not confine their aim to him alone. Lord North, the chancellor of the exchequer, was another prominent target. He had yet to provide "the first proof of his abilities." Junius heaped up the insults: "It may be candid to suppose he has hitherto voluntarily concealed his talents; intending perhaps to astonish the world, when we least expect it." Junius's sarcasm would come to be as much feared as admired.

Junius also had a knack for striking when his opponent was weakened. A second letter on the Duke of Grafton was published while the beleaguered prime minister's divorce proceedings were being heard in the House of Lords—an embarrassing legal process that required documenting his wife's infidelities. A footman, a butler, a waiting woman, a nurse, and two doctors from Grafton's household testified. They all told the same story, here in the footman's version: "that Lord *Ossory* frequently visited her Grace, and that upon her Grace's going to *Brighthelmstone*

Lord *Ossory* came there soon after, and lodged in a House facing her Grace's Lodgings, and visited her the same Day he came; that he continued to visit her constantly during her Stay there, sometimes in the Morning and sometimes in the Evening; that when his Lordship came in the Evening, he generally staid till 11, 12, and One o'Clock; that Orders were given by her Grace that Candles should not be brought up till she called for them; that Once, upon going up, he found the Door fastened when her Grace and Lord *Ossory* were alone together." It was scandalous, great fun for the chattering classes, and a prize opportunity for Junius, whose letter amplified Grafton's humiliation and political problems.

THE REPEATED EFFORTS OF the Grafton administration to avoid seating John Wilkes in Parliament were also irresistible to the pamphleteers. A third special election to fill the still empty parliamentary seat was held, and this time two other men ran against Wilkes. It made no difference: Wilkes finished first with 1,143 votes; a military man, Colonel Luttrell, came in second with 296 votes; the third-place finisher could muster only a meager 5. Yet on April 15, Parliament declared Luttrell the winner.

Now pro-Wilkes outrage boiled over. The press covered the issue relentlessly, having at long last broken through the Crown's prohibition on reporting parliamentary debates. As anger mounted, the Junius regiment was in full voice. They argued, "The right of election is the very essence of the constitution. To violate that right, and much more to transfer it to any other set of men, is a step leading immediately to the dissolution of all government. So far forth as it operates, it constitutes a house of commons, which *does not* represent the people."

On April 29, the Middlesex voters who had repeatedly preferred Wilkes submitted a petition to Parliament, asking that they be permitted to argue the case for the validity of their votes. Richmond's close associate, James Adair, was one of the two lawyers representing them. The effort to defend and support Wilkes now spurred the formation of new political associations. Alongside John Horne Tooke, Adair helped found the Society of Gentlemen Supporters of the Bill of Rights, which formalized itself to raise money to support Wilkes, his debts, and his legal bills. Political radicals were beginning to coalesce to resist the decisions of the Crown and government.

Hardening the conflict, Parliament voted once again to nullify the Wilkes votes and to seat Luttrell. Wilkes and his defenders petitioned the King directly, seeking redress from a Parliament that they felt no longer represented them. Redress was not forthcoming. The Americans, too, would soon be frequently petitioning the King for redress from grievances that they believed Parliament had inflicted on them. For the Wilkes voters, at stake was the fundamental question of whether the people's votes meant anything at all and whether the ordinary farmers, traders, and artisans who came to the polls controlled the House of Commons. It looked as if the corrupt dependence of members of the House of Commons on the monarchy for financial perks and privileges was reducing that body to a mere appendage of the Crown. Ordinary citizens now found themselves caught between a Parliament that no longer represented them and a Crown deaf to their petitions—a constitutional limbo where rights had no refuge. Junius drove home the point: The people's rights were disappearing.

NOR WERE THE PRO-WILKES forces the only people sending petitions to the Crown in 1769. In January, four days before the first Junius letter came out, something else extraordinary happened in British politics. For the first time in the history of the country, public sector workers coordinated nationwide to circulate petitions to the government for better pay. Thomas Paine's public service colleagues, excise officers in Wales and Scotland, submitted petitions to the Lords of the Treasury, the key cabinet officials overseeing the excise. The petitions listed their grievances and sought redress. Out of 3,000 excise officers, 79 signed the first petition, 179 on the second, and 29 the petition from Scotland—but this was just the beginning. Eventually, there would be nearly three thousand signatures, and every excise officer would also contribute three shillings to support the effort. Paine would be very involved in arguing the cause. The petitioners warned that their deepening poverty would leave the excise service vulnerable to corruption. Just as Richmond, a few years earlier, had increased his servants' wages and prohibited tipping to avoid corruption, now the excise officers were making exactly the same argument. Honest service required decent salaries.

Nor was resistance stirring only in England. The Wilkes protests were growing ever more interconnected to the American cause. The London petitioners complained about such innovations as standing armies and violations of press and political liberties, and they explicitly made the connection to America: "The same discretion has been extended by the same evil counsellors to your Majesty's dominions in America, and has produced to our suffering fellow subjects in that part of the world, grievances and apprehensions similar to those of which we complain at home." *The Boston Gazette* printed excerpts of the postelection petition to the King: "With great grief and sorrow, we have long beheld the endeavours of certain evil-minded persons, who attempt to infuse into your royal mind, notions and opinions of the most dangerous and pernicious tendency." On both sides of the Atlantic, the pro-Wilkes faction joined the excise officers in filling the political consciousness of the age with the clamor of their grievances. Ultimately, somewhere between one quarter and a third of all voters in Britain signed petitions to the King in the summer of 1769. The people were rising up.

In Lewes and Sussex, *The Sussex Advertiser* covered the Wilkes story over and above any other. In 1769, the fifty-one issues of the weekly paper carried 799 Wilkes stories or comments; the next most popular topic was the King and the Ministry, covered in 197 pieces that year. In America, a newspaper reported that "private letters from almost every county in England" remark that "there is no other language to be heard, from highest to lowest, but petition, petition, petition!"

Although Richmond was not participating in Parliament, he was very attuned to this petitioning movement, which he discussed in letters with Burke. One key question that emerged was whether voters should use the method of "instructions to their representatives" or "petitions to the Crown" to address their wrongs. Richmond, Burke, and Rockingham ultimately agreed that petitioning—the traditional politics of the disenfranchised—was the best strategy. They came to agree that having voters seek to tie the hands of representatives via instructions for how they should vote would be problematic. Representatives, as opposed to deputies, needed the freedom to make judgment calls. They also concurred that, while Richmond, Rockingham, and the other aristocrats should support the petitioners in their constituencies, as requested by their neighbors, they should not lead. It mattered that it was the voices of the people rising up, and Richmond, Burke, and Rockingham had no wish to co-opt or deflect the outpouring of popular spirit against the

Crown and Ministry. As they thought through the combustible politics of the moment, the three men were beginning to forge a theory of representation: Members of Parliament had a responsibility to communicate the will of the people; they needed to understand the will of the people in order to act on their behalf; but representatives also needed to be able to act as trustees, able to make judgments motivated by fiduciary duty, and not simply follow a predetermined set of instructions. The definition of political representation they developed shapes democratic chambers to this day.

THE JUNIUS CIRCLE DID not limit their criticism to the malfunctioning Parliament. Parliament was prorogued between the summer recess and January. Among his other failings, the Duke of Grafton was an indolent prime minister. In early October, Richmond traveled back again to France and, as well as visiting his lands at Aubigny, he was in the country exactly when, according to the French Secret Service, Thomas Mante was working on what would turn out to be the most important Junius letter of all, a letter directly addressed to the King.

Just when Richmond returned to London, "C" (Francis on behalf of the writing regiment) reported on the return of Junius to London in a private letter to Woodfall, of November 8, "Sir. I have been out of town these three weeks, &, tho' I got your last, could not conveniently answer it." In a letter from late November or early December, "C" (Francis again on behalf of the collective) wrote to Woodfall, "I am now meditating a capital & I hope a final Piece;—You shall hear of it shortly." Richmond also saw Burke during this time, who was also working on the essay addressed to the King, according to new computational analysis of the text recently completed by scholars. Burke reported to Rockingham that Richmond was speaking "without the least disguise"—politicking very actively, across a broad front and to his trusted co-agitators.

All the pamphleteering was creating a backlash. The letters between "C" and Woodfall in November and December 1769 convey the increasing pressure being placed on their printer, Woodfall, to disclose the identity of Junius. Woodfall expressed concerns that he might be prosecuted, and "C" sought to reassure him. Throughout the letters to Woodfall, "C" consistently promised Woodfall protection and financial backing, promises that could be made only because of Richmond's support. Adair's service for Woodfall as legal counsel was a concrete realization of that pledge. With such supports and despite his increasing anxiety, Adair Woodfall published Junius's Letter to the King of December 19, 1769, the most frontal assault on the dignity of the King in generations.

Still only thirty-one years old, George III had not yet stabilized his reign. After nine years on the throne, he had gone through six prime ministers. His efforts to suppress dissent with increasingly punitive treatment of critics weren't working; if anything, the criticism just intensified. The greatest direct challenge came from Junius, in the form of this December letter.

Although the King essentially never spoke to ordinary people, and spoke to the aristocrats around him only in a highly formal and stylized fashion, the regiment introduced the infamous letter by conjuring up an ideal situation of equality, where any honest man might approach the King for a conversation, human to human.

> It may be a matter of curious SPECULATION to consider, if an honest man were permitted to approach a King, in what terms he would address himself to his Sovereign. Let it be imagined, no matter how improbable, that the first prejudice against character is removed, that the ceremonious difficulties of an audience are surmounted, that he feels himself animated by the purest and most honourable affections to his King and country, and that the great person, whom he addresses, has spirit enough to bid him speak freely, and understanding enough to listen to him with attention. Unacquainted with the vain impertinence of forms, he would deliver his sentiments with dignity and firmness, but not without respect.

Then, with none of the customary invocations of the King's majesty, the letter began, "Sir, It is the misfortune of your life, and originally the cause of every reproach and distress, which has attended your government, that you should never have been acquainted with the language of truth." The simple fact of this address would have been breathtakingly shocking to contemporary readers.

Junius next proceeded to describe the urgency of the moment, one in which the vast body of the people was rising up in a spirit of resistance:

> When the complaints of a brave and powerful people are observed to increase in proportion to the wrongs they have suffered; when instead of sinking into submission, they are roused to resistance, the time will soon arrive at which every inferior consideration must yield to the security of the Sovereign, and to the general safety of the state.

Such a moment had arrived, Junius argued, and it required that George understand "the great duty he owes to his people," and seek advice for "how to gratify the wishes, and secure the happiness of his subjects." Junius was ready to provide that advice to his King because he had not yet given up on him and could still attribute his errors to "pernicious lessons" from Bute. They were far from thinking the King "capable of a direct, deliberate purpose to invade the original rights of British subjects."

The advice came in the form of a review of the entire policy of George III's reign to date—from his original identification of himself as a "Briton" rather than as an "Englishman"; his decision to alter the whole system of government when he ascended the throne; his misplaced confidence in Bute; the enormous attack on the constitution in the decision not to let Wilkes take his seat in Parliament; the "plunder and oppression" of the people of Ireland; and this provocation of the Americans who "divided as they are into a thousand forms of policy and religion, . . . all agree—they equally detest the pageantry of a King." The letter then bemoaned the degradation of the army: "those gallant troops by whom every hazardous, laborious service is performed, are left to perish in garrisons abroad, or pine in quarters at home, neglected and forgotten." Finally, Junius turned again to the undoing of the constitution by the decision of Parliament to overrule the selection made by the voters, and he added a threat. "The same pretended power, which robs an English subject of his birthright, may rob an English King of his crown."

Junius went on to tell the King how to right the ship of state: "You have still an honourable part to act. The affections of your subjects may still be recovered. But before you subdue *their* hearts, you must gain a noble victory over your own. Discard those little, personal resentments, which have too long directed your public conduct. Pardon this man [Wilkes] the remainder of his punishment, and if resentment still prevails, make it, what it should have been long since, an act, not of mercy, but contempt."

The brilliance of the advice to pardon Wilkes was that it solved a constitutional puzzle. The House of Commons had robbed the people of their vote by determining that Wilkes, a convicted criminal, could not serve on account of his conviction. If either the King or the House of Lords were to undo that decision, they would be violating the parliamentary powers of the Commons. The Wilkes event had stopped up the system of checks and balances and seemingly left no check that could operate without undoing the entire constitutional system. There was one solution, though: If the King were to pardon Wilkes, which was his prerogative, the House of Commons could seat Wilkes (since he would no longer be a convicted felon), the people would have their voting right restored, and no branch of the government would have had its own prerogatives violated.

The Junius letter brilliantly deployed Montesquieu's theory of constitutionalism to find a pathway out of the crisis created by the refusal to seat Wilkes. The letter explicitly articulated the point about separation of powers, invoking the King's duty "to prevent one of the three estates from encroaching upon the other two, or assuming the authority of them all." Maintaining the balance among House of Commons, House of Lords, and Crown was "the great constitutional line, by which all their proceedings should be directed."

Junius concluded by giving a chilling warning to the King—not to behave as the Stuart monarchs had behaved. Unspoken, but clearly implied, is the memory that one Stuart king had been toppled and beheaded, the next overthrown and forced abroad, and a pretender to the line brutally vanquished at Culloden:

> The people of England are loyal to the house of Hanover, not from a vain preference of one family to another, but from a conviction that the establishment of that family was necessary to the support of their civil and religious liberties .... The name of Stuart, of itself, is only contemptible;— ... The Prince, who imitates their conduct, should be warned by their example; and while he plumes himself upon the security of his title to the crown, should remember, that as it was acquired by one revolution, it may be lost by another.

No one had yet so directly threatened George III with revolution. The most radical Whig tracts from the late seventeenth century, like those associated with Algernon Sidney or John Locke's *Two Treatises of Government*, from the period of the Glorious Revolution which removed James II, had articulated a right to resist and remove a monarch. Those were theoretical texts. This was an immediate, practical threat to a Hanoverian monarch. The Junius regiment published this essay into the ponderous silence of a fall without a parliamentary session. It was the inaugural howl of the Age of Revolution. Immediately, there was "a hue and cry" after Junius, and Woodfall was charged with seditious libel—that is, defamatory speech against government, punishable with substantial fines, imprisonment, the public pillory, and banishment.

WITH SNOW FALLING AND black frost clinging to the city, the King opened the 1769–70 session of Parliament on January 9. What followed immediately was political collapse—swift, bitter, and almost theatrical in its disorder, largely owing to the Junius letters. Ministers turned on one another. Key figures resigned or were cast out in rapid succession. The government, barely held together by factions and royal will, seemed to be unraveling by the hour. The lord chancellor publicly attacked his cabinet colleagues over the Wilkes affair, opposing their continued resistance to seating Wilkes. The King dismissed him. Four other cabinet members were also immediately dismissed. Then commander in chief, Lord Granby, resigned on January 17. The new lord chancellor, Charles Yorke, died three days after accepting the role, and was generally thought to have killed himself. On January 20, the solicitor general and vice-treasurer of Ireland resigned. On January 27, 1770, the implosion was complete when the Duke of Grafton resigned as prime minister. "Nothing," wrote Horace Walpole, "could be more distressful than the situation into which the Duke of Grafton had brought the King and in which he abandoned him."

The government asked the great literary figure Samuel Johnson, who was on their payroll as a propagandist, to fight back against Junius. He obliged by caustically decrying Junius's "blaze of impudence," which "drew the rabble after him as a monster makes a show." His "impenetrable secrecy" was best understood as a symptom of utter shamelessness; he substituted vice for virtue as the object of his praise. His political effect was dangerous: "Finding sedition ascendant, he has been able to advance it; finding the nation combustible, he has been able to inflame." Johnson accurately captured how hot feelings were running, and the role of the Junius letters in creating that atmosphere. His accusations of a shameless overtopping of morals read, though, as the angry slanders of a defender of convention.

Thanks to Junius and the Wilkes movement, January 1770 brought a wholly new set of political arrangements to Britain. The Junius regiment had blown up the government and served notice to the King. Frederick, Lord North, a famously corpulent, sociable man and son of the Earl of Guilford, was now appointed prime minister and first lord of the treasury. Lord North agreed to accept the role very reluctantly. Yet he was able to pull George's reign back from the abyss opened by Junius. Surprisingly effective at stabilizing the government, North would serve as George's seventh prime minister from this point through the Battle of Yorktown in 1781, when Britain finally lost its American colonies. The fight between the Crown and radicals would grow fiercer during these years to come, but without the same dangerous destabilization of the throne. The threat of revolution would shift across the Atlantic, and the American War would bring internal unity in Britain and tamp down domestic pressures.

All of that was still ahead, however. For now, a complete transformation of the government had been achieved. In early 1770, it was unclear whether George would save his reign. The opening for change inspired new political energies. Richmond began to participate in Parliament again. It is as if the leadership of the Duke of Grafton had been positively repelling him from attendance in the House of Lords and forcing him to drive an agenda from the outside. Officially, Richmond was second fiddle to Rockingham in Rockingham's leadership of the Opposition party. In reality, Richmond, through the instrument of Junius, had set the agenda for the political debate in both houses of Parliament. For the following decade he would be the primary speaker for the Opposition in the House of Lords.

THE JUNIUS CAMPAIGN REQUIRED more than simply finding talented writers and articulating a coherent critique of the government. Richmond also needed "impenetrable secrecy" to protect his writing regiment and their shared work. He had learned in the brief period that he was an ambassador in France a set of practices to preserve confidentiality. One of the first things he did upon disembarking in Calais for his embassy was to probe the details of precisely how to get mail back and forth to England confidentially and quickly; during his embassy, he became accustomed to the use of a cipher.

At home he built up his own systems of correspondence. Between Richmond House in London and Goodwood in Sussex, Richmond employed about three dozen servants, who were steadfastly loyal. These included coachmen who essentially ran a private mail service for him, faster and more secure than the post. Across decades of his account books, the names of household servants and coach attendants solidly recurred. William Adair, a distant relative of the writer James Adair, handled his finances; the Buckner family for several generations served as stewards and in other roles; Captain Jones stayed with him well into Jones's old age. The letters that were sent to Woodfall were often sealed with signet rings, crowned by ancient Roman carnelian or agate stones with the head of a distinguished figure carved into them. Typically, aristocrats collected them on the Grand Tour. A few years after the Junius letter series was complete, such rings would proliferate through mass production of plaster imitations but as of the writing of the Junius letters, that methodology had not yet been invented. Such rings were still the mark of aristocrats, and whoever sealed the "C" letters had the use of many of them. Richmond's remaining account books include at least one payment to Captain Jones for the purchase of such a seal.

Richmond could also count on his colleagues. All of them, in one way or another, practiced misdirection. Despite being the result of a collaborative effort, the letters had such a consistency of opinion that all the drawing-room detectives assumed they were the work of a single author. As political London sought to solve the mystery of who could write at once so bitterly and so philosophically, fingers pointed first toward Edmund Burke, who aggressively and routinely denied authorship as a point of honor—"I now give you my word and honour that I am not the author of Junius." He also used an extended speech in Parliament in 1770, when he was criticizing the government for abusing the freedom of the press, to praise Junius. In so doing, he reinforced the notion that there was some single person behind the Junius letters and camouflaged his own involvement. He told Parliament that when he saw the letter to the

King his "blood ran cold." In a classic case of misdirection, Burke was disavowing the most important Junius essay in which he had a direct hand.

John Wilkes's tactic was different. He had the Junius regiment write private Junius letters to him, and he carried one of them around conspicuously so that he could tell everyone he had received a letter from Junius—the implication being that the recipient could not have been the author. Another deception.

Thomas Paine used his local community in Lewes as cover. He cultivated the impression that he was a regular excise officer who had stumbled across the political groups in Lewes—at the White Hart and the Headstrong Club. His neighbors were radicals, and he merely a marginal newcomer in 1768. (In fact, as scholars have recently shown, his political involvement had begun in collaboration with Benjamin Franklin a decade earlier.)

Richmond also needed to cover his tracks. At the very end of the period of Junius's writings, he conveniently claimed to have had a conversation with William Gerard Hamilton, a friend of Samuel Johnson and ally of George III, during which, he alleged, Hamilton had quoted from a Junius letter that hadn't yet been printed. This letter was supposedly addressed to the Duke of Richmond himself and was supposedly Junius's final missive, but then it never appeared. Richmond reported himself "anxious to see it," and surprised that "when the paper came there was an apology in it for its not appearing." It was a bluff—the same one that John Wilkes had used; the suggestion was that, since Richmond was the target of a letter from Junius, he could not be the author.

Richmond also began to spread the rumor that Hamilton was Junius. Hamilton was a good target. He would become known as "Single Speech Hamilton," for he gave one and only one speech during the entirety of his forty-two-year career in Parliament. He was described by one contemporary as "extremely tall and handsome, [with] an air of haughty and fashionable superiority, [and] intelligent, dry, sarcastic and clever." Just when Richmond accused Hamilton of being Junius, Junius made his single mention in all of his letters of the Duke of Richmond. Prior to the final four letters (published in October 1771 to January 1772), Richmond is the one politician conspicuously absent from the texts. Every other major cabinet figure from the preceding five years is referred to—often repeatedly. Not Richmond. Then, in the fourth to last letter, Junius tucks in a single reference: "The civil constitution . . . that legal liberty, that general creed, which every Englishman professes, may still be supported . . . even if . . . Savil, Richmond, Camden, Rockingham, and Chatham, should disagree in the ceremonies of their political worship."

Scholars have known that Richmond instructed one of his heirs to destroy many of his letters, and that his sisters' letters are missing from the years between 1769 and 1774—the Junius years. Few of Richmond's letters remain from this period. Richmond's account books are also missing from 1766, when his pamphleteers began publishing in the newspapers, to 1775, when they seem to have stopped. No explanation has previously been offered for the missing accounts and correspondence. The clear connection between the Duke of Richmond and Thomas Paine in advancing the voice and cause of Junius provides by far the most likely explanation. Richmond seems to have undertaken a meticulous destruction of any paper trail that could have enabled sleuths to discover who Junius was—or were. His precautions were understandable: To some, Junius's words were not merely scandalous or even seditious but treasonous. For years, it would be too dangerous to admit to being Junius. The seriousness of the stakes would soon be proved by 1771 sedition trials against the publishers of the Junius letters, and more sedition trials to come in the 1790s.

Richmond's allegation against Hamilton stuck for a while—the economist Adam Smith was still circulating it in 1789. Paine, too, continued to cover up, even after he went to America. He circulated the story that he had never written a word before crossing the Atlantic. *Common Sense* was published a mere thirteen months after he arrived. It has always been hard to believe that it was, as he claimed, his first political essay. In reality, he not only had a lot of practice with the Junius regiment but had written extensively in his own right.

IN THE DUKE OF Richmond's Large Library, Paine's first book-length publication, *The Juryman's Touchstone*, is bound in a simple volume labeled *Tracts*, in gold letters on the spine. The volume contains four other pamphlets connected to Richmond's political agenda, one about universal manhood suffrage, and the other three, just like *The Juryman's Touchstone*, relating to the Wilkes affair and the Junius sedition trials. Holding this volume in my hand beneath the weak sunlight coming in from immensely tall, heavily draped, south-facing windows, I came only slowly to understand that I held the key to a mystery more than 250 years old. The political and legal disputes of the period are so intricate that the texts yield neither their meaning nor their significance easily to a modern reader. I studied the book containing the pseudonymous dedication to Richmond on at least three separate occasions before I began to wonder whether the handwriting belonged to Paine. I considered several other candidates before I turned to him. I had needed to build up enough circumstantial evidence for the connection between Paine and Richmond before it could even become imaginable that they might be close enough for Paine to have dedicated his first book-length publication to the Duke. But he did. It was Thomas Paine who, with Benjamin Franklin, wrote *The Juryman's Touchstone*, and whose first book-length political writing is bound in a volume of pamphlets of central importance to the Junius letters and political agenda of the Duke of Richmond.

Thanks to the subterfuge and machinations of Richmond and his friends, it has been possible until now for Richmond's network and associations to remain obscure. Quite remarkably, in light of the later fame of the author of *Common Sense*, one of the secrets long preserved with these methods was that the revolutionary firebrand Thomas Paine's first steady political patron was the 3rd Duke of Richmond. Another buried truth: Paine and the Duke both cut their teeth as radicals by playing Junius.

Chapter
8

SPEAKER FOR THE OPPOSITION

1770–1774

Really to inform the understanding corrects and enlarges the heart.

—JUNIUS, FINAL LETTER

THE YEARS BETWEEN THE FALL OF GRAFTON'S MINISTRY IN 1770 and Thomas Paine's departure for America in 1774 marked a period of political transition—when one era slipped into the next. The age of the Old Whigs and aristocratic politics passed away. In its place, the foundations of the modern monarchy and modern party politics were taking shape. Richmond returned to parliamentary life and, working in sync through 1772 with the regiment of political writers who gave voice to Junius, forged a new partisan vocabulary for the Opposition. They rallied allies around a coherent policy agenda and spurred members of their party to refuse ministerial appointments that required abandoning core principles. With this discipline, and with political ideas at the center of their work, Richmond and his circle contributed significantly to British constitutional thought. They hammered home the connection between legitimate government and popular will, raised early arguments for expanding the franchise and reforming elections, and helped channel radical energy toward the American colonies. In 1770, Arthur Lee, one of the Lees of Virginia, claimed the persona "Junius Americanus" and joined their chorus, denouncing "the treachery and tyranny of administration, both at home and abroad." In 1774, when Paine—who was out of work once again—sailed for America, the revolution sailed with him.

IN FEBRUARY 1770, AS the impact of the Letter to the King continued to reverberate, Richmond was thirty-five years old, three years younger than George Washington, four months younger than John Adams, one year older than Thomas Paine, and eight years older than Thomas Jefferson. He was no longer a novice to politics. He had risen to cabinet level and fallen. His schoolmate, the Duke of Grafton, had risen even higher and fallen further. No longer did older men guide him. Newcastle was dead. His brother-in-law, Caroline's husband Henry Fox, was out of office and largely distant from politics. Nor was his father-in-law, Henry Conway, now a guide. Conway seemed to manage to cling to office from one administration to the next, preternaturally liked by all, but too pliable to lead. Richmond was by this point truly his own man. He developed his own measures, and the means to advance them. His country rather than his career had become his cause.

For the waning winter months and spring of 1770, Richmond's focus in the House of Lords was the right of the people to legitimate representation and the seating of those whom they had elected, resisting the erosion of this right by and in the House of Commons, and protecting the checks and balances that set King, Commons, Lords, and the judicial officers in relation to each other—in other words, all the issues raised by the continued exclusion of John Wilkes. Richmond's efforts would converge with grassroots efforts emerging out of London's middle classes.

On February 2, the Opposition lost a vote in the House of Lords that would have censured the Commons for its refusal to admit Wilkes. Richmond led the drafting and presentation of the Opposition's "protest" against the outcome and was its first signatory. His object was to defend the right to vote as the first and most important of all rights. He and the other members of the House of Lords held their own rights and powers not for personal interest but "as a Constitutional Trust," to be exercised "for the benefit of the People" and the preservation of "Laws and Liberties." The Lords were duty bound to protect the right to vote as a first priority.

In the protest statement, Richmond recapitulated precisely the argument the Junius regiment had been making. The House of Commons, by failing to seat Wilkes, was changing "the whole Law of Election," and the refusal of the Lords to censure the House meant that the people were being left "to despair of any Relief whatsoever." Failing to censure was abdicating the aristocracy's "ancient and unquestioned" responsibility to give the Crown advice when there was widespread, lawful public complaint about the behavior of their representatives. The House of Lords would be unable to fulfill its own constitutional duties if there were no legally constituted House of Commons with which to partner on passing laws. The decision not to censure the House of Commons undermined "the Purpose of which the Legislature has been divided into separate Branches" and "lower[ed] all the Constitutional Powers of the Kingdom, rendering the House of Commons odious, and the House of Peers contemptible." Richmond concluded the dissent by promising to persevere in seeking to block "this most dangerous Usurpation upon the Rights of the People." The refusal to seat Wilkes was, "by sapping the Fundamental Principles of this Government, threaten[ing] its total Dissolution."

While Richmond worked in the House of Lords on matters of core constitutional principle, his writing regiment kept up the attack politics. They worked in sync. Junius published on a theme, and Richmond advanced the same arguments in Parliament and vice versa. Similarly, at the same time that Richmond was working to keep the cause of the London voters alive inside Parliament, the voters of Middlesex were also carrying their own advocacy forward. In March voters of Middlesex—both Westminster and the City of London—sent up fresh petitions to the King. They asserted that a "secret and malign influence" on the King had violated the people's rights, and they demanded the dissolution of Parliament. The absence of a response to their petitions pushed them into a series of meetings to reconsider their tactics.

They settled on seeking an audience with the King to present a "remonstrance," an expression of grievances. The King agreed to receive them at St. James's Palace on March 14 at two o'clock in the afternoon. With that meeting imminent, "C" (Francis) wrote excitedly to Woodfall in a private letter, "Now is the crisis." He also confided to the printer his expectation that Lord Chatham would attend the public meeting in support of the Wilkes petitioners. The night before the scheduled visit to St. James's Palace, the lord mayor of London hosted a "great entertainment" at the Thatched House Tavern in St. James's Street designed to bring members of the Lords and House of Commons together in common cause with the agitators. The Tavern, despite its name, was an elegant edifice that hosted clubs and societies of various kinds. Its high-ceilinged and large meeting room could easily seat twenty for a served dinner under the wax candles in its three glass chandeliers. In attendance were the dukes of Richmond, Devonshire, Bolton, Portland, Manchester, and Northumberland, the Marquess of Rockingham, the Marquess of Granby, Lord George Manners Sutton, Mr. John Calcraft, and Mr. Thomas Thornton. After the event, the members of Parliament were escorted, "in procession, to the city by a cavalcade of City Liverymen."

The anticipated showdown between City activists and members of Parliament on the one hand, and the King on the other, did not go as expected. The violent rhetoric of the remonstrators had begun to fracture the Opposition. Chatham announced that he was suffering from gout and would not attend after all. This took much of the heft out of the effort of the activists. They appeared nonetheless in force: The lord mayor, the aldermen, sheriffs; 153 members of the common council, and the committee of the livery, in their proper gowns; all proceeded in carriages to the Palace through the bright sun and frosty cold. The King met them, seated on his throne. There was some confusion among the activists about who was supposed to read the remonstrance, but someone managed it in the end—only for the King to slap them down. His subjects were "misled," he said; their message was "disrespectful" to him, "injurious to parliament," and unconstitutional. The activists left angrier than they had arrived. John Horne Tooke published this account in *The Public Advertiser*: "When his Majesty was done reading his speech, the Lord Mayor, had the honour of kissing his Majesty's hand; after which, as they were withdrawing, his Majesty instantly turned round to his courtiers *and burst out a laughing. Nero fiddled while Rome was burning*." As soon as Horne Tooke's account appeared in print, the government threatened him with prosecution for seditious libel. He agreed to withdraw his allegations, which he then did simply by declaring, "Nero did *not* fiddle while Rome was burning." The effrontery of the radicals was too much for some more cautious members of Parliament. When the House of Commons voted on a statement in defense of the King later in the month, it passed with an overwhelming majority. The Opposition was shrinking.

The Junius regiment, though, tried to maintain the pressure by publishing an essay trumpeting solidarity with the voters in the City. The time had come for all "honest" men to speak up. The "least considerable man" was as worthy of having his rights defended as a "nobleman." They urged the act of last resort: "The time is come, when the body of the English people must assert their own cause: conscious of their strength, and animated by a sense of their duty, they will not surrender their birthright to ministers, parliaments, or kings." Here again was an expression, if tempered, of a right to revolution—recognized then as an extraordinary statement in the context of the limits of speech at the time. Junius's boundary-breaking rhetoric caused consternation among more conservative factions.

YET THE JUNIUS REGIMENT was not out to destroy the Crown. They wrote with a vision of what a constitutional monarchy might be. In early April 1770, they delivered a long essay outlining that vision. They also offered an argument about how kings ought legitimately to rule, and they offered King George specific pathways for performing a higher form of kingship. They issued a warning about the mood of the people: "Their speech is rude, but intelligible;—their gestures fierce, but full of explanation. Perplexed by sophistries, their honest eloquence rises into action. Their first appeal was to the integrity of their representatives:—the second to the King's justice;—the last argument of the people, whenever they have recourse to it, will carry more perhaps than persuasion to parliament, or supplication to the throne." Again, a veiled threat: The people might find themselves needing to move beyond persuasion and supplication into an unnamed beyond.

In his public role, too, and in contrast to Chatham, the Duke of Richmond remained stalwart in his support of the radicals. He advocated with his political associates for "wholehearted cooperation" with the Society of Gentlemen Supporters of the Bill of Rights, where his close associate James Adair was active, and where members were focused on supporting Wilkes, placing themselves at the center of the opposition to the King.

Edmund Burke also reinforced Richmond's willingness to criticize the King and his ministers publicly, with his own long-awaited pamphlet,

Thoughts on the Cause of the Present Discontents, which came out on April 23, 1770. Burke's caution shone through. He was forceful but careful to avoid insult or anything that might be construed as sedition. His pamphlet criticized the King's nepotism and cronyism and made the case that a counterweight to the crony associations of "bad men" running the government must be "parties": "bod[ies] of men united for promoting by their joint endeavours the national interest upon some particular principle in which they are all agreed." Replacing negative personal attack with philosophical reflection, Burke advocated for a politics of "men and measures" where some group of men formed commitments to one another based on shared convictions and steered their way through politics adhering both to principle and to those bonds of loyalty. With this pamphlet, the modern conception of ideological political parties—and not merely collections of families with overlapping interests—entered the public's political lexicon.

On the basis of this new conception of a political party, the Rockinghamites organized themselves as such a men-and-measures group around defense of Wilkes and the principle of needing to respect the will of the people through legitimate representation. To all appearances, they seemed to have the people with them. Five days earlier, on April 18, 1770, when Wilkes completed his prison sentence and was released to freedom for the first time in two years, sheep were roasted in town squares, and bells pealed across the country. A new peal, invented for the occasion and known as the "Wilkes and Liberty" peal, "consist[ed] of 720 changes, with 45 treble leadings." In Sheffield, a peal called "Wilkes's March" was rung "containing 5045 Changes"; it lasted three hours and twenty-two minutes. The bells rang again in Lewes when Wilkes visited that town en route to Brighton for a visit to the seaside with his daughter.

During his time in prison, and after the repeated refusals of the House of Commons to seat him, Wilkes had stood for election one last time, this time not for Parliament but for alderman for the City of London. He had also won that election. Following his release from prison, he was now able to serve. With his quest for elected office at last fulfilled, the Wilkes matter somewhat receded. The issues that the Wilkes case had put on the table—the rights of the people, in respect to the powers of the Crown and Parliament, and the nature of legitimate representation—did not disappear.

—

LATE APRIL BROUGHT STARTLING news from America. In Boston on March 5, 1770, British troops had shot into a crowd outside the Custom House near the Statehouse, the brick building topped by a lion and a unicorn, symbols of the British king. Five people were killed. The shooting was the climax of a testy period of low-level violence between the colonists, customs officials, and soldiers. The news brought American taxes back to the forefront of British political discussion, and raised again the question of how much Britain should conciliate the Americans. The new prime minister, Lord North, decided to stay the course. He had already repealed most of the Townshend duties, while keeping the tax on tea. The government understood this tax to be necessary from a symbolic point of view, an assertion of the right of Parliament and the Crown to tax the colonies, independent of any decisions by colonial legislatures.

Ireland too was restive. Charles Townshend now served as lord lieutenant there, the representative of the King in Ireland. In the previous months the Irish parliament, subsidary to Whitehall, had been complaining about British efforts to increase the size of the Irish Army. Irish politicians and citizens worried that standing armies were being imposed on them. They also complained about the revenue-raising bills that the government was trying to push through the Irish parliament. The fact that British taxation was moving through the British legislature did not make it any more palatable to them than to the Americans. In response to the Irish agitation, Townshend had simply prorogued—that is, closed—Dublin's Parliament in the fall of 1769. It would not convene again until 1771. This move failed to quiet activism against the Crown and government. To the contrary, the prorogation itself was seen as highly objectionable. Resistance and rebellion were gaining steam in England, America, and Ireland, simultaneously.

When the King opened Parliament in January 1770, his speech had stressed the importance of achieving reconciliation between his subjects in America and in England. Yet relations had grown only more strained in the intervening months, and the government had taken no steps to remedy the situation. Richmond chafed at the inaction. More than that, he also saw the actions of some of the royal governors—the dissolution of assemblies in Massachusetts and Virginia—as carrying into colonial policy the very same unconstitutional practice of undermining the representation of the people as had occurred with the Wilkes affair and the proroguing of the Irish parliament. All across the empire, the British monarch seemed to be eviscerating law and liberty.

On May 18, on the cusp of the closure of the 1770 parliamentary session, Richmond rose in the House of Lords to address a set of policy papers relating to America. When submitting them to the House, the government had expected a pro forma review of the materials, and everyone was looking forward to summer recess. Ignoring the mood, Richmond gave a lengthy speech proposing eighteen resolutions that repudiated current colonial policy. His desire to insert a new agenda despite the session being nearly at end stemmed, he said, from the urgency of the situation. He lambasted the administration for failing to make good on its airy, visionary promises to address the crisis, while warning that "the state of the British empire grows hourly more and more alarming." His parliamentary voice strongly echoed Junius. The ministers, he said, were shameless, had succumbed to "depravity of principle," and were about to be subject to "the storm of public wrath."

Richmond's eighteen proposed resolutions censured the policy actions recently taken by the administration on the treatment of colonial assemblies and taxation. When he finished, a long debate ensued. The final speaker for the ministry was Lord Gower, another former schoolmate, who proposed rejecting the resolutions and adjourning the session. He acknowledged, "To be sure the noble lords will call us a corrupt, a venal majority, and generously weep over the ruins of their miserable country." He stood, however, on the power of the majority. "Every sensible man knows that almost all majorities are branded as corrupt, by the ignorant or interested. . . . I trust the same remarks will be made in succeeding ages, when the public-spirited worthies of the present hour, are either consigned to oblivion, or hung up to the ridicule of posterity." With that, the ministry moved to adjourn for the summer. The motion carried.

Ten days later, on May 28, Junius followed up Richmond's detailed speech in Parliament with another long essay that offered a broad review of the state of the nation. The House of Commons, they wrote, had "assumed a power unknown to the constitution." In the House of Lords, in contrast, "the interest of the public was vigorously supported," albeit ultimately by only a minority. Lord North had failed to improve a nonviable system of taxation. Referring to the symbolic tea tax, Junius asked: "What is it then but an odious, unprofitable exertion of a speculative right, and fixing a badge of slavery upon the Americans?" Junius was ahead of the Americans in using rhetoric against taxation to place blame directly on the King. Junius suggested the King's errors stemmed from his excessive seclusion from the world: "Secluded from the world, attached from his infancy to one set of persons, one set of ideas, he can neither open his heart to new connexions nor his mind to better information. A character of this sort is the soil fittest to produce the obstinate bigotry in politics and religion, which begins with a meritorious sacrifice of the understanding, and finally conducts the monarch and the martyr to the block." Junius's words hit the mark in some specific ways. The King was remarkably well read but very poorly traveled. He never journeyed to Europe, Ireland, or the Americas, and scarcely made it far beyond London. Now, he was on track to follow Charles I who was executed right at home in London.

THE JUNIUS WRITERS PUT their pens down for the summer, but they were not idle. The conflict between Richmond and his Opposition colleagues, on the one hand, and the government, on the other, simply gained a new focus when the publisher of *The Public Advertiser*, Henry Woodfall, stood trial in June. On June 13 at nine o'clock in the morning he appeared in the Court of King's Bench, at the Guildhall, before Chief Justice Lord Mansfield. Five other publishers who had reprinted Junius's Letter to the King also were brought to trial that month. Mansfield gave the jury a set of instructions that ran counter to prior English legal practice. Historically, English juries had been able to decide matters of both fact and law. That is, they could vote to acquit someone because they thought a law inappropriately criminalized a given category of action, or because they thought the law did not apply to the actions known to have occurred, or because they thought the facts alleged were not themselves proven. The first two kinds of decision would be rulings on the law; the third a ruling on the facts. Any of these categories of ruling was available to juries. They had great latitude and power, as was widely recognized. For that matter, they could also vote to acquit simply because they felt like it.

Mansfield wished to avoid a circumstance in which the jury might acquit Woodfall out of sympathy for Wilkes's cause and so instructed the jury that they were permitted to decide on matters of fact only. They were not to rule on whether Woodfall had perpetrated seditious libel, but only on whether he had indeed published the Junius letters. The intention seems to have been that a ruling on whether Woodfall had published the letter would then leave it to Mansfield to evaluate whether the label of seditious libel applied to the texts. Outsmarting Mansfield, the jury returned the verdict that Woodfall was "guilty of printing and publishing only." They ruled only on the facts, as instructed, but in such a manner, introducing the word "only," as to preclude the application of any further guilty convictions, including a conviction on seditious libel. This then resulted in a flurry of competitive motions between prosecution and defense, and forced a new trial scheduled for later in the year. Surprisingly, by November, when the second trial began, no one could locate the physical copy of the newspaper that had been the object of the original indictment, so Mansfield declared a mistrial. Woodfall had escaped—as Junius had promised him—even if only on a technicality.

Despite the almost comical end to the trial, the issues raised by the proceedings were substantial, and the Junius regiment was irate at Mansfield's instructions to the jury. The trial sparked more than a year's worth of controversy over the chief justice's attempt to restrict the scope of a jury's powers. Here was yet another instance of the government undermining ancient rights and privileges. The Opposition in Parliament split over whether to advance a motion to prohibit similar instructions in the future, as Rockingham preferred, or to impeach Mansfield for unconstitutional actions, as Chatham wanted. Throughout the fall of 1770, the Junius writers continued to lambast Mansfield: "Our language has no term of reproach," they wrote on November 14, "the mind has no idea of detestation, which has not already been happily applied to you and exhausted." This letter was published a day after the opening of the new session of Parliament. Mansfield resigned his speakership of the House of Lords immediately. He had no interest in facing down Junius time and time again.

Mansfield's abominable ruling required even more, though, than just Junius's letter, Richmond and his colleagues believed. Thomas Paine took up his pen against Mansfield and wrote *The Juryman's Touchstone*, a ninety-five-page tract defending the rights of jurors. Paine's engagement in the theme of Mansfield's violation of the rights of jurors was personal, as well as philosophical. In Lewes, beginning in October 1769, Paine himself served on the local jury for the court leet, a court that handled minor offenses. He did not miss one of the annual court sessions during five years enrolled as a juror in Lewes, so dedicated was he to his jury service. No one had a better attendance record than Paine. His tract, which took its title from an important seventeenth-century work, stirringly defended that treasured role. Paine didn't work alone on the essay but collaborated closely on the text with Benjamin Franklin. Richmond also weighed in, editing at least one paragraph, and providing the final paragraph, which referenced procedure in the House of Lords.

Paine finished the essay and published it early in 1771 under the name "Censor-General," a pseudonym attributed to him several years later in a letter mocking his pamphleteering. In the pamphlet, after fifteen calm and measured pages traversing the history of the British constitution and the development of trials before a jury of peers within it, Censor-General turned to the subject of Lord Mansfield and his instructions to the juries in the various seditious libel cases. At that point he turned up the heat. The Scottish Mansfield was unfortunately "early im-*buted* with Jacobite principles," a scathing reference to the influence of George's still much-disliked Scottish tutor, the Earl of Bute. Worse, Mansfield was insulting not only the rights and responsibilities of jurors, but also their intelligence—by presuming they were not fit to judge a question of law. Paine went on to outline why juries in the case of the sedition trials should have no fewer rights than members of the House of Lords when dukes and marquesses and earls and other peers sat in judgment on one of their own—the original source of the idea of being tried by peers. The right to a trial of law and fact by one's peers was the cornerstone of English freedom for all people, not just aristocrats, he argued.

When this text appeared, Paine gave a copy to the Duke of Richmond. His full dedication reads:

> To the Duke of Richmond as A Tribute due to him for His Strenuous Efforts & unwearied perseverance in the Defence of Constitutional Liberty this Pamphlet is presented by the Author. Pray! If by his Grace's cursory perusal of it [the?] *Rank Errors* of Ld. Mansfields Judgment [in the] Case of Horne (which are to be argued before their Lordships tomorrow) shall be so [hei?]nously displayed by his Grace as to necessitate an immediate Reversal of the Judgment, attended with a Severe Reprimand of the Judge himself. *Nos non faciemus Justiciarios nisi de talibus qui sciant Legem et eam bene velint observare.* Mag. Chart. Johannis Regis Artic 45.

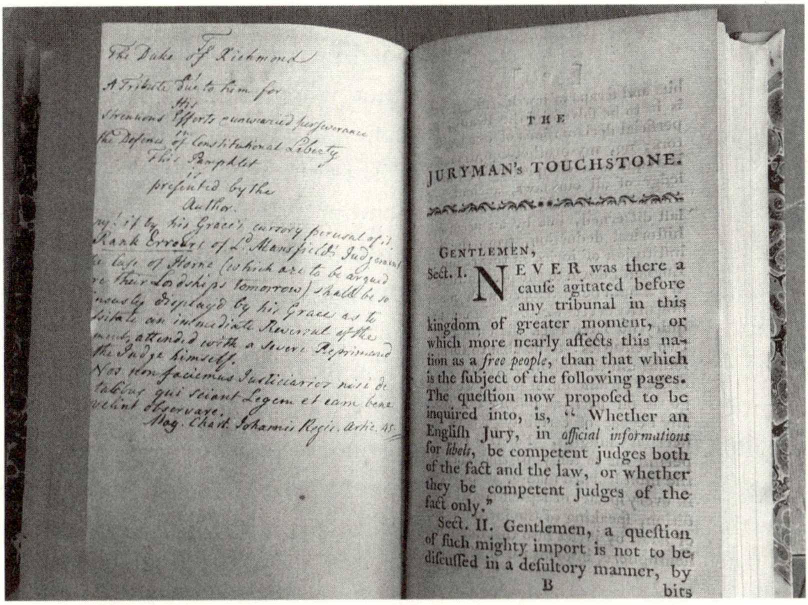

This dedication from the "author" to the Duke of Richmond inscribed in the 1771 publication of *The Juryman's Touchstone*, a book-length pamphlet about the sedition trials stemming from the Junius letters, is in the handwriting of Thomas Paine.

The concluding quotation from the Magna Carta provocatively modifies the original text, changing the phrase celebrating men who know "the law of the Kingdom," into one celebrating simply "men who know the law." In his first book-length publication, Paine was already showing his polemicist, anti-monarchical, republican hand.

The inscription also makes clear how closely Paine and Richmond were coordinating. Paine delivered the finished pamphlet to his patron the day before Richmond was slated to advance the same arguments in the House of Lords.

RICHMOND HAD BY NOW been a full-fledged member of the Opposition for several years. Members of the Opposition generally didn't attend the regal drawing rooms and levees, but Richmond took his self-imposed exile a step further. He wrote his own declaration of independence to the King.

The occasion was an opening for a position he had once desired. Back in 1763, he had made a request to be given command of the

Blues, the Royal Regiment of Horse Guards. His brother-in-law Fox had told Richmond that the King had promised it to him upon the death of Field Marshal John Ligonier, which would trigger a shuffle of senior officers opening a vacancy at the Blues. In April 1770, Ligonier passed away, but the King kept the incumbent in the post. When the incumbent then died, Richmond preempted any offer—or omission—by writing to withdraw from consideration.

Richmond could not accept the promotion without abandoning his role in the Opposition and his vehement arguments against the Crown and government. He wasn't the man he was when he had wanted the appointment, and he wasn't willing to give up the man he had become.

Pulling out one of the pieces of distinctive foolscap used for Junius's writing that was marked with a republican Pro Patria watermark, paper unlike the kind he used for the rest of his correspondence, Richmond

This Pro Patria watermark was a favorite of radicals and republicans, including Benjamin Franklin. The collected edition of Junius letters was printed on Pro Patria paper. The Duke of Richmond also used this paper for his "declaration of independence" letter to King George III. This paper was an alternative to paper with the royal watermark, which was more commonly used.
DRAWN BY NORA DOYLE.

wrote the King an extraordinarily convoluted note. Despite the letter's adherence to the conventions of indirect speech that characterized British politics of the day, Richmond's meaning was clear: He implicitly declared himself unavailable. He wrote: "As possibly it might be more convenient for your Majesty's present arrangements, if this engagement did not subsist, I most humbly presume to beg of your Majesty . . . to permit me to relinquish this claim to the Blues." Muted as the declaration appears today, it was a strong statement, and Richmond knew it.

Richmond immediately sent a copy to Rockingham, enjoining him to silence. "Pray do not communicate the copy to anybody, nor speak of it, till you hear the event from others." He didn't want the gossip about his plan to withdraw to reach the King before the letter itself.

With the letter, Richmond formally disavowed all conventional ambition within the established channels of patronage. He put himself beyond the temptation of the King's appointments. The watermark on the page was a token of his radical sympathies for the King to see. The King got the message and never replied to the letter. The two men would have no direct communication for more than ten years.

BRITAIN HAD REACHED AN important juncture. The question of how to govern its imperial holdings was increasingly entangled with how to govern at home. Abroad the government was swiftly sliding toward more and more autocratic measures—dissolving popular assemblies, and relying on the military to enforce measures. People worried that the same strategies would be applied at home. It was all too plausible. Britain desperately needed a new approach to the relationship between Crown, legislatures, and the people in Britain and in the colonies. Richmond saw an opening for his party to offer the necessary strategy.

His chance to enact it came in December of 1770 when Rockingham's wife fell ill, and the Marquess retreated to Bath to tend to her. In his absence, Richmond's associates appealed to him to take the lead of the party, which he did after many protestations of reluctance. His agenda was already clear. As he had been doing for four years, he stubbornly tried to unify the two wings of the Opposition: the Rockinghamites, who were committed to "measures and men," and the Chatham Whigs, who focused on "measures only." Unity had been tentatively advanced the previous spring, when Burke's pamphlet advocating for a party united by principle had advocated it. Real unity, though, required forging agreement around positions—not just on protesting Mansfield's mishandling of juries, where the Whigs were broadly already in agreement. On other increasingly volatile matters, the Opposition needed to stake out its platform: on America and Ireland, and a new conflict in the Falkland Islands, which the Spanish had recently seized. Ambitiously, Richmond also pursued closer rapprochement with the City of London radicals and members of the Society of Gentlemen Supporters of the Bill of Rights to widen the Opposition platform. But it was not clear if he could hold such a broad coalition together.

Throughout the frenzied year of 1771, Richmond maintained his double-barreled approach to driving the political agenda: His Junius team secretly published major policy essays nearly once a month. Richmond then used the essays to try to shape the agenda in the House of Lords. The schedule of a party leader was arduous: Richmond was in the House of Lords for debate on February 1, 4, 5, 8, 11, 14, 20, 21. On February 1, he also met in private conference with Chatham. On February 2 a group of party members met in Chatham's house for discussion. On February 3, Richmond met with six other party leaders at the home of the Duke of Manchester. On February 4, he met again in conference with Chatham and three others, and on February 5 with Chatham alone again. On February 5, he also had twenty men of the party to dinner in his home, including some of the City radicals. March and April continued much the same.

Under the pressure of an increased workload, Richmond seems to have turned again to his network of associates for support. Philo-Junius (or Friend of Junius) appeared regularly in the pages of *The Public Advertiser* in 1771. The network had developed the pattern of using the Philo-Junius persona to deliver shorter, punchier reviews of key points drawn from the long and philosophical Junius letters. Suspicions about the coordination must have been growing, because this is the period in which the writers' various attempts at misdirection emerged.

On February 12, Richmond wrote Rockingham—still in Bath looking after his wife—to report on how things were going for the party. One of the longest private letters he ever wrote, it runs to thirteen printed pages and contains much opinion recognizable from the Junius letters, such as a summary of Richmond's argument in the House of

Lords about the state of the British constitution. As Richmond saw it, George III was destroying the country's proudly mixed constitution by forcing his ministers into dependence on him. They took their sources of power from perquisites that he awarded them, rather than earning the support of the people. The best fix was to create a power base in the House of Lords independent from the Crown. What he wanted above all was a political system that could put limits on the power of the monarch. He concluded the long letter, "Adieu my Dear Lord, I can realy scarce hold my pen, my hand is so much tired, cramped, and cold."

THE CONSTITUTIONAL ARGUMENTS CONTINUED to evolve that spring—as the radicals pressed on the question of how to establish independence from the Crown and an increasingly unpopular King. Issues of transparency came up, and the question of how to root out the corruption of the election system. Checks and balances could operate only if the public could see what each branch of government was doing, and only if they were in a position to hold representatives accountable at free and fair elections. Neither lever of power had historically been reliably available to the people.

To fix this, John Wilkes, since his release from prison in 1770, had been working with printers to develop practices for reporting on parliamentary deliberations. Here he made perhaps his clearest contribution in the interest of the public, not just himself. Clerks attended the open meetings of the House of Commons, recorded what they heard, and passed their memoranda to printers, even though printing of the proceedings was illegal. Bringing matters to a head in the spring of 1771, the House of Commons declared that it wanted to suppress the growing practice of publishing its proceedings and once more pursued the arrests of publishers. When a messenger for the House tried to arrest one of the accused publishers, the sheriff of the City of London instead arrested the messenger and brought him before Wilkes, in his role as alderman. Wilkes promptly charged the messenger with assault and referred him to prosecution. This was just one of the flamboyant gestures with which Wilkes outsmarted the government. The House of Commons retaliated by throwing the lord mayor of London, a supporter of Wilkes, into the

Tower of London, which provoked popular rage. The King was hissed at in the streets; rotten apples were thrown at his carriage; and a mob made an attempt to assault Lord North. Volatile and theatrical, it was a moment made for Wilkes.

In April and June, Junius entered into the fray about whether debates in the House of Commons and House of Lords should be reported in the press. This was also an argument about how far the privilege of the House of Commons extended. Junius advocated for openness and for the check of publicity on the privilege of the House. Since Philip Francis, at least, and possibly Thomas Paine, too, were among the people attending sessions of Parliament and transcribing what they heard, the essays were effectively in self-defense. Francis passed the Junius text to the printer, Woodfall, on April 19, urging speedy publication on the following Monday, April 22. Woodfall obliged him. Richmond then attended the House of Lords on April 25, 26, 29, and 30, and on April 30 rose to address the question of whether the House of Commons had abused its privilege and should be checked. The timing bespeaks careful coordination.

Defending the right of the public to read the transcripts of the debates, Richmond laid out arguments familiar from the pages of Junius, urging the members of the House of Lords to stand up to the Commons. Invoking, as had Junius' December 1769 Letter to the King, the days of his ancestor Charles I, he exhorted his fellow peers not "to crouch to the Commons, and to humble yourselves before the Crown," and not to "become as contemptible as the Lords of Charles." He added, "You will lose all authority, and cease to have any weight in the scale of government. For what purpose was the legislature divided into separate branches? In order to be a check upon each other." Chatham seconded Richmond in the debate. At last, here was the united party that Richmond had been long seeking. Yet unity was insufficient for victory. The Opposition lost the vote.

The disappointment must have struck deep. Years of effort had gone into forming an agenda and browbeating his colleagues into coalition. At last he had them lined up together yet still they lost. With majority status still far from their grasp, the Opposition settled into a pattern of recording dissenting opinions against the actions of the ministry.

—

YET TRICKLING STREAMS OF radical reform thinking and political effort were merging with one another and growing stronger. Hindered in Parliament on matters of national policy, like a waterway dammed up by the fall of rock, radical efforts flowed in other directions. Finally, reform to election systems themselves, at least on a regional level, began to come into view as the necessary course to correct the growing disconnect between Parliament and the people. Opportunity lay not in London but in the counties.

While Richmond was blocked at the national level he made some headway in Sussex. On May 8, 1771, reformers secured passage of an act to clean up election corruption in the borough of New Shoreham, where a so-called "Christian Society" had been involved in selling parliamentary seats. The society was composed of individuals who had voting rights in the borough, and they sold their votes as a bloc, to control who would be elected to Parliament. The new law permanently barred all the members of the Christian Society from voting in parliamentary elections. The law also expanded the franchise. It allowed any adult freeholder (a landowning man with an estate worth at least forty shillings annually) within the jurisdiction to vote in elections for the borough. This broadened the pool of eligible voters beyond those traditionally in control, a critical early effort to extend the franchise. The act also introduced an oath before voting, with which voters would confirm that their property was genuinely theirs and not fraudulently claimed to gain access to the vote. Importantly, the act permitted religious dissenters, such as Quakers, who were prominent in the region, to "affirm" the validity of their property claim rather than requiring them to "swear" an oath, which would run counter to their religious obligations. In other words, the act not only broadened the franchise but also introduced an element of religious toleration. Finally, the law established election procedures for the borough, including the responsibilities of local officials, the timeline for elections, and the public reading of the act at elections to ensure transparency.

Reformers had at last notched a victory. Junius's, Burke's, and Richmond's arguments that institutional reform was needed to preserve liberty had at last carried the day. Paine wrote a poem to celebrate the victory, called "Farmer Short's Dog Porter: A Tale," which he recited before the Headstrong Club in Lewes. Farmer Short was, apparently, a voter who had refused to vote as directed by the corrupt officials controlling the pre-reform elections, and who had been punished by having his dog hung. After condemning the dog to hang, "The justices adjourned to dine / And whet their logic up with wine." The reform resonated in America, where colonial assemblies found themselves undermined by royal institutions that they considered corrupt. Corruption and arbitrary punishment were understood to go hand in hand. The poem was one of the first things Paine published after he arrived in America.

YET AS QUICKLY AS Richmond managed to forge party unity to advance the causes of transparency and reform, just as quickly during the summer of 1771 that unity began to unravel, much to the delight and benefit of the Ministry and Crown. Richmond had pulled together not only the Chatham and Rockingham Whigs, but also two different subsets of the City of London radicals. A path to victory is glue for a coalition; parliamentary losses made unity hard to hold. The City radicals now began to turn on each other.

John Horne Tooke, who had been in Paris at the same time as Wilkes and had been a founder of the Society of Gentlemen Supporters of the Bill of Rights, which backed Wilkes, had by now grown frustrated with Wilkes's gamesmanship and grandstanding. A bon vivant, Wilkes was profligate, and his financial needs continued to be very great. Horne Tooke proposed diverting 500 pounds from the society's fund of membership dues to support William Bingley, the publisher of *The North Briton*, the paper that had been first to broadcast its support for Wilkes. Wilkes objected to this proposal. He was now in the thick of running for sheriff of London, a step up from alderman. He believed he needed all the money. A heated debate emerged as to whether the reform agenda supported by the society should center on Wilkes's causes specifically or have a broader mission.

Horne Tooke took matters into his own hands, utterly shattering the unity of the society by deciding to find and assist candidates to run for sheriff against Wilkes. Pulled in both directions—their man and his measures—the activists now directed the violence that had been aimed at the government upon each other. Wilkes's supporters burned an effigy of Horne Tooke and physically assaulted Wilkes's opponent for sheriff. In July the

Junius regiment took sides and criticized Horne Tooke for the campaign against Wilkes. Offended, Horne Tooke replied in *The Public Advertiser*, which ran a series of acrimonious letters between him and Junius over the summer. Horne Tooke claimed Wilkes was supporting the Rockinghamite agenda—that is, the agenda crafted by Richmond—mainly in expectation of a financial payout. Since Wilkes *had* accepted bribes from Rockingham and some of his cabinet members to remain in Paris, the charge had bite. Indeed, Wilkes may well have been getting payment from Richmond for his participation in the Junius letters. This is perhaps as close as the radicals came to outing each other as writers of the Junius circle.

As a result of the infighting among the activists, the Constitutional Society, a new organization under the leadership of Horne Tooke, split off from the Society of Gentlemen Supporters of the Bill of Rights, with the original society retaining the more radical agenda. The original society, for example, advocated for having parliamentary elections annually instead of every seven years. They also committed "to restore to America the essential right of taxation by representation of their own free election." The domestic radical agenda was finally merging fully with the American agenda. Their North Star was a simple one: to make the institutions of Britain and its colonies truly reflect the people's will.

Under the pressure of the controversy, the Junius regiment used the back-and-forth with Wilkes to lay out their agenda for parliamentary reform. Horne Tooke's faction accused Junius and the Rockinghamites of failing to back reform. The Junius regiment used their letters to Wilkes to clarify their position—they were for shorter parliaments and widening the franchise; they just weren't sure yet how much shorter or how much wider. This exchange was important, not only because it threw the Junius hunters off the scent, but also because here for the first time the cause of widening the suffrage burst into public discussion. All the arguments that passed back and forth surfaced views that Richmond would soon be expressing in his own voice. As for America, the Junius regiment argued that the proposal to establish a system of representation for Americans to support their taxation came too late. The right to levy any taxes had already been lost: "Everything worth contending for is, in reality given up." They approvingly cited Burke's arguments on taxation in support. Richmond's journey toward a great reform bill would not culminate until 1780, but it had begun. His support for America was already solidly in place.

—

THE SUMMER OF 1771 was the last time the Junius letters made positive contributions to constitutional theory or helped to advance the cause of reform. Disunity among the radicals only grew through the fall and seemed to sap their confidence and direction. The letters no longer had the same clarity of purpose. More people joined the group and it was, in all probability, no longer as tightly directed by Richmond. The last essay, published January 21, 1772, attempting to drum up an impeachment of Mansfield, failed because of its length and tedium. Far more interesting to the British public was a coup in Denmark, five days earlier, when George III's sister, Caroline, Queen of Denmark and Norway, was imprisoned and then banished, while her lover, physician to her husband King Christian VII, was executed for having usurped the powers of the king whom he was treating for mental illness.

The writing network shut down; they certainly felt endangered. They recognized that they had comprehensively violated convention and genuinely put themselves at risk of charges of seditious libel. They understood that they would never be able to reveal their secret. In October 1771, Junius had written:

> When a man who stands forth for the public, has gone that length from which there is no practicable retreat,—when he has given that kind of personal offence, which a pious monarch never pardons, I then begin to think him in earnest, and that he will never have occasion to solicit the forgiveness of his country.

Despite the vulnerability, they were proud of the risks they had run; as they put it, "instances of a determination so entire and unreserved are rarely met with."

They were proud enough that they collected the essays for publication in book form. Still writing as "C," Philip Francis worked with Woodfall to edit and release the full set of letters in one volume, beginning with the letter of January 21, 1769. They must have understood that the collected essays constituted one of the most important contributions to British constitutional theory of the era. They had elaborated Montesquieu's theory of separation of powers and checks and balances to fit their contemporary context, using the theory to explain what was going wrong in British and imperial politics and declaring how it could be set right. They had discovered that maintaining an effective separate and checking mechanism to limit the monarchy depended on grounding the legitimacy of the government in popular sovereignty. They had subsequently realized that achieving this would require radical reforms to Parliament.

To bring the project to a close, they appended a new final paragraph, thanking God for the gift of a "reasoning intellect," but even more their collaborators for improving that reasoning, expressing the conviction that what had made the effort worthwhile was "that really to inform the understanding corrects and enlarges the heart." Woodfall printed the book on paper bearing the Pro Patria watermark and released it in May 1772. The epigraph came from Lucan's *On Civil War* epic poem: *Stat magni nominis umbra*. He stands in the shadow of a mighty name.

THE INTENSITY OF THE Junius years left Richmond depleted. They likewise left much of the British political world exhausted. People's lives had nearly been ruined because of the sedition trials. Swelling popular unrest both in Britain and America—juxtaposed with the coup in Denmark—brought home just how vulnerable any monarchy was, how real and near an alternative future might be. The glimpses of transformation enticed the radicals but did not effectively bind them in common cause. At the same time, the domestic turmoil distracted Parliament and the Crown. Little was done to address the situation in the colonies. But neither did the government heed the advice and suggestions of the radicals in London. Parliament did not meet at all in the autumns of 1771 and 1772. The government was marginalizing the people's voice not only in the colonies but also at home.

Richmond himself stayed more frequently away from Parliament in 1772. His sister Louisa, during a visit to Goodwood in April, reported him to be severely ill both physically and mentally. He suffered from "pain in his bowels," and it seemed possible that his "liver was being attacked." The difficulties were also mental. "His nerves are so oppressed," she wrote, "that he is quite miserable," and "anything of business seems to wear him to death." Louisa also registered a change in his orientation to his work: "I have seen [him] write a letter or two about business, and you can't think what an operation it was, and how much the worse he was for it." Louisa was not alone in registering a major change in her brother. Caroline too "was vastly struck with the great alteration in him." After stepping aside from Opposition leadership and from the leadership of the Junius regiment, Richmond clearly had some sort of collapse.

WITH HIS POLITICAL AGENDA disintegrating, Richmond was now able to release Paine from their joint work on the question of fundamental British rights. He did not, though, abandon him to his former poverty. Paine was no longer the impecunious, out-of-work intellectual whom the Duke had first met, and not only because of all the work he had done for Richmond.

In March 1771, Paine had married for a second time. The bride was Elizabeth Ollive, daughter of his landlord, Samuel Ollive, the grocer and tobacconist, and senior high constable, who had been running elections when Paine first arrived in Lewes. Sam Ollive had died in July 1769. A freethinker, like Paine, he did not believe in primogeniture, nor in female subordination. In his will he expressed that he wanted his daughter and three sons to "share and share alike" in his legacy. His sons were all watchmakers, and did not want to take over their father's grocery and tobacconist business, so that went to Elizabeth. She and Paine had been running it together, advertising their sale of "all sorts of Tobacco, Snuff, Cheese, Butter and Homemade Bacon, with every Article of Grocery (Tea excepted) Wholesale and Retail, at the lowest Prices."

After their nearly two years of commercial partnership and residing together above the shop at Bull House—a substantial, timber-framed building from the fifteenth century with carved satyrs over the front door—it made sense for them to marry. With Henry Verrall as a witness, they married next door in St. Michael's Church. They never consummated the marriage; its purpose appears to have been entirely economic. No doubt the joint proprietorship of the shop, and increased earnings, had given Paine the flexibility to travel back and forth between Lewes and London as he did frequently after 1770—not only for politics but also to attend lectures on natural philosophy. He certainly wasn't carrying out his excise duties; he wouldn't have had the time.

AFTER THE JUNIUS LETTERS wrapped, and before leaving for America, Paine was recruited, presumably on the recommendation of Richmond and on the strength of his gifts as a polemicist, by his "superiors in Office" at the Excise Commission—and historians generally think by

George Lewis Scott—to write an essay laying out the case for increasing the pay of excise officers. The goal was to prepare a pamphlet for publication just in advance of the start of the January 1773 parliamentary session. William Lee, the printer of *The Sussex Advertiser* in Lewes, was engaged to print four thousand copies.

Paine seems to have spent much of 1772 working on the essay. Now aged thirty-five, he wrote in the smoky, newspaper-strewn Excise Coffee House in London, no doubt swapping stories of grievance with the clerks, gaugers, and riding officers who passed through as they came in and out of the excise's administrative buildings.

In *The Case of the Officers of Excise*, Paine's second pamphlet before *Common Sense*, the development of his political voice is evident. His plain style dominates. He opens the pamphlet matter-of-factly, but his forcefulness has increased. He explains the economic situation of the excise officers in blunt terms. Inflation was raising prices but, as for the excise officers, "No increase comes to them.—they are shut out from the general Blessing." The wealthy needed to recognize that their "Affluence [has] become the Misfortune of others." Every step upward for the wealthy was a step downward for the excise officer. From this poverty, he argued, stemmed the problems of corruption in the excise.

Yet here too, Paine, and the reformers allied with him, found there were limits to the influence of pamphlets. On February 5, 1773, the lords of the treasury received the most recent petition from the officers, now with a full three thousand signatures, and the accompanying brief by Paine. On February 9, 1773, they read the petition and rendered judgment. They wrote on the petition one word: "Nil." After four years of work, the campaign was dead. Once again, the goal of reform met a brick wall.

Paine seems to have known that he needed to regroup. He immediately applied for a job at the Society of Arts, but was rejected. Clearly, Richmond was no longer offering him meaningful help. Just as Richmond's intense political effort, and its failure, had left the Duke exhausted, so too Paine's effort led to the disintegration of his professional and personal connections. Paine's time away from his excise duties in Lewes while he was writing in London seems to have cost him his job. He was dismissed in April 1774, despite penning a pleading letter. Then his wife sought a legal separation—divorce was too hard to obtain—which went through in June 1774. Elizabeth received the business assets; Paine, a settlement of somewhat more than a year's salary. Ejected once again from all obligations, Paine now pursued a fresh start. He sought help from his longtime collaborator, Benjamin Franklin. Paine's separation settlement was sufficient to pay for his passage to cross the Atlantic, and Franklin, who was still in London, gave Paine a letter of introduction to Philadelphia.

In October 1774, Paine left for his six-week journey to America on the *London Packet*, carrying *The Juryman's Touchstone* as well as poems he had written for the Headstrong Club. He also left with a philosophy—that the law could secure people's rights, but only if people controlled the law. Wealth drove poverty and corruption, separating the people from their power. Ensuring that the people could control the law required defeating this problem. Turning already to themes of economic inequality, Paine's radicalism had already grown more thoroughgoing than that of his patron, Richmond—whose focus remained primarily on constitutional order. Yet between them—and with the help of the broader network of radicals with whom they had collaborated for the previous six years—they had set the terms of the political debate of the age.

In 1762, when Wilkes had begun publishing *The North Briton*, British politics turned around life at the royal court, as different factions of the Whig elite jockeyed there at levees and drawing rooms for power. Thanks to his long-running feud with the government, his economic distress, and the rise of Junius, though, the dynamic changed to mass political agitation, public exchanges in the press, and the rise of popular radicalism. Politics moved from closed debate in the Houses of Parliament into the newspapers, coffeehouses, and streets. Some small but tangible victories had been achieved—freedom to report on parliamentary argument; reform to the corrupt borough in Shoreham; toleration for Quaker voters. Perhaps the most surprising feature of the period was how aristocrats themselves—the Duke of Richmond first among them—had begun to play a role in the radical project of reform. Bringing Enlightenment philosophy to bear, alongside thinkers from Burke to Burgh to Price to Paine, Richmond and his allies sparked a debate in Britain about the rights of man. Drawing heavily on Montesquieu, they taught the public about separation of powers and fired an ambition for limits on the power of the Crown and a House of Commons that authentically represented the people. As grievances accumulated—about economic immiseration, taxes, and the suppression of dissent—so too far grander peaks of reform began to come into view. Reform to Parliament, elections, and the franchise were now on the table, as well as a substantial broadening of press freedom. By October 1774, when Paine sailed for America, the stage was set for the American Revolution, and for modernization of the British monarchy.

PART III

SPREADING REVOLUTION

1774–1780

Chapter

9

ROMANCE AND A BRIEF RESPITE FROM RADICALISM

Proper *dans toutes les formes.*

—SARAH LENNOX, TO HER FRIEND SUSAN ON HER BROTHER'S LOVE AFFAIR WITH MADAME DE CAMBIS

AS THOMAS PAINE SAILED ACROSS THE ATLANTIC IN THE *London Packet* in the autumn of 1774, seriously ill with what was probably typhus, Britain and America were already on a collision course toward war. When Paine was carried off the *Packet* and into Philadelphia on a stretcher, a Continental Congress was meeting in Philadelphia, discussing what might be done to limit the prerogatives of Crown and Parliament and forge the cause of Massachusetts into the Common Cause of all. On April 19, 1775, less than six months later, British soldiers disembarked on the marshy northern bank of the Charles River well before dawn, and began their march toward Lexington and Concord.

By the time of what Longfellow later called "the shot heard round the world," Richmond was once again strenuously engaged in the cause of liberty—valiantly seeking to force a change of course from the British government to avoid the impending conflict. He rejoined the lists in 1774 as the government tried to pass what Britain called the Coercive Acts and what the Americans dubbed the Intolerable Acts. These included the Boston Port Act, to close the harbor and essentially blockade colonial trade; the Massachusetts Government Act, which revoked the colonial charter and decimated most forms of self-government in the colony; the Administration of Justice Act, which said that British soldiers accused of wrongdoing could be tried outside of Massachusetts; and the Quartering

Act, which required the Massachusetts government to house British soldiers in public buildings and, in cases of last resort, private homes. All were a response to the the events of the previous December 16, 1773, when the Sons of Liberty dumped three shiploads of East India Company tea into Boston harbor to protest Britain's enforcement of the company's monopoly.

Seeking first to fend off war, and then to end it, Richmond would, in the six years from 1774 to 1780, offer a novel strategy to reconcile British domestic liberty with empire, and simultaneously guarantee liberty for British subjects throughout the empire. Its centerpiece would be an argument for universal manhood suffrage, which he proposed in Parliament for the first time in history in June 1780.

War can often freeze domestic politics in place, locking in institutions and structures of power. In the case of the impending major conflict against colonial militias whose members had mustered under the banner of British law and liberties, radical energies at home in Britain gained new fuel from the revolution across the ocean. Right from the outset of war, Richmond argued for radical transformation as the only way to save British liberty. He also did this publicly. His use of masks and shadows was behind him.

Yet the Richmond who rejoined the lists in 1774 was not the Richmond of the previous decade. He had spent much of the 1760s attached to the royal court, or gravitating around it in one way or another, despite by the end of the decade his fierce opposition to the direction of government and Crown. He had helped bring down a ministry, yes, but at the same time the King had utterly bested him in the domain of cultural power. His positive victories had been few. He was now almost completely detached from the establishment.

When the Junius letters ended, in January 1772, Richmond had a midlife crisis. Aged thirty-six, he was at the midpoint of his life, though he could not have known, or even expected, that he would live to seventy-one. His father had died at forty-nine, so he must have had genuine uncertainty about how much time remained to him. Before Richmond would again be ready to advocate for a new vision of British constitutionalism, he would have to recompose his life. This was Richmond's work in the years immediately following 1772.

AFTER THE JUNIUS CHAPTER closed, Richmond remained a radical hero. In November 1772 Richard Price, a Welsh moral and political philosopher and dissenting minister, who was part of the Honest Whigs alongside Franklin, sent Richmond a copy of his pamphlet, *Observations on Reversionary Payments*. The book delves into mathematical methods for calculating the value of annuities and life insurance policies, helping to lay the groundwork for modern actuarial science, financial risk management, and policymaking in support of human progress. Price was also a prominent advocate for democratic principles and supported both the American and later the French revolution. Price's *Observations*, too, is still housed in the Duke's library and, as with *The Juryman's Touchstone*, it has an inscription: "Dr. Price presents his compliments to the Duke of Richmond and hopes he does not take an unwarrantable liberty in begging the honor of his Grace's acceptance of this Treatise as a small testimony of his respect and gratitude. Newington Green, Nov. 30th, 1772."

Richmond's closest collaborators, though, were directly encouraging him to reorganize his life. Recognizing the breadth of Richmond's efforts over the previous decade, Edmund Burke advised him to concentrate his energies on a single principal object. He exhorted him in the language of Richmond's beloved visual arts: "Though it is right to have reserves of employment, still some one object must be kept principal; greatly and eminently so; and the other masses and figures must preserve their due subordination, to make out the grand composition of an important life."

Richmond seemed at first to take this advice. Circumstances conspired to make it easy. The fall of 1772 brought something of a lull in the conflict with the colonies. Most of the Townshend duties had been repealed, the trials of the soldiers who had perpetrated the Boston Massacre proceeded without incident, and there was no major American legislation that year. Empire's attention lay elsewhere, and in fact, the East India Company was entering into a period of financial crisis. The government was seeking to take over control of the company from shareholders. King George III, now thirty-four and grown more comfortable in his authority, made this theme the top priority when he opened Parliament on November 17, 1772. For Richmond, the incredible wealth and imperialistic power accruing to a single corporation were not the worry, though they might have been. The Americans, after all, strenuously objected to how the British government was working to enforce the East India Company's monopoly over tea, to the detriment of the colonies' many small-scale traders. (Smuggled tea was much cheaper than East India Company tea.) Richmond was more anxious about the efforts of the Crown to override the chartered rights of the private citizens who were company shareholders. For him, the fight over the East India Company was an extension of the fight over seating Wilkes, voting rights, and the rights of jurors. He was nearly alone, politically in London, in seeing the rights of the East India Company shareholders as on level with those other fundamental rights. Focusing on this single issue, he used his usual methods: His associates wrote for the papers; and he worked to organize networks of activists, this time the shareholders of the company.

RICHMOND'S POLITICAL AND INTELLECTUAL network shifted alongside his change of focus. He parted ways with Philip Francis, with whom he disagreed about the best policy for the East India Company. Francis was put out when Richmond refused to accept his edits on a political memo. Francis was also more generally frustrated that he wasn't benefiting from his long-cultivated connections to Whig politicians. They were ineffective. He jabbed at "the Triumphs or Amusements of a Party that had almost all the Wit, and Popularity, and Abilities in the Kingdom" but that "never could carry a question in either House of Parliament." He despaired of all the time he had invested in them: "I saw plainly that my Connections would never lead me to any solid Advantage." Like Paine, Francis had also been dismissed from his public sector job, a clerkship at the War Office, toward the conclusion of the Junius letter-writing project. Now he changed face, embraced government policy and, in 1774, departed England for India, as a government man, accepting appointment as a member of the newly constituted Supreme Council of Bengal. He would remain abroad for a decade.

Also in 1774, another of Richmond's associates, Stephen Popham, a Wilkes supporter and lawyer for the extended Richmond and Lennox clan, was in personal and financial difficulties. We know less about him but, on May 5, in the House of Lords, Richmond presented a divorce bill "to dissolve the Marriage of *Stephen Popham* Gentleman, with *Ann Yate Whiteside* his now Wife, and to enable him to marry again." Popham too headed to India in 1774 to try to recover his fortunes. Richmond's activist circle was finding different reasons to shed obligations and leave the country.

In place of them Richmond grew closer to James Adair, his earliest pamphleteer and the lawyer who had supported Wilkes and Woodfall. The two men worked together on behalf of the East India Company against the efforts of the government to assert more direct control. This time Richmond did not pursue his political goals through Parliament—a sign of his greater distance and isolation from governmental power centers. While he wasn't completely absent from the halls of Westminster, his participation was episodic. He attended when matters relating to the East India Company were on the agenda but otherwise advocated outside of Parliament, including rousing his social network to buy shares in the company, as a route to controlling its board of directors. While Richmond's specific cause may now have been the East India Company, his underlying motivation was, as ever, a sense of the fragility of the British constitution. He lamented to Rockingham that their party had failed to destroy "that System of Government which has prevail'd amongst us constantly during this Reign" of George III. He resented what he considered George's autocratic control, governance "by his own Power and weight of His Influence" instead of governance through leading politicians, who are always "obliged to consult the Good of the People and court them as deriving their power from them." He described this as a conflict between "two Systems," one based on the King's personalism, and the other based on popular sovereignty. George's system, he wrote, "evidently tends to despotism."

THE DOWNSHIFT OF POLITICAL effort seems to have been good for Richmond's health. He had never been much of a drinker, in contrast to many of his aristocratic peers, but he seemed to suffer nonetheless from stomach ailments. When his younger sister, Louisa, returned to Goodwood on Sunday, January 17, 1773, for a visit of a few weeks, she reported in a letter to Emily that their brother's "nerves" were better, despite his still being susceptible to fainting fits and "over-fatigued" if he went out hunting. No longer consumed by politics, he had time to be more attentive to family. Louisa paid him lengthy visits, the first time brother and sister really came to know each other since their mother's death had parted them in 1751, at the ages of sixteen and seven and a half respectively. Louisa discovered him to be "always the kindest, dear creature that can be." She was struck by how insistently he asked for news about all their family in Ireland.

To all appearances, the Duke had accepted a more focused life at a comfortable remove from London and St. James's Palace, and with more time at Goodwood in Sussex. Nor was his focus on the East India

Company matter especially demanding. Also America was momentarily quieter. While committees of correspondence had formed in the American colonies, the acts of resistance of 1769 through 1771 settled into background murmurings through 1772 and much of 1773.

Richmond turned some of his unspent energy to sustaining his estates, traveling, and supporting his heirs. He hired the rising architectural luminary James Wyatt to add a wing to Goodwood as well as a greenhouse for orange and other fruit trees. He imported moose from Canada to explore anatomy and breeding. He had the large library redecorated, and its cabinets painted with images of antique vases from prints in books by Sir William Hamilton (not the same William Hamilton as "Single Speech Hamilton"). In 1773, he had a yacht built called *The Falcon*. For the first time he was able to go back and forth to France at his pleasure, or to sail houseguests down from London to Goodwood along the coast. Yachting captivated him enough for him to acquire a two-hundred-acre coastal farm at Itchenor, about a dozen miles from Goodwood. There he docked not only *The Falcon* but also a cargo sloop named *The Goodwood* and a barge. At Itchenor, he built a second set of magnificent stables and a riding school. His racehorses were exercised in the sea.

RICHMOND'S PERSONAL RETREAT WAS no mere vacation idyll. It was also a punitive, political exile from royal favor, a fact brought home periodically by George III. In an unprecedented move, the King left the environs of London and Windsor for the first time in his life from June 22 to 27, 1773. He traveled to Portsmouth, in the county of Hampshire, just over the border from Sussex, to conduct a review of naval vessels there. The naval base was just twenty-five miles from Goodwood. The weather was fine and everywhere the King went, he was greeted by enthusiastic, and surprised, subjects. Soldiers had to hold back massive crowds, and to at least one spectator, the King appeared "tall and full of dignity, his countenance florid and good-natured." The visit was considered a triumph by the court.

Richmond was obliged to attend the royal visit, but "the factious Duke of Richmond . . . was not invited to dine with the King as you may imagine," reported Lady Mary Coke, one of London's society gossips. She added, "I hope he [the Duke] will on every occasion receive marks of his displeasure which he well deserves." Richmond's vigorous opposition was not forgiven by the establishment. Just days before the visit to Portsmouth, the King had written scathingly to the prime minister, Lord North, about Richmond's East India Company politicking, saying that the Duke's machinations "showed blackness if it wanted any elucidation and that his whole conduct is dictated by malevolence." While George had written bitterly, and unfairly, about Richmond for years, this remark was perhaps the nadir.

THE FALCON SEEMS TO have encouraged Richmond to engage more frequently with France, and he developed increasing social connections with a network of French aristocrats. These included Armand Louis de Gontaut, duc de Lauzun; one of Lauzun's many mistresses, Louise Françoise Gabrielle d'Alsace-Hénin-Liétard, princesse de Chimay, whose married name was Madame de Cambis; and Madame du Deffand, who ran one of the most prominent social salons in Paris. The duc de Lauzun was rumored to be the illegitimate son of the French statesman the duc de Choiseul, with whom Richmond had gone toe-to-toe during his stint as ambassador to France. Madame de Cambis had a brother who had also fought, like Richmond, at Minden; her parents had visited Goodwood for a ball decades earlier. All were people whom Richmond and his duchess would have met in Paris in 1766 and 1767. Their connections had probably continued in the interim. When Sarah spent time in Paris in 1767 some months before she fell for William Gordon, the duc de Lauzun had paid her court, and had even followed her back to England, staying with her at her home in Barton, while Bunbury was away, just as Gordon later did.

By 1774 the duc de Lauzun's mistress, Madame de Cambis, was understood to be in love with Richmond. The Duchess of Richmond's mother, Lady Ailesbury, reported from a Paris visit to see the Duke and Duchess: "Madame de Cambis is our intimate acquaintance, and we seldom pass a day without seeing her. She is uncommonly sensible and lively, and sings 'Sans dépit et sans légèreté' charmingly." The duc de Lauzun may well have blessed the budding relationship. During this period, Richmond engaged the Irish painter James Barry, an Irish republican sympathizer who specialized in grand historically themed paintings, to paint *Antiochus and Stratonice* for him, a tale of lovesick Antiochus I, King of Syria, whose beloved, Stratonice, is married to another man, yet the first husband releases her so that she can marry Antiochus.

Richmond and Mary were still childless. Though they had been besotted with each other early in their relationship and would share a strong mutual affection until the Duchess's death in 1796, the Duke began to take lovers for the first time. Such liaisons probably started in the summer of 1773, with a young local woman, a commoner, from nearby Chichester, "a little dab of a miss 20 years younger than himself," as his sister Sarah put it. This first dalliance was embarrassing to the family. The subsequent relationship with Madame de Cambis, "a fine lady" and aristocratic peer, was much preferred. While Sarah had not approved of the Chichester liaison, she thought Madame de Cambis "very pleasing, & quite a proper age for him." The previous relationship was "very ridiculous," but this one was "quite proper dans toutes les formes," or appropriate in every dimension.

French society knew about the relationship between Richmond and Madame de Cambis, and there was nothing unusual in Richmond's behavior among aristocrats in Paris. This was the era of the erotic novel, *Les Liaisons dangereuses*, after all, a copy of which Richmond owned. While social mores were not as loose in London as Paris, the Duke of Grafton, his political rival, had sixteen illegitimate children. If anything, Richmond was more restrained than most, though not as restrained as George III, whose strict purity of behavior began a slow transition in English royal mores. Those members of British society who found their way to France guessed at Richmond's liaison. The great historian Edward Gibbon observed Richmond in Paris one summer when Mary had not traveled with him. Gibbon and Richmond dined together almost every evening at the home of Madame du Deffand. Madame de Cambis was often present. Gibbon wrote to a friend, "I am afraid poor Mary is entirely forgot."

Mary tolerated Richmond's relationships, though. She had no doubts about her primacy of place in Richmond's heart, her status as his "first object." What mattered to her was that his affairs be with women of appropriate social standing. Louisa discussed Mary's attitude with her sister Emily: "As to my brother's flirting, she don't mind it one bit, provided 'tis with what she reckons creditable and genteel." Jealousy did not factor in for Mary, just avoidance of "anything frippery or vulgar." Louisa was glad that her brother had the chance to divert himself because, as she wrote to Emily, "poor soul, . . . his spirits often want a little amusement." The Duchess's heart was so broad, open, and loving that in the same period (probably in 1774) she was able to incorporate into their household "a poor little girl," named Kitty, about whom "there was a mystery where she came from." Richmond confessed "that it was *his* child." Scholars think this may have been a daughter born from Richmond's young lover in Chichester. In the eighteenth century, illegitimate children of wealthy aristocrats were often folded into families as "wards" or "cousins." Louisa reports that her brother and the Duchess "were kind" to the child, and downcast when she died of illness in 1776. The Duke's French friends reported that the Duke was "fort affligé," meaning grief-stricken.

DURING THESE YEARS, RICHMOND was not the only member of the extended clan to experiment with new domestic arrangements. His sister Emily, Duchess of Leinster, also surprised her family. The roots of her own adventure lay a decade earlier. When Richmond and his brother George had gone to Paris in 1765, they had been initially supported administratively by the Scottish empiricist philosopher David Hume, who had served as secretary to the previous ambassador. That year the philosopher Jean-Jacques Rousseau was facing persecution and expulsion from Switzerland for his critiques of institutional religion. He needed a refuge. Hume wrote to invite him to England. Since the visit was official and Rousseau ultimately received a pension from the King, Hume must have made this offer with the assent of the Duke of Richmond in his official capacity as ambassador. In December 1766 *The Public Advertiser* reported that Hume even secured a retreat for Rousseau "in the Territory belonging to the Duke of Richmond." Although Rousseau seems not to have taken up that offer, he accepted the broader invitation to England and arrived in Paris in December to connect with Hume and prepare to cross the Channel. Rousseau was warmly greeted in Paris, in dramatic contrast to the dangers he had faced in Switzerland, including the threat of stoning by a hostile mob. Then, on January 4, with his large mountain dog Sultan and escorted by David Hume, Rousseau departed Paris for London. Emily knew of her brothers' close connection to Rousseau and asked them to convey to the philosophe an invitation to come to Ireland to take a role as tutor to her children. She wished to raise her growing brood—eventually twenty-two children—in accord with the naturalistic principles of Rousseau's *Émile*.

Rousseau never replied to her invitation, however, and Emily settled instead on hiring William Ogilvie, a highly intelligent Scotsman of obscure genealogy. So began a happy association and an experiment in modern education, radical politics, and romance. In November 1773, Emily's husband, the Duke of Leinster, died. Emily and Ogilvie's affair had till then been cloaked by the vast number of children in her household. (The last child recognized by the Duke was probably in fact Ogilvie's.) After the death of her husband, Emily had no cover left. She had the choice of abandoning her lover and her children's tutor or marrying for love, albeit well below her station. Emily chose Ogilvie, becoming the third Lennox sister to elope. Through a series of complicated maneuvers, white lies, and social diplomacy, she managed to depart Ireland with considerable property, effect a legitimate marriage, and establish herself anew in France with Ogilvie. They married in October 1774, with only one daughter and a serving woman as witness.

While Richmond had initially been hard on Sarah for her elopement with William Gordon, he came around much faster for Emily, perhaps because of her deftness or because of his affinity for Ogilvie, whose politics chimed with his and whom he adopted into his set of "particular friends." For a summer, Emily and Ogilvie traveled through France from one country inn to another, with most of her large brood of children, frantically trying to determine where they could establish a life in unconventional circumstances, until Richmond opened the chateau at Aubigny to them, and the newlyweds made it their home. Thirty years earlier, Emily had walked her older sister Caroline to the cupola by the Horse Guards, the ceremonial transition between courtly and governmental spaces, when Caroline had put aside her family's connections to the royal Hanoverian court and eloped with Henry Fox. Now, Emily had taken a similar fateful step, abandoning her role as Dowager Duchess of Leinster, the foremost peerage in Ireland, to tie herself to an unknown Scotsman with little property.

Caroline, though, was not there to accompany her sister. The sisters had recently reconciled after a bitter estrangement following Sarah's elopement. Emily's now deceased first husband had blamed Caroline for Sarah's fall from grace, and his passing opened space for them to reunite, which they did by way of correspondence. Then, in late July, Caroline had died, succumbing to an unidentified illness that had left her pain-ridden for many months. The first of the siblings to die in adulthood, Caroline had followed her husband, Henry Fox, to the grave after only twenty-three days of widowhood.

Now the only sibling who still had sturdy connections to the establishment was Louisa, whose husband Thomas Conolly, the wealthiest man in Ireland, was a leading Irish politician. Their parents' long service to the Hanoverians was now but a faint and fading memory. The whole family of this generation had chosen an independent path. Richmond and his household at Goodwood now replaced St James's Palace and Caroline and Henry's Holland House at the center of the family's life.

IN FAMILY AS IN POLITICS, the sense that one era was passing into the next had clearly begun to press itself on Richmond. The safe expectations of his own father for the continuation of a Whig aristocracy with assured social and political ascendancy no longer held. With ongoing rumblings of imperial conflict in the background, Richmond tackled the question of his own heir. Without legitimate children of his own, he would pass his ducal title on to the firstborn son of his brother George, named like himself, Charles Lennox.

Beginning in 1774, the Duke started to assume responsibility for ten-year-old Charles Lennox's education. Charles's parents, George and Louisa, kept to themselves, except for inviting George's military colleagues into their Sussex home in Stoke, about two miles from Goodwood. Despite their position in one of the great families of England, they kept their daughters out of society. Other relatives in the extended clan had to pluck the girls from Stoke's tight embrace for dancing lessons and to provide them opportunities to find husbands. Richmond did the same for his nephew. He hired a tutor for him and picked up young Charles's expenses for clothing and other amenities. He pulled other nephews, too, under his educative gaze. He enrolled Emily's son, Lord Edward, in his Sussex militia, so that he could acquire military training under his watchful eye, and also placed Edward's brother, Lord Henry, under the supervision of the family tutor.

During these years, Richmond sought to fill his home with children. His father had adored children, and the same passion now came alive in him. His siblings all described him as having a love of children, and this newfound focus endured even as Richmond returned to deep political involvement over the American Revolution. In the summer of 1778, when the widow of another nephew, Stephen Holland, passed away leaving young children, Richmond proposed to take the boy into his household. Death was so common in the age that orphans were frequently adopted by distant relatives. Sarah reported on this particular case to her friend Susan, explaining that her brother was "excessively fond of children & education." Sarah reckoned, though, that the extended family was unlikely to settle on Richmond as a guardian because of his political views: "My brother is as earnest to have the boy, but I suppose they won't trust him to a *rebellious* man."

There had been another addition to the household earlier that year. This time the child came from France. Her name was Henriette le Clerc. Louisa had traveled to Paris in March 1778 to see Emily and to meet Madame de Cambis. On April 6, when she set sail from Dieppe on the return journey, she brought a young girl with her. She explained in a letter to Emily: "We have had most heavenly weather and our journey went off vastly well, *all [but] the* poor little French girl, who 'spued' all the way; but it is so miserable at having left its friends, as is quite terrible; it said so many moving things and looked so meek that it set us all a-crying; but we have bought it playthings, and it is growing more used to us."

Henriette was born on October 28, 1773. The Duke and Duchess sometimes said they were looking after her until her father came for her. Sometimes Henriette was described as "Captain Jones' little girl," as though Richmond's former military comrade and long-serving aide were her father. This was clearly one of those fictions developed to cover the parentage of the illegitimate children of aristocrats, and the family generally came to believe that Henriette was Richmond's daughter by Madame de Cambis. Henriette's portrait was hung amid family portraits in the private quarters of the estate.

Yet Henriette was not Richmond's natural daughter, if the birthdate recorded on her tombstone is accurate. Richmond was both busy in London and ill in late January and early February of 1773, when Henriette would have been conceived. Nor did Madame de Cambis travel to England during these years. In the period of 1772 and 1773, she seems to have been involved with both the duc de Lauzun and with the chevalier Charles de Durfort. (There is some possibility that the name "chevalier Durfort" in letters was actually a cover for Lauzun.) Most likely, Henriette was the child of the duc de Lauzun, and Richmond, by now Madame's primary romantic companion, adopted her as a favor to her father and also to her mother, his own mistress. In 1778, France had recently entered the American War, and Lauzun had been called to active duty. In March 1778, he was assigned to form and head a legion, and it would eventually play a critical role in defeating Cornwallis. Louisa, who escorted the child to England, certainly understood herself to be acting on behalf of Lauzun (whose title had now shifted to Maréchal Biron because of inheritance). After the trip with Henriette, she wrote to Emily asking her to thank Biron for having made the journey "so easy and all *right* for me." He must have provided support and assistance, perhaps financial. Louisa also asked Emily to thank Madame de Cambis for the instructions she had sent for the journey. Lastly, she asked Emily to pass on to Biron a letter about the journey, as Madame de Cambis had requested.

The commissioned painting of *Antiochus and Stratonice* suggests a negotiated transfer of Madame de Cambis from one lover to another. Perhaps the adoption of Henriette was a part of that arrangement—perhaps recompense for a sexual betrayal, or perhaps a favor from one supporter of the American cause to another whose future, as he headed to war, was obscure. Henriette was a lively, intelligent child who charmed everyone, and took easily and well to Richmond's teacherly habits. They developed a pattern of working side by side in his study, she at her lessons, he at his political business. She became fully a part of the family and was educated and treated in many ways like the daughter he did not have. With her arrival, Richmond's personal universe was complete.

RICHMOND'S ROMANCE WITH MADAME de Cambis and his newfound place at the center of his extended family gave him new grounding. Rich intimate relationships and the calm pleasures of an increasingly beautified estate restored his energies. As Thomas Paine was separating from his wife and preparing to emigrate from the land of his birth, and Richmond's other "particular friends" were also departing for the outer reaches of the empire, the Duke seems to have attempted to put his radical politics behind him. He let his friends know that he was looking for new intellectual companionship, writing to Edmund Burke for recommendation of someone to help him "renew his acquaintance with the Classicks." He was also in the market for a tutor for his nephew, Charles Lennox.

Burke recommended a twenty-three-year-old named Walker King, who had recently graduated from Corpus Christi College, Oxford. Walker King eventually became a distinguished clergyman, lifelong friend to Burke, and editor of Burke's late works. In 1774, though, he was just another talented young man looking for good employment. When Burke passed on this job opening to King, he wrote a very cautious recommendation: "Such an acquaintance might lead to a further, a more serious, and a more useful connexion. It may also end in nothing, or worse than nothing."

Fairly quickly, though, Burke thought better of it and started to steer Walker King away from Richmond. Over the summer, Burke wrote three letters advising the young academic to avoid permanent employment with the Duke, cautioning him about Richmond's "singular opinions" and adding that the mistakes of wealthy men are dangerous "because they have means of supporting them so as to deceive others, and themselves into the Bargain." By the autumn he was adamant. The Duke of Richmond might be a considerate person, but he had the flaws of those with guaranteed wealth and standing. They "never feel thoroughly how much the fortune of a young man circumstanced" as Walker King was, without such financial or social resources, "depends upon every breath of rumour or every light construction" given to their affairs. Something had happened to Burke to make him wary of Richmond, or of recommending a post in his household to King.

What changed between the spring and the fall of 1774 was that Richmond had changed course and decided to re-engage more actively in Opposition activity in Parliament. Burke, it seems, was beginning to have doubts about Richmond's brand of politics and probably had no desire to go through again the kind of denials he had considered necessary to distance himself from the Junius project.

WHAT BROUGHT RICHMOND BACK to frontline politics was the now undeniable prospect of armed conflict with America. Part of the government's effort to stabilize the finances of the East India Company had involved giving the company permission to sell their tea directly to the colonies at a discount. The government had assumed the Americans would welcome cheap tea, which the Tea Act of June 1773 rendered more affordable than smugglers' offerings. Instead, they resented the monopolistic undercutting of their tradesmen, who were also importing, illegally, from Dutch, French, and Portuguese sources. Meetings of thousands of townsfolk voiced their outrage, assemblies so large they outgrew the space where the community normally gathered to deliberate. Then, on December 16, the Sons of Liberty dressed up as Mohawk tribesmen, stormed three ships, and dumped 340 cases of tea overboard. The Native costume was more than a disguise; it represented an identification with North America and its liberties, a rupture with British patriotism. The Sons of Liberty then followed this up by tarring and feathering the British customs comptroller for the second time. This news arrived in London a month later. A few days afterward, *The London Chronicle* reprinted a celebratory story that had run in *The Boston Gazette* about the "resolute men" who had sunk the tea in under four hours, without otherwise harming the ships or property, leaving the masters and owners of the ships "well pleased," while the city fêted "the happy event."

The times required serious people to engage seriously—too much was at stake for the future of Britain, for the future of liberty. Newly fortified by love and family, Richmond returned to parliamentary debate in March 1774 and, by May, was once again injecting arguments from his radical networks into the debates. Soon he would become the leading advocate of the American cause in the House of Lords and be well on his way to becoming the foremost advocate for radical reform in Britain. Each step in the progress of his ideas and arguments brought Britain closer, first, to the brink of a civil revolution of its own, and then to its transformation into a modern, constitutional monarchy.

Chapter

10

FRIEND OF AMERICA, FRIEND OF REFORM

1773–1776

All the real friends of England and of America, the true Whigs should come to a good understanding, and heartily unite to save the Nation. God knows if our utmost efforts can succeed; but I am sure that nothing less than such united efforts can have any chance.

—RICHMOND TO CHATHAM, FEBRUARY 1, 1775

FROM THE BOSTON TEA PARTY IN 1773 TO THE DECLARATION of Independence in 1776, when war was formally engaged, dark clouds of conflict piled up ominously, forming the hard line of a storm front on the horizon. Fear struck at the hearts of letter-writers on both sides of the Atlantic. The political questions that Richmond had been involved in on and off for the preceding two years—the case of the excise officers, the rights of the shareholders of the East India Company—paled in importance in comparison to the looming conflict with America.

In early 1774, Britain made its last effort to tamp down rebellion and secure its authority in North America through law—via the blunt, repressive force of the Coercive Acts. These would be the primary subject of parliamentary debate through the spring. As Richmond battled to avert intensifying conflict and pursue reconciliation with the Americans, he tried to solve the constitutional puzzles that seemed to make a break inevitable.

The question of how to solve the puzzle of the inclusion of the Americans in the British system of government forced intellectually serious people like Richmond to think hard about British sovereignty and the British constitutional order, and also about representation—what it was, how it should work, what role it should play in a whole system of governance. The pressure produced some new, radical ideas—for instance, that every colonial territory should have its own, fully representative legislature. The very fact that it was unclear whether Parliament or the King had sovereignty over America, and equally unclear how the Americans could or should be represented within the structure of British government, motivated Richmond to rethink representation in Britain itself. For Richmond, debating for the Opposition was not merely about winning power for his own party. It was also a chance to try to put his country, and its possessions, on a sound constitutional footing by advancing some novel ideas for how the government should be organized.

For this reason he spoke and spoke and spoke, pushing motions and forcing votes, even when the outcome of his effort would be certain defeat. He sought to familiarize some new ideas about the power of the government and Crown and the need for the independence of Parliament. He was constantly trying to make his countrymen clarify their thinking about the political structure they were creating, almost inadvertently, with every choice they made. Richmond saw, perhaps more clearly than anyone, that conflict with America was not simply a public order problem to solve but a wide-ranging constitutional crisis in the making. But Richmond's farsightedness, and the radical ideas of renewal that it provoked in him, put him at increasing distance from his former political allies. His correspondence with Burke and Rockingham trailed off in the years after the outbreak of the American Revolution.

As the government, and his friends, rejected his proposals, he grew ever more irate. The Crown and ministry took increasingly aggressive actions against the colonies, which Richmond called tyranny as early as 1775. Colonists had used the term to describe encroachments on their legislative prerogatives sporadically since the 1730s, and with increasing regularity since 1764. Calling the king himself a tyrant was newer, more radical. Paine followed Richmond to that rhetorical extreme in *Common Sense* in early 1776.

Richmond's radicalism is important for understanding the unfolding revolutionary dynamics. When the Americans had objected to the Stamp Act, they blamed Parliament. Franklin had expressed respect for the sovereignty of the King but an unwillingness to be taxed by a London legislature. By the time the Americans declared independence, though, they had shifted their focus from Parliament to the Crown. It was the King from whom they were declaring independence, and their case for their radical action was the King's tyranny. "A Prince, whose character is thus marked by every act which may define a Tyrant, is unfit to be the ruler of a free people," their representatives agreed unanimously in the Declaration of Independence in July 1776. Their characterization of King George III as a tyrant was new in their rhetoric, and historians have long debated whether it was fair. The Americans weren't the first, though, to put this accusation at the center of politics. That charge had already issued forth prominently from the tongue of Richmond and pen of Paine—that is, from British politics. As war drew ever nearer, Richmond's radicalism burst fully into the open, costing him his closeness to Burke and Rockingham. He, much more than they, was worried that the King might turn tyrant. The years from 1774 to 1776 brought his worries to a fever pitch, and his rhetoric of tyranny to full flower.

LIEUTENANT GENERAL THOMAS GAGE, an amiable, square-jawed man whose younger brother the twelve-year-old Richmond had campaigned against in 1747, was commander in chief of the British forces in North America in December 1773. His base was Fort George, at the southern tip of New York City. Immediately after the Boston Tea Party, he set sail for London to visit the King. The messenger carrying news of the Tea Party arrived scarcely before him. When Gage landed, he went straight to court. At a meeting at St. James's Palace on February 4, the general exhorted the King to respond with vigor to the events in Boston. He asked for twenty thousand troops. The King should be a lion, not a lamb, he argued. He also counseled that the Americans would prove "meek" as long as the British government was resolute. By February 19 the cabinet agreed: Britain would offer the strongest possible response. Excessively confident, they rejected Gage's request for troops. Two fresh warships had already been dispatched and, thinking that enough, they ordered Gage back across the Atlantic. The ministry believed they could secure America by force of law backed by a small military deployment. After all, they were facing only ragtag country militias.

The government then drafted and brought to Parliament what it called, with surprising honesty, the Coercive Acts. These were the measures to blockade the harbor; replace elected members of the colonial legislature with members appointed by the Crown; move trials out of Massachusetts; and improve accommodations for British soldiers by commandeering empty buildings and outbuildings. The Americans blamed the King for these Intolerable Acts, as they called them. In fact, they were mainly the doing of the prime minister, Lord North, though in North's own mind he was always deferring to the King.

Parliament opened its 1773–74 session late, not until January. Richmond himself rejoined only in March. Known by now as one of the most, if not the most, extreme radicals in the House of Lords, he returned with force, attending eight sessions that month as Parliament debated the Boston Port Bill. He voted against it, as did Burke in the House of Commons. On March 7, Richmond's nephew, Charles James Fox, also spoke out against the bill in the House of Commons. An exceptionally charismatic, witty twenty-five-year-old, Fox lived a remarkably dissolute life—gambling himself into extensive debt, whoring himself into disease, and drinking and eating with abandon. His parents, Henry Fox, Lord Holland, and Richmond's sister Caroline, had famously indulged him, treating their exceptionally bright son as a little adult from childhood. In his early years, Fox had rocketed to leadership of the Radical Whigs, but he was at the time more ambitious than principled and soon abandoned his Whiggism for government posts. By speaking and voting against the Boston Port Bill, he was once again throwing his lot in with the Opposition and consequently giving up his government appointments. Radical Whiggism would be his political cause for the rest of his life. Even the French Revolution did not put him off it. Of all Richmond's nephews, Fox was the only one for whom he felt no warmth. He disdained Fox's lifestyle and found him unreliable. In 1774, though, they were partners in Opposition—*measures, not men.*

In May 1774 Richmond spoke against the Administration of Justice Act and drew on two pamphlets that can still be found in his library. First, he invoked a newly published anonymous pamphlet called "Considerations on the Measures Carrying On with respect to the British Colonies in North America." Scholars have recently identified this pamphlet as having been written by Thomas Paine, making it the third long essay he produced prior to his departure from England, and the final point of coordination between the two men. In the pamphlet, Paine extended Richmond's arguments about Canada from nearly ten years earlier—that

Britain did have the right to tax the colonies, including to impose internal taxes, but that doing so required establishing genuine representation through local legislatures.

Richmond also drew on a sermon preached by Jonathan Shipley, the bishop of St. Asaph, in 1773 in front of the Society for the Propagation of the Gospel in Foreign Parts, "as containing the soundest doctrines and best policy." Shipley advocated for reconciliation and a far more moderate policy than the government was pursuing. Paine republished his own pamphlet in America, and Shipley's sermon also gained significant attention there for its pro-American sentiments. Benjamin Franklin had reported on it to his friends and sent them copies, and the text of the sermon sold rapidly in America. In London, though, innovative constitutional theory did not gain the Opposition the votes needed to defeat the government. All the Coercive Acts passed easily.

The acts raised fundamental questions of liberty—basic rights to jury trials before peers, for instance—and struck at the heart of self-government, legal due process, and local autonomy, principles that many American colonists believed were essential to British liberty itself. As Richmond later wrote, "in every situation of life my warmest affection [for liberty] will ever make me show myself," and he did not take this defeat lying down. During the May 18 session of the House of Lords, he immediately initiated a second debate to record a protest against the bill, and was the first to sign on to it. The protest registered four arguments: (1) there was no evidence that prosecuted officers could not receive fair trial in Massachusetts; (2) the bill showed the powerlessness of Parliament to deal with American discontent, and was effectively an admission of its guilt and an acknowledgment that Parliament had become odious in the Americas; (3) the bill amounted to a concession of the impossibility of civil government in America, which meant the colonies could be maintained only with military force, which would ruin Britain; and (4) the bill was one of the many misguided experiments toward an introduction of "essential [meaning: fundamental] innovations into the government of the empire." Richmond worried that the bill would create a corps of officers immune to accountability, not to mention requiring the shipping of witnesses across the ocean, which was both unjust and impracticable.

Richmond brought all the passion and craft of Junius at his most persuasive to his rhetoric. A vigorous speaker for the Opposition, he did not hesitate to prolong debate, extend arguments, and refuse to accept defeat, even when the chances of winning a vote were nil. His purpose was to put points on the record and shift public opinion and understanding.

Louisa wrote to Emily, "I really think he is one of the first characters in the world." Burke, too, acknowledged Richmond's "splendid reputation." It may have burned brightest across the Atlantic. In September 1774, when Massachusetts lawyer and member of a colonial legislature John Adams traveled from Boston to Philadelphia alongside his cousin Sam Adams to attend the first Continental Congress, he wrote home to his wife Abigail to describe how brilliantly he had been fêted along the way. The best way of capturing "the studied and expensive Respect with which" he and the Adamses had been treated was to say that they had been accorded "demonstrations of respect worthy of Chatham and Richmond." When Sam and John reached Philadelphia for their first Continental Congress, the session kicked off with a grand dinner for five hundred guests and all the city's worthies. After the meal, thirty-four toasts were drunk. The first two were to the King and Queen; the fifth to the "perpetual union" of the colonies; the eighth that Britain might be just and America free; the twenty-fifth to the Duke of Richmond; and the thirty-first to Dr. Franklin. Richmond was recognized far and wide as America's friend.

AT THAT GALA DINNER in Philadelphia, the Americans also raised a glass to "no unconstitutional standing armies." Of course, they had one garrisoned on their shores, and it was growing with every passing month. As Richmond watched the conflict with the American colonies intensify, his energies for political combat were stoked. While Richmond continued his friendship with Burke and was generally allied with the Rockinghamites in Parliament, he now more often charted his own course. He also found himself newly close politically to William Petty Fitzmaurice, Earl of Shelburne, who had succeeded him as secretary of state in 1766. Despite that friction, the two men had shared a military and political education under James Wolfe and, hence, a deep bond and mutual respect.

For Richmond, in whom Wolfe had first imbued "liberal notions of every kind," the interest of politics lay not merely in philosophical puzzles about sovereignty, representation, and constitutionalism, but also in the practical concern of how to bring novel political ideas to life. He wanted to be a philosopher statesman, like Frederick the Great of Prussia. Questions of what justice, peace, and prosperity required were irresistible to him, but the steps to take to secure those ends engaged him too. He always found the former easier than the latter, though, and the story of his political life was of trying to close the wide gap between his philosophical certitude and practical results. As his sister Sarah said, he was given to "high-flown ideas of right, which are apt to soar above nature." He also soared ahead of others and so found himself constantly fighting a system of political operations not ready for his ideas.

In the fall of 1774, there was plenty of fodder for philosophical consideration. The colonies had established a Continental Congress, and King George had signed the Quebec Act, which undermined habeas corpus and trial by jury by partially returning French civil law to Canada's seventy thousand French speakers. While the Americans took the act as repressive for these features, it was in fact meant to accommodate the customary practices of the French. It placed the administration of the colony in the hands of a "governor-in-council," meaning a governor with an appointed advisory body but without an elected legislature. Finally, the act provided toleration to Catholics. For this reason, when the King rode to Parliament to sign the Quebec Act into Law, he was harassed by a gathering Wilkesite mob shouting "Remember Charles I! Remember James II!" The threat was barely veiled. James had been a Catholic; Charles had been married to a Catholic. Both were deposed, and the former, judicially murdered.

Richmond supported religious freedom and this particular provision, but he thought the rest of the Quebec Act had created an executive branch with unchecked power. Although the act had its roots in his own prior work on Canada, he disliked its new directions and went on to argue for its repeal. He criticized the government's reasoning as continuously defending new constitutional innovations by reference to some "immediate necessity," while ultimately producing, over time, through the repeated application of emergency measures, an "engine of oppression and tyranny" and "arbitrary power." As he put it, the "end of all civil regimen, is the happiness and prosperity of the governed . . . the best government is that which is best exercised," a phrase that John Adams would echo in 1776 in his *Thoughts on Government*. The Quebec Act, Richmond argued, supported neither the happiness nor the prosperity of the governed. The argument that the act established conditions for tyranny marked him as belonging to the most radical of the Whigs. The aspersions he cast on the government now went farther than even Junius had.

BURKE CLEARLY WORRIED ABOUT Richmond's escalating rhetoric, hence his warnings to Walker King. Yet politics is a tricky business, and Burke's worries did not keep him from asking Richmond for help with his own campaign for a seat in Parliament from Bristol in August 1774. Burke was in the recognizably uncomfortable position of a talented man who, despite his own personal merits, inevitably required the patronage of those born into privilege to secure his own success. They were the patrons; he, the protégé. Though Burke respected the Duke's intellectual gifts, his mind was richer and more supple than Richmond's. The combination of intellectual superiority and social inferiority that Burke felt resulted in his often seeming to attempt to manage the aristocrats with whom he corresponded, rather than simply exchanging personal confidences freely as equals do. He flattered, chided, and warned them so as to coax from them the actions he hoped they would take. Political distance was growing between Richmond and Burke, as both men seem to have recognized, and this time Richmond declined to help him.

Richmond offered a breezy explanation. He could no longer be bothered with the hard work of electioneering because he had lost confidence in the parliamentary process. "The more I live, the more I grow to think," he wrote, "that few things are worth making one's self enemies for. After all, we can do no good; and why should we toil and labour so much in vain?" He tried to separate the political from the personal and added, "I grow very sick of politics, but not one jot less affectionate to my friends; it is impossible to love or esteem you more than I do; so pray don't look upon this letter as any want of friendship for you." Richmond often expressed a frustration with politics in his letters, even as his actions made clear that he was as deeply entangled as ever.

Burke surely recognized the distance between word and deed with Richmond. He wrote back with obsequious encouragement to Richmond to stay in the fray. Richmond's "constitution of mind" required a noble pursuit, he cajoled. Richmond had already achieved "a very splendid reputation." If he was frustrated, he needed also to recognize that he held "a high rank in [the] country, which kings cannot take from [him]." He also had a fortune equal to his rank, "though not," and here Burke laid it on especially thick, "to the personal dignity of [his] mind." Then Burke reached for a simile, as he often did when he sought to chivvy Richmond along, this one blending the fawning and the resentful. "Your birth will not suffer you to be private. It requires as much struggle to put yourself into private life as to put me into public. Pardon a slight comparison, but it is as hard to sink a cork as to buoy up a lump of lead." Burke's pleading yielded no fruit, though. Richmond wasn't willing to help. Something of a breakup between them was now occurring. Of course, Richmond wasn't really done with politics; he just didn't want to get involved in Burke's election. Burke needn't have strained so hard to convince the Duke; he won without him.

DESPITE RICHMOND'S RESPONSE TO Burke, when the fall parliamentary session started on November 30, the Duke engaged with a new upsurge of intensity on the American question. George III opened Parliament with a speech focused on the latest rebellious acts in Massachusetts. The Coercive Acts had transformed protest into widespread resistance. Gage was now governor of the colony, but the colonists boycotted all royal officials, refusing to obey them. Militia and townspeople marched to courthouses across the provinces and forced royally appointed judges to resign, shutting down the entire British judicial system in the mainland colonies. They revived town meetings, banned under the Coercive Acts, and began selecting delegates for the formation of a new Massachusetts Provincial Congress, calling that the de facto government of their colony. Minutemen companies began to form, and towns began stockpiling arms, powder, and supplies in anticipation of armed conflict. The majority in the House of Lords wanted to support the government by condemning the violence in Massachusetts. The single most important question of the subsequent months was whether the unfolding violence in Massachusetts should be classified as a "rebellion," like the 1745 Jacobite rebellion led by Bonnie Prince Charlie. The King's speech called that question.

Richmond, in contrast, wanted to de-escalate the language of rebellion. After the King gave his speech, the government supporters in Parliament proposed an address of thanks to the sovereign. Richmond took the floor to object. He anticipated aggressive policies toward the colonies and made preemptive arguments against such maneuvers. He also tried to pull power back to the House of Lords by offering an amendment that "exhort[ed] the King to share all intelligence on developments in the Colonies, so that the Lords can act on the 'fullest information.'"

Once again, however, the Whig Opposition was divided. On December 19, Richmond hosted Burke and Rockingham for dinner in his grand mansion in Whitehall to settle on a course of action. But despite a hospitable table laden with delectables and fine wines, fractures were evident. Earlier that month, Burke had argued against a motion "to give the government full support in any action in America that it thought necessary," but the party's members were split on how aggressively to pursue that line. Against them, the King's friends offered strenuous arguments in support of the motion. As one conservative MP said: "I think the Americans are a rebellious and most ungrateful people, and I am for assuring the King that we will support him in such measures as will be effectual to reduce them." Rockingham was wavering on whether to continue to prosecute the aggressive line that both Richmond, in the Lords, and Burke, in the Commons, had laid out, having come for the moment into alliance again.

Richmond was not willing to accept or confirm the label "rebellion," which he realized would provide the King with justification for extreme measures. While George and his ministers knew that the Americans were buying military supplies—for instance, "300 barrels of gunpowder, 3 tons of lead, 40,000 flints and four brass fieldpieces," probably from the Dutch, through Rhode Island—this wasn't yet general knowledge. The question most members were debating was whether the Americans' practice of assembling and sending petitions, and even of forming a Continental Congress and the Massachusetts Provincial Congress, should be counted as rebellion. To be sure, there were acts of political violence against British officials, but did these rise to the level of concerted rebellion, as opposed to being scattered actions better dealt with by police action? Richmond thought not. Under the pressure of these debates, Rockingham, the party leader who would settle the party's direction, was paralyzed. The men gathered at dinner to resolve whether to hold the line that no rebellion yet existed. The arguments must have been heated, and they failed to achieve agreement. Afterward Burke spent a sleepless night. Waking exhausted in the morning, he wrote Rockingham a note cautioning him to endorse the position he and Richmond had staked out, lest the Marquess weaken himself politically.

No sooner, though, had the men ironed out this issue than Rockingham next found himself in conflict with Chatham. Chatham accused him not of over-conciliating the Americans but of not conciliating them enough. Taking Rockingham by surprise, Chatham rose in the House of Lords to propose amending the Declaratory Act. Passed in conjunction with the repeal of the Stamp Act, it declared that Parliament had the right to tax the colonies. Rockingham considered its passage while he was prime minister in the 1760s to be his greatest achievement, and he, like the King and many other British politicians, understood the Declaratory Act to be the cornerstone of British sovereignty over the colonies. Chatham had given him no warning of the intention to undo it. Mild-mannered though he was, Rockingham was irate.

Chatham's proposal was that Parliament's legislative authority outside of England should be limited to matters that related to "the whole dominion of the imperial crown of Great Britain," and to those that were "beyond the competency" of local officials. As he saw it, Parliament could regulate trade but could not tax the colonies. Rockingham, who still considered the Declaratory Act good policy, now vigorously sought to defend it from Chatham's assault. Instead of uniting to fend off the King's declaration that the Americans were in open rebellion, the Whigs fell upon each other.

There was yet one more line of division. Both Chatham and Rockingham agreed that the British Parliament could legislate for the Americans and that the Americans were therefore bound to see Parliament as their sovereign. They disagreed only on the extent of the authority of Parliament over the Americans—everything, including taxes, as Rockingham thought? Or trade only, as Chatham thought?

But Richmond had a third view. While he was convinced that America should remain part of the territories of the British sovereign, he was not sure that Parliament had a claim of sovereignty over the colonies. As would become clearer over time, he thought the Americans needed their own legislature, much as he objected to the Quebec Act's having left the Canadians without a legislature. The Americans should accept the King as their sovereign, but not Parliament as their representative body.

This view produced a further constitutional puzzle. The British king was understood to be "King-in-Parliament." That is, the monarch held sovereignty only by virtue of delegation from the Parliament. The idea that there might be a separation between the sovereignty of the King and that of Parliament over the colonies did not make immediate sense in relation to the British constitution as it was understood at the time.

By the middle of January, the members of the Opposition vehemently agreed that the constitution was in crisis but equally vehemently disagreed on the nature of that crisis. Nor could they unite around a remedy. Richmond wrote to Chatham to express both his frustration and his sense that the Opposition needed to come together. He decried "the desperate temerity of the Ministry," and poured out a heartfelt wish "that all the real friends of England and of America," should "heartily unite to save the Nation." Richmond won Chatham over at least, though not yet Rockingham. On February 1, Chatham put forward the Provisional Act for Settling the Troubles in America. This was an expansive bill, which incorporated Richmond's idea about legislatures in the colonies, and called for (1) the withdrawal of standing British armies in the colonies; (2) the promise not to tax subjects without common consent through the provincial assembly; and (3) the restoration of trial by jury in civil cases (instead of martial law). It was a good proposal, one that would have had a prospect of success with the Americans and laid the foundation for a structure much like the modern Commonwealth. It was, in short, a brilliant attempt to avert war. The King and his ministers were adamantly opposed.

The initial response from the government was to agree to make the bill available to members for reading, ostensibly until it had been given due consideration, but the attitudes of various ministers during the initial debate were very hostile and eventually the government rejected it out of hand. Benjamin Franklin, still serving as a colonial agent for several of the colonies, wrote to America disconsolately to report that Chatham's bill, despite being excellent and moved by able speakers, was treated as contemptuously by the government as "a Ballad offered by a drunken Porter." Members of Parliament hadn't even been given adequate time to read the bill, and it was rejected without due discussion despite Richmond's best efforts. This was the moment when war became inevitable.

A few days later, on February 7, the debate in the Lords at last turned formally to the question of an Address to the King upon the Disturbances in North America, and whether the disorders in Massachusetts should be classified as a "rebellion"—in which case very harsh military measures must be used to suppress them. Rockingham had finally come round, and he and Richmond argued vigorously against the premature declaration. Once again the pro-government position prevailed. The Americans were declared to be in a state of rebellion. Richmond passionately if futilely protested the outcome. War could no longer be held off.

THE POLITICAL BATTLES BROUGHT to the surface the different possible answers to a conceptual puzzle—the question of where power really lay in a constitution where sovereignty was assigned to the "King-in-Parliament." Did Parliament have true power? Or had power been transferred completely to the King? What was the place of the colonial Americans in the structure? Should their ultimate loyalty be to Parliament, or to the King? What of their own legislatures? How did these relate to the legislature in Britain? Did a "provincial assembly" owe obedience to the Parliament in Westminster or only to the Crown?

Richmond bought more books—twenty-five—and did more hard thinking in 1775 than in any other year of his life. Many of the new purchases were in French and were works of political philosophy and politics, including *Maximes du droit public françois*, and Bigot de Sainte-Croix's *Essai sur la liberté du commerce*. He also bought a book on royal economies; Burke's speech on American Taxation; *Account of the Proceedings of the British and Other Protestant Inhabitants to Quebec to Obtain a House of Assembly*; *Observations on the Prevailing Abuses in the British Army*; and records of the 1774 election outcomes in Chichester and Lewes. His selections reveal a coherent and highly intentional taste—rooted in Enlightenment political inquiry, liberal constitutionalism, and practical political engagement, with a strong concern for both British and continental political structures. They are the books of a reader attuned to questions of liberty, governance, trade, and institutional accountability.

Richmond also bought Voltaire's 1731 history of Charles XII of Sweden, not because it was an entertaining piece of general European history, but because in Sweden the current king, Gustav III, who would be assassinated in 1792, had recently carried off a coup against Parliament. To understand this event, Richmond acquired Georg Georgson Stahlberg's *A History of the*

Late Revolution in Sweden. . . . Containing, in three parts, the abuses, and the banishment, of liberty, in that kingdom. Stahlberg had dedicated his book to "lovers of liberty." Richmond was his target audience.

The 1772 Swedish coup was a bloodless revolution that ended parliamentary rule and restored significant monarchical powers. Frustrated by the inefficiencies and factionalism within the *Riksdag*, the Swedish parliament, Gustav III capitalized on public discontent and the military's support to seize control. In August, he declared a new constitution that curtailed the powers of the *Riksdag* and empowered the monarchy with greater authority over governance, military, and foreign policy. By appealing to nationalist sentiments and promising to restore order and stability, Gustav III managed to secure broad support, successfully shifting Sweden toward a more autocratic but unified government.

Richmond read Stahlberg's *History of the Late Revolution in Sweden* carefully, marking passages that described the original formation of the Swedish parliament as well as comparative material about Russia, with whose politics Sweden was entangled. He noted the passage describing how another Enlightenment autocrat, the Russian Czarina Catherine the Great, convoked representatives from each jurisdiction to consult them in forming new laws and how "by her charms and virtues" she grew popular. Here was a monarch who, like Gustav, had further consolidated power; this was Richmond's concern as he watched George III. Would George seek to imitate Gustav and Catherine?

He paid particularly close attention to part two of Stahlberg's book, on the affairs of Sweden before the coup, and how representation had been organized—crucial questions for anyone trying to imagine the possibility of universal manhood suffrage. He noted the description of how "representatives of the kingdom c[ame] from four estates, nobility, clergy, merchants, peasants." He marked a passage describing practices, where "the Representatives taken from their own Body attend the Diet at their own expense, and [are] allowed to vote by Proxy or Warrant." He also closely studied how the Swedes defined qualifications for service: for representatives from the merchant class, "the Representatives must have carried on a trade for seven years." Also, he noted their number: "The whole of the representatives of the merchants number around 350." He noted that representatives of the peasants or "4th Estate," were "elected among themselves" and could hire a "Secretary from amongst the Gentlemen but chosen by themselves."* In other words, illiteracy was not in Sweden considered a barrier to participation, a critical detail for making the idea of universal male suffrage plausible. He was also quite interested in the subdivision of the Fourth Estate, the peasants, into four further subcategories. These were crucial details for understanding what it would mean to include the poor in the operations of government. He also noted various aspects of how a separation of powers operated in Sweden. For instance, the "Senate appointed ambassadors but the King gave their credentials."

Richmond was haunted by the Swedish precedent and concerned that exactly the same thing was happening in Britain. The imperial structure was clearly putting pressure on the British system to consolidate power in the hands of the King and to assign sovereignty to the King in his own right. Would this, as in Sweden, lead to an actual abrogation of the rights of Parliament?

Richmond signaled the extent to which he was consumed by the need to think through the expanding political crisis when he engaged the rising artistic talent George Romney to paint a portrait of him. Unlike the portraits Richmond sat for in his youth—in a costume reminiscent of the era of Charles II, with his dogs, and in his military uniform—now Richmond sat in muted dress, reading at Goodwood, with Chichester Cathedral, the English Channel, and the Isle of Wight in the background. He is the epitome of the philosopher statesman, and in his somber and discreet clothes he looks like he would be more at one with the American colonists than the embroidered and bewigged dukes in the court of King George.

Richmond had several copies of this portrait made for his "particular friends." He sent one to James Adair, one to William Adair, and another to William Ogilvie, his sister's second husband—people who understood how assiduously he was working to bring philosophy into politics and sympathized with his thinking.

WHILE THE WHIGS WERE struggling to convert their frustration with the government and the King into effective action, the Americans were pressing ahead. The two hundred British troops that disembarked in

* The use of the idea of a "Fourth Estate" to designate the public press had not yet emerged. The concept of estates was still limited to socioeconomic classes at this time.

The Duke of Richmond is shown here in his favorite activity of the mid-1770s—reading philosophy—at his estate. (In several variants, the spire of Chichester Cathedral and the Isle of Wight are visible in the distance.)

BY PERMISSION OF THE TRUSTEES OF THE GOODWOOD COLLECTION.

Cambridge, well before dawn in the early morning hours of April 19, marched onward to Lexington. Riding ahead of them were Paul Revere and William Dawes to carry the warning of the regulars advance. Militia scrambled from the farmlands around Lexington, and by 4 a.m. about seventy-five armed men had assembled on the town green. An hour later, still before daybreak, the redcoats arrived. In the dark someone fired a shot. Then the regulars fired a volley and charged with bayonets. Eighteen militiamen went down, eight fatally. One British soldier fell. The militia scattered and, undaunted, the British continued to Concord as the sun rose behind them. Militias from surrounding towns converged on Concord and, turning the tables, beat the British back by day's end, while thousands of armed colonists harassed them all the way back to Boston.

The Continental Congress reconvened in Philadelphia in May 1775 to plan a collective response. They appointed George Washington as commander of a new force called the Continental Army. Then, on June 17, at the Battle of Bunker Hill, the British suffered what would be their greatest casualties in any single engagement of the war: 228 killed and 928 wounded, including 90 officers killed or wounded, out of 2,300 who took part in the battle. The Americans had 3,200 militiamen, of whom 160 were killed, 271 wounded, and 30 captured. This battle upended the expectations of the British that they would immediately overmatch the American troops. On July 2, George Washington arrived in Cambridge, Massachusetts, to assume command of the Continental Army, the existence of which removed any remaining question as to whether the Americans were in open rebellion. He established a fort at just the location on the north bank of the Charles where the British had disembarked three months earlier. News of the rout at Bunker Hill arrived in London on July 25.

Despite the opening of hostilities and formation of an army, over the summer, at the instigation of John Dickinson, author of *Letters from a Farmer in Pennsylvania* and a member of Continental Congress, the Americans made one last attempt at reconciliation by sending a new petition to the King. Called the Olive Branch Petition, this missive asked the King to dismiss all of his cabinet members and to repeal the Intolerable Acts, restoring the *status quo ante*. The petition broke from the previous practice by petitioning the Crown directly, rather than Parliament. The American situation involved extensive confusion, for all involved, about which body in Britain was the real source of authority and who was setting policy. The Americans had come to believe that it was the King.

The King, however, redirected responsibility and declared the Olive Branch Petition to be an unconstitutional request for him to overrule Parliament. After all, the laws to which the Americans were objecting had been passed by that body. They were not royal decrees. He was, he insisted, simply executing the will of Parliament. Since the Americans were now in open rebellion, any petition for reconciliation had to be considered moot. The "Privy Council published a proclamation in the King's name, saying the colonies were in 'open and avowed rebellion' and 'Traitorously preparing, ordering and levying war against us' so the King would use 'utmost endeavours to suppress such rebellion and to bring the traitors to justice.'"

For the Americans, and most of the Whigs, the King's claim to be executing the will of Parliament had become a farce. The view of the Whigs was that the direction of influence ran from King to Parliament. The King invested money in elections to secure followers in the House of Commons, as well as putting members of Parliament into "places," lucrative roles given out as patronage. As one scholar has recorded, "[i]n 1780, the government payroll contained around fifty government officials, thirty sinecurists, twenty-five court officials, sixty-five military and naval officers, eleven contractors and eleven holders of Secret Service Pensions." Of the 558 members of the House of Commons, the government could command loyalty from about two hundred. Rockingham, who owned the next largest faction, could claim a party of about eighty. This math explained, quite simply, why the Opposition almost never prevailed in Parliament: They were continually outspent by the King.

AS THE FALL PARLIAMENTARY session opened, the political mood was edging toward crisis. Sixty thousand people lined the streets when the King rode to the Palace of Westminster. The session turned bitter quickly. Rockingham declared the administration incompetent, and he attributed this incompetence to the government's unwillingness to take advice and direction from Parliament. Richmond attacked the failures of the administration on military strategy, making the case that America could not be subdued by force. Like Rockingham, his point was not just that the government and King were substantively wrong, but that their error flowed from their unwillingness to listen to independent members of Parliament such as himself, and others who weren't on the payroll of the Crown. Both Richmond and Rockingham argued that Parliament should accept the Olive Branch Petition. They would have been happy to see Parliament agree with the Americans and tell the King to change his ministers. The very fact that he was unwilling to do so, they believed, was a sign that power lay truly with him, and not with an independent Parliament.

To some extent Richmond and his colleagues were right. The prime minister, Lord North—loyal, desperate, reactive, and increasingly isolated—continuously tried to resign, but the King steadfastly refused to allow him. North pleaded about his predicament, oddly speaking in the third person: "The anxiety of his mind for the last two months has deprived Lord North of his memory and understanding," he wrote to the King. The King was unwilling to accept a change of direction from Parliament. In doing this, he was consolidating power in the Crown and siphoning it away from Parliament.

To prove that the colonists were sincere in wanting reconciliation, the Duke of Richmond introduced Richard Penn, his age-mate (also born in 1735), childhood friend, and now governor of Pennsylvania, to testify in the House of Lords about the state of affairs among the American colonists. Richmond had spotted Penn in Parliament during a session of the Lords and called upon him to confirm the earnestness of the Olive Branch Petition's proposal for reconciliation. Richmond sent Penn the questions in advance of his testimony, causing another peer to challenge the propriety of Richmond's seeming to work in partnership with the American governor. To prove how serious the Americans were about reconciliation, Penn reported that the repeal of the Stamp Act was greeted by spontaneous celebration and that the Americans would have been satisfied by the status quo expressed in the Declaratory Act. He also emphasized that the Americans could not be vanquished militarily, because they were united in their resistance to the recent Intolerable Acts. Richmond argued that reconciliation was necessary, and that proposals for it were trustworthy, given the sincere desire among the colonists to settle the conflict. The government countered, though, by arguing that accepting the Olive Branch Petition—which the King had in fact already rejected—would amount to the surrender of sovereignty to subjects' demands. Again, questions relating to the conceptual puzzle of sovereignty were at the center of decision-making.

BY DECEMBER 1775 A debate began on what was called the American Prohibitory Bill. The bill would cut off the rebellious colonies from all trade with Britain. Under the law of nations, a trade embargo is an act of war. Consequently, the bill amounted to a proposal for a declaration of war against the thirteen colonies and treated them as a foreign nation. Richmond strenuously objected in his characteristically maximalist rhetoric: "I think it a most unjust, oppressive, and tyrannical measure. I perceive, my lords, that this Bill is a formal denunciation of war against the colonies; and on that ground, is not to be combated with arguments only applicable to a state of tranquility; or even some sorts and degrees of civil disorder." Once again, he objected to the premise of the bill "that the colonies are in open rebellion," and also castigated its cruelty. Richmond slammed the ideas that offending merchants would have their goods seized and taken prisoner on English ships and that the King would now be able to grant pardon to criminals without consulting Parliament. He warned that trade embargoes would hit the innocent, and that, if passed, such an act would communicate to Britain's other territories that any discontent would be met with brutality and plunder.

A month later in January 1776, the rhetorical battle reached new heights when Richmond's erstwhile protégé, Thomas Paine, published *Common Sense* in Philadelphia, which directly argued for American independence from British rule. Paine had landed in America in late November 1774 and found himself right at home among the many fellow Quakers in the City of Brotherly Love. He had been hired straightway into a job as executive editor for the new *Pennsylvania Magazine*. Now thirteen months after his arrival— freeing himself from tutelage, making himself a new man in a new country, and telling people he'd never written a word before arriving in America—he delivered his masterpiece. Paine could pick a fight with his own shadow—as Sarah Franklin wrote to her father, Benjamin, he had "at different times disputed with everyone"—but his polemical gifts were unrivaled. Written in his plain, vigorous style, *Common Sense* laid out the case against monarchical government and hereditary succession, emphasizing the natural rights of individuals and the inherent flaws of the British system. In explicitly arguing against monarchy, *Common Sense* went further than any previous treatise. Like Richmond in Parliament, Paine also charged the King with tyranny. He was a Pharaoh and the "Royal Brute." Paine highlighted the economic and political disadvantages of remaining under British control and inspired ordinary colonists to envision a self-governed republic based on egalitarian principles. The best-selling pamphlet was wildly popular, widely debated, and for many Americans, decisively persuasive. When John Adams returned to Congress a month later after the winter recess, his personal to-do list, scrawled into his journal, included "Declaration of Independency."

In March, Richmond put forward a motion to countermand the deployment of German troops—Britain had recently begun signing treaties with German princes to hire mercenaries. He also proposed suspension of hostilities in America, but the effort was in vain. At exactly that time the British also evacuated Boston. They were unable to safely resupply their garrison there, which was surrounded by the sea and by seething colonists determined to achieve American independence. News of the evacuation reached Britain weeks later. By May, the window for reconciliation had closed.

Something was at an end, and something new was beginning. As the colonists divorced the mother country, they forged a new union among themselves. British subjects were becoming American citizens.

DURING THIS PERIOD, RICHMOND'S attention was split between political and personal matters. In April, Charles Bunbury's bill to divorce Sarah Lennox was passed, and there too any window for reconciliation closed. Finally, that long, anxiety-inducing saga was over. The family was grateful that the Duchess of Kingston's bigamy trial was occurring at the same time in the House of Lords. Between that and what was going on in America, renewed gossip about Sarah was utterly drowned out. Shortly after the hearings on Sarah's divorce, Richmond departed for France. He and the Duchess, as well as the Duchess's half sister the sculptor Anne Seymour Damer, planned to go first to Aubigny to meet his sister Emily and her new husband Ogilvie for the first time. Eighteen months had passed since their marriage. Richmond also had his eye on Paris and Madame de Cambis. In the event, the plan changed, and the Duchess and her half sister returned to London, while the Duke sailed on his own to France, taking along his nephew Charles Lennox, Lennox's tutor, and Captain Jones to look after them all. Richmond enjoyed himself, and from Aubigny he wrote to Louisa that he found Ogilvie "sensible and attentive" to Emily and "very agreeable and pleasing in his manners." There reconciliation had succeeded.

Richmond's love affair with Madame de Cambis deepened that summer, as Madame du Deffand, who ran one of the great salons in Paris, regularly reported to her friend Horace Walpole. In mid-June, she wrote that Richmond was finding Madame de Cambis "much to his taste." Cambis sang and flirted with Richmond, she reported. She added that everyone was finding Richmond far more "amiable" or likable on this trip than previously. His sister Sarah, in a letter to Emily, later chalked this up to love: "Love, you know, is like a chameleon and takes its colour from the object. Of course, while he is in love with Madame Cambise he is '*amiable*.'"

YET EVEN AMID ROMANCE Richmond could not entirely pull his attention away from the question that utterly consumed him—whether the King was preparing a full despotic coup. His French business also brought his mind to this question. He had set himself the task for the summer of 1775 of formally securing the rights to his dukedom of Aubigny. He felt some urgency about it, in part because of his position within the Opposition in Britain. He wrote to Burke: "Who knows that a time may not come when England may not be worth living in, and when a retreat to this country may be a happy thing to have." He lamented his "gloomy prospects" and projected a future "not very far distant," when "England will be reduced to a state of slavery." He worried that George III now had it in his power "with the greatest ease and quiet, to imitate the King of Sweden." He even worried that beholden members of the House of Commons and House of Lords might "vote him complete despotism." Opposition was a hard word; retreat, a beckoning temptation.

The effort to secure his property rights taught him that France, too, was facing a constitutional crisis. As he told Burke, France's evolving political structures had produced a practice whereby all of King Louis XVI's edicts had to be re-examined, and many stakeholders could participate in this process. Clearly fascinated by what the process revealed about the French constitution, and the allocation of powers within it, Richmond wrote about it in detail. The French parliament was claiming the right to examine the propriety of every previously passed royal edict. The friends of the Crown argued that Parliament could revisit edicts only in such cases where the King had been thought to issue an edict contrary to "the *fundamental maxims* of the monarchy." The rub, though, was this, Richmond wrote to Burke: "What these fundamental maxims are nobody agrees with his neighbour." Montesquieu's own compatriots could not figure out how to harmonize judicial power with legislative and executive powers. The constitution was fundamentally unstable, Richmond recognized. He had noticed what would be seeds of France's Revolution without fully realizing the import of what he had observed.

While it was now clear to Richmond that constitutional crisis was a Europe-wide phenomenon, the Swedish case captivated him the most. He reported to Burke on an argument he'd had with the Swedish ambassador to Paris at a dinner party at the ambassador's residence. A lover of fine porcelain, Richmond had found himself drawn into an admiring conversation about the ambassador's table settings, until he realized that one of the serving dishes had a low-relief sculpture depicting Gustav III's 1772 coup or, as the ambassador called it, "the glorious revolution of Sweden." When Richmond realized what the dishware celebrated, he caught his breath so sharply that the ladies sitting near the two men commented on his obvious displeasure. The Swedish ambassador pointed out how the Swedish king was rendered on a throne between Liberty and Justice—and sought Richmond's approval of the iconography. Richmond's response was not satisfying: "I told him I was so unfortunate as to have been made to believe that the old constitution of Sweden was more consonant to liberty than the new one." The two men then proceeded to debate the question of whether Sweden was better off now that instead of "government by the country," there was "government by the King."

The conversation stayed with Richmond for some time and, as he mulled it over, the deeper application of the Swedish example came home to him. To secure alliances with other major powers, aristocrats in the Swedish parliament had supported Gustav's coup and the reduction of their rights. His empowerment, the King promised the lords, would bring their security. Richmond noted that the Swedish nobility had at least sold their rights for the sake of their own security. He and his fellow aristocrats in Britain, he thought, were on the cusp of doing something far worse. In failing to block George's accumulation of power, in voting him every power to reduce the Americans—their brethren!—often out of the desire to protect places and perquisites, members of the House of Lords were choosing "to sell themselves to sacrifice the liberty of their countrymen, to cut one another's throats, and to divide their empire." This degree of corruption, Richmond wrote despairingly, made the English "unworthy to be free." It would leave Britain in a worse situation than France, with Louis XV's domineering autocracy. Once the British constitution gave way to centralized control, the British would be subject to newborn tyranny, and "young despotism, like a boy broke loose from school, will indulge itself in every excess." Richmond saw only darkness ahead for Britain.

Chapter
11

A TOTAL CHANGE OF SYSTEM

1776–1779

It has been the government's object "to enslave America and to exercise a degree of tyranny over that extensive continent entirely repugnant to the spirit of the British constitution."

—DUKE OF RICHMOND, TO THE HOUSE OF LORDS, ON THE SUBJECT OF THE CONCILIATORY BILLS

RICHMOND RETURNED FROM PARIS A CHANGED MAN POSSESSED of startling new clarity about the constitutional stakes of the conflict with America. His recognition that not only possession of America but even the nature of the British constitution hung in the balance drove him incessantly over the coming years to find a solution to save Britain. The effort would ultimately lead him to a radical reconceptualization of the foundation of the British political system. Over a three-year period, he would conceive of a "total change of system" for British politics.

RICHMOND WAS OUT OF step with many of his compatriots, who generally had a cheery outlook about the war and were content to affirm the status quo. In August 1776, news of the American Declaration of Independence reached Europe, but the same month, the British took New York. News of this gain arrived in England just before the opening of Parliament on October 13. Things seemed promising for the British war effort.

The war in America would essentially have three theaters—in New England, centered around Boston; in the mid-Atlantic, centered around

New York and Philadelphia; and in the South, running from Savannah to Yorktown, and embracing the West Indies. This strategy replicated a core tenet of early modern European warfare: to control the capitol city was to win the fight. But the newly United States were a hydra, without a clear capitol, which spread Britain's fighting forces thin over great distances. Eventually, and especially once they directed significant energies to protecting the economically more valuable West Indies, it would be impossible for the British to control all three. This ultimately meant they could not win the war. The economic importance of the West Indies would drive them to hold on longer than they might otherwise have, but ultimately they could not form and administer strategy across three separate theaters from across an ocean, with constantly squabbling generals, and against the inspired leadership of George Washington. In the fall of 1776, though, with the capture of New York, things were looking bright for the government. The Declaration of Independence did not seem like something to be taken terribly seriously.

Indeed, the King opened Parliament on October 13 by insisting, as he had for several years, that the submission of the Americans must and would be achieved. News from America gave him "the strongest Hopes of the most decisive good Consequences."

Richmond thought this was outrageous and reflected an ostrich-like unwillingness to see plain truths—*common sense*, as his one-time protégé Paine had put it. He rose to object and once again moved an amendment to the usual pro forma address of thanks to the King for his speech. His amendment offered a dramatically different message. First, he provided a reality check. The agenda of punishing and reducing the Americans had simply introduced yet another "cause of war and revolt." He tweaked the King with the very phrase, "bloody and expensive," that the King had wanted to use to describe the war that he inherited when he came to the throne in 1760. The King's factious ministers, Richmond argued, had by now left Britain "almost inextricably involved in a bloody and expensive Civil War." This would exhaust the resources of Britain, making her vulnerable to the depredations of France and Spain and thereby bring "the most deplorable Calamities to the whole *British* Race." Richmond's rhetoric was, once again, maximalist.

Then he drove home his constitutional point. The government's foreign affairs strategy placed only two options on the table—causing the full subjection and submission of the Americans, or ceding their independence. All the acts that had been passed removed the liberties of the Americans, and all the military actions underway were directed toward destruction and subjection. Liberty-destroying submission was decidedly the wrong thing to wish on any part of the British Empire. The British were after all defined by their spirit of liberty, as Richmond saw it, drawing on Montesquieu, and it should cause feelings of "shame and horror" to attempt "to break the Spirit of any large Part of the *British* Nation." That spirit of liberty was what called the swirling starlings into formation. The goal should be to preserve the colonies as societies of free people, that is, as truly British *because* free, and as truly free because British. This agenda required a different sort of policy.

No piece of legislation had been developed to describe positively the relationships of connection and freedom that would be available to the Americans if they remained part of the British Empire. This was precisely what was needed. Much as Richmond had earlier sought to achieve clarity for Canada while he was ambassador to Paris, now he sought to accomplish the same with the Americans. The Crown's policy should be "to regulate, not to destroy" the Americans. What was also critical, Richmond thought, was to recognize that any victory that depended on stripping British subjects of their constitutional liberties opened the door to the same degradations at home. The treatment of the Americans, as it was being pursued by the ministry, risked "establishing Precedents the most dangerous to the Liberties of this Kingdom."

While Richmond did not explicitly formulate the legal puzzle here, he was pointing to it: The war, which demanded subjection of the Americans, also demanded their subjection to Parliament because of the structure of British constitutionalism. But their greatest concern was to be governed by their own legislative bodies. Saving British constitutionalism, Richmond was beginning to intuit, would paradoxically require limiting Parliament's power, and giving more power to the King, to be in direct connection to the colonies through their legislatures. This, though, would then produce another conundrum. How could Parliament relinquish some power, without itself becoming overpowered by the King? Achieving that would require constitutional innovations designed to reduce the power of the King, so that Parliament could continue to have independence in relation to the sovereign. Avoiding the independence of America meant finding ways to increase the independence of Parliament, even while shrinking the scope of its authority.

As usual, Richmond's proposed amendment to send a different answer to the King lost on the vote. He was a lonely voice, a Cassandra in a Parliament of Pollyannas.

ONE MAN, THOUGH, SHARED Richmond's cast of mind and his concerns. Major John Cartwright was a self-described "courteous and calm" naval officer. He was born in 1740 to a family descended from an archbishop of Canterbury, well-connected but now of modest means. His naval service took him from Cherbourg to the Bay of Biscay to Newfoundland aboard the *Wasp*, the *Spy*, and the *Guernsey*. Finally, while serving on the *Antelope*, his health suffered, and he had to abandon his sea career. He settled in London and turned to an intellectual life, reading voraciously as if to make up for years without books while at sea. He joined the reformers, became well known to associates of Richmond's such as the radical Richard Price, and would eventually publish more than eighty works advancing the cause of parliamentary reform. In late October and November 1776, after the King's speech, he began to circulate his recently published pamphlet, *Take Your Choice!* In it, Cartwright outlined his vision for a more just and representative political system. This would require, he argued, universal manhood suffrage, the secret ballot, annual elections, and equal electoral districts. His was the most far-reaching reform agenda yet published.

During the years that the American conflict had been growing sharper on the other side of the pond through thrust and counterthrust over taxes, the British radicals had been tackling the subject of the right to vote and the functioning of Parliament. The 1772 exchanges between Junius and Wilkes about whether parliaments should last three years or only one, instead of the status quo of seven years, were followed in 1774 by campaign speeches on the subject by a rising politician, Lord Mahon, son-in-law of Chatham. Then in 1775, James Burgh, Richmond's earliest and longest-serving pamphleteer, published his three-volume work, *Political Disquisitions*, which made an extensive case for annual parliaments and yearly elections. Cartwright's landmark pamphlet was thus the fourth published contribution on parliamentary reform. He sent copies to all the leading Whigs, despite dressing them down in the book as "factious demagogues," who "care not that [their country] sink in the pit of perdition." His basis for this charge was that the Whigs in Opposition had not embraced parliamentary reform as their top goal.

Richmond was insulted. He called on Cartwright, with the book in his pocket and "the offensive page turned down." As Cartwright reports in his memoirs, Richmond "complained vehemently" that Cartwright had been uncharitable and unjust in "doubting the integrity of men not yet tried." Cartwright and Richmond then spent several hours in conversation and came to a meeting of the minds that would become the basis of a friendship that lasted to the end of Richmond's life. They saw eye to eye on the danger of a clearly increasing dependence of Parliament on the Crown.

Richmond had already begun to express in his own voice that the solution lay in consulting with the people more assiduously. In September 1773, he had written to Rockingham and expressed the view that "royal corruption was steadily destroying the character of the nation 'as the falling water will perforate the stone.'" He argued that leading men such as himself were "obliged to consult the good of the people and court them as deriving their power from them." This formulation credited the British regime with having its foundation in popular sovereignty, a "peculiar view" for an aristocrat, as one scholar has put it. In Cartwright he found someone who agreed with him.

Their shared military background further united them. Cartwright hoped for citizen involvement in national defense and criticized reliance on standing armies. Richmond, as lord lieutenant for Sussex and the head of a citizen militia, agreed. One of the last books he bought at the end of his life was Cartwright's *England's Aegis: or the Military Energies of the Constitution*, which made an argument close to Richmond's core commitments, for a national militia system to defend England. Richmond had found a new intellectual companion who matched his appetite for solving national security and constitutional puzzles.

A second reformer also made his way into Richmond's circles at this time: Granville Sharp, a scholar, abolitionist, and one of the founding figures of the British movement to end the transatlantic slave trade. His tireless legal advocacy secured from Lord Mansfield a famous 1772 ruling in *Somerset v. Stewart*, which delivered such a stinging rebuke of slavery in England—"It is so odious, that nothing can be suffered to support it"—that it became a key judgment in the broader abolitionist campaign. Sharp would also later be instrumental in cofounding Sierra Leone as a settlement for freed African slaves, writing a constitution for the settlement. He was a committed advocate for human freedom. Richmond knew Sharp personally and collected his books, too—including *The Just*

Limitations of Slavery in the Laws of God and *Claims of the People of England on Parliament for a Reform in the Commons*, which developed policy visions for wider suffrage, participation, and democratization in England and for a free society for Africans. With Paine on the other side of the ocean, it was now through association with Sharp and Cartwright that Richmond participated in the day's cutting-edge policy conversations.

DESPITE RICHMOND'S GROWING CONCERN about danger to political liberty, Richmond's opinion of the King himself surprisingly softened after the arrival of the Declaration of Independence. The politics of the moment gave him new insight into the King, and he began to recognize that George III was in various ways limiting the exercise of his own power.

The fall of 1776 was a time of significant intraparty debate for the Whigs. While Richmond had now, once again, fallen into line with a circle of radicals from outside his social milieu, the Opposition Whigs in Parliament were themselves flailing as different factions among them sought to command the direction of the party. The Opposition was in agreement that the King's power must be reduced, but they found themselves strenuously at odds over the question of precisely how to constrain it. The debate ultimately focused on three possible approaches to limiting the King's power: They could try to undo the information asymmetry between King and Parliament by demanding transparency or pursuing investigations; they might pursue "economical reform" to reduce the number of members of Parliament who would be in paid service to the Crown; or perhaps they should advocate parliamentary reform to strengthen Parliament as a voice independent of the Crown.

Not only the Opposition's methods but also their end goals were in dispute. Should they reduce the King's power to ensure that Parliament could rule supreme including, for instance, over all British colonies? This was Chatham's position. Or did Parliament mainly need to be able to hold its own against the King on affairs in the home islands of Britain specifically and, as far as the Empire was concerned, mainly on the regulation of commerce? Richmond took this side. The Opposition Whigs debated this question among themselves ceaselessly for the next five years as the American Revolution ground forward—unabating, unforgiving, and increasingly unwinnable.

In the short term the Opposition's internal arguments availed little.

Even if they had been united, their numbers were not sufficient to outvote the government. Bruised by the unalterable mathematics that predetermined they would lose out in the votes, the Opposition politicians decided that their best course was to abandon trying fruitlessly to pass one after another bill or amendment. They concluded that they were better off "seceding" from Parliament and simply indicating their non-approval through non-attendance. This was a way, they thought, of communicating that they thought the whole business had devolved into illegitimacy.

Yet even amid all the frustration, Richmond continued to make progress on his understanding of the constitutional puzzles—including assessing the role and character of the King. The reflections on the contrast between Britain and Sweden had been important to Richmond. Like the King of Sweden, George III had at his disposal every tool he needed to take full autocratic control. Yet he had stopped short of doing so and continued to accede to his ministers despite their poor judgment. Nothing could explain this, Richmond realized, other than George's own surprisingly unshakeable commitment to the British constitution. Seven years earlier, working with his associates on the Junius project, Richmond had not been willing to attribute personal virtue to the King. Now, watching the King hold back from the full use of the monarch's power, Richmond recognized that George III might in his own way also be trying to preserve the constitution. Richmond continued to lament "the extreme degeneracy of government." He had now come to believe, though, that the problem could be "attributed to a want of wisdom in ministers, as well as a want of virtue in parliament." He was satisfied in his conscience "that nothing but the personal virtue of the sovereign prevented this country from a total loss of liberty." Although Richmond strongly believed the power of the Crown needed to be reduced, this period of intraparty debate left him no longer objecting to George III personally.

JUNIUS HAD SOUGHT TO drive change in British politics by putting pressure on the King directly, but Richmond's evolving view of George III motivated a new strategy. Despite his personal affinity for Cartwright and his broad agreement with his views, Richmond wasn't ready yet to fly the flag of universal manhood suffrage. He continued to seek an alternative means of reducing the King's power. He found the next elements of his strategy, once again, in Paris, in the form of advice from Horace Walpole.

Through the first half of 1777, as the war ground on, both Richmond in England and the Americans, too, devoted themselves to preparing for the next round of engagements. Since the Opposition had decided not to attend Parliament, Richmond spent his time primarily at Goodwood, funding and training the Sussex militia. He had for some time been anticipating that British overreach in America would lead France and Spain to enter the war to take advantage of Britain's vulnerability. For his whole life, he had seen the South Coast of England as a point of weakness in Britain's defenses. The last invasion of England, in 1066, had begun in Sussex, after all.

In America, in early 1777, the Continental Army was facing a crisis of morale in a bitter winter. They had recently been driven out of New York City and had fallen back to Pennsylvania. Thomas Paine, now famous and formally employed by Congress as a propagandist, had recently published the first edition of *The American Crisis*, a series of pamphlets intended to lift the spirits of the Americans. The first one opened, famously, "These are the times that try men's souls." There had been some inspiring victories. Washington led the Americans across an icy Delaware river in the middle of a nor'easter to catch the British by surprise at Trenton on Christmas night, defeating them there and then again just after New Year's Day at Princeton. Yet these victories were close-run things, and the army was suffering from lack of provisions and clothing amid deep cold. After these battles, Washington withdrew from action, camping his army from January through the end of May in Morristown, New Jersey, to rebuild its strength. With the arrival of summer, he broke camp and moved to force British troops back to New York, settling in for an ongoing series of skirmishes.

As Washington sought to take on the British in New York, Richmond sailed again to Paris for the summer. Once again, Duchess Mary stayed home. He resumed his effort to register his dukedom of Aubigny, and succeeded at last, which led to rumors that he was contemplating moving to France, converting to Catholicism, and taking up a seat in Parliament there. He dined frequently with Madame de Cambis, whose English was now good enough to translate Lord Chesterfield's 1774 *Letters* into French. He made another visit to Sèvres to buy porcelain for Walpole. Gibbon reported that "the air of Paris agrees perfectly well with him. He is easy, attentive and cheerful, pays court to young and to old women, and is extremely popular and even fashionable in the Society of Paris." Walpole was shocked that Richmond's romance was growing into such a fully formed and public relationship. Mary, Richmond's duchess, was the stepdaughter of his cousin, General Henry Conway, to whom he was close. Though never himself married or partnered, Walpole was devoted to family with a powerful sense of loyalty. Richmond's affair surely directly offended him. That was the way of the French, but not of the British.

Yet, in politics, shared purpose can transcend personal discomfort. Despite Walpole's disapproval of Richmond's private conduct, the two men—bound by family ties, mutual respect, and a commitment to the British constitution—continued to collaborate with remarkable clarity of purpose that summer. The son of the great first prime minister, Robert Walpole, Horace Walpole had, it seemed, learned some of his father's lessons. Probably better than anyone else, he gave Richmond sound, practical political advice. In their exchanges of letters, Walpole had long been urging on Richmond a strategy that might be boiled down to "Follow the money."

Walpole had urged Richmond to focus on the King's ministers, rather than the King himself. "Give the ministers no respite," he advised. "Press them with questions and motions; leave their poor heads no time to think of what they ought to think of, the next campaign." He urged him to overwhelm them with investigations of their waste, fraud, and abuse. "Talk of their waste, ask for pension lists, inquire after those scandalous ones to the widows or wives." He reminded Richmond to draw a connection between taxpayers and the wasteful corruption of the ministers. "Lament the hard fate of the poor country gentlemen who must pay for all this waste, and the enormous expenses of the war, too." He wanted Richmond to ask for documents about all the expenses of the war and of the sedition trials, all of which should be clearly communicated as being funded by taxpayers. Soldiers, who were getting only half-pay and even that delayed, were the other victims. Richmond should "lament the hard fate of the soldiers forced to go against their countrymen," who were then also left "without bark or bandages for their wounds, and with nothing but salt provisions."

The burden of the military effort was mounting, and the government had begun to seek new funds from British taxpayers. Richmond had long believed that "England will not much care whether America is lost or not, till they feel the effects in their purses or in their bellies." Walpole and Richmond must have discussed Walpole's strategy at length in Paris in the summer of 1777, for when Richmond returned to England for the fall he was at last ready to attempt it.

DURING THE FALL OF 1777, while Richmond was planning his new parliamentary campaign, the British and Americans were each also preparing new plans of attack on one another in the field. The hard-liner Lord Germain was now secretary of state for the colonies (he had managed to rise despite what should have been a career-crippling court-martial after the Battle of Minden). General Howe, an experienced officer, had replaced Gage in command in the field after the Battle of Bunker Hill outside of Boston in 1775, the Pyrrhic victory for the British where a rough and untrained militia proved how costly would be the effort to defeat them. Now, two years later, with both armies well-seasoned, the conflict had settled into a grim war of attrition. As the British military pursued a strategy untethered from reality, Richmond in Parliament continuously sought to douse the burning fires of war with the cold waters of realism, particularly the hard facts of the war's expense.

Lord Germain had dreamed up a grandiose strategy. He proposed to isolate and defeat the New England colonies by gaining control of the Hudson River valley. The idea was that New England was the hotbed of radicalism. If it could be subjugated, the rest of the revolution would be weakened and could be defeated. Trying to steer war strategy from the comforts of Whitehall, Germain concocted a three-pronged plan of attack. General John Burgoyne would lead British forces south from Canada down the Hudson River; a smaller force under Colonel Barry St. Leger would move east from Lake Ontario through the Mohawk Valley; and General William Howe would move north from New York City to meet Burgoyne near Albany.

The plan, developed in London, was ill-informed. Communication difficulties and arguments among the three military leaders sank it. Howe refused to play his part, leaving Burgoyne's forces isolated. At the second Battle of Saratoga on October 17, 1777, Burgoyne surrendered 5,700 starving men to an army three times the size of his own. This defeat not only meant victory for the Americans in the northern theater, but also attracted the attention of France and Spain, whose alliance Franklin had been assiduously courting. The calculus would be different if Britain's ancient enemies thought the ragtag Americans might potentially win. While the Americans took the rest of Burgoyne's army prisoner, General Washington cunningly sent Burgoyne himself back to London, knowing that his direct account of his defeat would be utterly demoralizing there.

Even before Burgoyne had arrived in London bearing his devastating news, British correspondents were writing anxiously about the fate of their young men abroad. When Sarah wrote to her friend Susan in November 1777, she revealed her worries about her two nephews in the war, Harry Fox and Charles Fitzgerald: "I am not much pleased with my friend Sr Wm Howe neither, for tho' a most humane man himself he has not contrived to keep strict discipline in his army, & I hear of horrible crueltys among them. . . . It makes one's blood run cold to think of it. I had some hopes that Harry Fox would come over with the next news, but I'm afraid he won't by what some military people tell me. . . . I have another nephew there, Charles Fitzgerald, who is a seaman; I wish they were both home & safe again." (Both young men would survive. Charles fought in the Battle of the Chesapeake in 1781 and remained in the Navy throughout his career, rising to vice admiral. Harry fought at Concord and Bunker Hill and was in America until the spring of 1779, when, home from leave, he informed his family of his view that "America *cannot* be conquered." Nonetheless, he returned from his leave to America that summer and served to the end of the war. The absence of his name from casualty lists was how his family tracked how he was doing.)

While these events were unfolding in America, Richmond had already begun to shame the government over the financing of the war. On December 2, even before the news of Burgoyne's colossal loss reached England, he rose in the House of Lords and moved an inquiry into the state of the nation. He proposed a comprehensive review of Britain's assets and liabilities. He emphasized that his proposal concerned only a retroactive enquiry, and that it would focus on the state of the Army and Navy, and on Britain's finances. In closing the debate, Richmond said, "The sincere wish of my soul is for peace—peace with America and the remains of the empire. A firm alliance with America would be a favourable compact indeed. Should this unhappy war continue, the ruin of both countries will be inevitable. England will most assuredly fall. Too late shall we find that by desolating America, we have only hastened the destruction of this country."

The House agreed with him. For the first time in his role as primary speaker for the Opposition, he won the motion. At last, he had won over some supporters of the ministry. For twelve years he had been trying to redirect policy on America. Finally, he had broken through.

What followed cemented Richmond's victory. The next day Lord North broke the news to Parliament of the devastating defeat at Saratoga. Everyone pointed fingers at everyone else and, according to Walpole, always a partisan witness, the King "fell into agonies on hearing the account." The catastrophe—total loss of an army—"unleashed a furore" and reinforced the importance of Richmond's investigative measure. How could a great military have failed so badly? Calls for further investigations came fast and furious. Richmond argued that the calamity should call into question not whether Britain *should* reduce America, but whether it even *could*. He advised the House of Lords to recall the remaining armies, under General Howe, and to focus on national defense, not American offensives. He had been warning that the overextension of the British military would tempt the French and Spanish into the war, and indeed the defeat of the British at Saratoga proved him right.

On February 6, 1778, Benjamin Franklin and two other American commissioners signed the Treaty of Alliance and a Treaty of Amity and Commerce with France. France's entrance into the war changed everything. For the next three years, the British would largely control the mid-Atlantic and southern theaters, seeking to protect their Caribbean possessions while both sides expended resources in innumerable small skirmishes. At the same time, the British now also found themselves fighting the French, and soon the Spanish too, across the breadth of their empire. By 1779 even Britain's own "sceptr'd isle" would be directly threatened with invasion. The contrast between military fantasy and economic and political reality hit home.

Richmond had intended to return to Paris again in April 1778, but the declaration of war by France on England made that impossible. He was too prominent a British politician to travel there safely now. This abated his growing relationship with Madame de Cambis. They wrote to one another for the remaining five years of the struggle, and after peace was signed in 1783, the Duke sent his yacht for her. She visited England again for a few weeks in 1786, which she spent largely in Richmond's company, and moved permanently to England in 1789 when the French Revolution broke out. After the war, though, they never did resume the intimacy that they had enjoyed in the summers of 1776 and 1777. War had begun to upend ordinary life in Britain itself.

FRANCE'S DECLARATION OF WAR pushed Richmond to pursue with even greater urgency a constructive path toward stabilizing British politics. Now came a stunning realization. Saving Britain, he had come to believe, meant liberating America. The time had arrived to recognize the colonies' independence. Richmond was moving fast in his policy thinking—from an agenda focused on waste, fraud, and abuse as a means of reining in the King's ministers to a proposal to rework the entire structure of the British Empire. Counterintuitively, he now believed recognizing independence was the best path for preserving British liberties and ensuring the viability of the constitutional system, even as Britain became an increasingly imperial power. Richmond put this question front and center to Parliament in the debates of the winter and spring of 1778.

The findings from his inquiry into the war's financial impact began with a focus on the commercial losses occasioned by the American War. He called a witness to testify about the extent of British trade volume lost to privateers during the war. The ministry introduced witnesses of its own. Then Richmond moved a set of motions phrased not as decisions to be taken but as mere records of fact documenting the hard economic truths. He wanted the House to confirm his analysis of the situation formally. He was trying to puncture delusion. As Richmond named how many trade vessels had been lost and how much the price of sugar had increased, the House listened sympathetically: Once more, his motions passed. He had never previously been able to accomplish such a sustained series of victories in Parliament.

Eleven days later, on February 19, Richmond rose again in the House of Lords, this time to report on direct expenditures undertaken by the British government to pursue the war. He moved a set of resolutions detailing public expenditure and again sought to pass motions on statements of fact. He began by baldly stating that the war had already rendered Britain "almost bankrupt," and asserted that his purpose was to investigate exactly how this financial ruin had come about. To isolate the effect of the war with America, Richmond expertly compared national accounts during wartime with the average expenditure of peaceful years. His conclusion: The war with America had reached a cost of almost 33 million pounds, while state expenditure during the same period, in a state of peace, would ordinarily have been only 3–4 million pounds.

The impact of the war was to raise public expenses roughly tenfold. The Earl of Suffolk objected that Richmond's presentation endangered the country by publicizing national weakness. Richmond countered that the weakness of Britain was already well known. The Earl's words were a warning. Richmond's wall of support was starting to crack, and this time his motion failed.

Rather than retreating, Richmond instead daringly sought to seize new argumentative ground, by demanding the British Army be recalled from America. The House of Lords was debating a set of bills called the Conciliatory Bills—measures to end the war in America. The bills repealed all parliamentary taxation in the colonies, promised not to tax the colonies going forward without their consent, and offered home rule, amnesty, and colonial representation, but not independence. They were designed to undermine American support for the war. They had already been moved and passed by the Opposition in the House of Commons. The Lords also approved the bills, marking a turning point: The bills amounted to the first serious British peace offer since the outbreak of the war. Surprisingly, the ministry remained silent throughout the debate, implicitly assenting to the bills. Richmond triumphantly "called upon some of the King's servants to explain to the House the reasons of their silence, and why they had abandoned all their former high-sounding terms of the supremacy of parliament, and unconditional submission, and now came to sue to America for peace?"

Despite his desire for peace, Richmond was skeptical that the Conciliatory Bills themselves were fit for purpose. He did not believe that they had been designed in good faith. They still trafficked in fictions about who the Americans were, what they wanted, and how Britain had treated them. The preamble insisted on the supremacy of British rule and proposed for peace negotiators precisely those individuals who had most aggressively "pursued the injustices of the war." In the House of Lords, Richmond read aloud the Declaration of Independence and showed how the peace commissioners could not possibly assent to its propositions without giving up British supremacy. The Declaration stated that the King had acted tyrannically and that the establishment of the admiralty courts and quartering of troops on American soil were an injustice. If the peace commissioners tried to ignore the

Declaration, as their bills did, they would have no credibility with the Americans. Richmond was not a reflexive defender of the Americans. In fact, he objected to the language in the Declaration calling King George a tyrant, but he did defend the American Declaration—and its basic liberties—as essentially a traditional Whig opinion. Any peace overtures, he thought, would have to start from that kind of mutual recognition.

As an alternative to this insistence on British supremacy and proposal to maintain policies that were anathema to the Americans, Richmond proposed that all the troops should be recalled. This, he thought, would best communicate Britain's desire for reconciliation. It was a reality-based solution to meet the true facts of the moment. He went on to shift the blame from the person of the King to the incompetent ministers who had acted in his name and besmirched it by doing so, showing how far he had moved in his own opinion of the King.

Although Richmond had been one of the first to apply the label of tyranny to the King's government, he now made a different argument. The Americans were mistaken to consider the King a tyrant. Yet their mistake had been made in good faith. The King's ministers had used the King's name, Richmond argued, to pursue their own unjust designs. Since ministers had presented their own unjust actions as royal resolutions, the colonists had quite reasonably mistaken the King for a tyrant, and according to good Whig principles, asserted that the King had deserted his post (just like in 1688) and declared their right to form their own government. Blame would be better placed on the King's ministers. Richmond was unsparing in his criticism of them, arguing, "It has been the government's object 'to enslave America and to exercise a degree of tyranny over that extensive continent entirely repugnant to the spirit of the British constitution.'" "The King," he declared, "was the 'first magistrate' but no more than that;" and "ministers were servants of the public as well as of the King." The entire war rested, in other words, on a profound misunderstanding brought about by a pernicious ministry. Rather than using the Conciliatory Bills that he was certain would fail in America, Richmond recommended that Britain simply withdraw its troops as a real sign of respect, and enter into favorable trade agreements with America, before France did the same. His arguments failed. The Conciliatory Bills passed, and his proposed withdrawal did not. Richmond was back to shouting into the wind.

Reality is unforgiving and, just as Richmond had predicted, the Conciliatory Bills failed to conciliate. American representatives in London speedily rejected the peace offer. They had already reached the point of full and irreversible commitment to independence. They had also already entered into a trade agreement with France. Knowing both these things and accurately seeing in them the signs that France was about to enter the war formally on America's side, Richmond objected to a proposal to withdraw the British ambassador from France. He believed such a measure "might involve the nation in ruin," because it was equivalent to a "declaration of war" on France, when France hadn't yet formally declared war on England despite having formed an alliance with the colonies. Richmond argued that British forces and finances couldn't sustain an additional war against France. That looming threat gave him an opening to push his policy point. Seeking to forestall the clear movement toward war with France, he argued that "instead of sending out commissioners to no purpose," Britain should arm peace commissioners "with powers to declare America independent, if they chose it." Only a full grant of independence could fend off war with France. He also thought independence would be the best method "to secure the friendship and commerce of our colonies." In March 1778, Richmond became the first member of the House of Lords to propose accepting American independence.

THE KING AND HIS administration remained committed to the vague cause of conciliation, even after its rejection, but not at the expense of any diminution of British supremacy over the Americans. The Whig Opposition remained split between those who would grant the independence of America, like Richmond, and those like Chatham who continued to insist on British sovereignty over the colonists.

The climax of the debate came on the morning of April 7, 1778. Richmond was preparing for a showdown in the Lords. He shared with the abolitionist Granville Sharp a letter he'd written to Chatham in which he pleaded for Whig unity and proposed to Chatham that the time had come to sue for peace and "to procure an accommodation with

America." Chatham, who at sixty-nine was very much a weakening elder statesman, nonetheless firmly rejected this policy. He continued to insist upon the sovereignty of England over America and let Richmond know that he planned to attend the House of Lords that afternoon to argue against Richmond.

That day's debates in the House of Lords were among the most dramatic in British parliamentary history. Richmond was surely in a state of heightened anxiety, knowing he was about to make one of the most important political arguments of his career, and that he would be opposed by a man who had been at his height the most formidable orator in the nation. Richmond rose and moved an address to the King upon the state of the nation. His remarks echoed precisely the themes of some of Junius's most powerful letters. He culminated with the investigations into the financial state of the nation and reiterated his belief that the war against America was highly unjust and pursued solely with the aim to enslave the continent. The text of the address that he proposed to send to the King conveyed all the alarming conclusions about expense and financial distress and expressed the House of Lords' lack of faith in winning the American War. His colleagues rightly heard this as a willingness to cede sovereignty over America and grant independence.

The debate reached its memorable climax when Chatham stood, unsteadily, supported on one side by his eighteen-year-old son, William Pitt the Younger, and on the other by his son-in-law, Lord Mahon, already a parliamentary reformer and the future Earl of Stanhope. Chatham had suffered a stroke recently, which had reduced his once commanding voice to little more than a whisper. He told the Lords that he strongly opposed the idea of suing for peace and thereby giving up sovereignty over America, which was the rightful patrimony of the monarch. Richmond replied by saying the patrimony had already been lost, and could not be recovered, but those responsible for the loss could and should be called to account. When Chatham rose again to respond, he suffered a sudden attack and collapsed. He "fell back upon his seat and was to all appearance in the agony of death," as Lord Camden reported it. His second stroke "threw the whole House into confusion. Every person was upon the instant upon his legs in a moment hurrying from one place to another." Pitt the

Younger and Chatham's son-in-law carried the Great Man out, and the House was adjourned.

Despite the extraordinary drama, the House was called to order the following day and the debate continued. The Earl of Shelburne, Chatham's second-in-command for his faction of the hawkish Whigs, argued in a long speech that the war could be continued and won if a new government were formed. Sympathy for Chatham's imperialist vision carried the day. Parliament could not bring itself to accept that it had to give up its rebellious colonies.

Yet within weeks, Shelburne had come round and joined Richmond in supporting the withdrawal of troops and independence for America. To have won round Chatham's faction to his policy—even without Chatham at its head, or perhaps *because* Chatham was no longer its head—was a major victory for Richmond. Like Richmond, Shelburne also supported parliamentary reform, including universal manhood suffrage. This moment of rapprochement between the two protégés of General Wolfe foreshadowed the important political movement toward radical transformation of Britain's institutions that was just over the horizon.

Chatham died a few weeks later. He had been a leading public figure for more than four decades, having served in Parliament for forty-three years. He had been vice treasurer of Ireland, paymaster general of the forces, secretary of state for the southern department, leader in the House of Commons, lord privy seal and first lord of the treasury, and prime minister. His name was synonymous with patriotism, and the growth of British imperial power. His rigorous adherence to policy commitments and unwillingness to traffic in patronage gave him an unparalleled reputation for freedom from corruption.

Britain mourned his loss handsomely. He lay in state for two days in Westminster Abbey, and thousands of mourners streamed by. Then he was buried in the Abbey in a funeral of magnificence unparalleled for any other eighteenth-century statesman. The House of Commons voted unanimously to attend his funeral. In the House of Lords, however, a similar motion brought by Shelburne was defeated by one vote. Richmond was not in Parliament that day, though we can imagine he would have voted with Shelburne, given their new policy alliance.

At public expense, and thanks to that unanimous vote in the Commons, a thirty-three-foot marble monument was installed in Westminster Abbey to memorialize Chatham. The inscription, etched in large block letters, reads:

> ERECTED BY
> THE *KING* AND *PARLIAMENT*
> AS A TESTIMONY TO
> THE VIRTUES AND ABILITY OF
> WILLIAM PITT,
> *EARL OF CHATHAM;*
> DURING WHOSE ADMINISTRATION
> IN THE REIGNS OF
> *GEORGE THE SECOND AND GEORGE THE THIRD*
> DIVINE PROVIDENCE
> EXALTED *GREAT BRITAIN*
> TO AN HEIGHT OF *PROSPERITY* AND *GLORY*
> UNKNOWN TO ANY FORMER AGE.

Chatham's death truly brought an end to an era. He was the last great leader from among the Old Whigs to fall. Richmond's speech was widely seen as having killed him.

YET CHATHAM'S DEATH, DESPITE its resonating cultural impact, did not distract Richmond from the larger task of making the British constitution resilient. Having put a marker on the board for American independence and forced his colleagues to contemplate eventual relinquishment of sovereignty over America, Richmond now needed to solve the remaining pieces of his constitutional puzzle. How could he claim that American independence would not diminish either Parliament or the Crown? His long-standing work on Canada, and his commitment to independent legislatures working in parallel and tied to the Crown, pointed him in the direction of a solution. America could be independent and still connected to the King if the new nation had its own legislature, a model that anticipated the British Commonwealth of the twentieth century. Richmond still had to resolve how the British Parliament could continue to be powerful under a new arrangement of this kind.

Richmond's constitutional philosophizing was interspersed during this period with increasingly demanding militia obligations. Britain's military position was now quite precarious, especially since Spain had joined France in allying with the Americans. In America, much as Richmond had predicted, the war continued to worsen for the British. The Continental Congress formally rejected the Conciliatory Bills in June and that same month, the Continental Army marched from Valley Forge and forced the British out of Philadelphia. By late July the French Navy was in the English Channel. On July 27, British and French troops engaged at Ushant off the coast of Brittany. The British repulsed the French, but without taking any prizes—broadly seen as a military failure. When Britain's two naval leaders (one of them Richmond's cousin, Admiral Keppel) returned their fleets to Portsmouth, they had to anchor at opposite ends of the harbor to keep their sailors from setting upon each other in their anger at one another for letting the French get away. The mood in Britain was ugly. By August an enemy fleet, combining the French and Spanish navies, and with thirty thousand infantry troops aboard, was visible in the English Channel off the coast of Plymouth, much as Richmond had feared. As one scholar put it, "The Year 1779 deserves to be remembered alongside 1588 and 1803 as a year of imminent, existential danger for the British isles." Richmond was among the first to recognize it. As well as raising his concerns in Parliament, and seeing them often voted down, Richmond took military preparations into his own hands and turned to bringing the Sussex militia into good order.

Though Keppel was under duress and would undergo a court-martial on account of the failure to capture prizes during the July 27 battle, he took time while near the South Coast to review its defenses. He noted approvingly the work that Richmond was doing with his militia, praising him for civilian recruits who performed "as well as regulars." Richmond's sister Sarah was proud of this compliment, though she thought it came at too high a price. She wrote to her friend Susan that Richmond was endangering his health from his exertions. She confided, "My dear brother has made himself excessively ill by his hard working & *talking* to the men, which has strained his stomach & done him a great deal of harm." She also reported to her sister Emily that the work with the militia was so demanding that it was "a total destroyer of all my brother's schemes and amusements and even business—for this summer."

YET SARAH OVERLOOKED HER brother's evolving thinking on the constitution. A publisher had recently gathered into one volume a whole history of radical efforts to change the King's policies. The volume collated several of the remonstrances against the King and the King's responding addresses, beginning with the Wilkes events in the spring of 1770. The exchanges between the King and his subjects addressed British constitutional structure. Richmond read this volume closely and annotated most of the pages, not only with check marks and underlines in the margins, but also with whole paragraphs of political and philosophical analysis scrawled in every unprinted portion of the page. This volume is the single most annotated book in his library. It was one of the last books I found during several summers of research there, shelved as it is in the very final tier of books. As I stared down at the age-reddened ink scrawls, I realized I held the pivot point in the development of Richmond's intellectual life. Here on the page in his extensive marginal notes, I could see him working through the puzzle of how to reimagine representation in the British constitutional order. His notes had never previously been seen or recorded by a scholar, and they brought to life just how intensely Richmond engaged in questions of political philosophy. They constitute, in effect, a minor treatise of political philosophy on the puzzle of representation.

This theme had preoccupied Richmond ever since the Wilkes affair, back in 1768, had squarely put it on the table. The decision by the House of Commons not to seat Wilkes, on account of his convictions and despite his electoral victories, brought a certain hypocrisy to the surface. Those who objected to Wilkes's exclusion protested that the representative nature of the House of Commons was being undone, and the legitimacy of the body therefore undermined. But of course, given how the British electoral system worked at the time, the House of Commons had never been a truly representative body. Only a small portion of the male residents of Britain had voting rights, and among those who did, only a small portion actually had the chance to participate in elections. Even for those who had a chance to participate, often their votes were controlled or dominated by those who could simply acquire properties that brought with them a certain number of votes. Its nonrepresentative dimensions were only getting worse with time, as shrinking rural areas were over-represented, and new and fast-growing industrial cities, were without representation. There were seats without constituencies—so-called rotten boroughs—as well as constituencies without seats. For example, Old Sarum, in Wiltshire, had once been a bustling, prosperous town but had since declined. It now had three houses, seven voters, and two seats in Parliament while the more than forty thousand souls in Manchester had not a single representative.

Even if Wilkes had gained his seat, he would still have been part of a woefully flawed assembly that scarcely deserved the description "representative."

As Richmond scrawled out his meditations on the problem of representation, underlining key ideas as he went, his thoughts were sparked by specific ideas appearing in the body of the texts he was reading. Although his lengthy comments on what he was reading are somewhat hard for a modern reader to parse, I include them here in full because they have never before been published—perhaps have never been read by anyone other than Richmond before I found them—and yet capture the moment when the modern concept of representation was born. They are an incredibly important milestone in the history of political philosophy and the development of the case for universal suffrage.

The authors of one of the remonstrances against the King had written: "It is the misfortune of your majesty; it is the misfortune and grief of your People; to have a Grand Council and a Representative; under an undue and dangerous Influence." Richmond marked the end of the sentence with an asterisk, and then linked the following note (with emphases in the original) where he complained that only one seventy-fifth of the population had the right to vote, and not all who held the right used it:

> This [undue influence] is the real source of all the evils and danger with which the Nation is at present afflicted; no Remedy, therefore, can be so efficacious *as a Reformation in that very point*. There cannot be a *legal* government in this kingdom, without *a due Representation of all the People* instead of which (partly through *inequality, undue influence, corruption &* want of due *Renovation)* the Grand Council is become rather a misrepresentation than a Representation of the People, especially as the small proportion of

> a 75th part of their number do at present Act for their whole body. Whereas on the contrary every individual ought to be esteemed in the State, what he is in the Christian church; viz a Member of it; because no inheritances of Land, Houses, Etc, are to be esteemed so valuable as that common inheritance in the Laws, to which everyone is entitled. The unjust Act, therefore, of the 8 Henry VI, cap 7, ought to be repealed and the ancient constitutional mode of New Annual Parliaments (or "more often if need be" as declared in the Act of 4 Edward 3 c14) ought to be revived and firmly established, both in England and Ireland, as the most probable means of saving the state. No man can be truly Loyal who opposes the revival of that just and ancient Law.

He continued on the next page:

> There can be no constitutional Authority without the free and uninfluenced assent of the Majority of the People and such a free and uninfluenced assent cannot be known nor obtained without a new Assent for every Session. Whilst this salutary, this necessary part of the English Constitution was maintained, there were no disorders, difficulties, or inconveniences attending general elections.

Richmond had at last arrived at his reconceptualization of the foundation of the British political system. He had come to understand that the best way for Parliament to have durable independence from the King was for it to incorporate the whole of the people. If Parliament could represent every adult man, and through him, every member of every household, and if each MP owed his seat to the broad population, he could no longer be bought by the King. Popular sovereignty was the key to having a monarch tethered to multiple legislatures across his realm, without those legislatures losing their own power, authority, and independence. Cartwright had been on his way to these ideas, but it was Richmond who saw that universal suffrage provided the solution to preserving British liberty in the context of a growing empire.

In one spot in the notes, when the King encouraged the colonists to express their affection for the Crown as subjects, rather than sending petitions for reconciliation, Richmond scrawled comments in the margin that sound as bitter and black as the Junius letters. George was offering not reconciliation but "subjection to the Crown," and

> those persons, therefore, who advised the Rejection of these just and reasonable petitions ought to be esteemed as enemies to God & to Human Nature! Blinded by the Mammon of Unrighteousness, they panted for the future sale and division of American possessions, the distant prospect of which hastily roused fresh Caledonian bonds to go & take possession; but (like the just fate of Ahab) the Coveted Land has been dyed with their own blood!

Once again, he was pinning the blame on the King's ministers. The Americans had made a reasonable offer of reconciliation, but the people's requests had been rejected because of ministers who were "Blinded by the Mammon of Unrighteousness."

The King, in his address of March 22, 1776, had declared, "I deplore with the Deepest Concern the Miseries which a great Part of my Subjects in North America have brought upon themselves." Richmond asterisked the line and scrawled in the margin: "*The Miseries of War seem at present to threaten this Country more than America! To whom, then, will the words 'brought upon themselves' be most applicable?" His note continues on the next page: "for a very great part of the people are still subjected (by the Act) to the Crown; whereby the Constitution of the Kingdom is perverted so that all persons who voted or advised for such a measure are guilty of high Treason to the State! Yet they remain unpunished, and the Act still subsists to the disgrace of the English name!"

Richmond went on to build the case to justify full inclusion of the adult male electorate in the political system on the basis that we are all children of God and all share in the only property that matters for defining political belonging, the "common inheritance of the laws." He hadn't yet discovered an ideal electoral method to deliver a fair vote, but he had laid down its foundational principles.

The dramatic argument against Chatham for American independence, the hard work with his militia, and now the intellectual breakthrough on constitutionalism took their toll. Moments of high stress always seemed to bring Richmond bouts of ill health, and in the fall of 1778, he was as sick as he had ever been as an adult. Sarah sped to him in London. She wrote to her sister Emily that his complaint had been "what they call spasms in his bowels, which occasioned a bloody flux with such violent pain nothing ever equalled it. But as there was no inflammation or fever attending it the danger is past, provided he is careful of himself, and he promises he will be so." He was still in recovery a month later, and the family had genuinely feared they would lose him. Richmond was forty-three; his father had succumbed to bladder cancer at forty-nine. Yet Richmond's greatest contributions lay still ahead.

AS THE REALITIES OF war with Spain and France began to bite, the nation seemed beset by challenges. Debts were high; taxes were up. Inflation was rising; trade disruption was putting pressure on agricultural markets. Crop failures and price increases were hitting ordinary people. Yet despite these troubles, Parliament stayed in recess throughout the entire fall. As the state of the nation spiraled out of control, there was precious little evidence of any government leadership in response.

Nor did the following year bring much improvement. In February, Richmond complained about the weakness of the Whig party agenda to his nephew, Charles James Fox, who led the Opposition in the House of Commons: "No system was proposed or even suggested by which the Dependency of America was to be recover'd, or its alliance as an Independent State procured. No foreign Alliances were in Contemplation. The Management of the East India Company and the great possessions in India were never once mention'd. I do not know that there was an inclination, still less any Plan for reducing the corrupt Influence of the Crown, and rendering Parliament more Independent. The dreadfull and immediately ruinous State of our Finances was never in Question; No Plan of future Resources, or of present Reformation and oeconomy was any part of the overture you communicated."

In the absence of a broad, ambitious, coordinated plan of the kind that he sketched to Fox, Richmond intervened where he could in debates to nudge his colleagues in the right direction. In the House of Lords, on May 11, 1779, the Marquess of Rockingham brought up the poor economic conditions in Ireland, advocating for relief measures to support Irish welfare and unity with England. In the debate that followed, Richmond supported an amendment advocating for a closer, fairer Anglo-Irish relationship without legislative union but with mutual loyalty. He remarked that "His noble friend [Shelburne] had talked of an Union. He was for an union, but not an union of legislature, but an union of hearts, hands, or affections, and interests." With Richmond's amendment, the motion passed unanimously. Here, Richmond at last began to install his innovative approach to constitutionalism at the heart of the British government, planting the seeds of what would eventually be the arrangement of the Commonwealth. The British Parliament would legislate for Britain only, while other countries within the Commonwealth would have their own independent legislatures, yet all would be bound by a union of hearts, affections and interests, not obligations and exchequers, to the British Crown. Richmond had conceptualized a wholly new structure for Britain's empire.

Using the Irish example, Richmond tried to bring his new model of constitutionalism to bear on American policy. In response to Spain's declaration of war on June 17, he once more proposed the withdrawal of British troops from America to focus on defending Britain against the combined threat of France and Spain. The proposal was compatible with the new kind of union he had in mind, and he was supported in it by Lord Shelburne. The proposal once again sparked heated debates, and once again Parliament was unready to give up its authority over the colonies.

The stakes were rising, though. Also in response to the Spanish declaration of war, another rising young reformer, Lord Abingdon, a close friend of Lord Mahon (Pitt's son-in-law), moved an amendment urging the King to eject his ministers. This was quickly defeated. Richmond then moved another more extreme amendment, recommending to the King a "total change of that system which has involved us in our present difficulties in America, in Ireland, and at home." Richmond's desire to see Ireland and America have legislatures as independent as the British Parliament established him in the absolute vanguard of radicalism. It made him nearly a republican, and the Crown took notice.

Chapter 12

A BRITISH LAFAYETTE

1779–1780

Many may think, and with reason,
that still greater reforms are necessary.

—RICHMOND TO THE SUSSEX ELECTORATE, JANUARY 10, 1780

BRITAIN'S FATE HUNG BY A THREAD IN JULY 1779, AND EVERYone knew it. The government was losing the war in America but was unwilling to admit it publicly. Not only was the country bogged down in a military quagmire abroad; it was also vulnerable at home. The powerful French and Spanish navies were now arrayed against a nearly unprotected island. The legitimacy of the government and Crown were in question. The populace's awareness of the corruption of the government had steadily increased, alongside the worsening financial pain of a debt-laden war economy. Richmond's refined distinctions absolving the King of tyranny did not lessen the heated rhetoric directed toward the monarch. American defense of liberties was ricocheting back to London where suppression of the press had stirred powerful resentments. Also, legislation from the fall of 1778 seeking to extend toleration for Catholics from England to Scotland was fueling reactionary anti-government mobilization. With domestic turmoil mounting and fractures widening, this was the nearest England would come to being invaded since the Spanish Armada of 1588 and until the Nazi occupation of France in World War II.

Against this backdrop, Richmond began to defy the Crown's military orders, leading to suspicions that the Duke, who had been arguing vociferously for American independence for more than a year, was also fomenting revolution at home. General Jeffery Amherst, who would later shock British consciences by intentionally giving smallpox-infested blankets to Native Americans, sent Richmond orders to use the Sussex militia to drive people and cattle inland away from the coasts so that they could not be captured and used by invading French forces. Richmond refused. He considered the command a violation of fundamental property rights and sent back a request for alternative orders. He also requested a supply of arms, so that he could raise twenty-four companies of men to defend the coast.

Rather than simply communicating this request in his own name, though, Richmond called a meeting of the voting electorate of Sussex at the Assizes on July 30, convening the high sheriff, grand jury lord lieutenant, and "other Lords and Gentlemen of the County of Sussex." He put to them the question of whether the county should follow Amherst's orders. This county assembly unanimously resolved that Amherst's letters "cannot be looked upon as Commands" that the Duke was bound to obey. Richmond's militia could not be put at the disposal of the army, including for the driving of cattle, unless martial law were decreed. They also passed a unanimous resolution requesting arms in order that they could effectively defend their county. In addition to sending these resolutions back to General Lord Amherst, the men also had them printed in the newspaper and proposed that another county meeting be held on August 27 to address the situation. From the perspective of the Crown, the refusal to obey a military order was insubordination bordering on rebellion.

General Amherst was furious and wrote back with tight-lipped displeasure: "I have had the honour to receive your Grace's Letter of the 31st past, with a Copy of the resolution . . . of the county of Sussex; at both which I Cannot help expressing my surprise." The matter rose to the attention of the prime minister, still Lord North, and the secretary of the treasury, John Robinson, the government's political manager. Robinson sought to activate other gentlemen in the county, including Lord Gage, elder brother to General Gage, to counter Richmond's efforts. Robinson, in trying to drum up government supporters to attend the second meeting, wrote, "What may be the intentions of the Duke of Richmond is difficult to guess. It is not however unfair to suppose that it will not be favorable to government." He was alarmed that Richmond might be trying to raise a private army, a use of his militia that would not be "apprehended legal."

The King was explicitly "unenthusiastic" about Richmond's "raising twenty-four companies of militia in Sussex." He worried that with this level of military power, Richmond might be able "to bring forward his own creatures," by which he meant threaten a coup. This was not a purely fantasized concern. Governments could change in an instant. Bonnie Prince Charlie had landed without men and raised an army to threaten the throne almost overnight. In Sweden, Gustav III had transformed the government at a stroke. In America, it was precisely the ordinary civilian militias that had risen up and proven themselves worthy of taking on British regulars. A decade's worth of petitioning and organizing meant that the people of Britain knew how to mobilize. The worry was that Richmond would use his militia to spark a revolution and force a change of government, much as, a decade later, the French monarchy feared Lafayette's revolutionary aims when the French marquis rode at the head of his own militia into Paris in the stormy days after the fall of the Bastille.

Richmond was probably not preparing to take the government by force. His own changed views on the King testify to his restraint. Yet his letters at the time reveal that he was working to prepare a new ministry—recruiting people to replace Lord North as prime minister and to take other roles. Was he perhaps hoping to force a change in national policy by musket, to remove not the King but at least his ministers? While it seems unlikely that Richmond ever intended his militia for anything other than defense of the South Coast, the government had good reason to be wary, and everything hung on its ability to channel Richmond into an approved course of action. Robinson negotiated terms: Richmond would be permitted to raise his desired twenty-four companies as long as he gave them commissions from the King, not himself; agreed to limit their movements to Sussex; and pledged to focus exclusively on defense from enemy invasion. The next meeting of the Sussex gentlemen and lords affirmed these terms, and so Richmond was empowered to raise an additional twenty-four companies and won a supply of arms from the Tower of London. The government's decision, in the end, to trust Richmond averted conflict. He was a loyal British citizen, and they would benefit from that. The relationship between Richmond and the government had quite nearly come to a point of no return. In that moment the stability of Britain's constitutional order was in doubt.

Richmond raised his militia rapidly, and on August 27 his companies were ready to move out to defensive positions. In a letter to her friend Susan, Sarah reflected on how frenetic the Duke's departure with his militia had been: "There is such a million things to do when one *leaves one's home fit to be taken*."

Out in the channel sat the sixty-three French ships with 30,000 soldiers. The British fleet had mustered only thirty-five ships against them. Eventual reinforcements brought the number to forty-one. The situation on land was even worse. Because of all the soldiers sent to America, Britain had only 21,000 regular cavalry and infantry, in addition to its 30,000 militia. General Amherst concentrated these forces inland, leaving the coasts undefended—save for the Sussex militia. For reasons the British could not discern, the French made no move to engage. The French Navy was, in fact, ravaged by disease, and commanders were struggling to field enough men to function. Then, rapidly descending foggy weather obscured the two fleets from each other. Ultimately, the Franco-Spanish fleet was forced to withdraw, owing to inclement weather and logistical challenges. Everyone understood that, had the winds blown another way, England could have succumbed to the French.

THE CRISIS, AS JUNIUS had written to his publisher a decade earlier, had truly arrived. Richmond thought Britain's parlous situation demanded radical action. Comprehensive reform to Parliament could no longer be postponed. Having clarified in his own mind that the necessary constitutional relationship among Britain, Ireland, and America was a union of independent legislatures, each attached to the Crown, he had one last constitutional puzzle to solve. How would the Crown, holding sovereignty over colonies separately from Parliament, not overpower each legislature? For new colonial arrangements to be compatible with the freedom of British subjects, the British legislature itself required reform to increase its independence from the Crown. This would be best achieved by ensuring within the legislature the full representation of all the people, so that it would be practically impossible for the Crown to get all of the legislators in its pocket. The time had come for one man, one vote.

Richmond for the first time not only embraced but even began to advance the cause of universal suffrage for adult men—the solution needed to achieve the independence of the legislature from the Crown. He clipped and saved a magazine article from that fall describing his political position as "founded on unyielding opposition 'to the introduction of a nefarious Court system'" that acted always and everywhere "in defiance of, public opinion." On November 5, just after his return from traveling to Exeter with the militia, he wrote a long letter to John Cartwright, who had proposed universal manhood suffrage three years earlier in *Take Your Choice!* Richmond praised Cartwright's arguments about parliamentary reform as "founded upon true principles" and affirmed universal male suffrage as the plan "fairest of any I know to destroy corruption and restore vigour to the Constitution." His primary concern was practical. He could not see a pathway to enacting the reforms because he found it impossible to imagine that the members of the House of Commons "could be induced to pass such a self-denying law." After all, because universal suffrage would make them accountable to voters, they would have to do their jobs, solving problems legislatively, through coalition and compromise, instead of simply currying favor with the King. They had an incentive to avoid this result.

Given how hard it would be to get elected officials to reform the system by which they had been put in power, Richmond could see only one path forward. Change would require the efforts of an awakened people. He wrote: "I am convinced that nothing but an irresistible cry from without doors, could induce them to vote it." He acknowledged that "it requires men of very peculiar talents to be able to convince a whole nation of their real interest, and to act with one voice in support of it." He was willing to try to make his own contribution to the effort: "I am far from refusing myself to any reasonable attempt." He also let Cartwright know that he had been assiduously trying to prepare people for such a moment. "I have constantly, in conversation, endeavored to prepare the minds of the people for such a consideration, and I am at this time engaged in forming a plan which, I believe, would very much coincide with your opinions."

Richmond's plan solved the puzzle of how to achieve universal manhood suffrage. It would require organizing representation not by municipality but by specially designed districts. Each district would encompass roughly one thousand men of voting age and would elect one member of Parliament. Divided in this way, Britain's new electoral districts would return the number of members of Parliament necessary to preserve the then-current number of MPs—558. With this idea, Richmond invented the district-based foundation of modern democratic representation, according to which districts comprise equivalent-size populations, a mechanism that had not been used since the democracy of ancient Athens. This contribution to modern politics by the 3rd Duke of Richmond has not previously been recognized; its significance was profound. Modern British "constituencies" are closely related to the districts that Richmond first envisioned. Achieving this monumental change, Richmond realized, would take mass action. He began to plot an organizing strategy that would bring the whole country into the conversation.

Richmond first shared these ideas with his Whig colleagues through Burke's protégé, Walker King, who had disregarded Burke's advice and signed on as Richmond's summer tutor in the classics and, ultimately, had enrolled as an ensign in Richmond's militia in order to tutor Richmond's heir, Charles Lennox. Walker King was Richmond's companion while the two men were traveling back from Exeter to Goodwood with the Sussex militia after the defensive operation against the French. After the journey, King lodged in Stoke with Richmond's nephew. From there, he wrote a lengthy tell-all letter to Edmund Burke communicating his shock about what Richmond had shared. This letter (printed in full in the appendix) reports on the invention of modern representation in Britain, and the complex politics involved in beginning to make it a reality.

Walker King wrote to Burke to report on, as he put it, "a dish of Politicks, with which the Duke of Richmond treated me one Evening at an Inn." He warned Burke that Richmond's "Cookery will not be altogether to your taste," and that Burke should expect to hear from Richmond himself soon. Richmond read to King "a sketch of a Plan" that he had developed "for securing the Liberties of the People, and improving the form of our Government." Richmond had confided that he intended to introduce the plan in Parliament that winter. It was linked to his efforts to achieve the dismissal of the sitting cabinet. Richmond thought the plan should be used as a basis for grassroots organizing. King then reported on the plan from memory. Its core elements were annual elections, extension of the right to vote to every man over twenty-one without exception, and the division of the kingdom into districts containing about a thousand voters each. In addition, Richmond proposed "a variety of regulations . . . for the proper management of Elections, Petitions &c &c . . . [and] a secret Committee for the examination of the expenditure of secret service money" so that the secret service budget couldn't be used for vote buying. Richmond also had a plan to clean up the succession rules for the bishops who were included in the House of Lords and to establish term limits for the chief justices. With the independence of Parliament and the other branches thus achieved, Richmond asserted, Parliament would then be able to clean up the revenues and regulations for the navy, army, and religion. It amounted to a comprehensive policy agenda, going well beyond the electoral reforms, which were its foundation.

Walker King assured Burke that he had explicitly expressed his reservations about the plan to Richmond. He worried about practical difficulties but also, above all, that Richmond seemed to want "to strike pretty deeply at the Power of the Crown." He thought that Richmond was in danger of embracing "levelling and republican principles." Richmond shrugged off the objection, saying that those results "could not be helped." When Walker King challenged him about what he would do if his plan should fail, Richmond said that he would publish it because "it contained sentiments, which he believed he should never alter." He would "leave it in the possession of the publick."

This remarkable letter provides a single complete review of Richmond's agenda—universal manhood suffrage, yes, but also reforms to the election system, the House of Lords, the bench of Bishops, all the public offices, and the Army, Navy, Clergy, and Revenue. Richmond had developed a complete constitutional overhaul. While scholars have known about the letter, which is lodged in Burke's correspondence, they have not previously recognized its significance to the birth of modern politics and history of political thought. The letter also reveals Richmond's mathematical mind at work, and the dawning power of mathematics to solve policy puzzles. The constitutional structure of British politics had rested on property and other establishment interests, for instance, the church. Representation was very skewed in relation to population precisely *because* it had never previously been organized in relation to population. It was the feudal lords, the landed gentry, the merchant members of city corporations, the freeholders in towns, the clergy, who had insisted on being heard by the King across several centuries. Their ability to press their claims had generated the representative structure of Parliament, organized by social sectors, but not by population. The idea that the whole nation should in fact be represented in Parliament reflected Richmond's deep exposure to the great political philosophers of the age and their theories of natural rights—a philosophy that required a radical reorientation of the basic foundation of British governance.

WALKER KING WAS SKEPTICAL about the viability of Richmond's plan to build a grassroots movement around parliamentary reform, but Richmond had read the moment right. Within weeks of his conversation with King, the people began to rise. First, on November 22, 1779, the voters of Middlesex, the London City radicals, quietly voted to establish a monthly meeting of freeholders "for the purpose of preserving the independence of this country." This monthly meeting initiated what would become a broad-based movement to form what the radicals called "associations," groups organized to redirect British politics and constitutional order, much like the many committees and congresses of the Americans beginning a decade earlier and still ongoing.

Most surprisingly, though, not only the people but also the Lords began to rise. When the King opened Parliament on November 25, 1779, the debate was ferocious. In a somber tone, the King acknowledged that the French and the Americans had now also brought Spain into their alliance and had attempted to assault the coasts of England. He called for unity to deal with "one of the most dangerous confederacies that ever was formed against the crown and people of Great Britain." The crisis notwithstanding, Rockingham moved a defiant Amendment to the Address to emphasize the total lack of cohesion among the deliberative bodies and offices, due to the court's corrupting influence. He hadn't yet embraced Richmond's most dramatic proposed solution, universal suffrage, but he was willing to carry the message about governmental corruption and move forward some of the more moderate reforms.

Then, out in the counties, country gentlemen, who were men of property but without aristocratic standing, also began to raise their voices, bringing together all three segments of society—urban merchants, rural landed voters, and the aristocracy—against the government and Crown. The movement was ballooning into the biggest challenge to date to

George III's reign. In Yorkshire, Rockingham's home county and also England's largest, an impressive new political activist, the Reverend Christopher Wyvill, was organizing. A handsome, square-jawed, charismatic man of independent family wealth and a champion of religious dissenters, he sought to restore the nation's morals and reground the constitution on its true principles. He planned to use legal assemblies of the people, petitions, remonstrances, associations, and requests for commitments from candidates for office to vote against corruption and corrupt men. He sounded very much like the Americans in their early days of organizing committees of correspondence and the first "association" of their Continental Congress.

Movements never grow without pains, though, as people seek to form coalitions despite different interests. As the movement gained strength, conflict also emerged among the three constituencies forming it. The City radicals wanted to remake the very foundations of government, transitioning from a property and interest basis for representation to a popular basis, proportional to population. They were fully on board with Cartwright and Richmond's agenda of universal suffrage. In contrast, the "Whig magnates" and "Whig grandees," as scholars often call them, wanted to reduce the power of the Crown but also sought to preserve the aristocratic foundation of the government. Led by Rockingham and Burke, their more conservative and privilege-protecting focus fastened on "economical reform" to reduce the extent of patronage the Crown could command, by shrinking the number of paid roles it could award. Burke's decision to reinforce aristocratic power now widened the split between himself and Richmond. The third faction was the newly mobilized county constituency. They shared with the Whig magnates a commitment to the traditional basis of the constitution in property, but they wanted to include the middle class and rising industrialists in the electorate. All three constituencies were united in wishing to rebalance power. They differed on the particulars and split over the degree to which the constitution should be popularized. Richmond's position, like that of the City radicals, was the most egalitarian.

Although his commitments lay with the City radicals, Richmond was the only leading political figure with a role in all the camps—as a long-term collaborator with both branches of Whigs, the Rockinghamites who were his home and also the Chathamites; in his close collaboration and connection to the City radicals from Wilkes to John Cartwright; and in leading a county constituency as lord lieutenant of Sussex, where there was above-average enthusiasm for republicanism, particularly in and around Lewes. On paper at least, he was the sole political figure positioned to unite the three constituencies as a new basis for a government.

THE NEXT FEW MONTHS saw much jockeying for position by different factions of the Opposition. Despite the political tension, business in London remained vibrant in the fall, and theaters were full, but coffeehouses and printing presses continued to spread dire news about the grinding descent of the conflict in America into guerrilla warfare. Also, prices were rising, the country faced bread shortages again, and an early frost arrived in October. The winter would turn out to be one of the coldest in British history. As the fog thickened and days shortened with winter's onset, a sense of foreboding grew.

Just days before George III opened Parliament on November 25, Wyvill and three associates met to consider "the troubled state of the nation." The question they asked themselves was whether they should call a meeting of all the voters in Yorkshire to discuss what was to be done. They concurred that the time had come and drafted up letters to seek support. They sought to wrest leadership of the county from Rockingham, while nonetheless incorporating him in their efforts. They also aimed to give voice to new constituencies. They decided to make the economy and corruption their rallying cry. For them the two issues were intimately connected. "From what I see," Richmond wrote to Shelburne, "a general spirit is rising. I do not expect such immediate effects as some do, but I think it will be gradual, only to become more formidable if commonly well managed." All over the country the enormous cost and the lack of success in the war were causing "general indignation." All the factions could tell that the moment of political opportunity had arrived and so the jostling to seize it intensified.

In December of 1779, the Opposition Whigs in Parliament aimed to set the agenda by focusing on widespread criticism of the government's handling of Ireland, public funds, and military expenditures. An expensive two-months' defense in September and October against a siege of

Savannah by a Franco-American force, including free black troops from Saint-Domingue, had succeeded but with no impact on the war's balance of power. On December 1, the Earl of Shelburne moved to censure the ministers for their neglect of Ireland, echoing an earlier motion from Rockingham calling for Irish relief. On December 7, Richmond advocated for "economical reform" of the civil list—the list assigning positions and roles, pensions to public appointees, and payments for the Royal Household—and urged the King to discourage wastefulness given Britain's dire finances. Then, a week later, Shelburne highlighted a dramatic rise in "extraordinaries" in army spending, attributing it to corruption in military provisioning. Shelburne estimated four million pounds had been squandered. Richmond proposed that an address be presented to the King asking him to speak out against extravagance and waste of public funds.

The aristocrats were laying out a clear agenda, and the country gentlemen were ready for much, but not all, of it. The day before the December 15 parliamentary debate, some two hundred miles to the north, 209 eminent Yorkshiremen—nearly a third of them clergy—signed a call for a meeting of voters to be held on December 30 to discuss reform. Two weeks later, on December 30, six hundred Yorkshire gentlemen gathered in the ballroom of the York Assembly Rooms. Constructed in 1735, the Assembly Rooms was a very fine and important classical building, part of an early eighteenth-century revival in England of classical architecture. Copying the Americans, the Yorkshiremen called their gathering in this grand space a "Congress," and signed a petition for economic reform, just as Rockingham and his allies had been arguing for in Parliament that month. The Yorkshiremen also signed on to the calls for inquiries into the gross abuses of public money via the civil list, and they favored peace with the American colonies, although they still rejected independence. Then they pushed further than Rockingham had been willing to go, much to Richmond's pleasure. They called for annual elections and adding one hundred more county members to rectify imbalances in representation. By welding together economic reform and electoral reform, the county men were trying to force the Whig magnates in a more radical direction.

Knowing the spirit of radicalism was rising, Rockingham and Burke sought to negotiate the agenda with Wyvill in advance of the meeting, hoping to rein it in. They produced seven resolutions, aiming to place power over the movement in the hands of members of Parliament. Wyvill, though, outmaneuvered them by keeping his own resolutions minimal. He wanted simply: "redress of the civil list, place, and pension grievances before the grant of any additional supply," meaning that the patronage system had to be reformed before Parliament approved a new annual budget for the King. Again copying the Americans, he also secured passage of a resolution to set up a committee of correspondence to communicate with other counties, firmly wresting control of the movement from the Whig lords. The committees of correspondence would be encouraged to set up allied associations on the same platform of "such measures as may conduce to restore the Freedom of Parliament." The resolution also added the language that "The Crown has acquired a great and unconstitutional influence, which if not checked, may soon prove fatal to the Liberties of this Country." The language of revolution had come to the shires of England. The different factions of the coalition might be struggling over the agenda, and who would lead, but the overarching goal of reducing the power of the Crown now had broad-based backing.

During those tough winter months, while the British Opposition wrestled itself into some sort of functional unity, the American Revolution settled into a strategic lull. The Americans were working to fortify Charleston, South Carolina, expecting a renewed assault there by the British in the spring. For the British, the city seemed pivotal for two reasons: Filled with powerful slave-holding merchants, it could catalyze an uprising of colonists with loyalist sympathies, something the Crown always expected, but which had yet to materialize at scale. Even more crucially, Charleston would serve as a key debarkation and supply point for what had become, since the entry of the French and Spanish, the most vital part of the war: the struggle to protect Britain's valuable colonies in the Caribbean. In the northern theater, at the Continental Army's winter camp in New Jersey, Washington encouraged his troops along through the coldest winter of the war. Meanwhile, in Britain the growth of the radical movement was electric. The publication of the Yorkshire petition and resolutions spread the reform message like wildfire. The Whig Party structure, which stretched across the nation, spread the gospel from county to county. Rockingham distributed the documents broadly through his network. Burke got six copies. Richmond received three, the numbers reflecting their relative degrees of influence within the official Rockingham party. Associations spread across the nation's counties, and cities joined in: Leeds, Manchester, Liverpool, Nottingham, Norwich, Birmingham, Exeter. This was the start of a modern representative nation. The industrial cities were beginning to insist on their inclusion, and all agreed with the demand for shorter parliaments. The Crown registered the growing movement—including its dangerous seeds of revolution—and started deputizing ministerial supporters in the different counties to show up at county meetings to try to offer counterarguments.

The earliest stages of revolution had arrived back in Britain. Ideas launched across the Atlantic had ricocheted back from America to the mother country in the form of practical action.

WITH THE PEOPLE NOW rising organically, Richmond was eager to engage in the building movement for reform. Wyvill's agenda was more moderate than his; it did not include one man, one vote. Since it came from the people, though, it was a real start. Until recently, Richmond had found the people of Sussex too "supine" to join a national organizing movement, but now things changed dramatically. Lewes had embraced Wilkes. The townsmen had nurtured the author of *Common Sense*. An appetite had grown in Sussex, perhaps an insatiable one, to join the national efforts to form associations and to lift grievances to the House of Commons by means of petitions. Richmond was suddenly in his element.

Seizing the opportunity, Richmond began to collaborate with the Sussex sheriff and other reformers to plan a county meeting. The winter was the hardest he and his neighbors had ever known. The county rivers froze, and ice appeared in coastal estuaries. Ponds and wells froze, too, dangerously limiting access to water. Frequent and persistent snow blanketed the South Downs and rural roads. To call people together in these conditions, Richmond paid for advertisements in the form of letters to *The Sussex Advertiser* of January 10 and 17 from himself to the sheriff and to the electorate proposing a general county meeting to be held on January 20. His letters were also republished in London papers, for instance, in *The London Chronicle* of January 13. On January 20, numerous nobility, gentry, clergy, freeholders, and other inhabits of the County of Sussex braved the elements to descend on the Lewes Town Hall.

At the meeting, the voting men of Sussex, with only five dissenting voices, passed a resolution to send a petition to the House of Commons that largely mirrored the Yorkshire petition. It began in high style. They could not stand by while viewing "the rapid decline of the British Empire"; they called on the members of Parliament who should be motivated by "every Tye of honor Interest and Religion," to avoid the "Ruin that Menaces this lately prosperous and happy nation." The petition then enumerated their grievances in fine detail, much as the Americans' Declaration had done. They condemned the "undue influence" of the Crown and insisted that no new taxes should be levied until the situation was rectified. They were angry about the mounting and "ruinous" war debt, "the extravagant waste of the public money," the many sinecures awarded, and "exorbitant emoluments of office" that had stretched "to an immense and still increasing amount."

As Yorkshire copied the Americans, so too did the Sussex meeting attendees. They committed funds to support the ongoing work of what they also chose to call a "committee of correspondence" to collaborate with the other associations. Attendees contributed to the fund according to their ability. The Duke of Richmond, not surprisingly, was the lead donor staking ten guineas. The participants resolved to print the petition in *The Sussex Advertiser* and to circulate copies throughout the county to gather as many signatures as possible.

The movement gained force through collaboration with other radicals gathered in London. The city was no less bitterly cold and angry than the counties, but there was strength—and warmth—in numbers. The Sussex committee held their next gathering on February 16, at St. Alban's Tavern in Pall Mall, in London, which soon became the meeting location for all the county associations, not only Sussex. Diasporas were forming, linking home counties to the metropolis. The Sussex gentlemen printed a record of their proceedings from February 16 not only in *The Sussex Advertiser* but also in the London papers: *The London Evening Post*, *The Morning Chronicle*, *The London Courant*, *The General Evening Post*, and *The General Advertiser*, in a deliberate attempt to inspire others.

The swelling movement that Richmond had hoped for began to emerge. The leaders of the York, Sussex, and London committees met together at St. Alban's Tavern on February 24. This brought Wyvill together with Frankland from Sussex, who was Richmond's man, and with the City radicals, John Jebb and J. Brand Hollis, who represented the London committee, and were Charles James Fox's men. No such broad-based Opposition coalition had previously formed in the lifetimes of any of these men. Their convergence was shaking the very pillars of government. Elections were in the offing. Everyone was aware that Parliament would be dissolved sometime in 1780, and Fox was courting the City radicals as part of an effort to win a Westminster seat. This group determined to call a meeting of leaders of the several committees for a March 7 to develop "a plan of association on legal and constitutional grounds for supporting the petitions and other measures conducing to restore the Freedom of parliament." The purpose of such a plan of association was to unite all their organizing and petitioning efforts. They were, in effect, bringing a grassroots party infrastructure into existence, coalescing around the reform agenda. Across Britain, the fabric of society was fraying under the pressure of imperial war, economic strain, and the bitter winter. Discontent rippled from country estates to city streets, as the war dragged on, bread prices soared, and petitions piled up—fueling a sense that the old political order could not long endure.

Between March and April, against Rockingham's desires, Wyvill added one more commitment to the Yorkshire platform. The associations would favor candidates ready to support an end to the war in America. Except for the cautious approach to suffrage expansion, the association agenda was Richmond's agenda. Richmond had good reason to believe he was on the cusp of building a party that might support his efforts.

THE BATTLE BETWEEN CROWN and country was now engaged, and each side moved aggressively.

Despite the building public sentiment for an end to the war, the King and his ministers pressed forward with the colonial conflict. Just when the several Opposition factions were finally forging a shared agenda, on March 29, General Henry Clinton crossed the Ashley River and began formal siege operations against Charleston. He had left safe Savannah behind to press for more. The siege would unfold over nearly seven weeks as a slow, tightening noose around the city. British forces built a series of siege lines and artillery batteries that crept forward in parallels, while the Royal Navy blockaded Charleston Harbor from the east; inside the city, American defenders were hemmed in between the Cooper and Ashley Rivers, with makeshift earthworks and redoubts stretched across low-lying, marshy terrain vulnerable to bombardment, disease, and encroaching British trenches.

Just as stubborn as the King, Richmond too, in this moment when his decade-long pursuit of Opposition unity was finally coming to fruition, pressed for more. He tried to push the movement toward the full embrace of universal manhood suffrage. Here the British radicals were ahead of the Americans, by generations. In April, Major John Cartwright and the City radicals, with Richmond's blessing and support, formed the Society for Constitutional Information to flood the country with the idea of universal manhood suffrage. The society began rapidly printing and disseminating its pamphlets throughout Britain. Soon there was one concrete victory. On April 12, the Westminster Committee formally recommended "universal manhood suffrage, annual parliaments; equal electoral districts, single-member constituencies, vote by ballot, removal of property qualifications, and payment of members." This at last embraced Richmond's full program of reform and added salaries for members of Parliament.

While Richmond had been feeding the grassroots movement over the winter and into early spring, he had also been working to drive an aligned agenda in Parliament. The dynamics of synchronization between tavern and Westminster were the same as during the Junius years, except that now Richmond was acting publicly. On February 8, 1780, the Earl of Shelburne proposed a motion in the House of Lords to form an impartial committee, free of government employment or pensions, to investigate public expenditure. Although he didn't win the vote, his new motion reignited the furor over corruption in military provisioning contracts and prompted an unusually lengthy debate. After the motion was rejected, Richmond signed a protest against the decision, reinforcing core Whig principles of accountability and anti-corruption. At that same meeting of Parliament, Wyvill presented the initial York petition to the House of Commons. On February 11, Edmund Burke formally introduced his own motion for "economical reform," which would eliminate sixty government patronage "places" or jobs. Richmond fully supported this measure, but with it Burke was trying to limit further expansion toward Richmond's more radical ideas.

John Adams, minister plenipotentiary in France at the time, recorded Britain's astonishing degree of political turbulence. He made note of the petitions, "numerous committees of correspondence," and associations, reporting that these had "alarmed the King and his Ministers to great degrees." The government tasked its loyalists in Parliament with carrying the message that the nation faced "faction, sedition, and rebellion." The King was advised to dismiss lords lieutenant of counties, such as Richmond, who were supporting "meetings of the people." The King held off this extreme step but did seek to suppress meetings of the people. Adams perceived a dynamic of radical action followed by royal suppression that looked likely to him only to intensify the conflict. "One would think," he wrote to the American Congress, "that the Nation was really at the Brink of a Civil War."

Britain had reached something of a hinge in history. Pressure might ratchet up and produce full revolution, as in America. Or the King and his ministers might double down on repression and secure full autocratic control, as in Sweden. Each side understood the stakes. John Dunning, one of the Opposition Shelburnite Whigs, introduced a rallying cry for the clearly momentous reform movement. On April 6 he proposed a vote on a very simple motion, namely "that the influence of the Crown has increased, is increasing, and ought to be diminished." The Opposition Whigs delivered a breakthrough victory, passing the resolution 233 to 215. It seemed that the dam holding back constitutional change had broken. Dunning's sentence became the rallying cry not only of the Opposition in Parliament but also of the City radicals and the county associations. It was the motto of the civil revolution unfolding in Britain.

Yet the forces arrayed against the reformers were stronger than that victory made them seem. Ten days later, on April 24, there was another test of the strength of each side in this near civil war. The House of Commons convened to debate Burke's bill on "economical reform." Burke's bill plainly struck at the root of the power imbalance between the King and Parliament. It gave concrete form to Dunning's statement of principle that the influence of the Crown should be diminished. The stakes could not have been higher. Did radical and reformist or royalist voices now rule the nation? Attendance was the largest it had been in living memory. The Opposition had invested strenuously in preparation through organizing, and petitioning, but for nought. The bill failed. The King and his ministers had successfully whipped the vote, turning out every last member of Parliament dependent on them for some favor or other. It was a signal victory for the Crown. Now the conflict was in equipoise. The wave of reform was cresting. Would it break for the Opposition or subside in support of the King?

RICHMOND RECOGNIZED THAT THE whole country was by now engaged in a battle for the future of Britain. Committees of correspondence were spreading the reform message everywhere, including into the industrializing cities of Birmingham and Manchester. Even lazy absentee members of Parliament were being dragged from country homes and forced to participate. This, he believed, was the moment to put universal manhood suffrage on the table—a chance to deliver wholesale transformation of the British constitution, a soft revolution through grassroots organizing, a popular movement and law, rather than through bloodshed.

On Friday, June 2, 1780, Charles Lennox, the 3rd Duke of Richmond rose in the House of Lords and made a motion for universal manhood suffrage—that every man over the age of twenty-one, regardless of his ownership of property, should have the right to vote. It was the first such motion in British history, a proposal to put the constitution on a fully popular and national footing, instead of its long-standing feudal footing. It was the first proposal in Europe for universal manhood suffrage on a national scale, and quite probably the first in the modern world.

On the very same day, fourteen thousand disorderly anti-Catholics descended on Parliament carrying a petition for repeal of the 1778 Relief Act legislating religious toleration. The mob, organized entirely separately from the reformers by Lord George Gordon, an eccentric Scottish MP in the House of Commons, was consumed by not only passionate prejudice but also rank violence. As members of Parliament struggled to gain entry to the House on their way to hear Richmond, they were roughed up by the rowdy crowd. They arrived disheveled and badly shaken.

While the county associations had been organizing throughout the country all spring, anti-Catholic activists had been doing the same. Their efforts had originated in Scotland, away from the main action of the conflict between the Crown and parliamentary reformers. As one scholar has put it, if the first was the movement of light, the second was a movement of darkness. In 1778, the House of Commons had unanimously passed a bill for the relief of Catholics. While the proscriptions against Catholics had long gone unenforced, they were still on the statute books. This bill removed them as part of a general movement toward liberal toleration. Yet that formal decision to protect the basic liberties of Catholics awakened a sleeping dragon of bigotry, particularly in Scotland.

Between 1778 and 1780, just as the county associations were developing their plans to organize around economic reform, constituencies in Scotland formed associations to petition for repeal of the Relief Act. The effort was shot through with the dark passions of extremism; and violence against Catholics broke out, largely centered in Scotland but also in large English cities such as Bristol. Homes, shops, and chapels were destroyed; the government dithered before it brought the violence to an end and required the Scottish Protestant activists to pay compensation to those whose property they had pillaged. Neither Richmond nor his associates were tracking this other populist wave. The anti-Catholic activism began to peter out, and would probably have died out but for one person: Lord George Gordon.

Gaunt and wild-eyed, Lord George Gordon was the brother of William Gordon, for whom Richmond's sister Sarah had abandoned her husband. This family was somehow destined perpetually to upend his hopes. In March 1779 the Committee for the Protestant Interest in Edinburgh had recruited Gordon to serve as their parliamentary spokesman. They hoped he would combat the pro-toleration arguments of Burke, Fox, and Wilkes. He had the passion but not the discipline to do this.

From one of the great Scottish families, and with a brother in the House of Lords as a duke, Gordon was himself a vehement orator but functioned independently of any of the parties. He was energetically opposed to the American War. He was equally opposed to the King, whom he called "A Tyrant King," and to what he called "a Venal Parliament, and a flagitious [or criminal] Ministry." He was unwilling to take direction from the leaders of the Opposition in Parliament, or to associate with anyone at all as a partner. He was a fanatic with a populist's messianic desire "to find a safe harbor in the affections of the People, as they find me a true Pilot of their own Interests." As government response quelled Protestant agitation in Scotland that spring and summer, Gordon took it into his own hands to drum it up in London. He made dangerous proposals, for instance, that Protestants should be armed and that there should be a Presbyterian Congress, more mimicry of the Americans. In November 1779, as Richmond had begun to circulate his radical proposal for universal manhood suffrage, Gordon took up the presidency of the Protestant Association, dedicated to repeal of the 1778 Catholic Relief Act. More moderate elements of the coalition began to fall away and by May of 1780, Gordon was surrounded by diehards.

On May 5, 1780, he met with his committee and proposed that the Protestant Association should draft their petition for repeal of the Relief Act, assemble throngs of supporters, and then parade the petition en masse to the Houses of Parliament. He summoned his members together and filled Coachmakers' Hall to capacity on May 29. There he dared his supporters, telling the standing-room-only crowd that they should be prepared to "run all hazards with him" as "he would run all hazards with the people" or else they could "get another President."

On Friday, June 2, 1780, Gordon gathered fifty thousand people for a rally in South London on St. George's Fields, site of the fateful massacre of Wilkes supporters in 1768. Then he led fourteen thousand incited Protestants, wearing blue cockades and cursing Catholics with shouts of "No Popery!" in a parade to the Houses of Parliament. The Horse Guards had to be brought up to clear the area. That initiated a week of rioting in the city that did more damage to London than anything since the Great Fire of 1666 or until the Blitz of 1944.

The rioters attacked the homes, shops, and chapels of Catholics. Then, on the night of June 6, they opened the gates of Newgate Prison, released the prisoners, and burned it. As a result, "a hardened criminal element was injected into the ranks of the rioters," as one historian has written. From that point on, a mob of impassioned and emboldened advocates transformed into a force for systematic violence throughout the city—going door to door, robbing and extorting people. The rioters attacked the homes of members of Parliament from both parties. Members of the Opposition avoided blame for the riots mainly because they were victims equally with royalists. The mob burned Lord Chief Justice Mansfield's extensive law library. A distillery was attacked. Gin ran through the gutters, and rioters lapped it up from the street, and then were incinerated when the alcoholic rivers were accidentally set on fire. All of London was ablaze, as if the Great Fire of 1666 had been reignited, but this time by rage, not accident.

The authorities were paralyzed. Only the King kept his head. For once, he did in fact take matters into his own hands and called out the army to restore order. Militia and regular troops were put on forced marches to London. Some three hundred people were killed by the soldiers. In perhaps one of the greatest ironies of the event, John Wilkes, the

London sheriff, led soldiers to defend the Bank of England against a mob attempting to enter and loot it.

On the first Friday of the Gordon Riots the only topic on the minds of parliamentarians was the mob outside, whose violence put Richmond on the defensive. There was no possibility of bringing his motion in favor of wider representation for the people when a mob was baying at the door. The House was adjourned to reassemble on the following day.

The Lords returned to their chamber on Saturday, were called to order, and began their deliberations by debating and unanimously passing a motion recommending that the King deploy force to control the riots. Only after that did Richmond have his chance to present his bill for universal manhood suffrage. He made the best case he could in the circumstances, and took an hour and a half to read through the details of his bill. Unsurprisingly, given the context, the Lords were unpersuadable. Richmond's bill was rejected without an official vote. The debate about Richmond's radical idea was over before it began. The cresting wave of reform had broken, and the seething seas of civil revolution yielded to the urgency of turmoil in the streets, ebbing back to support for the King.

EVEN RICHMOND NOW FOUND himself siding with the Crown. On June 12, he wrote morosely to Rockingham to advise him not to give in to the rioters' demands for repeal of the Catholic Relief Act. The contrast between his aspirations for the people and the behavior of some of them left him in despair. The nation had borne so much through the war and the people had endured "evident loss of their own liberty" in the King's now two-decades-long suppression of dissent as well as the reduction of parliamentary independence. Yet rather than fully "stirring," the people had consented "to being led by Scotch fanatics, and to the tune of bagpipe—set Newgate loose and burn London." In attacking even the Opposition members of Parliament, they had turned "against the best friends of liberty." "Such a nation," Richmond was emphatic, "*cannot* be saved." Once again, he forswore Parliament, projecting that he might never attend again. Britain's nascent civil revolution had been overwhelmed by sulfuric paroxysms of endemic bigotry.

Reports from America changed the mood again, and not in

Richmond's favor. News that the British had captured Charleston in early May arrived in London in mid-June. This was one of their greatest achievements of the war. Alongside offers of 100-pound rewards for the "arrest and conviction of any leader of the late Riots or Tumult," *The London Gazette* simultaneously carried the good tidings. Suddenly, the efforts that Richmond and his allies had undertaken for months to elevate the voice of the people had been subsumed. The King's ministry knew full well that the tables had turned. War Secretary Charles Jenkinson marveled in a letter from on July 20, 1780, that the country's "strange Convulsions" had produced an effect "the very reverse of what might have been expected." They had strengthened the government and restored Britain to a tranquility that it had "not for a long time experienced." The combined uprisings had indeed been a "Crisis," but the violence of the final riots discharged all the "noxious Humours, which had for a long time been collecting." King George III had won. He had fended off a true threat of broad-based revolution, by staring down and ending the violence of a fanatical faction. He, not his ministers, had directly, personally, earned the victory.

Richmond knew he was defeated. When he had first shared with Walker King his plan of introducing a motion for universal suffrage for adult men, he had imagined a possible future in which it would be rejected. He anticipated that in that eventuality, "as a man, whose political sentiments did not entirely agree with those of any party he should retire." This was now the future he faced. For more than a decade, he had sought to understand, define, and protect British liberties. He more than anyone had seen how the strains of empire were undermining a tradition of liberty at home. Broadly humane in his outlook, he was ready to accept the Americans as peers, yet neither did he wish to see a weakening of the great strength of Britain. He cared not about liberty in the abstract but about British liberties, an ancient inheritance as he saw it. The intensity of his desire to resolve the tension between a tradition of citizen liberty and the outspreading reach of empire led him, in effect, to invent the intellectual architecture of the Commonwealth. The keystone of the edifice was to be universal manhood suffrage. His vision was noble, far-sighted, and creative. In contrast to his years with the Junius brigade, this attempt to lead his nation had in fact achieved great practical success—he had at long last united his Whigs. He had persuaded the more traditional Whigs to embrace reform and settled the City radicals enough for them to partner, at least momentarily, with the country moderates. Not alone, but absolutely at the center of the work, he had truly inspired a movement. No one had challenged the King with the force of Richmond. Yet an old saw has it that, if you're going to take a shot at the King, you'd better not miss.

PART IV

GOD SAVE THE KING, GOD SAVE REFORM

1780–1806

Chapter
13

RECONCILIATION WITH THE KING

1780–1782

My Dear Lord if you Think my Services in the present Administration useful, you must support me in this Measure. You know it was my Bargain.

—RICHMOND TO ROCKINGHAM, MAY 11, 1781

AS RICHMOND SANK BACK DOWN DEFEATED TO HIS BENCH in the House of Lords, he could not have known that the next twenty years would bring tremendous change in Britain toward the constitutionalism he sought. The war in America was about to end disastrously and destroy Lord North's government, creating an opening for new leadership. After a major storm, the ocean doesn't quickly return to calm. A storm-whipped sea pulses with chaotic, residual energy even after thunder and lightning have passed. The swell may come in multiple directions at once, colliding in unpredictable patterns. This dynamic captures the state of politics in Britain between 1780 and 1806—the period from the Gordon Riots and the Battle of Yorktown to the ministry of William Pitt the Younger, encompassing the French Revolution and Terror, and the rise of the French autocrat and empire builder, Napoleon Bonaparte.

To try to ride the waves of postwar politics was more about managing chaos than performing grace; it was, for Richmond, the ultimate test of political nerve and skill. As in the first years of the King's reign, Britain would once more cycle rapidly through prime ministers—with five serving over the three-year period from 1780 to 1783. In despair, the King drafted secret abdication letters. Britain truly was on the brink.

Also in this decade, George would suffer a second, far more severe bipolar episode that could not be hidden from the public and that plunged the nation into a deeper regency crisis than had unfolded in 1765, with allies of the dissolute Prince of Wales maneuvering to place him on the throne.

In 1789, a mere four months after the regency crisis came the fall of the Bastille, and the French Revolution brought more full-throated, and even violent, calls for revolution in England. These were enthusiastically encouraged, if not instigated, by Richmond's long-standing "particular friend," Thomas Paine, who, like revolution, crossed the Atlantic and returned to Europe.

Yet despite Paine's overwhelming influence, neither he nor any other individual was in control of the political maelstrom that was unleashed in Britain and France between 1780 and the close of the eighteenth century—as Europe ricocheted from one war and revolution to another. By 1780, Richmond's intent to shape the course of events—through pamphleteering, the Junius group, the Society for Constitutional Information, grassroots organizing, and parliamentary oratory—might seem not only to have been thwarted but even to have been a strategy fully wiped out by the disordered times. Yet those efforts of a decade and a half left him uniquely positioned to surf the political turbulence. He had always looked out ahead, beyond the gaze of others. He had never relied on the status quo to chart his course. In the chaos, he could see opportunities where others saw only collapse.

The choice of the age was not in fact binary—between the revolution and republicanism of America and the coup and autocracy of Sweden. Richmond had long been pursuing a third way—a transformed constitutional monarchy wherein the true sovereign was the people, and the Crown accepted limits on its own authority. He would spend the last phase of his life realizing this possibility through a set of counterintuitive political moves that read to some as acts of hypocrisy but which were in fact smart adaptations to chaotic times. The coming two decades would be an era of surprises—strange bedfellows and new coalitions; broken friendships and fresh enmities—and out of them a modern Britain was born.

The first major surprise of this period was Richmond's reconciliation with the King and the introduction of reform efforts into official government policy. No one saw it coming.

AFTER THE GORDON RIOTS and without an ability to see the future, Richmond must have been filled with dread about punitive measures he might face from the King. Retreat to France was off-limits because of the ongoing war. He would have to bear the brunt of whatever came. For the summer of 1780, he withdrew with his militia to Ranmer Camp, in the woodland, grassy meadows of the North Downs northwest of Dorking in Surrey, about twenty-five miles south of London.

Richmond had reason to be alarmed. His main confidant now was no longer Edmund Burke but the Earl of Shelburne. He wrote to Shelburne to lament that the "much alarmed" ministry would now treat the suppression of disturbances as "the main object of all their government." Indeed, he and Shelburne were both under attack by the government, which had branded both men as "traitors."

The Duke was not alone in his sense of despair. He had been defeated, yes, but the King too had been wounded. At forty-one, George III was still physically vigorous—an avid horseman—and, in the summer of 1780, he and his queen Charlotte were expecting the fourteenth of their fifteen children. He also remained disciplined in his sense of duty to preserve Britain and its territories—but he was under siege. A sizeable percentage of his population, and of members of Parliament, were on record saying they wished to see his power reduced.

In the King's family, his heir, George Augustus Frederick, Prince of Wales, had just turned eighteen and was beginning to display the hedonism and financial indulgence that would drive him apart from his father, and attract opportunistic Opposition politicians toward him, eager to capitalize on the split between father and son.

Nor would the King receive any more good news from the thirteen North American colonies—only from Jamaica—after the capture of Charleston. Just as Richmond had overreached in seeking to fold universal suffrage into the agenda of his now united Opposition members, so too the British military in America was overreaching, choosing to fight on from Charleston for the sake of the Caribbean instead of leveraging that victory into a peace treaty on advantageous terms.

The Gordon Riots had not improved the situation. The King had been compelled to take matters into his own hands because of Lord North's ineffectiveness. The beleaguered North had long wanted to quit, and now the King also began to think he might want him gone. George III had always been politically canny and diligent in tracking his nation's politics. With Chatham dead, the King's twenty years on the throne made him the most experienced politician in the realm. George III was not one to idle in inaction when he was at risk of failing in his duty to safeguard the nation. He could not bear North's ineptitude; nor could he afford, he believed, to let the Opposition gain any further strength. Both problems required his attention.

North's widely recognized failure to staunch the rioting gave the King an opening to tackle both problems together. The King reached out to Rockingham, still the leader of the Opposition Whigs, to see if he would consider replacing North as prime minister. There was a hefty condition, though. Although Rockingham and the members of his party, such as Richmond, had for a decade been pursuing a steady and consistent policy of conciliation with America and economic and political reform to rebalance the constitution, the King would not admit Rockingham into the premiership unless he agreed to abandon these policies. The King also had a list of men from his own party whom he wanted Rockingham to include in his cabinet. George hoped to dispatch North and the Opposition in the same shuffle.

Rockingham had the power and influence of a wealthy, exceptionally charming man, with a wife who was his equal and helped him keep his political relationships warm and active. He was not, though, a hard-nosed tactician. That work had always fallen to Burke and others. True to the mildness and honesty of his character, Rockingham told the King he could not accept the King's list of men but would otherwise consider the offer. He drove out from London to visit Richmond to discuss it. That he went in person rather than writing reflected his style. A human touch was his strong suit. Yet as always, Richmond's reading of the politics was far clearer than that of his leader. He warned Rockingham that the King was setting a trap.

Rockingham and Richmond had been building an Opposition party for more than a decade. They had tried to maintain party coherence around a set of policies—reconciliation with America, stable union with Ireland, reform to the government, reform to the exercise of the public purse, and protection of juries. They also sought to maintain bonds of personal loyalty. The Chathamite Whigs, in contrast, now under the leadership of the Earl of Shelburne, pledged to support "measures, not men." They claimed to be 100 percent focused on policy, and totally free of corrupting patronage. When they differed with men, they would break with them, rather than trying to maintain the coalition. In the absence of Chatham's magnetizing oratory to bind the people to them, this cavalier approach to relationships ultimately made their version of the Whig Party weaker than Rockingham's. The scale of the Chathamite bloc was limited precisely because of the weaker commitment to personal loyalty, and, from Rockingham's point of view, that rejection of a commitment to men made Shelburne fundamentally untrustworthy.

The King, though, wanted neither the full set of Rockingham "measures" nor the complete set of Rockingham "men." Most particularly, he did not want Richmond. When Rockingham had proposed Richmond for secretary of state back in 1766, the King had personally rejected him. Rockingham was ready to try again and, surprisingly, the King indicated a willingness to consider the possibility. Rockingham had come to Ranmer Camp to convey the message that if Richmond hoped to join any kind of Rockingham administration, the time had come for the Duke, who had not shown his face at a levee at St. James's Palace for ten years, to reconcile with the King.

Richmond followed up with a letter to Rockingham that possessed none of his usual vehemence. He accepted the charge to communicate with the King but implored Rockingham to let the King know that he had in no way asked for a role in government; he had not even "the smallest Inclination" to claim a place. He wanted to make a stand-alone apology, not as part of a transaction. He was willing to make an honest apology but not to humiliate himself.

Richmond also recognized that the real negotiation underway in these exchanges was not between Rockingham and the King, but between the King and himself. With Chatham gone, Richmond and the King were the two most principled, independent, and stubborn politicians in Britain. They had been squaring off since the 1750s. Given the force of

Richmond's attack on the power of the Crown that spring, the King's response had been notably restrained. He had not stripped Richmond of his role as lord lieutenant. Receiving Rockingham there at Ranmer Camp, at the head of his militia, Richmond had to know, deep down, that he remained there only by the grace of the King. Richmond's decision to apologize was a response to an implicit invitation the King had proffered by leaving his leadership of his militia intact, even as he removed others from office. Thus, with restraint, George led his wayward sheep back toward the fold.

Richmond warned Rockingham by letter that the King had made an offer that Rockingham should know was impossible to accept. The sovereign was not negotiating in good faith. Since Rockingham had already told the King that he would not take into his administration some of the men whom the King wanted, Rockingham had already killed any possible deal. All the conversations after Rockingham's initial conference with the King were shadow theater. "My Belief," Richmond wrote, "is, not that the Sentiments of His Majesty and His Advisers are changed, but that from the beginning there was no real Intention of taking you in, still less of giving You the lead in Administration."

Richmond thought George was now toying with Rockingham just to tease information out of him about the relative strength and weakness of alliances among different politicians. Richmond's analysis was spot on. The King was not serious about bringing Rockingham in and the negotiations came to a quick end. Still, the false start had put wheels in motion for a reconciliation between the King and his most threatening opponent. While the King had not solved his problem with Lord North, he had begun to neutralize his opposition. It was only a start at restoring his control but, after twenty years on the throne, he knew how to play the long game.

George abandoned the idea of removing North—proving Richmond right that he hadn't been terribly serious about it—and sought rather to strengthen his prime minister and his own hand against the Opposition by having North call snap elections. The King wanted to test the strength of the Crown's party with the electorate. The King's ministers could be expected to benefit from the pro-government sentiment in the wake of the Gordon Riots. The frugal King—saving monthly since 1774—had amassed a war chest for the election of more than forty thousand pounds, or more than ten million dollars in present-day terms. He also had the best political operatives and vote counters in the country. He had every reason to hope for success.

The King's election managers fanned out throughout the country to do their job. Even George III himself took part. Violating protocol and scandalizing the Opposition, he personally campaigned in Windsor against Richmond's cousin, Keppel, who would lose his seat. As returns rolled in, the Crown had some other notable wins: Edmund Burke was defeated in Bristol; John Sawbridge lost in London. On the other side of the ledger, Fox fended off a government challenge, and although Burke and Keppel lost their original seats, both then won alternative seats in other constituencies in the same election. Overall George's victory was less healthy than anticipated. The grassroots basis of the reform movement was more genuine and durable than the King and his election managers had thought.

Still, the elections somewhat shored up North's faltering administration. Thanks to independents, he could count on healthy margins for parliamentary votes on the Crown's policy goals, which would continue unchanged, including the resolute but unrealistic focus on defeating America. Yet the narrowness of the Crown's victory also taught the King's men and their opponents another lesson—the people were tired of the expense of the war.

In the immediate aftermath of the Gordon Riots, the King modestly improved his political position and dealt impactful blows to the Opposition radicals. Ironically, in turning to elections to fend off the threat of reform, the King had actually also accepted a key concept of radical thinking—that the people, fundamentally, were sovereign. The tepid victory showed the King that the people would indeed place limits on his power. This relatively small moment in 1781 was the beginning of a redirection of the British constitutional system.

LETTERS FROM THE PERIOD are full of the energy and anxiety of the elections—stories of threats the King made to voters in Windsor about Keppel, of why merchants in Bristol turned against Burke for his advocacy of free trade for Ireland, and of how the government sought to pressure Charles James Fox by driving up the expense of his election through prolonging its timetable. For Richmond's allies among the radical reformers, the question of the moment was clear. The King's strategy to neutralize their work by coopting the Rockingham Whigs and channeling pro-government popular energies in the election targeted them above all—the City radicals led by John Cartwright, who had established the Society for Constitutional Information in the spring; the charismatic dissenting clergyman, Christopher Wyvill in Yorkshire; and a rising generation of members of the House of Commons, who had entered political life fully committed to the reform agenda from the outset. This group included the two young men who had escorted Chatham to his final speech in the House of Lords—the twenty-seven-year-old Lord Mahon, who had been raised in republican Geneva and who had begun campaigning for parliamentary reform during the 1774 elections, and his twenty-one-year-old brother-in-law William Pitt the Younger, son of the great Chatham, who now in 1781 was standing for Parliament for the first time.

How would these three groups of reformers handle this reactionary turn? Lord George Gordon was in the Tower of London. His trial for treason would come after the New Year. The radicals had to consider their next steps under the shadow of his uncertain fate. His cause was quite different from theirs but, like him, they had sought to rouse the people. They too had to navigate churning political seas and dangerous undercurrents that might easily doom a man.

Most of the reformers refused to blink. Cartwright and the Society for Constitutional Information did not slow down their publication of radical materials. Cartwright had spent many months in consultation with the Rockinghamites before launching the Society for Constitutional Information in April 1780. Now Richmond was the member of the party with whom he was in the closest touch. In essence, the society would continue work reminiscent of the Junius letters. The society would support publication and wide distribution of pamphlets about the core principles of constitutionalism to educate a broad public. Membership was not exclusive in terms of class or background, though there was an annual membership fee of one guinea. The organization was committed to distributing its publications for free. To do the work, they formed committees to make editorial decisions about what and how to publish. Any member could attend any committee meeting.

A network of like-minded thinkers and politicians—initially many who had long been connected to Richmond—contributed essays over their own names. The difference from the Junius days was that this work was public. If anything, the Junius letters, and the subsequent strenuous defense of printers and the press over a decade, had paved the way, broadening the space available for free speech in England. As Cartwright, Horne Tooke, and other founders and leaders of the society would say consistently over the years, they established themselves for the sole purpose of advancing the Duke of Richmond's political and intellectual agenda for parliamentary reform: "a radical Reform in the Commons House of Parliament." When the work later became the subject of sedition trials, Cartwright would testify that he "had had many conversations with the Duke of Richmond on that subject" and that the Duke's reform plan had met the approbation of the Society. Publishing vigorously despite the Gordon Riots—and the tinge of revolution now attached to all populist endeavors—the society ensured that the public's understanding of the reform agenda continued to grow.

The American Revolution was defined by the 1776 Declaration of Independence. The French Revolution would be shaped by the Declaration of the Rights of Man. Less famous than either of these but with the same purpose, the Society for Constitutional Information's first publication was by Cartwright himself, entitled *Declaration of Those Rights of the Commonalty of Great Britain without Which They Cannot Be Free*. This British declaration of rights presented a theory of natural rights that the constitution should respect and advocated universal manhood suffrage and annual parliaments. On what turned out to be the final day of the Gordon Riots, the members of the Society for Constitutional Information ordered and distributed four thousand copies of the *Declaration of Those Rights*. Scarcely a month later, on July 7, they distributed an additional ten thousand.

The men of the Yorkshire Association also moved forward, though they focused only on the less controversial part of their agenda—economic reform. Even during the summer, when Lord George Gordon's actions had so broadly discredited the practice of political organizing, they kept at it. They proposed to gather for a Yorkshire meeting in early January and to elect representatives to a second annual meeting of delegates from all the counties. The young parliamentarians united with their effort, trying to keep the movement alive. In January 1781, after the Yorkshire meeting, Lord Mahon wrote to Richmond requesting that Richmond bring a contingent of delegates from Sussex to the second annual convention. Mahon's role signaled a change in dynamic. A younger generation of reformers was willing to take the lead.

For his part, Richmond spent the last few months of 1780 trying to keep the older parliamentarians behind the radical agenda. He was concerned that the strands of reform were unraveling. With the additional pressure from the government to undermine the Opposition, the movement was in danger of giving way because of internal division; he once again took on the task of trying to pull the factions together. Richmond focused especially on trying to bring Rockingham round to the cause of moderate parliamentary reform, and on uniting Rockingham and Shelburne. He pleaded with Shelburne to come up to London for in-person conversations, but despite his efforts neither Rockingham nor Shelburne was willing to yield to the other.

Richmond decided that the failure of rapprochement meant forward progress on parliamentary reform was out of reach. He replied to Mahon's request to re-engage Sussex by averring that the time wasn't right: "Every Day produces greater marks of disagreement between those who must be united before any good can be done," he wrote. He similarly complained to Rockingham in January that the reformers were all "split into miserable little palliating politics," with "fatal consequences."

If anyone needed a reminder of the fatal stakes of politics in those years, Lord George Gordon's trial for high treason began in Westminster Hall on February 5, in the same complex of buildings, Westminster Palace, as the Houses of Parliament. Gordon's conviction might have been considered a foregone conclusion, but he was defended by the thirty-one-year-old Thomas Erskine, a brilliant young barrister, whose defense struck all who heard it for its eloquence and constitutional clarity. Erskine contended that Gordon had never intended violence nor conspired to levy war against the King, that he was driven by sincere religious and political conviction, not treasonous intent, and that it was constitutionally important to maintain a distinction between mere incitement and treason. Gordon might be guilty of the former, but he hadn't committed the latter.

Stunning all of London, Erskine won Gordon's acquittal and cemented his own reputation as the brightest lawyer of his generation. Like the fall's weak election results, which reinforced the importance of popular sovereignty to British constitutional order, the Gordon jury too insisted on robust protections for civil liberties and limits to state prosecution. Crosscutting political waves were colliding unpredictably.

Perhaps the most important choice made in the late winter of 1781 about how to handle the next stage of reform was made by William Pitt the Younger. Erskine was not the only young star to emerge that political season. Two and a half weeks after the close of the trial, on February 26, nearby in the House of Commons, the twenty-one-year-old Pitt gave an eloquent maiden speech in Parliament. Burke commented that Pitt was "not merely a chip off the old block but the old block itself."

Pitt, though, was the reformer who blinked. He used the oratorical gifts he had inherited from his father to endorse moderation. He supported Burke's bill for economic reform in his maiden speech and then a few months later gave a speech arguing for the moderate electoral improvement of replacing rotten boroughs with redrawn county constituencies, a policy that took only a modest step toward universal suffrage. Pitt wished to leave the City radicals behind.

Richmond was right when he told Mahon and Rockingham that the reform movement was too miserably split to be effective. The King's attempt the previous summer to neutralize the Opposition was working. By dangling the prospect of the premiership before Rockingham, the King had managed to divide the Opposition between those who pressed ahead with the radical agenda and those who wanted to compromise to seize what looked like an opportunity. The weakening of the Opposition was most obvious when John Sawbridge made his annual motion for annual parliaments. It failed 59 to 29, another loss. Even more significant was how few of the 558 members of Parliament in the House of Commons even turned out for the vote. Parliamentary reform was fizzling.

Richmond rode the waves as they came. Just as he had rightly seen the growing political energy of spring 1780, he now recognized that the moment had passed, at least for the time being. Rather than fruitlessly trying to unify a badly splintered reform movement, he turned his attention to his other area of major concern: repairing relationships with America. He spent July 1781 advocating for better treatment of American prisoners at Mill Prison at Plymouth in Devon.

Thomas Paine was at the same time briefly in Europe for the first time since he had left England in 1774. He had sailed to Paris with the South Carolinian John Laurens, to join Benjamin Franklin in seeking to raise money from the French. By August, they would return to America with 2.5 million livres in silver as the first installment on a gift of 6 million livres and a loan of 10 million livres.

Their other mission while they were in Europe was to secure the release of John's father, Henry Laurens, a former president of Continental Congress who had been taken prisoner while sailing to Amsterdam on a top-secret diplomatic mission. When his vessel, the *Mercury*, was intercepted by the HMS *Vestal*, he threw a bag of his papers overboard but had failed to weight the bag sufficiently to sink it. The British recovered the papers and found a draft treaty between the United States and the Dutch Republic, grounds then for their December 1780 declaration of war against the Dutch. Laurens was the only American prisoner to be held in the Tower of London during the war, and Richmond wrote to the head of the Royal Navy seeking better treatment for him. It seems likely that Paine solicited Richmond's assistance. Richmond was taking a great personal risk in maintaining contact with the Americans while the war was still actively being fought. His known links led to the accusation that he was a traitor.

WITHIN MONTHS, THE END of the war at last arrived. On October 17, 1781, forty-two-year-old Charles Cornwallis, the most aristocratic of all the British generals, surrendered an army of more than seven thousand men to George Washington at Yorktown, Virginia, the battle that ended the American Revolution's North American theater. The repeated British error of underestimating the Americans led to the fatal blow.

After years of guerrilla-style warfare in the South, Cornwallis needed relief for his exhausted army. Rather than attempting to reach New York City, which the British still securely held, Cornwallis decided to rest at Yorktown, in Virginia, near the mouth of the Chesapeake. He marched his wearied troops there over the summer, as the British Navy formed a plan to meet Cornwallis there in the middle of August, either to bring new troops or to evacuate him.

The war had ground to a stalemate. The British held coastal cities in the South, while the Americans were garrisoned in New York state and from there blocked the British from any decisive victory in the mid-Atlantic.

Just as Cornwallis understood he was reaching the end of his resources, Washington also understood that his own forces were depleting. During 1781 he had to suppress six mutinies. Washington grimly determined that he needed to force the war to a close, or lose it.

The American general faced a choice. He could try to take the British in New York City, or surprise Cornwallis—who was much farther away—at Yorktown. While Washington understood that the material assets of the two sides were still closely matched, and running down for both, he realized that he could gain the upper hand through two resources that were his to create: surprise and bold ambition. In the largest movement of forces in the war, Washington marched twenty thousand troops some four hundred miles to Yorktown, catching the British by surprise.

While Washington was marching, Richmond's sister Sarah was marrying a veteran of the war in America. She had met her husband-to-be, George Napier, in the autumn of 1776 at the home of her brother George Lennox. Recognized as one of the handsomest men in the British Army, Napier served in George Lennox's regiment. He was a military man with strong intellectual interests, having been born in Edinburgh and educated by the philosopher David Hume. Although Napier was married with children when he and Sarah met, the two fell for each other quickly. Whatever affection developed between them was sufficiently evident to those around them that in 1778 Napier had been banned from the Lennox home and reassigned to a different regiment.

With his new regiment, he had been deployed to America, arriving in Brooklyn in August 1779 with his wife, Elizabeth, and their three-year-old daughter and infant son in tow. War involved whole families then as now, and this unhappy family, ejected from lovely Sussex, arrived at a crowded, unsanitary city that had been occupied by the British for two years. Yellow fever was spreading unchecked. In 1780 Napier's wife and young children succumbed to the dread disease. Then soon enough Napier sickened. When Napier, too, was thought to be dying, he was put on a ship back to England. Death came for two out of every three patients in the disease's toxic phase, but Napier was lucky. He recovered on the sea voyage to England.

Once home, he had to start from scratch, and that included paying court to Sarah. When Richmond learned of Napier's pursuit, he offered neither approval nor support. Napier had few prospects, and Richmond seems to have thought that Sarah owed perpetual penance for her earlier adultery. Despite all the help he had given her since her disgrace, he refused even to pay for her wedding dress. Yet on August 27, 1781, Sarah married Napier anyway—yet another Lennox sister charting her own path. Her elderly Aunt, Lady Albemarle, was her only witness. Napier, she wrote poignantly, "made me like this world."

Together they would have eight children, including five sons, four of whom became distinguished British officers. On her birthday, in 1783, Sarah wrote to her beloved friend Susan, "This is my birthday. I am 38, & I see nothing 'new under the sun,' except that till I was past 36 I find I never knew what real happiness was, which from my marriage with Mr Napier till now is much greater than I had any idea of as existing in human life, & it is no small satisfaction to be able to say that at 38, as at least it secures that happiness from all the dangers of change, in consequence of youth's flying away."

A world away, three days after their wedding, on August 30, the French fleet under Admiral François Joseph Paul de Grasse arrived in Chesapeake Bay, beating the British Navy that was racing to aid Cornwallis. This determined the outcome of the American Revolution. From then, events unfolded as if in slow motion, almost as a matter of mechanical necessity. By the time the Royal Navy reached the Chesapeake on September 5, the French were well positioned to repel them. They drove off the British ships, which abandoned Cornwallis's army of nine thousand on a narrow peninsula, where the troops had been waiting to be picked up. The French then encircled the peninsula, waiting for Washington to block escape by land. The general and his twenty thousand men arrived on September 28. The trap was sprung.

For twenty days, Washington's artillery blasted away at the British fortifications, and squadrons sallied out for raids. Some two thousand British soldiers were killed; nearly all the remaining seven thousand were wounded. The Americans suffered only 389 casualties. On October 17, 1781, the Americans spied two figures on the British ramparts, one waving a white handkerchief from the end of a sword. A drummer boy banged out "parley," signifying a desire to negotiate.

Word of the Yorktown surrender arrived in London on November 25, forty-eight hours before the King was due to open Parliament. It was brought from Cornwall by a messenger who delivered the news to the home of a cabinet member in Pall Mall who in turn took it to Downing Street in the early afternoon to tell the prime minister. Lord North despairingly exclaimed, "O God! It is all over!"

The King's speech was hastily rewritten, though the King enjoined Parliament—with both Houses assembled together as was custom for Parliament's opening—to recognize the permanence of his principles, even in the face of the catastrophe. He regretted that his "assiduous endeavours" had not been "attended with Success equal to the Justice and Uprightness" of his views. He closed with the jaw-dropping pronouncement that, Yorktown notwithstanding, he intended to stay the course and expected to win the war.

The Opposition was incredulous and instantly revived. Charles James Fox led a chorus of disapproval. He mockingly parodied the King's words, "Our losses have been singularly calamitous: The blood of my subjects has flowed in copious and unavailing streams. The treasures of the country have been thrown away, and the weight of taxes imposed with such a heavy hand, upon an overburthened and sinking people, is grown at length almost intolerable. Yet I will tax you to the last shilling." Still savagely mocking the King, he continued, "When all hope of victory is fled for ever, and the operations of the war must accelerate the ruin of the empire, I will forbid you to think of peace; for my thirst of conquest is not quenched; my revenge is unsated; and nothing short of the total subjugation of my opponents is capable of appeasing it."

On the streets of London, the arrival of news of the Yorktown surrender was met with stunned, solemn quiet. Deep shame seems to have been the overwhelming sentiment, mixed with some relief from the end of a miserable endeavor.

Thinking not only of Yorktown but also of Saratoga, Horace Walpole noted to a correspondent that only the Romans had similarly ventured so far and wide as also to lose two whole armies. He was struck by the irony of Henry Laurens being in the Tower of London while his son, John, received Cornwallis's capitulation papers and took him prisoner. He was equally staggered by the disgrace of Cornwallis having acceded to the American request to hand over American Loyalists for hanging. Still, he had also to admit, "I cannot put on the face of the day and act grief. Whatever puts an end to the American war will save the lives of thousands—millions of money too."

In Parliament, shock quickly turned to action. Fox demanded, as Richmond had earlier, "a total change of system," meaning that Lord North's administration should be replaced. But despite the magnitude of the loss at Yorktown, the broken mathematics of a rotten Parliament prevailed: Fox's motion was defeated 218 to 129. Yet a swelling corps of members knew that they—and the British people—had had enough. The war was done, and so was Lord North. Over the coming four months, he would have to fend off one after another motion of no confidence, or other parliamentary attack. He began pressing the King again to let him resign. George, who could still see no alternative prime minister he could tolerate, continuously refused.

The consequences of Yorktown unfolded, piece by agonizing piece. On December 1, North's cabinet voted to pursue peace talks with the Americans. Despite the King's insistence on continuing to fight, the cabinet was ready at last to take policy in a different direction. They still resisted recognizing the independence of America, however, and to prevent further losses, they decided to reinforce the British troops in America. Their actions were incoherent—seeking peace on the one hand and maintaining the conditions of war on the other. The Rockinghamites, in contrast, were ready to recognize American independence, a position the King still could not abide. The independent landholders in Parliament from the rural parts of Britain began to turn on the Crown and government. They had suffered enough losses through taxes and military casualties and wished to bear no more.

In January 1782, the government received definitive word from Benjamin Franklin, who was in Paris, that the Americans would not accept peace without independence. By February, North's administration began to collapse. Several junior members of the cabinet refused to vote or speak for the administration in Parliament any longer. Some resigned. Opposition members began preparing to take votes of no confidence in the prime minister.

In early March, building on the call of Charles James Fox for a new government, Rockingham began laying out his terms for serving as prime minister, in expectation of an invitation from the King. He would require recognition of American independence, Burke's economic reforms, and reforms concerning excise men, revenue officers, and contractors. Parliamentary reform itself was not on Rockingham's list of terms because the Opposition Whigs could not agree among themselves on which variant to pursue. When Rockingham made this policy agenda known to the King, George recorded in a memorandum that he found the demands "so strange" and an "indignity" to his person.

The King flatly rebuffed them. This led the Rockinghamites simply to put a motion on the parliamentary calendar for March 20 to vote on replacing North with Rockingham. They were no longer going to defer to the Crown in the appointment of the prime minister but simply claim that power for themselves. That would rebalance the constitution!

In this moment of high stress and brinksmanship, George III drafted a statement of abdication, taking the prospect seriously for the first time. Speaking of himself in the third person, he began, "His Majesty, during the twenty years he has sat on the Throne of Great Britain has had no object as much at heart as the maintenance of the British constitution." Parliament's "sudden change of sentiments" left him "totally incapacitated" and forced him "To the painful step of quitting it [his native country] forever." He concluded "His Majesty resigns the Crown of Great Britain and the Dominions appertaining thereto" to the Prince of Wales. He never showed the text to anyone, but he kept it close at hand in a drawer.

It's unclear who was emotionally the more overwrought at the time—the King or his prime minister, but George plainly didn't want to be in the fight for control of the government nor dealing with the repercussions of the military defeat alone. Lord North continued to press for the chance to resign, which he desperately hoped to do before being voted out. Only on the morning of March 20, with a parliamentary no-confidence vote looming later that day, did the King at last relent. The wretched prime minister rushed to Parliament in a hackney cab so that he could announce his resignation before the question could be called. He won that small battle, but he had comprehensively lost the war.

Lord North announced not only his own departure but the dissolution of his entire cabinet and provided no information on replacements. This was unheard of. Even the Duke of Grafton's collapsing ministry in 1770 had not disassembled so totally. London was abuzz as people tried to determine what negotiations might be underway with the King. Inveterate gossips like Horace Walpole trafficked in information of who was coming and going to audiences with the King.

North had resigned on a Wednesday. On Thursday London saw snow all evening. By Sunday word was spreading that Shelburne was negotiating on Rockingham's behalf. While everything hung for the British on these events, they mattered little to the Americans, who were now simply preoccupied with their own economic realities, such as the collapse of their currency, and the terms of peace. The war had shut down diplomatic relations, so London was empty of Americans who might report on the reshuffle via letters, except for Henry Laurens, and he did not. Many colonial newspapers had also failed during the war, and the content of Loyalist and American papers had utterly diverged. American indifference to Lord North's plight was a sure proof that independence was real.

THE COLLAPSE OF NORTH'S administration and prospect of a second Rockingham administration (the first had been from 1765 to 1766) offered a chance at last for Richmond to move some of his policy agenda forward through a cabinet position. If Richmond wanted to serve, he would first have to repair his bitter rift with George III.

There was much to overcome—his objection to the King's regency proposal, his secret newspaper writing, his long tenure in the Opposition, his charge of tyranny against the administration and the King, his investigation of the government's finances, his radical proposals, and the pressure brought to bear on the King via economic and parliamentary reform. Over time the King had expressed so many complaints about Richmond, and so many negative characterizations (the worst being that "his whole conduct is dictated by malevolence") that reconciliation must have seemed all but impossible.

Yet the job at hand wasn't personal but political. Richmond did not need to make the King like him or even forgive him. He merely needed to pledge allegiance to the monarch. This meant undoing the specific act with which he had declared independence years ago: his 1770 letter preemptively declining regimental leadership of the Blues. Through Rockingham, he sent the King another circumlocutionary letter, dated March 24, 1782, to retract his earlier letter. With a cabinet job finally within reach, Richmond was willing to forswear his independence.

In a convoluted sentence of 175 words, Richmond sought an audience with the King to assure him that his earlier letter had not arisen "from any disinclination to serve his Majesty in any situation his Majesty might command." This was the phrase in his letter that mattered. These were the words of a liege swearing fidelity to his lord on bended knee. This loyalty oath won Richmond his audience.

When the two men met on Wednesday, March 27, their minds must both have been on a lifetime's worth of rivalry, as well as each man's youthful missteps—Richmond's overreaction to the slight to his brother George; the King's ill-judged seduction of Sarah. Richmond had last closely interacted with George III in 1766 when he was secretary of state. Each man—the one forty-seven and the other forty-three—must have been curious about how the other had changed. Both taller than average, Richmond was by now tending to portly and still eschewed wigs despite a balding pate. The King, always bewigged, had grown slimmer and sterner in his features—his mouth now settled in a slight frown. Stress was taking its toll. There is no record of what was said during their meeting, but after two decades of bitter mutual resentment, they came to terms. George III had deftly neutralized his opposition. Richmond had gained new power.

In this painting from 1782, King George III no longer has the gentle smile of his earliest portraits as monarch.

ROYAL COLLECTION TRUST; COPYRIGHT © HER MAJESTY QUEEN ELIZABETH II.

During the royal levee later that day, the King was "civil" to Richmond, as men reported at White's Club that evening. When Rockingham was appointed premier that same day, Richmond was able to join him in office as master-general of the ordnance. Secretary of state for the southern department was to be Charles James Fox, Richmond's nephew, a role that then evolved into the country's first foreign secretary. Secretary of state for the northern department—which is to say foreign affairs with Europe—was the Earl of Shelburne, first a rival and by now a long-time collaborator of Richmond's. At last, there was to be a government that united all the Whig factions.

The master-general was responsible for British defenses, fortifications, munitions, military hospitals, artillery, engineers, and logistics and was a peer in authority to the commander in chief of the armed forces. In this role, which Richmond's maternal grandfather had held, and which existed until 2013, he also took a seat in the cabinet. To formalize Richmond's renewed allegiance, the King admitted him, along with the Earl of Shelburne, into the Order of the Garter—the most ancient order of chivalry and the highest honor the Crown could bestow. The gesture capped a remarkable rehabilitation of Richmond's political standing and demonstrated that George III fully recognized the gravity of Britain's military losses in America and the precarious state of affairs at home. The monarchy required broad support if it was to endure the crisis.

RICHMOND'S RETURN TO THE cabinet meant more time in London, away from Goodwood, and more time entertaining political allies. He hired James Wyatt, who had done beautiful work on his Sussex estate, to remodel Richmond House in Whitehall. He continued his involvement in the Society of Arts and stands next to Burke, though pointedly not turning toward him, in a grand history painting by James Barry from this period depicting the society's annual awarding of prizes. He seized the opportunity of the cabinet role to integrate the reforms he'd long sought into government policy—richly succeeding with economic reform although only marginally advancing parliamentary reform, despite persistent effort.

Richmond didn't wait to bring reform through legislation but used his own executive powers to eliminate waste, fraud, and abuse. The day after

In this painting of the Society of Arts by James Barry, Edmund Burke and the Duke of Richmond can be found in the right third of the painting. They are the third and fourth men from the right edge of the painting in the middle row of figures. They stand beside each other while also being turned away from one another—an apt visual metaphor for their relationship. The Prince of Wales is holding court on the far left of the painting, a harbinger of his engagement with the radical Whigs later in the 1780s.

his swearing in as master-general of the ordnance, he was already hard at work cleaning house. He visited the Tower and fired sixteen employees, with salaries from two to five hundred pounds each, and proposed to abolish the role of lieutenant of the ordnance. He raised wages to drive out tips and corruption and made the operations of the office efficient.

Aside from fiscal issues, Richmond and the others who joined Rockingham's cabinet committed themselves to peace for North America, and to a proposal that "no person holding Place under or who are influenced by the Commissioners of the Customs or Excise [should] have a Vote for members of Parliament." They didn't want those who controlled the collection of taxes to have any hand in setting their rates.

The papers noted Richmond's reformist energies. A week into his tenure, *The Public Advertiser* reported that Richmond was "to be pronounced the most indefatigable Man of Business at present extant in Europe." Not even Frederick the Great could match him, they editorialized.

Richmond set the pace for his colleagues, and the whole cabinet moved fast and with big, bold steps to advance reform measures. The threat of Burke's economic reform bill to reduce the civil list and the King's ability to make patronage appointments led the King to do some anticipatory pruning of his favorites. In March, even before the administration turned over, "many persons of high rank disappeared from the King's person and Court." In April Burke's bill successfully passed as the Establishment Act of 1782, also known as the Civil List and Secret Service Money Act. This gave the government's treasury department oversight of the finances of the royal household. That same month Parliament delivered on Richmond's plan for a Commonwealth structure by granting legislative independence to Ireland while retaining the tie to the crown through the office of a viceroy. April also saw the repeal of the resolutions that had blocked John Wilkes from taking his seat in Parliament, closing a long, sorry chapter and restoring the integrity of parliamentary elections. On April 19, the Netherlands recognized American independence, which increased the pressure on Britain to do so. The Rockingham administration was eager to achieve this, though peace negotiations were to drag on for another seventeen months, while war continued in the Caribbean.

As they raced through their agenda, the new cabinet stumbled in the one area that mattered most to Richmond: parliamentary reform. Rockingham had never grown comfortable with changing the election system and put off dealing with it. To try to address the roadblock presented by Rockingham himself, Richmond began convening meetings on his own authority. In the House of Commons, he partnered with John Sawbridge and his younger allies—Pitt the Younger; Lord Mahon; and in the House of Lords, he allied with the Earl of Shelburne. He hosted dinners at his house and the Thatched House Tavern to corral people into shared strategy. Just as Pitt had pivoted toward pragmatism, so too the whole movement now did. Richmond, Pitt, Mahon, and Shelburne settled on their key priorities, including the idea that rather than pursuing any specific reform to the election system, they would instead put forward a bill for a committee to study potential reforms and propose a pathway.

Richmond had at last installed parliamentary reform in the routine legislative agenda, a remarkable accomplishment. Getting there required embracing Pitt's pragmatism. On May 7, 1782, Pitt, slender and still fresh-faced but already one of the leading orators in the House of Commons, introduced the first of what were ultimately a series of motions on parliamentary reform over several years. This first bill was not expansive. He called simply for an inquiry into the state of representation. Yet despite the ideological moderation and political planning, the bill failed by twenty votes, a sign of its quiet momentousness. Still, the vote was as tantalizingly close as an election reform bill had ever come. Richmond sensed an opening.

The loss resulted partly from Rockingham's lack of enthusiasm for the policy and so Richmond determined to do something about that. He could not hide his irritation with the prime minister and wrote that Saturday evening, to reproach him: "My Dear Lord if you Think my Services in the present Administration useful, you must support me in this Measure. You know it was *my Bargain*. I do not wish to tie you down to my plan, or to any particular measure. I only ask to have the Committee; I trust to them for the measure, and only contend for some plan being adopted." He warned Rockingham that the people themselves would eventually rise to "demand their rights" if political leaders did not themselves advance reform. He also had a conversation of several hours with Shelburne on similar themes. Despite Richmond's having sworn him to secrecy, Shelburne reported to the King by letter. Shelburne's letter reveals that Rockingham was not fully in charge of his own ministry and that Richmond's loyalty was still under close watch.

With Richmond and Pitt ready to twist arms to get parliamentary peers on board, the reform movement had the best opportunity for change it had ever had. Seizing the moment would require total alignment of all factions on a shared agenda. Richmond called a meeting on Thursday, May 16, 1782, over dinner at the Thatched House Tavern in St. James's Street to discuss where the parliamentary reform effort should go next.

The Society for Constitutional Information was represented and so was what was called "The Quintuple Alliance," a metropolitan coalition of London, Westminster, Southwark, Middlesex, and Surrey. This group brought the radical reform agenda into the conversation. Also present were members of the Yorkshire group of moderates. The only group absent were the Whigs associated with Charles James Fox, who vacillated between the radical and the moderate course.

The large clubroom in which the meeting was held was visible from the street. The flickering, candle-lit chandeliers illuminated the portraits on the walls inside, and the guests too, to passersby. That evening, the guests included Pitt, John Wilkes, Lord Mahon, John Sawbridge, Major John Cartwright, Mr. John Horne Tooke, and Doctor Jebb—a who's who of radical reform. Two were collaborators with Richmond from the Junius days—Wilkes and Horne Tooke.

The purpose of the meeting was to come to some sort of resolution—to try to unify the different factions of reformers around a shared vision, which Rockingham might be brought to endorse. As he had been doing for a decade and a half, Richmond was, once again, indefatigably pursuing a unity agenda. This time, though, he was a cabinet minister so that agenda would define governmental policy. The reformers had never had such an opportunity.

Pitt kept the minutes of the meeting. The assembled company took formal votes and memorialized their plans. They resolved that since Pitt's motion on May 7 had not passed, the time had come to rouse the people. They would work over the summer to encourage popular petitions from their respective districts for "a substantial reformation of the Commons House of Parliament." These petitions would be submitted to Parliament early in the fall session when they thought the agenda was light enough for ample discussion of measures without which, as Pitt underlined, "*neither the liberty of the nation can be preserved nor the permanence of a wise and virtuous administration can be secure.*"

Richmond was weaving together now the several political techniques he had learned over time—herding his parliamentary colleagues toward unity and drawing on grassroots organizing "out of doors" to apply the pressure needed to achieve and activate that unity. Here were the basic ingredients of modern party politics where political leaders understand that their most effective power always comes from the people. The pursuit of parliamentary reform was itself igniting the practice of pulling the people into politics.

Fate was to intervene once more, though, just when Richmond's efforts were gaining momentum. In June 1780 it had been the reckless Lord George Gordon. Two years later it was a pandemic. While the candles flickered inside the tavern, a novel influenza virus, recently arrived in Europe from Asia, was quickly spreading in London. Naval ships that left port on May 2 with healthy crews were by May 29 so ravaged that they had to return. As Sarah wrote about the situation to Susan, "*so general* an illness has never been known here in the memory of man."

Before the group of reformers could execute their summer agenda, the pandemic claimed their prime minister. The Marquess of Rockingham caught the flu at the end of June, and after an illness of only three or four days died on July 2, 1782, at the age of fifty-two. The decline was so rapid that when Rockingham's death was reported to George III, he marveled that he had not even known that his prime minister was sick.

When Rockingham died, Richmond lost someone that he had admired since they were both scholars at Westminster School and Rockingham had run off to fight Bonnie Prince Charlie. Despite their differences, Rockingham had been his steadfast supporter, insisting on bringing him into government each time the opportunity arose even in the face of the King's opposition. While their relationship had waxed and waned, Richmond had remained personally loyal to Rockingham throughout. As Richmond had done years earlier with James Wolfe, he had a death mask taken. These two men were unquestionably his most important mentors.

RICHMOND'S GRIEF AT ROCKINGHAM'S death clashed with his ambition. Perhaps the power vacuum was now an opportunity for him to push farther, faster in integrating his policies into government. Perhaps he should be the next prime minister.

Richmond might not have had Rockingham's charm and wide net of patronage, but he had been the principal Opposition speaker in the House of Lords for a decade and had shaped his party's platform. He had been the best bridge between the Chathamite and Rockingham Whigs. He was held in high regard by most moderate and radical reformers alike. The brightest talents of a rising generation of leaders looked up to him and were working closely with him.

While the Tory press abused him—and Fox and Keppel—for supposedly dominating the King with the rapid implementation of the Whig agenda, the Whig press lavished him with compliments for his work at the ordnance. He had good working relations with the Americans, and with Benjamin Franklin in particular, as Britain was negotiating its future relationship with America. He had worked harder in Parliament and been more consistent in his principles than just about anyone. The King might consider the Rockinghamite agenda "so strange," but Parliament and the people were behind it. The Gordon Riots were receding into memory. The time was right.

Besides, who else was there? Charles James Fox was a brilliant orator and commanded the largest personal following in the House of Commons. He was huge fun, always up for a party, and spent more time at the club than anyone else, but he was also unreliable, of loose morals, and disliked by the King. Keppel didn't really have the parliamentary presence. No one trusted Shelburne, even if he was—or perhaps because he was—one of the King's most frequent correspondents. Also, Shelburne and Fox were locked in counterproductive rivalry. Because Fox's cabinet portfolio included America while Shelburne's included France, they were running two separate channels of negotiation about the peace treaty and driving two different agendas. They had choked up diplomacy. Even under Rockingham, with his general attitude of "firm kindness" toward the Americans, Fox and Shelburne were making the final accomplishment of peace very difficult.

Richmond still had a problem in the King, though. Their rift had been exceptionally deep. Also, despite their restored relationship, Richmond had gone straight back to importuning the King on behalf of his brother, George, who had at some point been promised that he would be appointed governor of the fortifications at Portsmouth when that role came vacant. Even while working on parliamentary reform in May and June, Richmond had been persistently advocating on behalf of his brother to the King. The King must have found it shocking that Richmond could advocate so aggressively for an anti-corruption agenda and then pursue patronage for his brother incessantly. Also, the King had heard about a very public dispute with Lord Rawdon that ended up with Rawdon demanding satisfaction from Richmond via a duel. The duel was ultimately averted but Richmond had to apologize. The King received many letters about the altercation. It made him unwilling to rely on Richmond.

That left one possible candidate to succeed Rockingham—the Duke of Portland. Three years younger than Richmond, and also educated at Westminster School, Portland had been serving in his first, and minor, cabinet post as lord lieutenant of Ireland when Rockingham died. A nonentity of no intellectual or political distinction, Portland lacked the ambition, ideas, or energy to shape events, but he was inoffensive.

Richmond was blindsided when his party recommended Portland to the King. The party recognized that Richmond, for all his talents, suffered from what his nephew Charles James Fox recorded as "[his] extreme unpopularity, his intractability, and what he terms his speculative visions, and romantic and impracticable schemes about parliamentary reform." Years later, Fox sarcastically wrote that, in his view, "the best thing" about Richmond's plan for universal suffrage was "its utter impracticability." Fox was simply not as brave or farsighted in his understanding of the needs of reform as Richmond, but Richmond paid a price for being a visionary.

Fox was tasked with communicating the unpleasant news to Richmond. He delayed and prevaricated, uncertain how best to pass on the message to his uncle. Finally, he determined to point out that if he, Fox, with his strong following in Parliament, was too radical for the King to take in as his prime minister, his "noble relation," whose views on reform were more extreme than his own, was certainly never a viable candidate.

Richmond must have felt some satisfaction when the King ignored the recommendation of Portland. George recognized that Portland was just a vessel for Fox, with his faction in the House. To keep both Fox and Richmond at bay, he decided to switch Whig horses—from the Rockinghamites (as they continued to be called in the immediate wake of Rockingham's death) to the Chathamites. Disdaining the large following in the House of Commons that Fox would bring to Portland and that would ordinarily justify a premiership, the King decided to choose the enigmatic Earl of Shelburne. The blow to Fox was as severe as the cut he had delivered to his own uncle: Fox resigned as foreign secretary immediately.

Now the question of whether the King could form a government hung in the balance. If the rest of the Rockinghamites followed Fox out of office, Shelburne would have nothing to lead. Edmund Burke, who had been serving as paymaster general of the forces, determined to follow Fox. The question was how everyone else would break. Party meetings were called to discuss the matter.

Richmond at first considered resigning too but then changed his mind.

He was deeply hurt by his colleagues' preference for the simple-minded, ineffective Portland. Portland was ever the follower, never a leader, whereas Richmond had broken the path into the new world. Probably he also understood that Fox's explanation of the choice was deceitful and that the choice of Portland was a case of the nephew seeking to leapfrog the uncle. He and Shelburne had squabbled but at least they were allied on the importance of parliamentary reform, and Shelburne had in no way humiliated him.

Richmond also had reason to believe that Shelburne could be trusted to move their shared agenda forward at least as energetically as Rockingham had done. One of Richmond's close confidantes, John Cartwright, told Richmond that in a conversation he had with Shelburne, Shelburne had emphatically insisted about Richmond "that where your Grace leads, he will follow." The radicals were willing to trust Shelburne on the principle of reform, and Richmond was willing to trust him with his pride. He determined to remain in the cabinet and stay on as master-general of the ordnance.

All these internecine feuds worked themselves out in a matter of days—as Britain's leading parliamentarians rushed back and forth among one another's homes for party meetings. Decisions were not slowed down by ceremony. There had been no national mourning for Rockingham. He was respected but not beloved. Also, despite the anxiety provoked by his passing, gossip spread less quickly than at other moments since London was still in the grip of the influenza pandemic, which was only just peaking. All were equally laid low—aristocrats and message-carrying servants alike. The political maneuvering played out in the newspapers, though, where debate was fierce over constitutional reform. It was a high point of publication for the Society for Constitutional Information—which seemed to move forward come what may.

Richmond's July 1783 break with the Rockinghamites proved to be a decisive turning point in British political history. In choosing to remain with Shelburne, Richmond chose measures over men, abandoning Rockingham's political approach. Many of Richmond's former colleagues would now be in opposition to the administration in which he served.

Before his decision was final, the Rockinghamites descended on him in force, trying to badger him into remaining with them. They recognized that their own strength as an Opposition party to Shelburne, whom they continued to distrust, would be much weaker if Richmond stayed in the government.

Horace Walpole reported on his efforts to mediate between Richmond and Fox: "I intreated both him [Fox] and the Duke to argue without passion, and to remember, that being such near relations, they must come together again, and therefore I hoped neither would say what the other could never forgive. I did prevent any warmth, and they parted civilly, though equally discontent with each other."

If Walpole was gentle and softening, others were implacable and crushing. At another meeting at the London home of Earl Fitzwilliam, Rockingham's nephew and heir, Burke held forth against Richmond for two hours. Other attendees, associated with Fox, attacked Richmond so violently for his decision to remain in government with Shelburne that the meeting concluded when Richmond "so pressed and stung in this nest of hornets," "at length . . . burst into tears." Despite the rhetorical assaults, Richmond remained steadfast in his decision to stick with Shelburne. It was a strange form of courage, but courage it was.

Some of Richmond's former Rockinghamite allies were unforgiving. His friendship with Burke was at an end. Later when Fitzwilliam built a memorial mausoleum to his uncle that included statues of all Rockingham's key allies, he left Richmond out. A life-size white marble statue of the marquess is surrounded by similar-sized statues of Burke, Keppel, Fox, John Lee, Lord John Cavendish, the Duke of Portland, Frederick Montagu, and Sir George Savile. In just two weeks, Richmond had lost a lifelong friend, his pride, and his party.

RICHMOND'S DECISION TO STAY in office saved Shelburne's administration; others stayed in because he did. The rupture with Burke was complete, and also a break with the past. Shelburne was influenced not only by the war hero Wolfe but also by figures like political economist Adam Smith. For the first time in history, Britain would have a government led by Enlightenment progressives who believed in American independence, universal manhood suffrage, and strength through free trade alliances rather than strict colonial control—a trio of commitments that laid the foundation for modern politics.

Fox continued to try to rouse his followers to break Shelburne's government. On July 8, Richmond wrote to his brother: "To-morrow it is expected there will be very warm debates in the House of Commons. Mr. Fox, but still more some of his warm friends, are very warm indeed." An American observer writing to Adams and celebrating Richmond's steadfast support for the United States also acknowledged how important his decision was: "I fancy the Duke's Staying in place is a concerted Measure," that is, an intentionally coordinated plan by those who shared Richmond's policy agenda.

Richmond's and Shelburne's actions demonstrated that they had been acting in coordination throughout the turbulent transition. They meant to steer the country in the policy directions they had long advocated, or as Richmond called it, the "the measures on which we came in." On July 10, 1782, in the House of Lords, Richmond was the first person to speak. He rose to clarify the objectives of the new Shelburne administration. The "great principles" of the Shelburne ministry were, he declared, the independence of America, a peace treaty, and a diminution of royal influence in Parliament. Shelburne then affirmed that Richmond had correctly represented his agenda.

With Shelburne's triumph over Fox, peace negotiations with America would at last progress. The British still occupied New York, Charleston, and Savannah, and American forces remained mobilized. Washington had kept the Continental Army active and encamped in New York and New Jersey, in case of failed negotiations and renewed hostilities. The war in the Caribbean remained hot, and even in North America skirmishes and local raids continued—especially between Patriots and Loyalists in the Carolinas, the New York frontier, and the Ohio Valley. Despite Walpole's fears, the Americans did not execute Loyalists, after Cornwallis failed to achieve protection for them during his capitulation. Many were simply pardoned, exiled, or had their property confiscated.

The emergence of Shelburne and Richmond at the head of government meant that war would at last conclude. Peace abroad did not, though, calm the rough waters of British politics. Shelburne was too politically weak for that, and Richmond and the King would have to navigate several more leadership crises before Britain's modern government emerged. The period is broadly recognized as a constitutional watershed for British constitutional monarchy, and Richmond played a pivotal role.

Chapter
14

RICHMOND SAVES THE KING

1782–1784

The King is reported to have said that "There was no man by whom he had been so much offended, and none to whom he was so much indebted, as the Duke of Richmond."

—CHARLES JAMES FOX

SHELBURNE'S PREMIERSHIP WOULD BE BRIEF—NINE MONTHS. If ever any political phenomenon could count as a riptide sucking someone back out to sea, it was Charles James Fox—whose exuberant, combative, fiery oratory won him an unmatched following in the House of Commons. Shelburne could not resist its force, and both the King and Richmond would also suffer losses from the conflict between those two Whigs—each brilliant, each egotistical.

The turbulence would sink Shelburne's ministry; leave the nation adrift without a government for a second time, this time for an excruciating six weeks; drive the King once more to consider abdication; and push Richmond out of office, thwarted and demoralized.

Yet, as ever, Richmond and the King stood out from the crowd. Both had their eye on Britian's future—not on personal gain. Deftly harmonizing after years of adversarial distance, together they spotted a means of charting a course: They both bet all on the rising talent of William Pitt the Younger, the King for the sake of his crown and Richmond for reform—seeing in the young leader's moderation but a steppingstone to a fuller program. With Richmond's help, the King would soon make Pitt prime minister at the age of twenty-four, the youngest prime minister in British history. In so doing, the two men laid the foundation block of modern Britain. To get there they had months of dangerous politics to navigate.

ONCE IN OFFICE, IN July 1782, Shelburne moved quickly to advance an initial reform agenda—rooting out corruption in government offices. He also immediately drafted preliminary articles of peace with the Americans—essentially a rough draft for the full treaty. Their ethos was pragmatism and conciliation to restore relationships and spur a commercial alliance. These preliminary articles were ratified in Britain on November 30, 1782.

Richmond would have been largely pleased with the start of the administration. His contributions to the debates over the treaty also had the backing of the Americans. Thomas Paine, for one, wrote to Shelburne from Philadelphia, with a copy of his 1782 *Letter Addressed to the Abbé de Raynal*, which he intended—as he explained in his cover letter—as a defense of views expressed by Richmond. Shelburne passed the pamphlet on to Richmond, and it remains at Goodwood to this day.

The anti-corruption work also advanced, thanks especially to the partnership with Richmond. Shelburne sought to stamp out a practice of bureaucrats' accepting fees for every little transaction they touched. He wanted to replace this essentially corrupt habit with regular salaries for civil servants. Richmond had already undertaken just such measures on his own authority at the ordnance. As Shelburne said in his memoirs, the Duke of Richmond was the "one man in Administration or Opposition [who] was in earnest in the support of any reform."

Richmond's earnestness, though, had its limits. He did not fully live by his own principles. At the ordnance, he hired his nephew and heir as secretary and also, after much prodding by his sister Sarah, her husband, George Napier, as superintendent of the Woolwich Laboratory, which handled gunpowder production for the nation.

Still, while Richmond did indulge in some patronage, he certainly bucked the norms of the period. The Woolwich Laboratory role brought in only 300 pounds a year, and Sarah continued to hope for something better. Her family, which would soon grow to eight children, was struggling financially, but Richmond refused to help beyond the one small, modestly compensated job. This created a source of great bitterness for his sister that would separate them for a decade. To this extent at least, Richmond lived by—and felt the bite of—the policies he advocated.

Shelburne found himself constantly having to fend off onslaughts from Fox. Fox was the leader of the House of Commons and, without him, Shelburne could not effectively move his agenda forward. Casting about for a solution, he settled on appointing the second-best speaker in the House of Commons into his cabinet, a man who had been in Parliament for only three years. At the age of twenty-three, William Pitt, tall, slender, fair-skinned, and ruddy-cheeked, was made chancellor of the exchequer. A man of the library and study, not the hunt or the battlefield, he was immensely talented, intellectually and politically, as well as ambitious. He was also still very young. He could not yet counterbalance Fox.

Political conflict with Fox now consumed Shelburne. Shelburne's commitment to parliamentary reform had always seemed authentic to Richmond and other radicals. Now Richmond could not get the Prime Minister's attention for this, nor for work at the ordnance. Richmond found it demoralizing and pulled back from cabinet attendance. His desire to integrate his top policy goals into the government's agenda was undiminished, however, so he turned back to his grassroots organizing outside of Parliament.

THE REFORM MOVEMENT HAD been drifting away from universal manhood suffrage and toward a moderate course of merely removing rotten boroughs and improving enfranchisement of underrepresented counties. Striking out on his own, Richmond now sought to reaffirm the movement's commitment to the more ambitious goal. He continued to work closely with the Society for Constitutional Information. In October 1782, Jeremy Bentham, the father of utilitarianism, spotted Richmond in close conversation at a reform event with John Cartwright, "a bird of his own feather."

Richmond called his network together again—first at St. Alban's Tavern in London in December and then at the White Hart in Lewes in January. Ultimately unable to escape London to attend the Lewes meeting, Richmond sent a lengthy letter to be read aloud. The moderate reforms, he charged, just swapped out one form of "partiality" for another. They might successfully increase the proportion of the population that could vote from

2 to 3 percent—an improvement, to be sure. But that was far from what anyone should make a goal if they were serious about protecting natural rights. The activists debating in the smoky, low-ceilinged rooms of the White Hart vigorously approved the Duke's sentiments and decided to publish his letter supporting universal manhood suffrage in *The Sussex Advertiser*. The Society for Constitutional Information also published it. They distributed two thousand copies throughout Yorkshire and elsewhere alongside yet another ten thousand copies of Cartwright's *Declaration of Rights*.

Richmond's political methods befuddled his contemporaries, including his sister Sarah, who was personally devoted to Charles James Fox. Fox had by now claimed the banner of leadership of the Whigs. Sarah expressed exasperation with her brother and professed an inability to understand how he could claim to be of service to his country when he was on the opposite side from the Whigs and serving in a cabinet without even going to its meetings.

Fox himself was still fuming at the King's decision to turn to Shelburne, and so he cast about for any coalition that would allow him to topple the government. Ultimately, he chose an alliance with Lord North, a despicable compromise from the point of view of Richmond and other Whig stalwarts. It made no ideological sense at all but was simply a way to wreck the government and motivated by Fox's egotistical fury.

The Fox-North coalition soon proved strong enough to force Shelburne out of office. On February 17, 1783, Shelburne lost a vote in the House of Commons, 224 to 208. Two days later Richmond paid a visit to his sister Sarah. They talked politics "very freely," she reported to her friend Susan. Perhaps Shelburne would hold on, Richmond mused. Perhaps Fox would end up as prime minister. "As to the chaos," Richmond told Sarah that his view was that "all is possible *now*." A week later, Shelburne resigned.

THE ENSUING CHAOS WAS even more severe than after North's departure. When North had stepped down, the King had already opened discussions with Rockingham, and the economy, although bloated with war debt, was still artificially supported by that massive investment in the military.

Less than a year later, in the wake of the preliminary articles of peace, demobilization was underway, and Britain was in the early stages of a postwar industrial contraction. As public spending ramped down, returning soldiers struggled to enter a contracting labor market. A hard winter and poor harvests exacerbated the situation, leading to spikes in food prices. Britain was headed into a season of food riots as laborers, who could no longer afford their daily bread, demanded fair prices. The King lacked an obviously steady hand to whom to turn. He desperately wished to avoid having the Fox-North coalition lead the government, so he spent six weeks trying to find an alternative. Meanwhile, the cabinet staggered along, and the country raged. The Yorkshire Volunteers mutinied over demobilization. The 104th Regiment of Foot, stationed on Guernsey, also mutinied. Women and workers rioted in Newcastle, attacking granaries and bakeries and seizing and redistributing bread.

The King understood that his most fundamental duty was ensuring stable government. He felt himself sickeningly close to failure. For a second time, he considered abdication. He also appears to have weighed a stark alternative—following the example of the King of Sweden and carrying out an autocratic coup. George III was losing faith in Parliament. Yet he did not choose autocracy. Like Richmond, ultimately, he remained resolutely committed to constitutionalism.

FOR RICHMOND, THE MESS actually provided an opportunity to install his vision in the heart of government. His greatest preoccupation in his role as master-general of the ordnance was with hardening the fortifications of the South Coast. Richmond hoped to win 400,000 pounds over eight years from Parliament for dockyards improvements. In the political tumult of January and February, he had had difficulty securing Shelburne's attention for expansive plans to extend and rebuild the fortifications at Plymouth and Portsmouth with innovative star-shaped fortifications. Rather than giving way to frustration, though, Richmond plowed forward on his own.

While the King was looking for a new prime minister, Richmond opportunistically presented both of his two major ordnance projects in Parliament in the form of a request for a budget approval. The budget contained two important policy moves: first, it reorganized salary scales, cut staff, and reduced use of the civil list and, second, it provided funds for the dockyard improvements. The first move would entrench the economic reform agenda; the second, Richmond's heterodox defense policy of a fortified coast, rather than a mobile navy, as the foundation for

Britain's safety. Richmond continued to steer by his double north star. Distracted by maneuverings elsewhere, Parliament voted Richmond's budget through. Won in such conditions, Richmond's victory would prove fragile.

After the King steeled himself to staying on the throne, and finally swallowed the Duke of Portland as a figurehead prime minister for the Fox-North coalition, Portland asked Richmond to remain in the ordnance and join the cabinet. Richmond refused. He explained in a letter that Lord North had declared himself against parliamentary reform, and Richmond was sure North would have "the power to prevent any Measure he may not like." Richmond's focus was constant. No one else held on to his own compass so firmly.

The conflict had tossed the major players of British politics around so violently that the King and Richmond in the spring of 1783 found themselves, astonishingly, aligned politically. Not only that, they were aligned *against* the government in power, a circumstance that would have been unthinkable three years earlier. Richmond was officially in opposition, but the King was secretly in opposition too. They were also aligned in a second way. Each man had recognized the potential of William Pitt the Younger.

NEITHER GEORGE NOR RICHMOND considered the ship of state in safe waters under the leadership of the Fox-North coalition, with Portland in the premiership. Indeed, the Fox-North coalition was not destined to last much longer than the one it had displaced. In a supreme irony, the politics of reform that the King had so long fended off would be central to the undoing of these ministers, whom he so despised.

The new coalition sought to rein in the territorial concessions to America, but the momentum of the Shelburne plan ratified the previous November carried the day. When the preliminary articles were ratified by Congress in April 1783, church bells rang throughout the United States, cannons were fired, and fireworks went off everywhere. General George Washington symbolically chose April 19, 1783—the eighth anniversary of the Battle of Lexington and Concord—to issue his ceasefire order. In London, the mood was not celebratory, however. The nation's circumstances were simply too dire.

Right from the start of the Portland ministry, George III continued to seek an alternative to it. He was a desperate man—and emotionally raw because of the recent deaths of his two youngest sons from smallpox contracted after inoculations for the disease. He persistently sounded out Pitt to see if he might take the premiership. As he had with Rockingham, though, the King conditioned the offer to Pitt on a promise to drop reform. Pitt refused. In fact, he kept moving his moderate reform bill in Parliament, for which Richmond was his partner.

Once the official ceasefires were in place, Richmond made plans to travel by yacht to France in the summer to "frisk for a month to Paris," as Sarah put it. Before he left, he continued to press the reform agenda forward. In the House of Lords, he stood and argued for establishing a committee "to consider further regulations to secure the independency of the judges," another idea he had first presented years before.

In the House of Commons, Pitt reintroduced election reform legislation—to combat bribery, disenfranchise rotten boroughs, and add representatives for London and the counties. Both men were grateful to have new reinforcements for the reform cause in the House, including a new member of Parliament, William Wilberforce, an evangelical Anglican social reformer who would become the leading voice for abolition of slavery. Disappointingly, though, the 1783 motion fell even further short than the previous year's motion: 293 to 149. Despite the defeat, Pitt's leadership in the cause would soon give him access to the political power of the grassroots movement that Richmond had built. That power, once combined with Pitt's oratorical gifts, would pose a substantial threat to Fox and North, which they could not yet see. Richmond, however, could.

AS A MODERATE REFORM caucus emerged in Parliament for the first time. Richmond had a timely opportunity to explain his thinking about reform late in the summer of 1783. After an unseasonably hot summer in Paris, made hazy by a volcano erupting in Iceland, he found a letter waiting for him at home from Colonel William Sharman, chair of the combined local militias in Ireland. Colonel Sharman had written to six leading reformers—Richmond, Wyvill, Cartwright, Jebb, Price, and Lord Abingdon—posing eight questions about parliamentary reform. All six men's answers were published together in pamphlet form in Ireland. Richmond's response, though, was best suited for stand-alone publication, so the Society for Constitutional Information as well as a second London publisher reprinted it separately.

In his *Letter to Colonel Sharman*, Richmond reprised the arguments he had been making for years. Only the prospect of a complete reform of the franchise could motivate people for change. Anything else would simply adjust which elites controlled the electoral system. But the British subject had an unalienable birthright—here he quoted Paine's letter to the abbé de Raynal—to be governed only by laws to which he has consented. This required universal participation. To every man "should be given his own." Political rights, though, didn't mean social homogeneity. He wrote that "the equal rights of men to security from oppression, and to the enjoyments of life and liberty" are "perfectly compatible with their unequal shares of industry, labour, and genius, which are the origin of inequality of fortunes." Although he affirmed social hierarchy, for political matters he insisted on pure equality, writing about his view that "it is true that the poorest man in the kingdom will have an equal vote with the first, for the choice of the person to whom he trusts his all; and . . . he ought to have that equal degree of security against oppression."

Then Richmond reminded his readers of Montesquieu's conception of a balanced constitution. He acknowledged that, if the House of Commons was merely a vessel for the expression of popular will, and if there were no other branches of government, Britain would approach "a pure democracy," which would be "more than our constitution warrants, or than I wish to see."

Years earlier Richmond had brushed off warnings that he should be worried about being seen as a leveller or republican. Now he emphatically stated that he was neither. "I am not for a democratic, any more than for an aristocratic, or monarchic government, solely." His commitment was to constitutionalism: "I am for that admirable mixture of the three, that our inimitable and comprehensive constitution has established."

Richmond held constitutionalism itself in such high esteem for the very reasons he had learned from Montesquieu, and he drew on the French philosopher's theory of separation of powers to account for his views, explaining their application to universal suffrage. He wanted to see the executive branch of government "where the constitution has originally placed it, in the hands of the crown to be carried on by its ministers." Those ministers in turn needed to be "under the control of parliament." Parliament, in turn, needed to be "under the control of the people."

Parliament should not micromanage; its core purpose was simply "its superintending and controuling power, which is the main end of its institution." The people would check Parliament, Parliament would check the ministers, the ministers would check the Crown. The Crown would execute on behalf of all.

This system of separating powers, and establishing an order in which one power could check another, would ensure that no institution or individual could amass the kind of excessive power that led to tyranny. British liberty would be well protected, while the nation would also have a strong executive capacity. With this argument, Richmond gave a great gift to the monarch: an account of how popular sovereignty and royal power could be fused.

George III, as he sought to protect a stable balance among the Crown, the House of Lords, the House of Commons, and the people at large, had also drawn extensively on Montesquieu to guide his thinking. While Montesquieu had advocated that a mixed constitution—blending democratic, aristocratic, and monarchic elements—was best, he had also allowed that any given constitution could tip in the direction of one of those elements and become simply a democracy (or a republic), an aristocracy, or a monarchy. Richmond had used Montesquieu to develop a conception of a balanced constitution led by aristocrats. The King had used the same framework to develop a conception of balance anchored by a monarch. What the two men—King and Duke—could agree on was the principle of constitutional balance, and that finding that balance would be the secret to establishing the stability of constitutional monarchy.

In addition to the *Letter to Colonel Sharman*, Richmond wrote a second, similar letter to Scotch reformers in 1784. The *Letter to Colonel Sharman* was reprinted twice in 1792, and would stay in print until 1859. For several generations, Richmond's letter would lay the foundation for the reform conversation, as parliamentary reformers steadily advanced a program of radical constitutional reform that remained fairly stable all the way through to the Third Reform Act in 1884—still only partway to Richmond's goal of universal manhood suffrage.

Richmond had provided King George III and Britain with the

conceptual foundation for a modernized constitutional monarchy—a theoretical framework to transition the government into the era of popular sovereignty while retaining a monarchical structure. He had also taught this framework to Pitt and other young parliamentarians—handing the baton to them. Richmond delivered this gift just as the Treaty of Paris was signed on September 3, 1783, bringing an end to the wars with America, France, Spain, and Holland. The treaty introduced the world to the United States of America, a republic constituted on a larger scale than any yet seen in human history. The era of popular sovereignty had arrived.

THE KING HAD GOOD reason to adapt. Popular sovereignty had arrived not only on foreign shores but also at home in Britain, and already the movement was beginning to reach for more. That fall the Society for Constitutional Information also reviewed and decided to endorse Quaker petitions against the slave trade. Fox and North, though, were unaware of just how much political power was growing in the grassroots reform movement.

The success of economic reform turned out to be the second danger that caught Fox and North by surprise, advantaging the King and, in another twist, placing him on the side of reform. Burke's Establishment Act had reduced the number of jobs that could be doled out as patronage to secure support in Parliament. If the King had had good relations with Fox and North, he might have been willing to apply his remaining patronage powers for their benefit, but instead he fully withheld that tool from them.

With fewer resources for maintaining allegiances and order in parliament than before, Fox and North sought new means of patronage. Returning to a hot button issue of the early 1770s, Fox proposed nationalizing the East India Company. His rationale was not purely financial. He did want to co-opt the revenues of the East India Company for his government's use and dispersal—but he also had political goals. Control of the East India Company would give him vast patronage power.

All the committed reformers, who had been steady in their purpose, were ready to resist such a measure. Nationalization of the company would clearly reverse the work of the economic reform bill. Fox had betrayed them by allying with North; they were unwilling to let him perpetrate a second betrayal with a bill whose purpose would have undermined their hard-won victories.

Fox's planned extension of parliamentary patronage angered the King. After Fox's bill passed the House of Commons on December 8, George III felt himself pushed to the limits of his tolerance. In an uncharacteristic but adroit act of interference with legislation, on December 11, he secretly authorized one of his allies to let members of the House of Lords know that he disapproved of the bill. His usually meticulous correspondence record, with letters sent and received recorded to the minute, is blank for a week, obscuring any communications about the meddling.

That simple knowledge of the King's disapproval was enough to sink Fox's bill by 95 votes to 76 in the House of Lords. Though the King typically—and more often than one might expect—left legislative politics to the politicians, he was ruthless when he decided to play. For the King to defeat his own administration was tantamount to dismissing his ministers. He waited a day for Fox, North, and Portland to take the hint and resign. When they did not, he directly dismissed them at midnight on December 18.

Then George III took one of the most risky and inspired steps of his reign: He appointed William Pitt as prime minister. The King's desperation for a government he could trust led him to drop his requirement that Pitt abandon the cause of reform. The instrument the King wanted to stabilize the nation was also the instrument Richmond had fashioned to secure the reform agenda. Both the King and Richmond boldly reached for the future by turning without ego to a twenty-four-year-old.

The London Chronicle marveled over the turbulence of the reign of George III—that snap elections dissolving Parliament had been called three times, peace had been made twice each with France and Spain, Britain had lost thirteen of its twenty-six colonies in America, and Parliament had given up legislative jurisdiction over Ireland. The paper glumly predicted that Pitt's appointment was hardly likely to steady the ship.

RICHMOND'S NEXT STEP WAS his greatest gift to the King, and the first of his two greatest gifts to his country. Pitt faced a daunting prospect. The King understood that the British nation was in a perilous state and undertook desperate measures to steady it. When Pitt's appointment was announced, sixteen peers and thirty-two commoners resigned from government offices on the spot. Or, as the *Chronicle* put it, "Every body resigned. Even those to whom the text of the poet . . . may be applied, 'that to resign's the last, mad thing they do.'"

If Pitt's government was to succeed, the young prime minister—whose obsession with work would render him a lifelong bachelor—needed the ballast of experience in his government. He also needed the weight of authority. A naturally gifted politician and campaigner, Pitt, green as he was, would also need help extending his reach in elections, to gain a majority to govern. Richmond agreed to join Pitt's cabinet and to resume his role as master-general of the ordnance. By shoring up Pitt's ministry with needed legitimacy, Richmond gave the King the stable government he craved, placed at last in the hands of a man George could both respect and trust.

Richmond's motivation was uncomplicated. He believed that Pitt would carry forward the reform agenda. That was always his priority. Also, even in a reformed government, Pitt was able to offer Richmond a few choice patronage opportunities: for Lord George, oversight of the Tower of London and the governorship of Portsmouth, which George had long desired; and resumption of the secretaryship at the ordnance for his nephew and heir, Charles Lennox. Richmond was coming to settle on measures *and* some men.

The value of adding Richmond to the cabinet was immediately apparent. Parliament was to be dissolved for snap elections soon after Pitt's appointment. The purpose of this quick pivot to campaigning was to give Pitt a chance to consolidate his authority by winning seats for more allies in the House of Commons. Richmond's strong standing with the City and county reformers would serve the ministry well in the elections. The power of his grassroots organizing was about to be revealed.

The election had more contested seats than any other in a century. The central battle was between Pitt and Fox. It was also a contest over the direction for the reform movement. Pitt was still committed to Wyvill and moderation—Richmond had accepted his pragmatism—but Fox, who had once captured radical hearts, had betrayed them by allying with Lord North. The Duke of Richmond, Lord Mahon, and Sir Cecil Wray, then the president of the Society for Constitutional Information, worked to bring the Quintuple Alliance radicals from the City away from Fox and over to Pitt, despite Pitt's moderation. All the work educating the public about reform had paved the way for Pitt's campaign. An indication of Richmond's success at campaigning was that in April he was himself elected a president of the Society for Constitutional Information.

The young prime minister's victory was emphatic. He blocked and diminished Wyvill's power and massively reduced Fox's. The King, seeking to reinforce the electoral victory, also gave Pitt the power to create peers. In one stroke, that undid the power of the old aristocracy.

Fox reflected acidly in his memoirs on the outcome of the election. He recognized that "the defection of a man of such weight and abilities as the Duke of Richmond" had kept other members of the cabinet attached to Pitt. He acknowledged that it was Richmond's "firmness during the memorable contest of 1784" that had kept Pitt strong, in the face of a gargantuan challenge. The elections of 1784 were the occasion, he reported, when George III declared that "there was no man in his dominions by whom he had been so much offended, and no man to whom he was so much indebted as the Duke of Richmond."

RICHMOND'S HOPES LIFTED WITH the new administration. On April 25, 1784, he wrote buoyantly to the Duke of Rutland conveying his belief that popular opinion was moving toward parliamentary reform. He was impressed by Pitt's success on the stump and awestruck by the degree of his popularity. Pitt, he wrote, had "the fullest support of the people from all quarters." With that support, the prime minister would be able to carry the measures "to which he is pledged," Richmond added, very much having parliamentary reform in mind. He also confided that Pitt was someone "very well disposed to keep his word."

In this letter, Richmond was reporting on the strengthening of modern popular party politics. Pitt would carry out his work not because of his careful management of elite networks, but by taking his cues from the people. He would bring popular power to the Crown and reinforce the strength of British institutions, not cling pitiably to George's good graces as he sought to chart his course. In Pitt's person, Richmond was already winning the cause of parliamentary reform, restoring the independence of Parliament from the Crown through the power of the people.

Pitt would serve as prime minister for nineteen years, from 1783 to 1801—years in which Britain would confront Revolution and Terror in France and the rise of Napoleon. His would be the second longest tenure of any prime minister in British history. Thanks to the assistance of the

Duke of Richmond, Pitt and George III were able to fashion the parameters of modern constitutional monarchy—a reinforced commitment to limits on executive power.

With Pitt's elevation to the premiership, a nation long managed exclusively in the private dining rooms of aristocrats passed into the age of popular politics. The Duke of Richmond was the pivot around which the ages turned. He carried the country and the King from Lord North through the Marquess of Rockingham and Earl of Shelburne and delivered it to William Pitt, in a period of chronic and almost catastrophic instability, chop, and change until finally the country found a prime minister who could hold a government together.

Richmond had been ahead of his own generation in his commitment to reform, and this won him the allegiance of a rising generation who took the project forward. Just as he had bridged Whig factions, he bridged generations. His perseverance peaceably birthed a future for popular sovereignty in Britain. The King was indeed indebted to Richmond, because the monarch and the monarchy survived, in an age when other monarchs fell.

Chapter
15

HURRICANE SEASON

1784–1792

The internal convulsion in France had but just begun; and it was then asked, whether we would think of repairing our house in the hurricane season.

—MP CHARLES GREY IN PARLIAMENT, 1793

WHEN RICHMOND ENTERED THE PITT ADMINISTRATION, he was nearly forty-nine, the age at which his father had died of bladder cancer. He had already suffered for years from bouts of bad health—liver ailments, bowel indispositions, gout. The beauty of his youth was gone. Newspaper caricaturists seized on the paunch and pate that betokened age. His three remaining sisters would all outlive him.

Richmond himself was free enough of vanity and honest enough about the changes wrought by time to let George Romney paint a final portrait, in this case in his role as master-general of the ordnance, with a sword at his hip and a cannon in the background to signify his domains of responsibility. He was, though, a senior figure, not a dashing youth.

Richmond was remarkably comfortable passing the baton on reform to Pitt and redirecting his energies to the ordnance. Perhaps his father's early death and his own age gave him a sense that it was time to lay in a succession plan. He was certainly accelerating his investment in his heir, Charles Lennox, and also in his other nephews. He reappointed Charles as his secretary at the ordnance and spent time touring Lord Edward Fitzgerald, or Eddy, as his nephew was called, around Portsmouth and

This caricaturist mocks the Duke of Richmond for treating his responsibilities at the ordnance as the hobby of a sleepy old man playing war games.

BY THOMAS ROWLANDSON, 1786.

The Duke of Richmond turned to one of his favorite artists, George Romney, for this formal portrait in the insignia of his office as master-general of the ordnance.

BY PERMISSION OF THE TRUSTEES OF THE GOODWOOD COLLECTION.

the Channel Islands, to review and discuss fortifications. Eddy did not appreciate all the attention. Rushing around at Richmond's pace made him feel that his thoughts would "all go *harum-scarum*."

Eddy's sense of feeling overwhelmed by Richmond is understandable. The energy that Richmond had directed for so many years toward reform legislation he now redirected toward innovation. At the ordnance, he sponsored the first hot-air balloon trials in England. He pursued technical improvements in firearms—from revamping the flintlocks in use in British rifles with the introduction of the Nock lock, which improved speed and reliability of firearm ignition; to changing the source of the flint used in the locks for improved materials; from quick-reload rifles and an improved bayonet scabbard for infantry to a musket that came to be known as the Duke of Richmond's Musket. He dreamed of surveying and mapping every inch of Britain, and thus was born the Ordnance Survey, which exists to this day, now known as "Britain's mapping service."

This shift of focus was made possible *because* he had passed off reform to Pitt. In backing the young prime minister, Richmond had accepted that the government's approach to reform would be Pitt's gradualist moderation. Richmond could live with that; he did not abandon his ambitions for universal manhood suffrage and a new contract between the monarchy and the people, but he had accepted that *he* could not impose them. The times would not bear it. Pitt would move at a different pace, with different priorities. He was working to unite the goal of full and equal representation with a gradual approach to reform that respected the monarchy.

Richmond might well have thought that his most intense political days were behind him, but he would have been wrong. The perpetual rabble-rouser, his one-time partner-in-arms, Thomas Paine, was about to return to Europe and reenter his life.

Over the coming two decades, Britain's activists would radicalize further, especially under the impetus of the French Revolution and inspired by Paine's writings, particularly *The Rights of Man*. Not content with the soft revolution Richmond was engineering, some people wanted the whole conflagration, including the end of the monarchy, by violence if necessary. There were two assassination attempts against the King in 1786 and 1800—as well as a third conspiracy alleged by the government in the 1790s, which became a justification to suppress dissent. Richmond would have to work harder than he anticipated to protect his agenda from the government but also from his oldest radical friends, first among them Paine.

WHEN THE JUNIUS PROJECT wrapped up in 1772, the national conversation about reform had barely begun. There was a certain vagueness about precisely what was entailed by a commitment to universal manhood suffrage. The debate among radical and moderate reformers throughout the late 1770s and early 1780s flowed from this ambiguity and was, roughly speaking, a disagreement about whether popular sovereignty required American-style republicanism—with replacement of monarchies and administration by elected officials—or could be made compatible with monarchy. There could be overlap between the moderates and the radicals because of the vagueness—because the answer to this question was not clear. This overlap sustained a political coalition, as long as the question of how far reform should go was never directly answered. Richmond's success in uniting different factions in the grassroots movement depended on not resolving this ambiguity.

With his *Letter to Colonel Sharman* in 1783, Richmond had forced the issue into the open and chosen a side. He was not for democratic, aristocratic, or monarchic government but for a blend of the three. Specifically, he had chosen not republicanism but monarchy welded to popular sovereignty and governing through popular ministers. Once America had become a full-fledged constitutional democracy—the world's first in the modern era—the terms of the debate shifted. No longer could one hold a position for universal manhood suffrage and not also clarify whether that went with a republican, aristocratic, or monarchical picture of politics.

In Richmond's view, the choice was obvious. Like Montesquieu, he deeply revered the British constitution with its balance among the three estates of monarchs, aristocrats, and commoners. Throughout his entire career, he sought to stave off two threats to it: invasion from France and disequilibria in domestic politics occasioned by one or another branch overreaching its role. This commitment to monarchy and aristocracy, alongside a commitment to reform, had, in fact, always characterized his writings and those of his propagandists.

The letters written in 1768 and 1769 under the pseudonym "C," for instance, simultaneously argued both pro-monarchy and anti-corruption lines. The same was true for the Junius letters. Those letters violated convention with respect to how Junius addressed the King, but at the same time Junius expressed consistent and steady support for the monarchy, albeit for one cured of corruption. This feature of the Junius letters had confused readers and made it difficult to identify authorship—the strange paradox of reverence for the monarchy coupled with fierce criticism of King George III specifically.

By the time Thomas Paine published *Common Sense* in 1776, the former exciseman was a full-blown republican. His deep involvement in the American War only intensified his conviction. The ocean between them since 1774 meant he and Richmond had not yet had to face their differences. Their confrontation would prove fierce. First, though, Richmond had to reckon with disappointment in Pitt.

WHEN PITT ENTERED OFFICE, the British economy was laden with war debt. Prices and taxes were both high. Ordinary people felt the pinch. The governance challenges within the East India Company also continued to destabilize both the Empire and the economy. Pitt understandably chose rebalancing the economy as his first priority.

In addition to pursuing sound finance, debt reduction, and stable governance of India, Pitt also planned to continue Shelburne's administrative reforms, parliamentary reform, an end to the slave trade, improved commerce with Ireland, and stable relations with Canada. The twenty-four-year-old had a lot on his plate. Richmond was the "only member of cabinet interested in three of Pitt's most important reform proposals—Parliament, slave trade, and Irish commercial restrictions." Richmond might reasonably have hoped to accomplish great things. But Richmond was, frustratingly, only Pitt's second most important ally.

The prime minister's most important ally was George III. For the future of parliamentary reform, the single most important fact of Pitt's premiership was his strong sense of partnership with a king who did not approve of it. The King had not made Pitt renounce the agenda but neither would he favor it. Pitt, by virtue of being committed both to the King and to parliamentary reform, was trying to fashion a new path for the future of British constitutionalism—one that more clearly welded monarchy and change together.

Richmond was ready to endorse such a path. Even John Wilkes had come to endorse it. At the London Guildhall, Wilkes presented Pitt with the "Freedom of the City" (we might say "the keys to the city") to honor him for "his support 'for the legal prerogative of the Crown, and the constitutional rights of the people.'"

Pitt was trying to square the circle, and as he worked on that, he, like Richmond, drove a wedge between reformers supporting constitutional monarchy and those in the republican camp. While Pitt was trying to steer the massive energies stirred up by the American War toward a modernized monarchy, welded to popular sovereignty, his political nemesis, Fox, flirted with outright republicanism. The question of the direction reform would take—of whether Britain would shift from a soft to a full revolution—depended on who won. In the Age of Revolution, no political question was more important.

Pitt kept his promise—to Richmond and also to Sawbridge—to introduce a third and (for him) final bill for parliamentary reform on April 18, 1785. Bowing to the power of the King, he introduced the bill not as prime minister, but as a private member of Parliament. He therefore signaled that the bill was not a government measure and could not be presumed to have the King's support. That set it up for failure.

Pitt had crafted the bill to bring on board those who "reverence the constitution so much as to be fearful of touching even its defects." He also sought to win over members of Parliament who could see defects and wanted to fix them but held back simply from fear that cracking open a habitual avoidance of change would set free "the daring enterprize of Innovation" with "no foreseeing to what alarming lengths we might progressively go, under the mask of reformation." The bill was consequently the most moderate reform legislation yet presented. It proposed eliminating thirty-six "rotten boroughs"—jurisdictions that no longer had significant population but still had seats in Parliament. The seats were to be reallocated to the counties, to London, and to the unrepresented new industrial centers like Manchester. In addition, Pitt proposed monetary compensation for the current borough owners to redress their loss of representation. Richmond had said he was open to supporting whatever bill his colleagues considered best.

Pitt's proposal was so tame, so limited in its ambition, so directly responsive to a clear and agreed upon problem, and so generous to those who would lose out from the change that it should have passed. Yet the politics of reform had changed. Richmond and Pitt had driven a wedge between those reformers who wished to glue reform together with appropriate protection of royal prerogative and those who wished to reform right up to the line of republicanism. Now that wedge was used against them. Charles James Fox stood on the other side. Purely for the sake of his own political ambition—to hand Pitt a loss—Fox worked to kill the bill. He had no real substantive grounds to object to it, but he unleashed Burke to argue against the bill, counter to his prior practice which was to silence critics of the reform bills. Burke's eloquence drove the wedges in the reform movement deeper. He lambasted Christopher Wyvill, the original proponent of moderate reform, whom he called witheringly, "this reforming divine." The bill was rejected in May with a vote of 174 to 248.

Moderate reform was dead for a generation—paradoxically killed by those for whom no step at all was now better than a step in the right direction. The bill had been defeated by exactly the same margin—seventy-four votes—as Sawbridge's effort the previous year. Pitt had done no better than the wild-eyed radical in getting reform through Parliament. It was a sobering result for reformers, and put Pitt off the project for the remainder of his parliamentary career. After this defeat of Pitt's bill in 1785, it would be forty-five years before a government once again placed parliamentary reform seriously on the national agenda.

Richmond was a policy visionary, but Pitt was a pragmatist. His goal was above all to maintain power so that he, partnered with the King, could continue to lead the country. The sequence of events from 1784 through 1785—the need for sound economy; the anti-tax resistance; the failure of complicated policy change—led him to shrink the scope of his action and ambition. He moved in the direction of his more conservative supporters and chose as his priorities "keeping government cheap, taxes reduced, and commercial prosperity encouraged." Thus Toryism was born out of reformist Whiggism.

The field of reform now belonged wholly to the republicans. This would give Richmond an entirely new set of problems.

RICHMOND MIGHT HAVE GENTLY drifted out of public life in favor of his sylvan world at Goodwood and society life at Richmond House—

in 1787 he launched a series of lavish private theatricals in his home attended by the royal family and other luminaries—but for two ghosts of the past that re-entered his life. The first was political instability. The threat of a war with Holland caused Pitt and Richmond to speak confidentially—in the office or home of one or the other of them—almost every day during the summer of 1787. There was even some loose talk that Richmond might take over as foreign secretary and pass the ordnance to someone else.

Then, George III fell into his second bout of manic depression in November 1788. This period of crisis lasted for some six months, as the Prince of Wales, who was now tightly allied to Fox, jousted with Pitt for control of the government. Pitt and Richmond worked strenuously to preserve authority for the King. Only George's recovery in March 1789 averted a deepening constitutional crisis.

The second ghost came from France. On April 26, 1787, a week after the opening night of Richmond's first season for his home theatricals, Thomas Paine, that uncompromising champion of reason and rights, set sail for Europe. Once more, letters from Franklin paved his way, this time bearing introductions to Franklin's French associates. The ocean was now blissfully free of danger from military vessels thanks to the peace treaty, but Paine was sailing right into the building storm of the French Revolution.

Paine's life had been rocky in America. During his thirteen years there, he had inspired a revolution but irritated many revolutionaries—ceaselessly cycling through heady success followed by crushing failure. Like many another immigrant, he set out once again, this time for France, to improve his fortunes.

His departure from America would not have been predicted a decade earlier. The publication of *Common Sense* had made his name in 1776 and put him in the middle of revolutionary action. He was close enough to the production of the Declaration of Independence to have assisted in its first publication in book form on July 8, 1776. Then, in 1777, the Continental Congress hired Paine as a propagandist on account of his obvious talent for rousing prose to help rally public support for the Revolution.

Within two years, though, the investigative journalist and newspaper polemicist in Paine got the better of him. In an effort to fight corruption, he revealed some secret congressional information when writing an essay in defense of a friend. This cost him his job and saw him assaulted in the streets of Philadelphia by men who thought he had betrayed the cause. Without other income, Paine took a job as a personal secretary to a private citizen in Philadelphia until the Pennsylvania Assembly hired him as a clerk. Ever the committed partisan and careless about his own money, he plowed a third of his salary into donations to Washington's army.

By 1781 Paine, on the up again, was traveling to France with John Laurens to raise money for the American military. Upon his return, Paine found all his personal funds exhausted and was once again unemployed. He was too poor to rent a horse. He wrote to George Washington seeking help, asking for compensation for all the good he had done on behalf of the new nation. Washington attempted to secure Paine a secret contract from Congress to carry on with propagandistic writing, but Congress referred the matter to a committee where it died. Paine continued to write nonetheless and earned small amounts from his writing, sponsored by one friend or another, but he remained deeply impoverished.

George Washington truly admired Paine and went out of his way to help him, trying again in 1783. He wrote to all the state governments seeking support for Paine, but once more, Paine's outspoken personality got the better of him. He chose that time to publish his argument that the sovereignty of the states didn't matter because only the sovereignty of the United States should be recognized. The result of this impolitic expression was that only two states made contributions. Luckily for Paine, both gifts were generous; one, extraordinarily so. Pennsylvania gave him a grant of 500 pounds, and New York gave him an estate of 277 acres in New Rochelle that had been confiscated from a Loyalist. These two gifts rescued Paine from immediate financial anxiety; he was able to buy himself a horse.

Paine's next political campaign, in the winter of 1786–1787, was on behalf of the re-establishment of the Bank of North America. For this work, he partnered with James Wilson, a Philadelphia-based, Scots-born and trained lawyer, who had been a signatory of the Declaration. Like Paine, Wilson advocated for a popular basis for the new government. In the spring of 1787, the two men and their allies at last succeeded in securing renewal of the bank's charter.

During the advocacy work of that spring, both men were in Philadelphia, where they were both also involved, alongside Benjamin Franklin, in preparing the intellectual foundations for the work of the Constitutional Convention. Paine had previously secured access to congressional archives to support his writing work, and now Wilson did too, equipping himself with copies of the Declaration. Franklin founded the Society for Political Enquiries, a small group, of which both Paine and Wilson were original members. This society was like the political networks Paine had been part of in Sussex, both in the Junius regiment and in Lewes.

Paine's life had never, though, been only about politics. He was also a tinkerer and inventor, another passion he shared with Franklin. Alongside his political endeavors, Paine had been at work designing a single-arch iron bridge, a long-standing obsession that he believed could become a commercial venture. With war concluded, and his prospects mixed in America, by 1787 Paine had decided to seek expertise, interest, and investment in Europe for construction of the bridge. With Franklin's introductions paving the way, Paine set sail for France in April 1787, departing from New York, probably on another packet ship, with a model of his iron bridge in tow.

Over the course of his life, Paine had few stable, lasting intimate relationships. While in Europe, he also intended to visit England, where he hoped to see his parents in Thetford. He arrived at Le Havre de Grace on May 26. In September, after some months in Paris seeking conversations with French engineers and innovators, Paine made his way to England to see his family and reconnect with other old friends. For all of Paine's frenetic correspondence with political associates, he was completely out of touch with his parents. When he arrived at Thetford, he learned that his father—his first teacher, whose Quaker egalitarianism had surely formed him—had died a year earlier, in November 1786. Only his widowed mother who had worked so hard to help him enter the excise service was there to greet him. Little had she known then how far away the role would take her son. As if to make up for lost time for filial duty, while he was in Thetford, Paine set up a weekly financial allowance for her.

Even while Paine was in Thetford rediscovering his elderly mother, his mind remained as fixed as ever on politics. He had left Britain in 1774 a virtual unknown except to his "particular friends." Most of his work had been in the shadows. Thanks to *Common Sense* and the *Crisis* essays, he returned to London as one of the most famous figures of the age. He felt on a level with the country's elite politicians. Soon after his arrival, he wrote an essay to advise the Pitt ministry, which included Richmond, on its foreign policy and to warn against war with Holland, the very subject on which Pitt and Richmond were conferring daily. He also wrote a letter to the Marquess of Lansdowne (formerly the Earl of Shelburne), seeking to make his acquaintance.

The iron bridge, though, was his obsession—whether for financial interests or a vision of social progress. To carry on with that work, by December Paine was on his way back to Paris both to see the American diplomat, Thomas Jefferson, and with hopes that Parisian urbanization, including efforts to bridge the Seine, would soon lead to interest in his project. Nine months later, though, he had made no progress in France, so he returned to England to try to sell his bridge there.

Paine's old connections kicked in. The estate of Francis Ferrand Foljambe, a Yorkshire MP and Wyvill protégé, was not far from the Walker ironworks, where Paine had a contract for the construction of his bridge. Foljambe needed to span a river near his home with a bridge of about one hundred feet. He offered his site to Paine to model his creation. Foljambe belonged to the world of parliamentary reformers, and he was also a vice president of the Society of Arts, serving alongside the Duke of Richmond, who still continued as a vice-president.

When Edmund Burke and Lord Fitzwilliam, Rockingham's heir, came up to the ironworks to see Paine's concept, Fitzwilliam invited Paine to his estate, Wentworth, and Paine accepted. Then Burke invited Paine, secretly his former colleague on the Junius letters, to visit his estate in Buckinghamshire, and Paine traveled there for a week. In December, Paine, listed as "the author of *Common Sense*," was elected into the Society for Constitutional Information. Paine was back with his people—the same network he had left behind in 1774. His election mirrored a sea change in the society. Its charter members, who were linked to Richmond and who had put the society on a moderate footing, had been replaced in leadership of the society by more radical reformers, most importantly John Horne Tooke.

Paine also visited sessions of Parliament. He attended on December 4, when Richmond was also there. He connected with Lord Edward Fitzgerald, who had been eleven when Paine left for America, and the two became fast enough friends for Fitzgerald to lodge with Paine in Paris four years later. Paine may even have been in touch with Charles Lennox, Richmond's nephew, whose cricket club made Paine some sort of honorary member.

Paine's letters from London to Jefferson in Paris in 1788 and 1789 reveal a person who quickly reintegrated with London's intellectual and political world of parliamentary reform. His letters name all the key players—Pitt, Burke, Fox, Stanhope, Foljambe, Price, Vaughan, Shelburne/Lansdowne. Only one name is conspicuously absent: the Duke of Richmond.

From Paine's letters to Jefferson, one would never even know that Richmond existed, let alone that he was a cabinet member and the leading spokesperson for the issue of parliamentary reform, for which Paine cared so passionately. What might have happened? The depth of the silence disguised a profound rupture.

WHILE IT IS IMPOSSIBLE to say for sure, it seems likely that Paine sought out Richmond's patronage when he first returned to England. If so, he was rebuffed. When Paine wrote from Thetford to the Pitt ministry about negotiations with Holland, which Richmond was publicly known to be working on, it is probable that he also wrote to Richmond directly. He does appear to have paid Richmond a visit at this time. Two items from the Duke's library are likely to have been gifts from Paine.

The first is a history of Thetford, Paine's hometown, where Paine had just been visiting. Within the library at Goodwood, there are very few volumes about specific municipalities—Berlin and Vienna, from the Duke's Grand Tour. Among UK locales, there are only a cluster of three books about Kent, a book about Scarborough in Yorkshire dedicated to William Wilberforce, the abolitionist, and the book about Thetford, a regional market town of no distinction but for being Paine's birthplace. It's hard to explain why the Duke of Richmond would have been interested in Thetford if not for Paine, nor why he would have taken the trouble to purchase the book. It has all the marks of a gift.

The second item, housed now not in the Duke's library but in the West Sussex Record Office, is the parchment Declaration of Independence with which the mystery of this book began: what is now called the Sussex Declaration, and which has to date been visited by dignitaries from Prince Harry and Meghan, the current Duke and Duchess of Sussex, to a US president, Donald J. Trump. The first time I saw the Sussex Declaration in person I felt time collapse between the two and a half centuries from the American Revolution to our present. The parchment is so stately in its simplicity—its text so pristine and easy to read compared to the faded and buckled version in the National Archives—that it felt like a gift directly for me, something to treasure.

I can imagine no better token of gratitude for Richmond, the first member of the House of Lords to recommend recognizing American independence—the one member of the House who had read the entire Declaration aloud during debates. Yet there were puzzles to resolve. If the parchment had been presented as a gift, why was it not framed and hanging in a place of honor at Goodwood, as a copy of it hangs now in the front hall

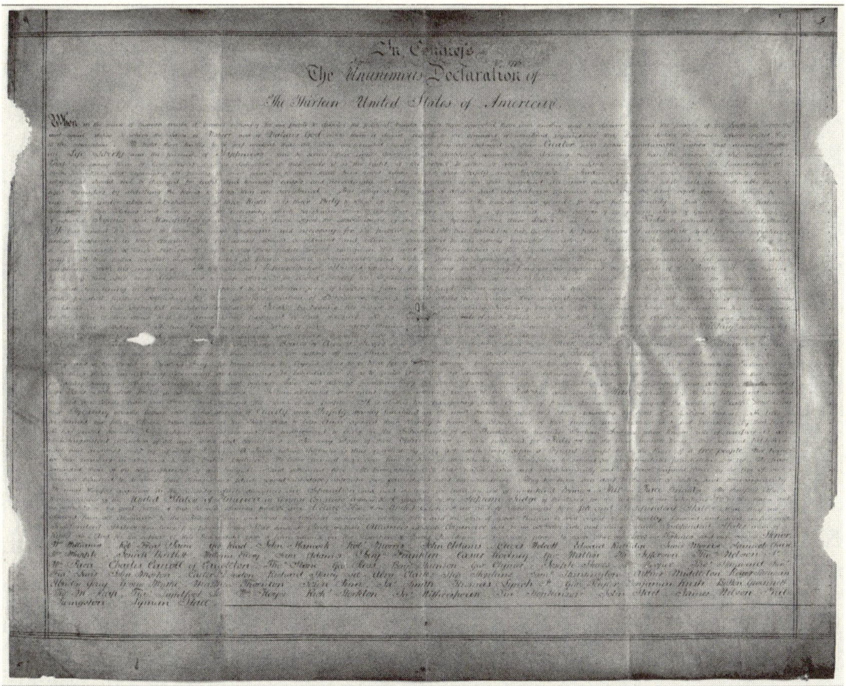

In Congress

The Unanimous Declaration of

The thirteen united States of America

At 24 × 30 inches, the Sussex Declaration of Independence is one of two parchment manuscripts of the Declaration of Independence rendered on this scale. The other is in the National Archives in Washington, DC. While there are still mysteries to solve about this parchment, it is likely to have been produced in Philadelphia in the 1780s.

WEST SUSSEX RECORD OFFICE, ADD MSS 8981.

of my own home? When I arrived to view the Declaration, it was folded into eighths, like any old working paper, like something confidential to hide. Its deep creases tell the story of a certain kind of burial. Something had happened to keep this glorious document a secret. I believe it was the dramatic rupture between the Duke and Paine provoked by Richmond's choice to support constitutional monarchy and Paine's for republican revolution.

IN EVERY COUNTRY WHERE he lived, Paine found his way into the protection of the most elite member of that country's radical circles: the Duke of Richmond in England in the 1760s and 1770s; then the very wealthy George Washington in the 1770s and 1780s; and then the Marquis de Lafayette in France. Upon his return to England, he is likely to have returned to the Duke quickly, hoping to receive protection once again. His effort to form a bond with Lansdowne, formerly Shelburne, reflects a similar effort. Lansdowne rebuffed Paine, and Richmond must have too. The Duke had very recently disappointed others. It was just a year earlier, in October 1786, that the writer Thomas Northcote complained to John Adams about Richmond's "cruel desertion."

Paine might have expected this. The two men's political paths had utterly diverged, as Paine would have known. He had followed how the debate about parliamentary reform had unfolded since his departure in 1774. He knew Richmond's arguments in the *Letter to Colonel Sharman*, but Paine rejected monarchy instead of embracing it. He was now a thoroughgoing republican and disdainful of Montesquieu's other two realms—the aristocracy and the Crown. He was uninterested in balancing the people's sovereignty with either of them.

In a 1789 letter to his business partner, Paine declared that "the English Nation is composed of two orders of men—Peers and Commoners" with "distinct and opposite claims." The conflict between these two orders provokes the emergence of a "regal power" to establish order. True reform would dispense with both aristocrats and the crown, so that the people might truly be sovereign. Paine lambasted Pitt's approach to reform, the very agenda that Richmond had crafted. He thought Pitt's half-hearted reforms had taken power from the people. Rather than protecting their rights, Pitt had increased the power of the aristocracy. Paine asked, "How then can the Rights of the People be asserted and supported by absorbing them into an hereditary house of Peers?"

Paine thought he knew why Pitt was doing this. It all boiled down to money. Economic reform had been a fig leaf, simply transitioning power over patronage from the King to the most powerful members of Parliament. Paine concluded, quoting Jonathan Swift, "Spit on such Patriotism."

Paine's criticism of Pitt tells us what he thought of Richmond by 1789. He had come to disdain him. Critics of Richmond had begun to hold his income from the coal duty over his head, and to call out the hypocrisy of a reform movement led by a man who held the ultimate "place," an annual income of seventeen thousand pounds, funded by the British taxpayer, just for being the descendant of the bastard son of a king. Paine was willing to accept handouts from aristocrats—and was in fact dependent on them. At the same time, he abhorred his own dependence, resenting those whose funds he needed, and a political economy that made dependence necessary.

The regency crisis during King George's incapacity only widened the political chasm between Richmond and Paine. Citizen Paine believed that Pitt should have taken the opportunity of "the King's insanity" to call a national convention and create a new constitution for Britain. He proposed that on his recovery the King should consider himself "as more properly the servant than the sovereign" of the British people.

Instead of doing this, Pitt had, as Paine saw it, "absorbed the right of the nation into a right of Parliament." In other words, Paine credited Pitt with achieving independence for Parliament and reducing the power of the Crown, goals that Richmond had been seeking for his whole career. The problem, though, for Paine was that Parliament itself had not been reformed. One of the Houses was purely hereditary and the other "elective by only a small part of the nation." Not only was universal suffrage needed to reform the House of Commons, but also the House of Lords had to go. Such an attack on the peerage would have been intolerable to Richmond.

Richmond's response to the regency crisis differed completely from Paine's. Rather than seeing it as an opportunity to spur transformation, he worked aggressively with Pitt to stabilize the monarchy, in the face of the challenge from Fox and the wayward Prince of Wales. When the King recovered, Richmond probably joined the service of Thanksgiving at St. Paul's to celebrate. Every householder in Lewes got beer money. Simply put, Richmond, whose instinct for unity was consistent throughout his life, preferred to protect his country and its constitution in a moment of crisis, whereas Paine would have used the crisis to revolutionize it. Their division was sharpened to a lethal cut by the added wound, as Paine saw it, that Richmond had money that he didn't really deserve.

THE DIFFERENT POLITICAL INSTINCTS of Paine and Richmond were thrown into even starker contrast by events unfolding across the Channel. A revolution in America was a source of shame and embarrassment in Britain, but it was 3,500 miles distant; one in France was a cause of panic since it reached scarcely twenty miles from Dover, not to mention the Duke's beloved Aubigny.

In 1788, France trembled on the edge of insolvency. Hoping to gain support for new taxation measures—and under pressure from nobles who resisted paying taxes and reformers who demanded representation—Louis XVI assembled the Estates General for the first time since 1614. Paris was already seething with radicalism, so the King resolved to host the meeting at Versailles and installed seating for a thousand attendees in the Salle des Menus-Plaisirs, a vast, austere hall typically used for royal entertainments. Like the British Parliament, the Estates General included representation from three orders of society—the clergy, the aristocrats, and the commoners, though organized into three estates instead of the two houses.

But the Estates General was no Parliament. It had no power. Once assembled, members of the Third Estate, the commoners, seized the opportunity to demand fairer representation. Suppressed by the other two estates and the King—and even locked out of the assembly hall—they occupied an indoor tennis court on the palace grounds. There they declared themselves a National Assembly representing the will of the French people, and insisted they would not stand down until they had drafted a new constitution for France. Meant to resolve a fiscal deadlock, the convening of the Estates General instead unleashed the French Revolution.

By late June 1789, the old order teetered. The elite had split—always the beginning of rapid change. Some members of the First and Second Estates, including the Marquis de Lafayette, supported the claim of the Third Estate to be the National Assembly. After unsuccessfully attempting to force the three estates to deliberate separately, Louis XVI gave up and ordered the aristocrats and the clergy to join the National Assembly, yielding to popular sovereignty.

At the same time, troops massed around the capital, bayonets glinting in the sun, and rumors spread like wildfire that they'd been dispatched to stage an aristocratic counter-coup against the fledgling National Assembly. Citizens of Paris began to arm themselves, looting armories, blacksmiths, and gunsmiths. Gunpowder was stored in the Bastille, a fourteenth-century limestone fortress used in the eighteenth century as a prison. On July 14 some eight hundred fiercely angry working men and women, backed by a swelling crowd, stormed the Bastille in search of the gunpowder. Ninety-eight were killed in the attack, but the crowd prevailed. After the fortress fell, the mob turned on the prison governor and officers, capturing and killing them. In the French countryside, hunger was pervasive due to poor harvests and starting in late July, in village after village, peasants rose against their feudal landlords. For British aristocrats and political elites, this news would have triggered memories of bread riots and the Gordon Riots.

The rising French radicals struck not only at the material bases of society. They also went for the institutional heart of the ancien régime. On August 4, the National Assembly passed a raft of directives: feudalism abolished, serfdom ended, tithes erased, and the special privileges of nobles and clergy swept away. On August 26, the assembly issued the Declaration of the Rights of Man and of the Citizen—a document not merely declaring political freedom, like its American and British cousins, but claiming an end to privation, and asserting the people's right to economic justice, to property, and to a fair and progressive tax.

Before long the French royal family had become a target. On October 5 and 6, 1789, a crowd of thousands of women and some men marched on the royal palace of Versailles, driven by the need for bread for their families. They were followed by twenty thousand members of the Paris militia, led by the Marquis de Lafayette, precisely the scenario King George had feared when Richmond demanded arms for his militia a decade earlier. Just thirty-one years old, Lafayette was already a war hero, having served as a major-general in the American Revolution. He heartily embraced the principles of rights and popular sovereignty, but he shared Richmond's ambition, not Paine's, for a constitutional monarchy, where the King would reign under the rule of law restrained by the will of the people.

The day after the fall of the Bastille, Lafayette accepted command of the National Guard, on the condition that its symbol—the blue, white, and red tricolor cockade—honored both the people and the Crown. Now, he was following behind a popular uprising, ostensibly to maintain order and limit violence. In this his militia largely succeeded. No blood was shed on those first two nights, and the King agreed to sign the Declaration of the Rights of Man and of the Citizen.

Despite the good beginning, things turned ugly on the final morning, and an altercation between one of the King's guards and the crowds led to the deaths of three or four people. The violent attacks on feudalism in the summer and the deaths at Versailles in the fall—even if only a harbinger of the vastly more terrifying violence to come in 1793–1794—fundamentally transformed the conversation about parliamentary reform in Britain.

DIFFERENT BRITISH POLITICAL COALITIONS had toyed with the idea of a national convention over the preceding two decades: Wilkes's supporters, the excise officers, Christopher Wyvill, the efforts of the association activists in 1779 and 1780 working to create reform associations in every county and to knit them together via an annual convention in London, the Scottish activists both during the time of the Gordon Riots and also in subsequent years. All had studied the many American national conventions closely—first the Stamp Act Congress, then the two Continental Congresses, and finally the Constitutional Convention, which had just delivered a new constitution for the United States. Now the example in France killed any prospect of a national convention for Britain—it looked too dangerous, too violent, too destructive.

Richmond had direct exposure to the blunt and bloody impacts of the rapidly unfolding French Revolution. Not only did he lose his titular and property rights at Aubigny, but he was involved in assisting French friends with their escape. In October 1789, his former lover, Madame de Cambis, mother of Henriette, left Paris for London, this time for good. While no record of her escape exists, she probably used a disguise, false papers, and carriage convoys, as other escapees did. She traveled with her cousin, Amélie de Boufflers, the duchesse de Biron. Also with them were Amélie's stepmother and two other relatives, including a child. They took a house together on the south bank of the Thames, near the royal retreats at Richmond Lodge and Kew Gardens.

Londoners marveled at the flood of French people into their city that fall, and one visitor to the Boufflers-Cambis lodgings reported them to be quite pitiable, "more like an hospital than anything else," with "such a crowd of miserable wretches, escaped from plunder and massacre." They had left so quickly that they were largely penniless. Richmond assisted the refugees. He began paying Madame de Cambis an annuity, which continued for a decade.

The refugees themselves, and much of London, read Edmund Burke's 1790 pamphlet, *Reflections on the Revolution in France*, with gratitude—as bringing sanity to a delusional age. Burke saw the French Revolution as a catastrophic upheaval—an ill-conceived approach to governance likely to brutalize people and ordinary life because it was driven by abstraction and the belief that social life could be reengineered. Burke argued for the importance of tradition and the organic evolution of social life as the best way of respecting and building on human nature, for pursuit of the common good. He offered a defense of monarchy and hereditary privilege. With this essay Burke broke with Charles James Fox and completed his own philosophical and political journey—from reformist and pro-American Whig to inspiration for modern conservatism—a road Pitt had already traveled through his embrace of partnership with the King. The Burke of 1789 was a different man than the radical thinker who had contributed alongside Paine to the Junius letters project.

In stark contrast, Paine passionately embraced the French Revolution and republican absolutism. In Piccadilly in April, he had visited the Opposition bookseller John Debrett, who informed him that Burke's text was in press, but that Burke was struggling with revisions. Paine immediately determined to write a rejoinder. From the bookseller, Paine went to meetings with pro-French politicians Lord Stanhope and then Charles James Fox, where Stanhope greeted him with the words, "Have I the pleasure of shaking hands with the author of *Common Sense*?" The two men discussed Burke's pamphlet and Paine's resolve to answer it and to defend the French Revolution, to prosecute the case against monarchy, and to defend republicanism. The conversations continued the next day over dinner with two radicals, Samuel Vaughan and Dr. Richard Price, another former member of the Honest Whigs, and intellectual collaborator of Richmond's at the time of the Junius letters.

By February 1791, Paine was ready to publish his response to Burke, the first volume of *Rights of Man*. It is a fiery defense of republican government and condemnation of monarchy and aristocratic privilege. After its publication, Paine kept up his travel around England, now to sell a revolution, not a bridge. Lord Edward Fitzgerald, Richmond's nephew, wrote glowingly to his mother, "My friend Paine is there [in the North] preaching his delightful doctrines."

In the summer of 1791, between the publication of the first and second volumes of *Rights of Man*, Paine traveled briefly to Paris to oversee the publication of a French translation of the first volume. He was there in June when the royal family unsuccessfully sought to escape the capital in a lumbering and conspicuous coach drawn by six horses. They hoped to make it to a royalist army near the border, but their heavy coach required frequent stops. The King was recognized from his picture on currency. Local officials intercepted Louis, Marie-Antoinette, and their children and returned them to Paris, their credibility destroyed and all remaining hopes of channeling the uprising into stable constitutional monarchy smashed.

The worst violence of the revolution lay still ahead. Paine was able to return easily to London by July 14, 1791, where he planned to attend an anniversary celebration of the fall of the Bastille at The White Bear in Piccadilly. The danger of association with the French revolutionaries was beginning to sink in. At the last minute, Paine decided not to attend the dinner. It didn't matter, though. The proprietor of the tavern himself thought better of hosting the gathering and refused admittance to the dinner guests.

Now led by radicals, the Society for Constitutional Information plunged ahead with their support for Paine. On August 20, John Horne Tooke chaired a dinner meeting at the Thatched House Tavern—where Richmond had often assembled his reformer associates—at which Paine delivered an "Address and declaration, of the friends of universal peace and liberty," and the society took the occasion to endorse—and have members personally sign—a manifesto written by Paine congratulating the French on their revolution and advocating for reforms he was about to propose in the second volume of *Rights of Man*.

While Paine's first volume began to circulate, and the Society for Constitutional Information began to distribute it broadly, Paine lived in London with a friend and kept writing. By the time he delivered the manuscript of the second volume to his publisher, on February 1, 1792, the violence in France was increasing. The British government wanted to stop it from spreading. The second volume laid out a plan for republican government and social welfare provision that Paine believed should inform new constitutions. Paine's publisher considered the book now too dangerous and backed away from it. Another publisher, J. S. Jordan, who wanted to produce a cheap version for working people, stepped up instead and published it.

In addition to laying out Paine's economic and welfare vision—a prescient anticipation of the post–World War II British welfare state—the second volume also continued his blistering attack on aristocracy and hereditary privileges. In this volume, though, Paine got personal. Society needs leaders, Paine acknowledged, but should not seek to secure them by having the past tie the hands of the future. The kind of meritocratic leader he admired was clear. He dedicated the first volume to George Washington and the second, to the Marquis de Lafayette. (Ironically, even as recently as 1790 Paine had described himself as a supporter of Louis XVI, whom he saw as a reforming "republican monarch.")

The kind of leader Paine was trying to defeat was also clear: those who depended on rents and protected their rent-seeking habits through hereditary privilege. There was an implicit question in those two dedications. If America had Washington and France had Lafayette, who was the reforming aristocrat that could lead England forward? Years earlier, the obvious answer would have been Paine's own patron, the Duke of Richmond. Certainly, the Americans thought that way. When John Adams many years later, in 1817, sought to provide a historical account of the great British leaders for the cause of universal suffrage, he named "the Duke of Richmond, Dr Price, Dr Jebb &c. These three great Statesmen Divines and Phylosophers." Instead of dedicating a volume of *Rights of Man* to Richmond, though, Paine used the book to lay waste to their former relationship.

The argument of the second volume focuses broadly on the theme of aristocratic corruption, but Paine named only one example: the Duke of Richmond. With hundreds of peers he might have chosen, he made the Duke alone his exemplar of the exploitative excesses of the British aristocratic system. He churned out whole paragraphs of criticism against him: He took from the public purse as much as would "maintain two thousand poor and aged persons"; the coal tax was "iniquitously and wantonly applied" (underlined in the original) in supporting the Duke of Richmond; and Richmond lived off "the distresses of a community."

Paine did not mince his words about his former mentor. Richmond was a member of a "band of parasites, living in luxurious indolence, out of the public taxes." Punning on Richmond's role at the ordnance, Paine charged the Duke with being part of the "outworks to protect the citadel" of monarchy, sarcastically reflecting that in "this species of political fortification, all the parts have such a common dependence that it is never to be expected they will attack each other." Richmond's work on reform should be seen as a hypocritical puppet show. He depended too much on the Crown for his own subsistence to ever have been serious about reform constraining royal power.

Paine then took his attack on Richmond into the footnotes, underscoring Richmond's moral offense. No principle of justice could legitimate the wealth Richmond possessed: "Humanity dictates a provision for the poor; but by what right, moral or political, does any government assume to say, that the person called the Duke of Richmond, shall be maintained by the public?" Paine knew what should be done about the situation: "The enormity is too serious to be permitted to remain."

Paine made Edmund Burke, too, a target of the second volume of *Rights of Man*, but the onslaught against Richmond stands out for its force, length, and bitterness. Paine concludes the rhetorical assault on the Duke with a disavowal of personal animosity: "In stating this case I am led by no personal dislike." He clearly protests too much.

Richmond's dependence on rent-seeking was neither distinctive nor new. Yet Paine had not sought to criticize it earlier when he benefited from Richmond's largesse. As Washington, Lafayette, and Jefferson could all attest, Paine was a difficult protégé; he fell out with all of them. Too proud to be a dependent, too undisciplined to be independent, Paine bitterly resented the aristocratic order that both enabled and humiliated him. He kicked at his patrons to lash out at a world made wrong.

RICHMOND WAS STILL MASTER-GENERAL of the ordnance when the second volume of *Rights of Man* came out. With its blistering attack on a sitting cabinet minister, the government could not ignore the book, as it had the first volume. On May 21, 1792, the King issued a royal proclamation against seditious writings, and the government immediately sued the publisher and Paine. The publisher, Jordan, was removed from the case when Paine stepped up and took sole responsibility. This would turn out to be only a temporary reprieve for Jordan, who was sued directly a year later, convicted, and jailed for sedition.

Paine was eager for a trial, believing that he would easily acquit himself on the grounds of having done no more than make reasonable arguments for the improvement of the British constitution. He appeared in court on June 8, 1792, but was disappointed to learn that the trial would be postponed until December. That summer, while he waited for his trial, and during the height of the political controversy surrounding his books and sedition indictment, George Romney, Richmond's protégé and friend, painted Paine's portrait over the course of six sittings. He still appears handsome and trim—he had plainly aged much better than Richmond. Despite the political intensity of the moment and his own personal endangerment, he is gently smiling.

The government actively sought to suppress distribution of Paine's

This portrait captures Thomas Paine at one of the most politically intense and dangerous moments of his life.

works, yet his books circulated widely—through the Societies for Constitutional Information in Manchester, Sheffield, Leeds, and Edinburgh and the London Corresponding Society. Copies of the two volumes continued to sell, eventually reaching a distribution of 200,000 copies. At a time when printing was expensive, postal systems rudimentary, and literacy far from universal, that level of circulation—equivalent to millions of copies today—was astonishing. It was a feat of both political messaging and underground distribution. In an age when most pamphlets sold only a few hundred copies, the two volumes of *Rights of Man* reached a level of circulation that was exceeded only by almanacs and the Bible. *Common Sense* had been no accidental stroke. Paine was the best-selling author of his age.

The rapid spread of Paine's ideas energized England's radical republican movement, which had now become the project of the working class, and infused it with pursuit of economic justice. In a change from the reform effort of a decade earlier, Paine's elite allies fell away. When Paine wanted to donate the volume's earnings of one thousand pounds to the original Society for Constitutional Information in London, its leaders decided, for safety's sake, to refuse the gift. The societies that now took up his work were often workingmen's associations.

WITH PAINE'S FRONTAL ATTACK on Richmond, battle was now joined between the republican apostles of revolution and reformers pledged to constitutional monarchy. Richmond found himself called back to the reform movement—to preserve what he had built from threats created by those who now sought to carry it to extremes. The Junius brigade of two decades earlier, once a united front against what had appeared to be emerging tyranny, had split. Its veterans now trained their fire on each other.

In response to Paine's unsparing attack on Richmond in *Rights of Man*, the London Society for Constitutional Information in June republished Richmond's 1783 *Letter to Colonel Sharman* in a clear rebuke to Paine. The new release preserved the front matter from 1783, which sought to assure readers that reform and republicanism were separate things. "Evil designing men" might seek to conflate "the Friends of Parliamentary Reform" with "Republicans and Levellers, who wish to overturn all government," but such a mistake would be a "calumny." Paine and his arguments were one thing; Richmond and his, quite another. In a blunt rejection of Paine, the society advertised the publication by explicitly communicating that their own reform efforts still followed in the Duke's footsteps.

As Richmond strove to disassociate himself from his former protégé via a pamphlet war, equally angry debates raged in Parliament. The stark example of spiraling violence in France cleaved the parliamentary reform movement into those who thought the franchise must be widened to stave off revolution, and those who thought acting amid revolutionary ferment would be like "repairing our house in the hurricane season." In 1790, a new generation of reformers in the House of Commons, including future prime minister and earl, Charles Grey, chose the first path and revived reform motions in Parliament, hoping to fend off the bloody descent of France. Like Sawbridge in the 1770s and Pitt in the 1780s, he settled into a pattern of annually introducing the same bill, drafted in the mold of Richmond's original proposals, yet far more moderate.

Richmond, however, aligned himself with those who thought it reckless to attempt renovation during a political hurricane. In the House of Lords, he argued that the time was not right to agitate reform. Grey countered with a sharp distinction between British reform and "French principles," insisting that "it was impossible that any set of men, who had not actually lost their senses, should ever propose the French Revolution as a model for imitation." Linking his reform bill to the French Revolution, Grey argued, was not a sincere critique but a pretext—a disingenuous tactic to justify opposition.

Richmond's plea for delay until the storm had passed landed him in another rhetorical battle. He faced charges of hypocrisy—and found himself waging a two-front political war. He had to separate himself from Paine while also deflecting the accusation that he had abandoned his reformist principles. During a May 31, 1792, debate in the Lords over the King's proclamation against seditious writings, which Richmond supported, the Earl of Lauderdale called the Duke a hypocrite, and accused him of using his militia to "awe the people into submission and suppress any attempts at a parliamentary reform." Lauderdale then sarcastically remarked that no general was better suited to such a job than Richmond, with the exception perhaps of Benedict Arnold. He explained that "if apostasy could justify promotion, he [the Duke] was the most fit person for that command." Richmond took extreme exception to this comparison to the American traitor and challenged Lauderdale to a duel. Lauderdale was obliged to retract the insult.

Through it all—the flattery from friends, the cuts from former allies, and the rising tide of panic sweeping the political class—the Duke of Richmond did not disavow the core principles of political reform. On the contrary, standing to speak after Lauderdale in the House of Lords and defending himself against attacks on his loyalty and judgment, Richmond reaffirmed his intellectual kinship with the arguments laid out in *Rights of Man*. He invoked Paine's insistence on the universality of natural rights and also echoed the language of "unalienable rights" in the American Declaration of Independence—a striking move at a time when both documents were understood as totems of republican revolution. He declared himself "an advocate for the rights of man," even "for the unalienable rights of man." He explicitly acknowledged adopting "the principles of Mr. Paine." The problem with Paine was not his core ideas, but that his actions had crossed a line. The Duke now believed, "from one passage in Paine's second book," that Paine was operating as a French spy. In the passage in question, Paine advised the destruction of the British Navy.

Having separated himself from Paine's Frenchified radicalism, Richmond then countered the charge of hypocrisy. His repudiation of Paine was no rejection of reform itself. He continued to think, he said, that reform of the House of Commons was "an indisputably right thing," including all the way to universal suffrage; he also thought "it should be when the people wished for it, and at present he heard no such wish."

Grey and his colleagues had brought their motion without any great extra-parliamentary petitioning movement to back them up. Nothing like the piles of petitions that Richmond and his colleagues had delivered years earlier was now heaped upon the tables at the front of the House of Lords. Reform was, Richmond declared, a measure that ought to be "called for by the people themselves." Strikingly, the Duke made no mention of Paine's attack on him despite clearly having closely read the second volume of *Rights of Man*. Philosophically consistent and temperamentally resolute, Richmond explained his life, as he stood at his bench in the House of Lords, the seat from which he had risen repeatedly for three decades to defend liberty and advance reform—work he had first begun in the now distant era of the Stamp Act crisis.

Charles Grey had been but one year old when the Stamp Act passed. He would scarcely have understood the particulars of the legacy Richmond sought to defend, had he been in the House to hear Richmond's speech. Yet it was to him, not Pitt, that the baton of reform ultimately passed. Pitt would develop the modern Tory Party and put reform utterly aside. Grey followed Richmond, remaining resolute in his convictions and taking seriously the idea that the right time would come. He would reintroduce his motion for decades until, in a surprising turn of events, he became prime minister in 1830 and two years later won passage of the Reform Act, the greatest change in England's political institutions since the Protectorate of Cromwell in the seventeenth century. This act broadened suffrage and equalized the allocation of constituents across districts, finally accomplishing at least one of the Duke's reforms proposed generations earlier. It did not achieve universal suffrage, but did set Britain on its path toward it.

Through his speech in the House of Lords, Richmond planted seeds that would keep reform alive in the political wilderness. He was however not done steering the small bark of election reform through yet another storm. He went out of his way to finish Paine off.

RICHMOND RIGHTLY OBSERVED THAT in the last decade of the eighteenth century the people were by and large not calling for reform, despite the growing vitality of workingmen's associations. A petition movement was in fact underway but against reform—or at least against Paine. Probably boosted by government operatives, people raised their voices to thank the King for his proclamation against sedition. At Staines, Leeds, Camberwell, Bristol, Chelmsford, and hundreds of other towns and villages—scholars estimate more than five hundred—town meetings and county associations came together to vote to condemn Paine and to burn him in effigy, along with his banned books when available.

Crowds gathered in town squares and village centers to fire guns and ring church bells and cheer as a straw effigy of Paine dressed in old clothes and tarred to burn well, with his book beside him, went up in flames. Often the effigy wore the liberty cap known from the Pro Patria paper Richmond had used during his Junius days. Sometimes signs were pinned to the effigy, like the one in County Durham that read: "Tom Paine, a sower of sedition, and libeller of our happy and envied constitution—Britons beware of his democratic principles, and avoid his merited fate."

The Sussex sheriff called one such meeting for July 4, 1792, in Lewes. The meeting surely had Richmond's support; it may even have originated with him. It was to be held in the Assembly Room of the Town Hall, across the street from the White Hart, where Paine had spent so many happy evenings in the jocular company of Lewes's political and intellectual vanguard. July 4th that year fell on a Wednesday, an unusual day for a county meeting, which more often took place on Saturdays. Perhaps the date was intentionally chosen. It certainly makes a dark irony that the American founding holiday, one that Paine often celebrated with a special dinner party even in London, should be the occasion of his cruel rejection by his neighbors.

Paine chose not to attend and, in advance of the meeting, wrote an impassioned letter to his former fellow townsmen, to be read aloud (and later published). In it, he implored them to stand with him. He tenderly reminded them that eighteen years earlier, as a resident of Lewes and "officer of the revenue" for more than six years, he had seen their "numerous and various distresses" from the government's taxes but had never been found by anyone to have treated them with severity. Then, casting tenderness aside, he twisted a knife in Richmond's back, claiming that his book was alarming only to those who were "insensible of the burthen of taxes which the general mass of the people sustain" while "living in luxury and indolence" thanks to sinecures, pensions, and family connections. Attendees would certainly have understood the thrust at Richmond and his coal duty.

Paine closed by justifying his now more extreme radicalism in economic terms, straining to recruit his former neighbors to his cause. For too long, he had found his heart shocked by things he knew they too had seen: "ragged and hungry children," "persons of seventy and eighty years of age begging for bread," "the dying poor being dragged from place to place to breathe their last," a subject he had written a column about for *The Sussex Advertiser* years earlier.

The Poor Laws were simply, he expounded, "instruments of civil torture." The time had come to dispense with them and to provide social support—equivalent to modern welfare—so that widows might easily have a subsistence income for themselves and their children and so that petty crime, "the offspring of poverty and distress," might be reduced. He knew his audience would largely consist of voters and thus men of property. He urged them to cease speaking and feeling for themselves alone. Only with a moral reorientation—to embrace the cause of economic justice—could they expect the riots and tumults that shot their lives through with fear to come to an end. Well before Marx, Paine had transformed the cause of political liberty into the work of economic emancipation. His emotional plea was intended to move hearts and change minds.

Richmond came from Goodwood to preside at the meeting in Lewes as lord lieutenant. He stood at the end of the long, rectangular wood-paneled civic hall on a raised platform to address the dozens of neighbors Paine had known so well, with daylight streaming in from the sash-windows on the sides of the high barrel-vaulted ceiling. He knew they felt great affection for Paine and, indeed, years later, Lewes residents continued to record fond memories of Paine in their diaries. When Paine's letter was announced, instead of being read out, it was, the local paper reported, thrown unopened on the table and then "torn to pieces with distinguished marks of contempt"—in all likelihood a reference to Richmond having himself torn up the letter. As the letter was torn, some in the crowd—Paine's friends—hissed and called for it to be read, but they were overwhelmed by the shouts and groans of the majority.

With Paine's eloquent letter neutralized, Richmond moved that the people of Lewes send an address of thanks to the King to express their gratitude for new laws against sedition. He already knew that he had the majority with him, and his motion carried. Paine's defeat was an exercise of raw power by an establishment duke, the dominant patron of the county, who had been cultivating support for the King in Lewes at least since the regency crisis. Here the radical Junius partnership ended for good.

IN AN ACT OF stupendous courage and defiance, Paine stood his ground against the tremendous rage unleashed against him all over Britain in the summer of 1792. He continued to make speeches until early fall, yet fending off the rising fright would ultimately be beyond his power. As the violence in Paris grew, British fears intensified. In the first week of September, 1792, Parisian mobs slaughtered more than a thousand prisoners—clergy, nobles, and common criminals—in a wave of terror-driven vigilante justice as foreign armies approached Paris. Reports of the massacre began to reach London on September 6 or 7 through personal correspondence and then hit the newspapers in the following days, with increasingly graphic descriptions.

On September 12, Paine was back in London to deliver an impassioned address at a dinner of the Society of the Friends of the Liberty of the Press. The following night found him at yet another dinner, this time in the company of the poet William Blake. More perceptive than others in Paine's circle about the danger the revolutionary faced, Blake strenuously advised him to flee, saying, "You must not go home, or you are a dead man." For once, Paine took someone's advice. He departed the dinner for Dover, leaving his belongings behind, and found the first boat available to cross the Channel. An order for his arrest reached Dover just twenty minutes after he sailed.

On December 18, 1792, Paine was tried in absentia for seditious libel in London's Guildhall. The defense attorney was Thomas Erskine. This time Erskine's eloquence could not overcome the outcry. Paine was condemned to perpetual outlawry. He would never return to his native land.

Hounded out of Britain, the unrepentant Paine landed in his second adopted land just as it was sliding rapidly toward the mass executions of the Terror. With no apparent hesitation, he embraced the hero's welcome the revolutionaries gave him and accepted election into the French Assembly and French citizenship, alongside (in absentia) Joseph Priestley, Jeremy Bentham, William Wilberforce, George Washington, Alexander Hamilton, and James Madison. As an assemblyman, he was asked to serve on a committee with eight other people to write a new constitution, despite his poor French.

At first, he was glad to do so but, in the end, a year later, he and three other members of the committee were arrested and condemned to the guillotine. In Paine's late-in-life telling, when the guards were marking the doors of the cells of prisoners to be executed the next morning, his door was propped open and marked on its inner side. In the morning, when the executioners came to collect the assigned prisoners, Paine's closed door looked unmarked, and he was passed over, by the grace of God, like the Israelites in Egypt, or, as he would have said, by sheer chance.

Small wonder that stories of revolution from France filled the British political class with cold dread. Paine remained in prison for nearly a year. There he would write *The Age of Reason* before being rescued by the

American diplomat and future president James Monroe in 1794. When he returned to America in 1802, it would be for good.

The Age of Revolution—from which our own modern era was made—strained the human soul to extremes. The noble Enlightenment visions of what should be possible for humanity roused hopes that found no easy passage into reality. When radicals finally gained power, the challenge of turning ideals into lasting human prosperity proved far more difficult—requiring not years, but generations. It was an age of reason largely in prospect.

Liberty is easy to love and hard to realize; its mundane reality in institutions and careful control of power through steady constitutionalism do not fire the imagination as do shouts and cheers on the ramparts. Zeal was needed to inspire people to shake off old orders. Paine was right in this. But zeal needs its partner, moderation. Zeal can capsize the ship, while moderation steers it on a grueling journey through perpetually stormy seas until it at last reaches the long-sought port. Richmond understood as much; Paine never did.

Chapter
16

WITNESS FOR THE DEFENSE

1792–1806

Unattainable as perfect Happiness in this world is, the Constant Pursuit of it seems to be the natural occupation of Man and Expectation the Sum of Happiness intended for Him here.

—DUKE OF RICHMOND, "THOUGHTS ON REPRESENTATION," JULY 25, 1804

THE FRENCH REVOLUTION, AND THEN WAR WITH FRANCE remained the constant background for the rest of Richmond's life. The Duke slipped into his twilight years after the 1792 summer of battle with Paine. He was nearing his sixties. His long public service would soon come to an end, and his circle of associates shrink to his immediate family. Even in these years, though, he would make one last, great contribution to the cause that inspired his warmest affection: parliamentary reform. He would testify in the greatest sedition trials of the decade. He would rescue the legacy of his radical friends while putting rather little energy into his own.

That Richmond's contributions have gone unknown for so long reflects his own harsh judgment on himself. He had failed to win universal suffrage. He had no principal victory to report. His ambition had led him, as he would tell his heir, just to vexation. He destroyed many of his papers. For too long, historians have taken him at his word.

Yet as we shall see, he remained devoted to his cause to the very end of his life, always moving it forward whether in action or thought. His forty-five years of sheer, unrewarded persistence make him the father of universal suffrage.

THE TERROR OF THE increasingly destructive violence in France struck Richmond personally. Shortly after the September massacres and Paine's headlong flight from London, Richmond received a message at Goodwood that came from the coast and reported that a woman was wandering on the beach in a confused state asking for him. He sped to the shore and found the duchesse de Biron, cousin of Madame de Cambis. After her initial flight with Madame de Cambis, she had returned to Paris. Now the duchesse had fled the anti-aristocratic insurgents for a second time, this time on her own, with no servants. She had talked her way onto a boat traveling to Portsmouth. Richmond rushed a message to Madame de Cambis to come to her cousin's aid. They then settled the duchesse in a home in the southwest of London, with her aunt, seemingly just in time.

British politicians constantly feared that France would export its revolution. In November 1792, the French National Assembly proactively began attempting just that. On November 19, the convention proclaimed universal revolution in all lands. Before two weeks were out, in cities such as Sheffield British radicals mounted public processions to celebrate the proclamation, and posters appeared on city walls and in dockyards "demanding the immediate 'free and equal representation of the People in Parliament.'" The battle lines had been drawn; the class conflict that would define the nineteenth century had begun to spread.

The revolutionary urge reached Ireland, thanks in large part to Richmond's nephew Lord Edward "Eddy" Fitzgerald. Eddy followed Paine to Paris and took a room with him, amid a circle of Paine supporters who lapped up his witty, cheerful conversation.

Years earlier Eddy had come to know his uncle's pamphleteer, Thomas Mante, in Dieppe. He had been imbibing republican principles since his teens. Now he gladly adopted the revolutionary principles. He gave up his title, becoming simply Mr. Fitzgerald. In Paris with Paine, he met and married Pamela Seymour, the illegitimate daughter of Louis Philippe II, duc d'Orléans—cousin to King Louis XVI and one of the wealthiest men in France. Like his son-in-law, Louis Philippe also renounced his titles and became Philippe Égalité or "Equality." Sarah Lennox wrote to her friend Susan to share the news and said: "Edward Fitzgerald has acted a romance throughout all his life, & it is finished by his marriage with Pamela Seymour. Adieu." Adieu indeed, to Edward and all his happy world of romantic revolutionaries, for the Terror was about to begin.

King Louis went to the guillotine with bravado in January 1793; Marie-Antoinette mounted the platform pale and stoical that August. When the news of her death reached London, King George III canceled his social calendar and dressed in mourning.

Paine must have been horrified. In the National Assembly, he had argued that the King should be tried, but he had also argued against the imposition of death sentences. On account of Paine's poor French, Eddy was his translator during the arguments. Fitzgerald's father-in-law, Philippe Égalité, was also executed at the guillotine, as was, crushingly, the duchesse de Biron's husband, the duc de Biron, who had been Richmond's friend and Madame de Cambis's lover, and was probably Henriette's father. Tragically and astonishingly, the duchesse de Biron, despite her rescue from the beach, inexplicably returned to France in 1793 after the Terror began. She too died at the guillotine in 1794—the third casualty of the revolution in Richmond's immediate circle. A fourth was imminent.

In 1796, Fitzgerald returned to Ireland to help lead the Society of United Irishmen in fighting British forces. He wanted to invite French forces to assist them, just as the Americans had done. In 1793, his aunt Sarah had anticipated how events in France would tempt the Irish into revolution. Writing to her friend Susan, she prophesied that if the government would just permit reformation of the election system all would go well, but that if it rather persisted in its tricks to sow division, they would inculcate in the Irish "a strong inclination to join the French." Fitzgerald, too, recognized signs of spiraling discontent that would soon "be beyond the power of man to stop." He watched the Irish people lose faith in both the government and the Opposition party and become determined to take the law into their own hands. He saw it as his duty to answer their call.

Before long, he was a wanted man, and the British military sent troops to arrest him. When two soldiers caught him by surprise, he stabbed them and they fired, shooting him in the shoulder. Despite entreaties from his family members, the British refused him medical treatment—the very kind of inhumanity that had provoked rebellion in the first place. Eddy died in prison from his untreated wounds, devastating his mother, Emily; widow, Pamela; and three children. Richmond gave Pamela and the children refuge at Goodwood and unsuccessfully implored the government to transfer Fitzgerald's property to his family, despite his status as a traitor.

DURING THESE TERRIBLE, DARK YEARS, Pitt utterly abandoned the cause of reform. He led his government in a hardline direction, issuing proclamations against Paine and sedition. Richmond broke aggressively from Paine but was unwilling to reject reform. Instead, he was consumed by the need to protect his ideas from association with the French Revolution, to maintain the tie he had developed between universal suffrage and constitutional monarchy, and to fend off the charges of hypocrisy.

This focus also meant separation from Pitt, who had developed significant frustration with a cabinet full of members not fully aligned to him. Pitt was especially frustrated with his lord chancellor, Edward Thurlow, who also held the role of Speaker in the House of Lords. Pitt initiated the process of easing Thurlow out of the cabinet by removing him from the speakership. Richmond expected that it might fall to him to serve as interim Speaker, presiding over the House of Lords. By 1790, he had served for two decades as a leading speaker for the Whigs, after all. Yet Pitt promoted someone else over him. Richmond felt deeply betrayed. His fury made him feel justified in more absenteeism from Parliament and cabinet meetings. Goodwood appealed more and more.

Then personal tragedy made Goodwood Richmond's only true home. In December 1791, a fire broke out in Richmond House from the grate in Henriette's room while the Duke was breakfasting. The fire raged all day and destroyed the mansion. Fire brigades on barges fought the blaze from the river. Cabinets were thrown out of the windows to save books and papers. A worker was paid what amounted to a year's salary to rescue the Duke's favorite spaniel. Because the house was uninsured, Richmond was unable to rebuild it. (Now it is the site of government buildings.) Though he rented a house in London, it was not the same.

Richmond's absences from Parliament and cabinet meetings meant that people began to reorganize authority at the ordnance and in the cabinet and cut him out from decision-making. He made no effort to reverse this. His chronic bowel and liver illnesses and gout were also disabling. He spent much of the summer of 1793 at Goodwood nursing his ailments.

Richmond's attenuated attention to his official duties became consequential in the early winter of 1793 when France declared war on Britain. While Britain feared that France was exporting revolution, France feared Britain was supporting counterrevolution. In February 1793 the Duke of York, King George's second son, was given command of British forces on the Continent. Richmond's job as master-general of the ordnance required supplying the army with the weaponry—innovations and all—that it needed for victory. The first objective was to besiege Dunkirk, which was vulnerable to assault precisely because Richmond, a man of unusual foresight, had achieved the destruction of its jetties in 1765 when he had been ambassador to France.

Although the vulnerability of Dunkirk had been Richmond's first strategic goal as a statesman, he now left the job unfinished. Rather than seeing the logistics work through to the end, he left for summer camp with his militia on July 19 and handed over administration of the ordnance to the sixty-three-year-old Lieutenant General William Howe, the former commander in chief of the British forces in North America, and to the fifty-one-year-old foreign secretary, Alexander Dundas.

Before leaving Richmond had planned for two ships of gunners to be sent out to Dunkirk, but mistakes were made. The gunners were loaded on one ship, and the guns on the other, which never left England. The Duke of York had to abandon his siege for lack of artillery. He fired off a furious denunciation of "ministers [who] have sacrificed their duty to the holiday mummery of camps or to the amusements of Partridge shooting." It was the single worst mistake of Richmond's career. Rather than taking responsibility for it, he fired off rounds of defensive, blame-shifting letters, further alienating his colleagues.

This error—and the surrounding disputes—hastened his transfer of responsibilities. The ramp up to war would be taxing. The ordnance was suddenly turning into a more than full-time job, and Richmond wasn't physically up to it anymore. He had a bout of illness in 1794 that made his sisters fear for his life, and the family doctor advised that only giving up work would save him. This transfer improved Richmond's health and spirits. Now aged fifty-nine, he was at long last putting down the burdens of a frenetic life.

Retirement wasn't official yet. He was still notionally master-general of the ordnance, but he was using the privileges of aristocracy and seniority to convert the job into a sinecure, precisely the kind of soft corruption he had railed against for years.

He was glad, though, for the extra time with family. Much like the period after the conclusion of the Junius letters, when he enthusiastically turned his attention to the extended Lennox clan and restored Goodwood to the center of the family's life, his sister Sarah now found him grown good-humored again. The decade of their estrangement after her marriage to Napier dissolved in newfound warmth. Sarah thought age itself explained why "family affection" had recovered "her power in his heart."

Goodwood had plenty to occupy him. Richmond resumed improving his estates. He moved the hunting dogs kenneled at nearby Charlton to Goodwood and renamed his annual hunt The Duke of Richmond's Hounds. He rebuilt the small theater in Chichester that he had originally constructed in 1765. He installed his heir, Charles Lennox, as a member of Parliament for Chichester for the Tory Party, creating a transfer of the ducal line from Whig to Tory for the foreseeable future. He moved the new horse artillery he had created at the ordnance to Goodwood, stabling them in his own stables and training them himself—fully erasing the line between private and public as was the distinct privilege of the aristocracy. In his mind, his life had always merged fully with his country's life; such was the burden and honor of a duke.

THE WORK OF PARLIAMENTARY reform, though, would always draw him back to London. He had described himself accurately when he long ago had said to Newcastle that the warmest affection of his life—namely, liberty—would always make him show himself. Even well into semi-retirement, this held.

Charles Grey's moderate petition for reform had failed in 1792 because that year the people were petitioning instead in support of the King's proclamation against sedition. Yet just as quickly as Paine had gone from famous native son to outlaw, the political dynamic reversed course. John Horne Tooke took over leadership of the Society for Constitutional Information. He gave wholehearted support to Thomas Hardy, a Scottish shoemaker who, learning from the publications of Wyvill and Richmond, founded the London Corresponding Society in 1792 to fold the lower-middle and working-class populace into the organizing effort. The Corresponding Society charged only a shilling to join, and one penny a week after that, instead of the guinea of the Society for Constitutional Information. This effort renewed energy and momentum around universal manhood suffrage and annual parliaments. By June 1792, even as Paine's effigy was burning around the country, a thousand people had enrolled.

Similarly, the Whig Party, now consolidated under Fox, founded the Association of the Friends of the People. Ever the populist, Fox sought to inspire "a public clamour for fundamental constitutional reform" in the growing industrial towns where tradespeople and shopkeepers were joining the movement. Philip Francis, now back from India and elevated as *Sir* Philip Francis, joined and recovered his older commitments to full-throated reformist Whiggism. As radical forces grew stronger, against the backdrop of violence in France, moderates fell away from the movement.

Seeing revolutionary plots everywhere, the government now took an even harder line. When the Society for Constitutional Information raised relief funds for Parisians, the government interpreted this as a sign of their involvement in revolutionary planning. In December 1792—the same month as Paine's trial in absentia, Lord William Grenville, son of former Prime Minister George Grenville, introduced an immigration law in the House of Commons, to require foreigners entering Britain to have a passport and to register upon arrival. The goal of the Alien Act, a precursor to the American Alien and Sedition Acts of 1798, was to block infiltration by French radicals. Burke thundered on behalf of the bill, famously whipping a dagger out from his coat and throwing it to the floor, as he alleged that radicals at Birmingham had placed an order for three thousand blades.

The receiver of public offices, John Reeves, was granted new police powers to suppress radical activity. To counter the Society for Constitutional Information, the Corresponding Societies, and Fox's Association of the Friends of the People, he built the Association for the Preservation of Liberty and Property against Republicans and Levellers. Within two weeks, he successfully stood up local chapters in every region of the country. Despite the hard work and agitation of the radicals and incredible sales of Paine's books, Richmond had correctly anticipated that more of the English public opposed the revolution and radical ideas than were for it.

Reeves's effort ratcheted up and turned into an aggressive campaign of prosecutions against printers and publishers. Matters came to a head in the summer of 1793 when the Scottish associations took the lead and decided to summon "a great Body of the People" for a national convention to make the case to Parliament for reform. The government understandably interpreted the call to convention as akin to what had transpired four years earlier in France, an effort to establish an alternative legislative assembly. They moved to prosecute participants not just for sedition but for high treason.

The two most important men to be put on trial were Thomas Hardy, the Scots shoemaker, and John Horne Tooke, Richmond's lifelong intellectual and political connection. A conviction on the charge of high treason would earn each defendant a sentence of death by hanging supplemented by drawing and quartering. Both Richmond and Pitt were called as witnesses for the defense.

HARDY'S TRIAL WAS IN October; Horne Tooke's in November. Because of their public significance and the expectation of a large audience, they were heard in the gothic fifteenth-century Great Hall of London's Guildhall, the administrative center of the City of London, instead of the Old Bailey, the usual site for criminal proceedings. Each man was to be represented by Thomas Erskine. Hardy's trial ran for eight days, with a break on Sunday. Horne Tooke's trial ran straight through in six from a Monday to a Saturday. The trials unfolded against the backdrop of shocking government allegations that the London Corresponding Society had been plotting to assassinate the King with a poisoned dart.

London in 1794 was reeling from a steady stream of grim reports from Paris—executions of royalists, revolutionaries, and priests alike filled newspapers and refugee accounts. The large émigré community, many of them aristocrats and clergy who had fled the Terror, kept public anxiety high with harrowing stories of radical violence. After several relatively calm years, the combined pressure of a costly new war with France and poor harvests in 1793 and 1794 also triggered renewed bread riots across southern and eastern England—including in London, East Anglia, and major naval ports. Conditions looked ripe for revolution. Hardy and Horne Tooke looked like they just might be real revolutionaries.

Erskine's entire legal and political career was marked by a willingness to take on high-risk, high-profile, and often unpopular causes—especially in defense of liberty and against overreach by the Crown. He had lost his role as attorney general to the Prince of Wales because of his defense of Paine. He seemed to thrive under the pressure. With supreme self-confidence, he formulated a beautifully simple defense for Hardy and Horne Tooke.

Each man had advanced policies proposed a decade earlier by the Duke of Richmond, currently a member of the King's cabinet. Those very same policies had at the time been endorsed by William Pitt, currently prime minister. How could anyone be charged with high treason for following in the footsteps of Britain's leading statesmen?

Some radicals considered the defense insulting to their own energies and efforts. The abolitionist William Fox, for instance, wrote in a 1794 political tract: "The progress of Jacobinism is amply secure, without the aid of the Duke of Richmond or Thomas Paine, inciting the body of the people to assume government." There was no need for "Citizens Richmond and Paine [to] ransack all the Ginshops to form a National Convention." The defense might have downplayed the creative energies and contributions of a new generation of radicals, but as a legal strategy it was sound.

When called to testify, Richmond and Pitt appeared in civilian dress—waistcoat and dark coat, knee breeches and buckled shoes—before a bewigged judge robed in black with purple trim. Erskine would have worn the short, white, tightly curled, and well-powdered horsehair wig of a barrister. During court days that ran from 9 a.m. to 9 p.m. with few breaks, the razor-sharp Erskine laid out a case honed already from his earlier trials of publishers for sedition. The logic was clean: "It was the abuses pointed out by [Paine] that led the Right Hon. Gentleman [Pitt] to associate with many others of high rank, under the banners of the Duke of Richmond, whose name stands at the head of the list, and to pass various public resolutions, concerning the absolute necessity of purifying the House of Commons." The Society for Constitutional Information had "adhered strictly to" the Duke of Richmond's plan and "adopted as much of Paine's works as was consistent with that plan." The entire case turned on the content of the Duke's writings and parliamentary motions. His *Letter to Colonel Sharman* was read aloud in full.

Richmond's fulsome but careful parliamentary testimony two years earlier about his relationship to Paine had tracked precisely the line of argument Erskine now used. Arguing at that time against Lauderdale, Richmond had both distanced himself from Paine and, within limits, acknowledged his debt to his former protégé. Erskine made exactly the same delicate moves now—acknowledging some debt to Paine while also repudiating him. The close parallels suggest possible coordination but, whatever the case, Richmond had clearly made defense of the radicals one of his projects. Now the moment had arrived for his starring role.

In Horne Tooke's case, Richmond was called to the stand and examined by the defendant himself. Horne Tooke had been arrested six months earlier and held in Newgate Prison since then. In Parliament Richmond had already offered the complete arguments being used to defend the radicals, so now he could be brief.

Horne Tooke asked him whether, on the occasion when he had paid Richmond a call to discuss some young men, Richmond had asked him to share his opinion of Mr. Pitt's plan of reform. Richmond answered that he could not recall. Horne Tooke probed for more details of that conversation about Pitt's bill. Richmond again could not recall. Horne Tooke asked Richmond if he did recall attending a "Convention of the People," consisting of 1,200 men from different counties at a London tavern. Richmond had some recollection of a meeting but could not confirm that it corresponded to the meeting under discussion. Horne Tooke then asked if Richmond could remember Horne Tooke having ever taken a position of his own in a meeting and brought the whole meeting over to his own opinion. Richmond confirmed that, while he had often heard Horne Tooke argue with great ability, he could not recall any instance when he had seen him stake out a new position and then bring everyone else over to it. Lastly, Horne Tooke asked Richmond if he had ever heard him say anything against the King or the House of Lords. Richmond answered, "Never."

The jury deliberated for eight minutes and returned their verdict: Not guilty. The surge of relief must have been immense for Horne Tooke. It would also have been felt by every radical, the light of freedom for their efforts restored. The earlier Hardy trial had been more complicated. In his case, the jury deliberated for three hours, but they too delivered a verdict of not guilty. Hardy's acquittal was met by jubilation from the radicals.

The acquittals and public rejoicing broke the fever of the government's efforts at suppression. Here in these trials, Richmond had accomplished what was arguably one of his greatest feats of public service. He had secured the acquittals on the basis that Horne Tooke and Hardy had never spoken against the King and could not therefore be guilty of treason. It was a brilliantly deft conjoining of popular sovereignty, personified by Horne Tooke and Hardy, to the monarchy—and a redefinition of radicalism in support of constitutional monarchy.

The value of Richmond's obstinacy and consistency shone brightly forth in the moment of these trials. With his steadfast support for the monarchy, his equally unyielding support for the rights of man, and his firm refusal to engage with the reform movement while it was under the spell of the French Revolution, Richmond helped save the monarchy in England from the revolutionary pressures of the age, and the reform movement from the fever of revolution. His precise, respectful testimony for Hardy and Horne Tooke made their radicalism respectable enough. He saved their lives and laid the foundation for the modernization of constitutional monarchy through the reforms of the nineteenth century. When he had joined Pitt's ministry—and stabilized the government—he had made his greatest gift to the King and the first of his two great gifts to Britain. With this testimony, which saved radicalism, he made his greatest gift to the radicals, and his second great gift to Britain.

FOR THE GOVERNMENT THE Hardy and Horne Tooke trials were embarrassing. Subsequent trials grew shorter, each acquittal coming more rapidly, until the government simply decided to dismiss the remaining cases.

The trials seem to have revived Richmond's appetite for politics. In December, a few weeks after he testified, Richmond wrote Pitt proposing to resume cabinet attendance. He heard nothing in reply for a full month. Then in January 1795 Pitt wrote curtly and coldly: "I see that your resuming a seat in the Cabinet must prove equally unpleasant and embarrassing to public business." On this basis, Pitt dismissed him. To advise on military planning for cabinet discussions, Pitt would now draw not on Richmond but on General Cornwallis, who had lost an army at Yorktown and was now recently returned to England from a period of distinguished service in India.

Richmond's defense of the radicals meant he had little common ground left with Pitt, who was increasingly an establishment Tory. The slender, severe prime minister had his eye always on business. He wanted a cabinet that would in no way distract from his project of reforming and improving the economy. Richmond's dismissal communicated Pitt's desire that the Duke also leave the ordnance. He did so, painfully, in July 1795, after eleven years of service.

The King gave Richmond a warm exit interview and consolation prizes: He was appointed colonel of the Horse Guards Blues, the role that had been promised him three decades earlier and that had been the pretextual issue that the two men—King and duke—had used to negotiate their relationship—their total rupture and then their reconciliation. A year later Richmond was also appointed field marshal, and he kept a military title at the ordnance, equivalent to emeritus status.

While Richmond had clearly been easing himself out for some time, he was shocked by the harsh way the end came, despite the grants from the King. Later he wrote about the moment to his heir, complaining that Pitt had forgotten all that he owed to Richmond and had ignored the warmth of Richmond's faithful friendship. Pitt had turned him out of office "in the most shuffling manner," by which Richmond meant dishonest, evasive, and underhanded. Richmond developed a biting anger at Pitt that would last for the rest of his life.

The grand political moments of Richmond's life ended in 1794. In his final twelve years, broader events regularly aroused his political appetite, but he no longer had a meaningful part to play. Edmund Burke also left politics in 1794. He retired from the House of Commons that year, after the devastating death of his only son, Richard Burke. When they retired, Richmond was fifty-nine; Burke, sixty-five. In their youth in the 1760s, they had been New Whigs to Newcastle's Old Whigs. Now they were the last remaining links to the men who had shaped British politics under George II, and their time of service had come to an end. Those left had known politics only under George III. A new era had fully arrived.

FOR RICHMOND, PITT'S COLD dismissal of him was a painful humiliation. He wrote to the Duchess who was at Goodwood, in ill-health herself, for solace. She could not come to London, so he asked that she send Henriette up to London to keep him company. "I do want some of my females just now," he wrote.

In his early years, Richmond had taken affirmation from the men around him—the Duke of Newcastle, General James Wolfe, Edmund Burke—who had all called him a "considerable" man, meaning worthy of esteem. The opinion of these mentors mattered to Richmond and also those of his small circle of particular friends. Now that circle had shrunk. Paine was gone from it, and Francis. The only ones left were Adair and Ogilvie.

Richmond had always counted on the many women in his life to carry him through times of tribulation—his wife, the Duchess, especially; and his four sisters. Madame de Cambis had buoyed him for a season but that closeness appears to have ended with the American Revolution. Sarah recognized that Richmond was generally a man of low ego. His willingness to join the ministry of a man half his age, as William Pitt was when he came into office, was proof of that. Sarah also rightly observed that attention of his "females," as he called them, could puff him up.

Mary especially adored him, and Richmond's sister Sarah sometimes worried that this caused him to cultivate an "inward consciousness" of his own worth as being greater than that of other men. Richmond had an intellectual bond with all his well-read, learned sisters, as well as with Madame de Cambis and Henriette, but what Mary gave him was the sense that he could do no wrong. In the final years of her life, she wrote him hundreds of pages of scarcely legible letters scrawled in haste throughout the course of her day. The set runs from November 1792, after Paine left Britain, to February 1795, when Richmond was dismissed from the cabinet and returned to Goodwood for good. She was constant in her attention, giving him, simply, presence. Walpole, who had known her since she was five years old, understood what she gave—a friendship and confidence "more steady" than was to be found with anyone else. For the last year and a half of her life, from February 1795 until her death, Richmond returned that gift. He was constantly at her side. Henriette too would join them, playing music after supper to relieve the Duchess. By November 1796 she was gone.

Mary's passing left Richmond lonely. He remedied this through affairs—one with the Lady Elizabeth Foster, who had previously been notoriously involved in a long-standing ménage à trois with the Duke and Duchess of Devonshire. The relationship worried the family, not only because of Lady Elizabeth's bold sexuality but also for fear that he would marry her and displace Charles Lennox as his heir. They may have helped bring an end to that relationship. His other late-life affair was with one of his housekeepers, Mrs. Bennett, by whom he fathered three daughters, bringing the total of his natural children to four, all girls. He provided handsomely for his lover and their daughters both in life and in his wills, and they, like Henriette, were folded into the extended family.

IN HIS FINAL YEARS, Richmond's most important resource was simply his own restless mind. Still immersed in the twin passions of his life, military strategy and political philosophy, he resumed anonymous pamphleteering, producing a published essay entitled *Thoughts on the National Defence* in 1804, and an unpublished essay on representation, also from 1804, on whether voters can bind their representatives with instructions to vote in specific ways. He also tackled the headache of his own domestic economy.

Thoughts on the National Defence laid out Richmond's vision for a national militia system, with citizens who are properly trained and organized, the first line of Britain's defense. He still distrusted standing armies. The pamphlet brought him back in touch with his friend Major John Cartwright, now sixty-five and still a perpetual motion machine of reform energy.

In 1806, Cartwright also published a book on national defense, his under the title *England's Aegis, or the Military Energies of the Constitution.* In that book, Cartwright wrote, "I cannot close this work without expressing my sentiments on a pamphlet entitled *Thoughts on the National Defence,* which, not only from strong internal evidence, but from the information of the bookseller, I understand to come from the pen of the Duke of Richmond." He went on to express his appreciation for the book's author as "one in whom the knowledge of a soldier is united with that of a constitutional statesman." Forging such a unity was always Richmond's goal, and it must have pleased him to read those words.

Despite the long hiatus in their friendship, Richmond quickly read Cartwright's book and sent a brief note of thanks on March 23, 1806, affirming that he found himself still approving of Cartwright's general principles as well as of his criticism of "the base corruption and servility of the age." Above all, though, he expressed gratitude that Cartwright had praised his "attachment to the constitution," as being manifest on every page of *Thoughts on the National Defence.* Richmond had been recognized as he wished by someone who had known him well over many years—a small oasis of happiness in a landscape of bleak disappointment.

Less happy was his work on the finances of his estate. He had amassed significant debts over the years through his building projects. Now he spent his time making endless calculations and working assiduously, if futilely, to form plans to pay them off. He took at least one step to relieve himself of a thorn. In 1799, he had finally sold the family's coal duty back to the Crown for an annuity of nineteen thousand pounds, freeing himself of the painful charge of rent-seeking that Paine had cast against him.

His worries about the finances of the extended family, though, led him wrong in one very important particular. In 1806, his nephew, Charles James Fox, spent seven months in the cabinet as foreign secretary. The window was brief and closed with his death, but during it, Fox achieved what had been the project of a lifetime: abolition of the slave trade within the British Empire. When the Foreign Slave Trade Bill came up for a vote, Richmond, the lifelong defender of natural rights and early friend and patron of William Wilberforce, gave his proxy to vote against it.

While he did not attend the parliamentary debate, he asked his great-nephew, Lord Holland, who was Fox's own nephew, to carry his proxy. Lord Holland's wife held a plantation in Jamaica. Richmond had disrupted the finances of his heir by giving up the coal tax; he didn't wish to damage Lady Holland's economic position also. He wrote to Lord Holland that, although slavery was an "inhuman practice" and immoral, "it is impossible for us to reform the world and one must take it as it is." This was his lowest act. The world's blows had finally drained Richmond's idealism.

By the time Richmond sent that proxy, he had outlived, or was on the cusp of outliving, the towering statesmen of his generation—comrades and rivals alike, men who had steered empires, toppled ministries, and shaped the turbulent decades of revolution and reform. The men he had known were all gone: Rockingham (1783), Conway (1795), Burke (1797), Shelburne (1805), and Chatham (1778). His nephew Edward Fitzgerald (1798) was also already gone as was his brother George (1805). He would also see the deaths of Charles James Fox (September 1806), and even the ever-young William Pitt the Younger, who died in January 1806, at forty-six. George III had only seven years left of his very long reign. The Prince of Wales would become prince regent in 1811, when his father grew too ill to continue. And Thomas Paine would die in 1809. In his final years, Richmond was well placed to reflect on what their shared striving during the Age of Revolution had ultimately achieved—what hopes had endured, what ambitions had faltered, what price had been paid, what might lie still ahead.

Richmond launched his 1804 essay on representation with a meditation on happiness that reflects years of living with the language of the Declaration of Independence and Enlightenment and utilitarian political philosophy. He despaired of the possibility of ever achieving intellectual satisfaction, writing that "whoever duly considers the State of Man in this World must be convinced that it is not one of Happiness, such as can content His Mind."

Neither, though, can those who labor with their hands find perfect happiness. Regardless of whether one labored with head or hand, "all is Contention and Strife attended with more or less painfull Circumstances, but always with considerable disappointments." A misplaced hope that politics might bring happiness will instead leave people frustrated.

Richmond found it necessary to affirm the thirty-year-old philosophy of the American Declaration of Independence as fundamentally wise. He wrote: "Indeed unattainable as perfect Happiness in this world is, the Constant Pursuit of it seems to be the natural occupation of Man and Expectation the Sum of Happiness intended for Him here." The new forms of politics that were being built in the Age of Revolution to protect liberty can bring no perpetual peace, no perfect happiness, only protection for people's constant striving in directions they choose for themselves. This is a bleak but true view. Richmond's dedication to Enlightenment ideals over a full life yielded this clear-eyed realism.

RICHMOND MADE NO EFFORT to record his legacy. Instead, in his final years, he prepared the destruction of his papers, giving specific instructions to Henriette. To his heir, Charles Lennox, the 4th Duke, son of his brother George, he left no charge to carry on the mission of reform but only the lessons of his life's conflicts distilled to their most concentrated form—stoical lessons about self-discipline and taking one's reward from one's family. His valedictory advice to Charles Lennox in a letter of June 5, 1806, included lessons that paint a picture of happiness achieved through freedom and self-government in private life. These lessons were as follows:

- Ambition only leads to vexation;
- Be prudent, rationally economical and above all things regular with your routine, or
- Be what it may, you will be ruined and you know not why or how;
- A domestick Life is both the happiest and the most creditable you can pursue;
- Don't have your House always full of companions inclined to encourage you to drink and which will only promote dissipation and idleness, but a few rational friends;
- Your main resource will be always in yourself, your family and your Home concerns.

This end-of-life realism—fermented from a harvest of disappointment and frustration—should not, though, be understood as a repudiation of the work of reform. Richmond would not at the very end of his life have been writing yet another essay on representation if liberty were not still the cause that most captivated him. That dedication to the cause of natural human rights was a gift to posterity—as the gifts of reformers ever are. Richmond could not live to see the fruits of his reform work. Nor could the early African American scholars in the United States who began to document lynchings and other atrocities in the late nineteenth and early twentieth century. Their efforts to secure civil and political liberties for all Americans would not flower into wholesale legal change until the 1960s, long after they were gone. To work for the cause of human rights is always to have faith in posterity.

When William Pitt died in January 1806, he received a state funeral like his father before him and was buried near him in Westminster Abbey. When Charles James Fox died in September 1806, his funeral, though not a formal state funeral, also took place in Westminster Abbey, attended by widespread public attention and high honor.

After Fox's death, Sarah, with whom Richmond was now fully reconciled, came to Goodwood to nurse her brother through the last painful months. His feet and one hand were crippled by gout; his senses and busy, anxious mind were dulled from the opium used to kill his pain. On Sunday, December 29, 1806, after lying for several days "insensible but without pain," he died. He had given instructions that his body be slaked in lime and that his funeral should be conducted in a "private and inexpensive manner." With few people attending, he was laid to rest in the family vault in Chichester Cathedral, whose spire is visible from Goodwood.

RICHMOND'S LEGACY WAS ALMOST buried with him because he wanted it that way. Partly, that must have been to hide the extent of his early radicalism. Partly, the disappearance of his work was the consequence of British cultural habits. In France, philosophical and literary writing might have been a sign of intellectual prestige and public service, but British aristocrats, by contrast, often wrote anonymously, worked through parliamentary speeches, or used proxies, due to different norms of decorum and political caution. Partly his vanishing act reflects harsh self-judgment. He believed he had failed, or at least not succeeded. His ambition had brought him only vexation—even if for the rest of us it laid a foundation on which to build. Richmond hid himself so well that the one scholarly biography written about him summed him up as a "minor politician" of "limited mental abilities."

That is far from the truth. As Burke said, Richmond had an anxious, busy mind. Seeing Richmond's powerful intellect and radical vision required stepping into his library, a privilege that I am the first scholar to have had. Without meaning to, Richmond recorded the full life of his constantly working mind in the margins of the nine thousand books held there. They are not all annotated, but enough of them are to reveal the shape of his intellectual life and an unrivaled political project for reform from the beginning of his career to the end of his life.

For a bibliophile and political philosopher such as myself to find the pathways of a life crisscrossing the pages of the great books of Enlightenment philosophy collapsed time. I too had read many of the books Richmond had read. I had my own musings about them. I could follow his mind because I had wandered in the same groves of the imagination. As I sat in his gorgeous library, reading his notes, I felt we were not 250 years apart but in the same room.

Once I understood that Richmond's mental abilities were very far from limited, I could not cease in my pursuit to understand their development and consequence. With assistance from other scholars wielding new technologies to make author identifications, the pieces fell into place. Richmond was no metaphysician, no moral philosopher. Cartwright recognized him rightly, though. He was one of the most creative and visionary constitutional thinkers of his day. At life's bitter end, the one achievement he was willing to claim, as he did in his note to Cartwright, was his fierce commitment to the constitutional project: to the painstaking task of restraining power through form. The Americans were right to hold him in high regard.

Ultimately, not Richmond's nephew and heir but rather one of his carefully selected rational friends, John Cartwright, the longest-lived of them all, shouldered the burden of communicating Richmond's legacy to the next generation. In 1816, Cartwright wrote to Shelburne's son, the new Marquess of Lansdowne, to encourage him with his own father's example. The Marquess's father, at the time the Earl of Shelburne, had assured Cartwright that he was ready "to march side by side, and to keep pace with the Duke of Richmond." If the young marquess was to live up to his own father's legacy, Cartwright now exhorted him, that meant living up to Richmond's legacy and refusing to shop short of anything other than annual parliaments and universal suffrage. There is always a way to pass the message on. It moves through the souls we touch.

EPILOGUE

THE UNITED KINGDOM HAS NEVER ADOPTED ANNUAL PARliaments, but in 1911 it did reduce their length from seven years to five. Legislation for electoral reform began in 1832. Charles Grey, after first introducing election reform motions in the early 1790s, kept at it every year for decades. He was heir to Richmond's persistence—as are all true reformers.

As the transforming economic forces of the Industrial Revolution wreaked havoc in the lives of Britain's working people, the problems of skewed representation only worsened, and the illegitimacy of a narrow, self-dealing elite grew ever more visible and pronounced. A movement for reform reignited—but the target now was not monarchy but the aristocracy.

When Pitt's Tories collapsed in 1830 and the Whigs had a fresh shot at power, a massive working- and middle-class movement—sending heaps of petitions for reform to Parliament—made Grey prime minister. Richmond had rightly prophesied that the cry of the people would be needed to win reform. This moment of crisis was Grey's to seize, and he did, successfully winning passage of the Reform Act of 1832. His government also won passage of the Slavery Abolition Act of 1833, ending enslavement in the British Empire. They also ended the economic monopoly of the East India Company. Reform, kept constantly alive by little more than stubbornness, was ready to bloom when the moment came. Earl Grey, as he became, is world famous to this day, his name affixed to a popular tea, which is a very strange kind of honor for the man who finally put Britain on its path toward universal suffrage.

The 1832 Reform Act was only the first step. Reform could finally take off only when Richmond's ideas about universal manhood suffrage were supplemented with yet newer ideas of secret ballots and pay for members of Parliament. In the end, there were four Reform Acts with the last, which finally delivered universal male suffrage, coming only in 1918. Women were included in 1928. The Duke of Richmond had been more than a century ahead of his time. From 1770 to 1785, he made universal manhood suffrage and parliamentary reform the orienting project of his political life. When he changed course, he became a stabilizer for the monarchy. His political transformation was crucial to King George's efforts to stave off revolution. Yet his social vision laid the foundation for nineteenth-century reform.

Richmond's writings would provide the basis for the reform movement for decades to come and help weld together monarchy and popular sovereignty. The *Letter to Colonel Sharman* was reprinted twice in 1792. Its last publication was in 1859. As that letter made clear, Richmond sought reform not for the sake of upturning old orders but to balance a constitution under new strains because of the imperial project. Not only this dimension of imperialism but also Richmond's unwavering support for the role of the hereditary House of Lords are now seen as indefensible aspects of the balanced constitution that he defended.

Yet Richmond confronted the challenges of the day and sought to renovate political institutions in the direction of support for the liberty and well-being of ordinary people. He hoped the colonies and motherland would become an association of free peoples united by head and heart. He thought the Lords should function as a second parliamentary chamber with a specific obligation to examine the constitutionality of legislation emanating from the commons (or the Crown)—a reasonable view in a country where there is no Supreme Court.

Nor did he see this right of peers as inalienable. If they misused it, he imagined them losing it. At the time, the peers were the only available second chamber. There wasn't an alternative to the peerage performing this role in 1770; there simply wasn't a similar educated cohort with any experience in government.

While there is no longer a need to place this responsibility in the hands of hereditary aristocrats, and certainly no need to accept slavery as something unreformable, Richmond's constitutional insight was acute. The role that he imagined for the House of Lords needn't be played inevitably by "lords"; but every balanced constitution needs an informed constitutional safeguard.

For Richmond's friends across the Atlantic—we, Americans—the Duke's constitutional insight also affords lessons. Freedom, he insisted, depends on a legislature fully independent from the executive. The Founders agreed with this and first fought a revolution and then drafted the US Constitution to secure government conducted by their own legislature. When, in the 1770s, Richmond and his allies faced their own challenge of a legislature too dependent on the executive, they eschewed revolution but fought a decades'-long campaign against governmental corruption. Now, 250 years later, the British would seem to have bound their executive more tightly, thanks to that campaign, than did the Americans. Parliamentary supremacy endures in Britain; it is unclear whether that can still be said for legislative supremacy in the United States. Yet the Duke's tale, and that of his political heirs, offers hope. Not revolution but the steady, unflagging work of reformers—dedicated to renovating the rights of the people and tethered to the ancient idea of British liberty—sufficed to achieve their distinguished result. They whisper to us fiercely and command us urgently: Do not underestimate the power of reform.

A man of commitment and courage, Richmond's contemporaries did not consider him a savvy politician. This is because he didn't specialize in the inside game, nor make his own political weather by cultivating relationships and alliances.

As a legislative politician, he fell below the greats of his era: William Pitt, Earl of Chatham and William Pitt the Younger, the Marquess of Rockingham, and even the Duke of Grafton. He played the outside game, and the long game. His involvement over several decades in rousing the people—to support Wilkes, to support the excise, to support parliamentary reform—made popular sovereignty real in Britain for the first time in the modern era.

His unusual gift was penetrating vision. Those "superb eyes" noted by Joshua Reynolds are a metaphor for what he had. He could see through the chaos of his age to what his society would ultimately need for durable stability and health: universal suffrage; an end to the dependence of society's leaders on the public purse; economic and penal reform to improve the lives of the working poor; and sturdier national defense. Edmund

Burke formed a party through force of intellect. Thomas Paine fired human hearts across two continents with a passion for human rights. Together William Pitt the Younger, King George III, and the Duke of Richmond forged Britain's modern constitutional monarchy, and none would have made it through without the others.

ACKNOWLEDGMENTS

My debts are many and I doubt that I will be able to discharge them fully. Thanks go first to Emily Sneff who found what we now call the Sussex Declaration and who worked doggedly with me to understand its provenance and significance. Also, I owe great thanks to all those who helped in that process: Wendy Walker and colleagues at the West Sussex Record Office, Fenella France at the Library of Congress, and Christina Duffy and Cordelia Rogerson at the British Library and, of course, my mother, Susan Allen, who always pitches in when archival matters come up. Liam Klein and Annie Walton Doyle provided invaluable research assistance for early stages of the work. Next come those who welcomed and helped me at Goodwood: the 10th Duke and 11th Duke and Duchess of Richmond, Goodwood curators James Peill and Clementine de la Poer Beresford, as well as their colleagues Amanda Sharp and Tony Mountford. Then there are the dedicated scholars of Thomas Paine who are revolutionizing our understanding of his work: Paul Myles, Gary Berton, Gregory Claeys, Jonathan Scheick, Scott Cleary, and Leanne O'Boyle. I am also indebted to experts of the period, Timothy McCann, David Bromwich, and Rosemary Baird. While Lord Andrew Roberts did not directly assist, I could not have written this book without his wonderful biography of George III, *The Last King of America*. Among its other contributions, it alerted me to King George III's paraphrase of Montesquieu's *Spirit of the Laws*, which I downloaded from digital archives and gave as a Christmas present to my father, William Allen, himself a translator of *Spirt of the Laws*. This led to countless conversations about eighteenth-century British, American, and French politics and political philosophy, which profoundly shaped my thinking about Richmond's contributions and provided great joy in this late stage of my father's life. I am also so grateful to the brilliant historians who also happen to be among my dearest friends—Elizabeth Eger, Ruth Scurr, Jane Kamensky, and Paul Cartledge—for conversations about writing and British and American history, as well as to Paul for an unrivalled eye for typos. My agent, Tina Bennett, kept the faith when this project looked impossible. Thank you for all the deft interventions that have brought this book to term. A true case of wise midwifery! My profound thanks go to Bob Weil for sticking with an improbable subject and providing peerless editorial guidance. Clive Priddle was indispensable for wrestling a first draft of some 250,000 words into something others could bear to pick up. I knew I could count on the Norton team—Peter Miller and Luke Swann—and indexer Dave Luljak to get me through any difficult project with grace and good humor and so it has been. Their patience is miraculous. Thank you, team! James Doyle, Nora Doyle, and William Doyle have been living with this project for more than ten years and have been dragged to Sussex more often than they probably have wanted, even beautiful as it is. My greatest thanks are due to them. They had to listen to oral renditions of chapter drafts over countless numbers of Premier Inn breakfasts. And to my kiddos, especially: Thank you, Nora and William, for allowing the Duke's portrait to live alongside your school photos on the fridge with such good humor and for so many years! I really do love you vastly more than the Duke.

APPENDIX A: PLAN FOR ELECTORAL REFORM (1779)

LETTER FROM WALKER KING TO EDMUND BURKE FITZWILLIAM MSS (SHEFFIELD)

STOKE, NOVR 5TH 1779.

Dear Sir,

I have waited some days for an opportunity of sending you by a private hand, an Account of a dish of Politicks, with which the Duke of Richmond treated me one Evening at an Inn, on our Journey from Exeter, instead of a Supper—I imagine his Cookery will not be altogether to your taste; but you and your Friends may expect to be invited to the same entertainment, I think you will not be sorry to know what kind of fare you are likely to have.

It is not necessary to trouble you with an Account of the loose conversation, which led him to read me a sketch of a Plan, which he said he had been thinking of some time, for securing the Liberties of the People, and improving the form of our Government. This Plan he means to bring forward, in some way or other, this Winter. He said, he thought it but fair both to the King and People, to let them know, what those, who were so vehement for the dismission of Ministers, meant to do, if they were put into their places. If making a declaration of this sort should fall in with the Ideas of your Friends, he should then propose the plan he had formed, as a ground for Associations or, if his plan should not be approved of, he would be ready to support, to the utmost of his power, any other, that pursued the same object. But if your Friends should object to the making any publick declaration of their Intentions at all, in that case he meant, in justification of the part he had hitherto taken, and of the conduct he should in future pursue, to publish, as his political testament the Plan he had devised and to retire from Parliament and Politicks entirely.

His Plan, as far as I can recall it to my memory, is as follows—The Election of Members to be annual; and the right of voting to be extended to every Man of 21 years of age and upwards without exception. The Kingdom to be divided into districts containing about 1000 Voters each, which he computes will be the proper quotient for electing one Member, in order to make up the present Number. A variety of regulations follow for the proper management of Elections, Petitions &c &c. By these means he thinks the Independence of Parliament will be secured, and of course an effectual control be established over the conduct of Ministers. A secret Committee for the examination of the expenditure of secret service money [so that the secret service budget couldn't be used for vote buying], and a scheme for a more strict and a more intelligible method of passing the publick accounts, are, I think, the only Regulations he introduces into your House.

Amongst the Lords, the Integrity of the Bench of Bishops is to be secured by establishing a sort of Succession amongst them—I told him he should also make a law, that they should have neither Sons, Brothers, nor Cousins. A similar Regulation is to be adopted in the Courts of Law. The Chancellor is to be confined to his court and the Chief Justices to theirs; but after a certain term of service, they are to succeed to a peerage and a pension—All the Offices at the publick Boards, excepting such as are ministerial, are to be for Life, with the Right of Succession—The putting the Navy, Army, Religion and Revenues under proper regulations he leaves to his independent Parliament. I am afraid my want of memory may have prevented me from doing justice to his Plan, though I am pretty confident I have mentioned every thing that is very material.

In order to let you farther into his views, I am afraid it will be necessary for me to trouble you with the part which I also had in the Conversation—I told him, that I was very much inclined to think with him, that it would be exceedingly useful to hold out some specific propositions to the People, as a ground for Associations, and that this was a proper time to do so. Indeed, it appears to me, that no thing would be so likely to make the People, what one cannot say they have hitherto in the smallest degree been, a part of Opposition: It is a sort of appeal to their Judgement that flatters their vanity, and gives them, together with a strong desire of proselytizing, all the Ardour of self-consequence, and the strength of Connection—

At the same time I observed, that it was a measure, which I conceived might be liable of itself to objection, and in its execution, to numberless difficulties. I imagined, I said, that he meant to strike pretty deeply at the Power of the Crown—

He must be sensible, that the avowal of such an intention, would not only set the whole power of the Court for ever against him, but would also raise great jealousies and fears amongst a numerous set of Men, who either really are, or affect to be, alarmed, at, what they call the levelling and republican principles of Opposition. He said, that could not be helped—that as to the King, he thought it but justice to acquaint him at once with their Intentions; that for his part he could never think of coming into his service upon other ground, and afterwards making use of that power to attack the Prerogative. I answered, that though the King might and no doubt would, positively refuse to employ Ministers who openly professed a design of lessening the Influence of the Crown; yet that even the same King might be induced, by keeping good company, to make, of his own accord, as large concessions as might be wished—That the same kind of reasoning would apply to a Party, who at present might oppose with the utmost violence the appearance of any attempts to innovate in the Constitution. As for the present King, if what some people say be true, that he is as weak as he is bad, I should not be surprised, after he had once tasted popularity, to see him run as violently into that extreme, as he had done into the other.

He afterwards heard me with great patience make a number of objections to his plan of Reformation—I particularly observed to him that I imagined one of the principal advantages to be derived from the associations [county-wide grassroots organizations] would be, in giving a turn to the next general Election: but that he had taken care, by depriving them of their exclusive Rights, to set the whole body of Freeholders and Electors against him.

I lastly took the Liberty of desiring him to explain to me more fully, upon what plan he would have the associations formed, and what he meant to do in case his proposal should not be adopted by his friends. He said, that his plan went no farther, than that after the points to be reformed were agreed on, all the members in the minority of both houses should subscribe to them in a strong form—(This he said he meant at Lord Shelburne) that afterwards associations might be formed by their friends throughout the Country: people be invited to subscribe, and either petitions sent up or things be put in a train for the Election. If this plan should not be accepted of, he should publish it himself with the reasons that might be given him for not adopting it, and leave both in the possession of the Publick. I then asked him if he meant to put himself at the head of a Party, in case the Publick should seem inclined to fall in with his Ideas.

He said, by no means—that he meant to say, that his plan, not having had the fortune to meet with the approbation of those, whose opinions and judgment he valued much higher than his own, he had not a doubt but that it was defective or . . . at the same time, as it contained sentiments, which he believed he should never alter, he should leave it in the possession of the publick, that he should always be ready to come forth, whenever a change of circumstances might bring about a coincidence of opinions between him and his friends; and in the mean time as a man, whose political sentiments did not entirely agree with those of any party he should retire.

I think I have given you the substance of our long conversation. I hope you will excuse the liberty I have taken in introducing so much of my own poor sentiments on the occasion. When we had finished he told me he would get me to look over his plan when it was done; but as I have been ever since at Lord George's, I have heard nothing more of it. I imagine we shall not come to town many days before the meeting of Parliament. The Duke since he came home has had a very violent attack from his old disorder and is but just recovered. I beg you to present my best respects and my most Affectionate Compliments to Mrs B. Mr W. Messr R and Mr Z.

I have the honour to be your most obliged and faithful humble Servant,

Walker King

APPENDIX B: STATEMENT OF POLITICAL PHILOSOPHY (1780)

CONTAINED WITHIN DOCUMENTS FROM GENERAL MEETING FOR THE COUNTY, 1780–1783, ESRO REFERENCE: L/C/X/1/1, EAST SUSSEX RECORD OFFICE.

January 1780

Sirs, You may easily believe that being one of those who joined in requesting you to call a county meeting nothing but illness can prevent my attending it, and it is with infinite regret I submit to the decision of my physicians who pronounce that it is not safe for me to leave London.

I trust that my sentiments on the subject of parliamentary reform are in general sufficiently known, and that without further assurances I might be depended upon for giving it every support in my power; but some circumstances made me wish to state them as briefly as possible to the County of Sussex.

They were formed on the experience of 26 years, which whether in or out of Government, has equally convinced me that the Restoration of a genuine House of Commons by a Renovation of the Rights of the People is the only effectual Remedy against that system of corruption which has brought the Nation to Disgrace and Poverty and threatens it with the Loss of Liberty.

I take the grievances of the present state of Election to be its gross inequality. All the Electors in Great Britain do not amount to one sixth part of the whole people and a still greater inequality subsists in the elections made by that sixth part; for one seventh part of them select a majority, so that one 42nd part of the Nation disposes of the property of the whole and have their lives and liberties at Command. And this 42nd part, far from consisting of the most opulent part of the Kingdom, is composed of the small boroughs, most of which are come either the private property of Individuals, or are notoriously sold to the best Bidder; so that the Counties and great Cities are, in Fact, as well as the great mass of the people, swallowed[?] in this system of corruption.

My ideas of reform undoubtedly go to one that shall be compleat and general throughout the Kingdom. I see such fatal consequences arise from the present partial and accidental state of elections that I cannot take upon me to propose any new mode that partakes of the same Defects. If we do not differ from the abettors of corruption upon the broad principle of inequality in election and the universal right of the people to be represented and are contending only for a degree of partiality more or less, I fear our ground is not sound; if we mean only to substitute partiality for partiality, and are struggling but for its extent, one man's whim may be as good as another's conceit, and we have nothing certain to direct us; and if inequality is still to subsist, the advocates for the present system will have the sanction of time, and the risk of changes to oppose us, which will have their weight when it is but for a change of partiality that we contend.

I have thought that a parliamentary reform had much more simple and unerring guides to lead us to our end; I mean the true principles of the Constitution and the Rights of the people. If these exist, I do not consider myself at Liberty to speculate upon systems. I have no choice but to give to every man his own.

But this it seems is by some thought impracticable and the Rev. Mr. Wyvill of his Letter of the 7th of December to Mr. Alderman Crosbie, as Chairman of the Committee of the Livery of London, which has been published, very concisely decides it to be so. For I presume his objection of Impracticability is not confined to my plan, which I believe he has never seen, but to the Extent of the Idea; and yet Mr. Wyville in the second address of the Yorkshire Committee to the Electors in Great Britain, speaking of the more and less extensive plans, says "that the Diversity of Sentiments does not arise from a Difference of political principles, for in them there is an entire Agreement but soley from Consideration of a prudential nature."

How far it is wise for those who entirely agree in principle upon the Rights of Men to endeavor to persuade them that the Recovery of the Birth

Rights and most essential Interests "are not reducible to practice nor attainable by any regular constitutional Efforts of theirs," is what I must leave to others to determine. But the truth of this Assertion is what I never can subscribe to. I cannot but think that this Nation ever has its own powers by peaceful and constitutional Efforts to do itself Justice and that nothing can render Attempts for this purpose impracticable but either a general indolence and indifference to all that requires Exertion, though for the noblest purposes, or such prejudice to Favourite systems as shall divide the people.

To guard against such an Imputation falling on me, I am most ready to agree to an address in the most general Terms, not pointing to my specific mode of reform in the Petition, or by instructions to our Members, or by Resolutions—but submitting the Remedy, as in my opinion it ought to be in the first Instance, to Parliament itself; which I Conceive to be at least as equal to such consideration as any provincial committee.

Should Mr. Wyvill's first or second plans be proposed in Parliament or anything like it, although I shall amend that We for a moment quit our advantageous ground of the Constitution and the Rights of Men, yet I shall certainly give every support in my power to this or any other amendment. And it certainly will be a considerable improvement that instead of a 42nd it should be 36th or 30th part that shall decide the Concerns of the whole people. It will be something material they will have gained and may become a step to the more easy attainment of their full priviledges.

I shall most sincerely hope that that plan may be found attainable; but I never can consent to tell the people, and I hope in God they never will believe, that the Recovery of any Right which Nature and the Constitution has given them is impracticable. On the contrary, convinced myself I wish them ever to believe that whenever they please to claim them they shall and must have the full extent of their rights.

I have thought it necessary to say this much on an Impression I cannot think indifferent the public should entertain.

The Measure for which you are assembled meets with my hearty concurrence and I shall be happy if these sentiments, which I beg you would communicate to the Meeting of the County of Sussex, should meet with their approbation.

It is with the highest esteem and regard that I have the honour to be
Sir Your most obedient and most humble servant
Richmond Etc.

APPENDIX C: THOUGHTS ON REPRESENTATION (1804)

GOODWOOD MSS. 1622 (FILED WITH ACCOUNT BOOKS IN ARCHIVE RECORDS), WEST SUSSEX RECORD OFFICE.

July 25, 1804

Whoever duly considers the State of Man in this World must be convinced that it is not one of Happiness, such as can content His Mind. The more perfect we may suppose the Enjoyments of His Life can make it, the more we must regret its short Duration. But how few are in that situation! The generality of Mankind spend their Lives in daily Labour only in the search of those Earthly Enjoyments which they never attain. All is Contention and Strife attended with more or less painfull Circumstances, but always with considerable disappointments. Indeed unattainable as perfect Happiness in this world is, the Constant Pursuit of it seems to be the natural occupation of Man and Expectation the Sum of Happiness intended for Him here.

These general observations have been premised to prepare the mind of the Reader not to feel too much dejected at the many Imperfections in Matters most interesting to him that will herein be pointed out, as they are only the necessary consequences of the imperfect State of Man. Laudable as it always is to seek Perfection, with a view of approaching towards it, yet we ought to make up our minds, to the Mortification of finding that in all our undertakings we must fall very short of it in which as we have often to blame ourselves for Neglects and Errors, and human Frailities, we ought not to be too severe on others.

In no Instance will these Reflections apply with more truth than in that of Government which it is the object of this writing to consider.

By some it is thought of no use to enter into the origin of societies, that we can never trace with any accuracy their first beginnings or gather that there never was an original Institution, but that Time and accident have produced them and by Degrees introduced the establishment of these Principles by which they are now governed.

But altho there never may have existed an original Compact, yet some advantage may be derived from considering the Foundations on which at least it ought to have been equitably established, and if we can suppose that man ever existed in what we call a free state independent of all other men, and that a number of men so circumstanced met to consider and agree upon the Terms on which they should enter into and form a Society, it will be very right to examine what, according to Reason to attain their object, those Forms must have been; and establishing them as the Foundations of all Societies to esteem them as sacred Principles never to be departed from.

This Idea of having some certain and fixed Rules for the general Benefit of Mankind to which all Governments should be obliged to bend, is so pleasing to the Mind, that it is no wonder men should be anxious to have [chased] them out and therefore we will now enter into this search.

But alas in the very outset we shall find ourselves much embarrassed by the Imperfections attendant upon our Human Institutions, in the Grand Question: What Consent was necessary to establish the Compact? Will it be said <u>universal Consent?</u> And that it is evident it was given, as all being free to enter into it or not, those who did not consent would not of course have become members of the society. This supposition may be true as far as concerns its first formation but before we can draw any consequences from this admission, we must understand what we mean by the word Consent.

Consent to what? Do we mean that universal and separate Consent was necessary to every act by which individual Liberty should be restrained for the Good of the whole, or in other words, by which we should be governed; or that by one universal Consent at first, our remote ancestors agreed for themselves and their Posterity to be for ever governed by such Laws as were then assented to and (which in another Part of the Question) by such future Laws as a Majority of the Society should from Time to Time deem necessary.

Let us now examine these three Points.

The Inconveniency of Laws, such as we are told those of the Medes and Persians were, that never altered, must be evident; because no human Prudence can foresee every Circumstance and guard against it, and that the Ingenuity of Man is much more fertile in finding means to evade than to enforce Regulations that restrain His Passions. New Laws must therefore be made to meet new Cases, and experience may teach us that what might have been thought right and perfect some Centuries ago does not suit our Present Manners and Circumstances and may be amended. That a spirit of Innovation by continual alterations and mistaken Improvements may be carried too far is what we have far too much Experience of. But it would be still worse, if from the first origin we can trace of British Government, for instance, under our Druids, no alteration would have taken Place: Then arises the Question what Consent shall be necessary for such alteration? And the first supposition is, that the same universal Consent that was necessary for the first Institution must be necessary for every alteration as otherwise those who would now be called upon for such further Consent would then be governed by Laws to which they had not consented, which is contrary to what is supposed to be the origin and only just Foundation for all Society, the Consent of those who enter into it.

But altho' alterations in Laws need not be so frequent as we have seen them, yet the necessity of them, must too frequently occur, to be able on such occasions to obtain a fresh consent of every individual of the Society. If from a small Beginning when we may suppose the whole could have been assembled, it afterwards is grown into a great Nation it must be evident that the whole can never be again collected together. Resort much therefore upon this supposition that universal Consent is again necessary to be had to the collecting that consent separately in smaller districts or assemblies, and then must arise another Inconvenience, which is, that as the Propriety of adopting or rejecting such alterations ought to be surely considered the Discussion which is to obtain universal consent cannot be the same in all Places and therefore may produce different Determinations. But a further and insuperable Inconvenience must arise if the Principle is strictly to be adhered to, that no man is to be governed but by Laws to which he has personally consented, because in that Case a single negative must put a stop to every new Proposition tho' ever so essential to the rest of the Community and accordingly it has been seen that the Veto in Poland, established upon this Principle, and undoubtedly just in itself but impracticable in the Execution, was always attended with the worst Consequences; the meanest and most unprincipled Party could always counteract the most salutary Provisions, and the Rage of the most numerous Party against one individual who would so disappoint their measures was such as often to induce them to sacrifice him to their Resentment; so that in these tumultuous assemblies which in Poland consisted only of nobles who were all on horse back, the Person who meant to veto, took care to be mounted on the swiftest Horse He could get, and the moment he had pronounced the word from the Outer Part of the Circle rode away to save himself by instant Flight. And such or similar confusion must arise if the impracticable tho' ever so just Principle in theory is to be maintained, that is man is to be governed but by Laws to which he has personally given His Consent.

But it is contended that personal Consent is not necessary to maintain the Principle, and that provided universal Consent is given, it matters not whether it be directly in person, or indirectly by any other Means and that a written consent sign'd and surely attested or by deputation, are methods equally secure of conveying the real vote and opinion of the Individual. If they really were so, the Principle would undoubtedly be maintained by such a Substitute for oral consent. But as to the finish Who is there who has seen Petitions carried about for signatures who can for a Moment doubt but that such means are so liable to Frauds, mistakes threats and corruptions as by no means to convey the genuine sentiments of the Subscribers; and as to the latter, who will contend that deputies may not also be corrupted. But supposing either of these methods to be so far perfect as to be free from abuse, yet the mere recurrence to universal vote upon every occasion of alteration in the Law or of public, Regulations, must be so manifestly inconvenient as in fact to stop the whole Machine. This Principle of the consent of every man, given either oraly, by writing, or by deputy, to every act by which he is to be governed, must therefore be abandoned.

Well, but may not this Principle still be supported by relaxing one step further in the means? It was before conceded that Consent might be given by Deputation from each individual for each particular act, and why instead of such Deputation might not we admit of Representation, that is, one deputy for many Individuals, and instead of being told how He is to vote in each case to confide in Him the Power of voting for all those He represents in all cases that may occur.

But instead of maintaining the Principle in any Degree is not this completely giving it up? [July 27, 1804]. It is only playing upon words in contradiction to common sense to say that by consenting to be governed by the will of others, we are still governed by our own Consent, as well might we say that Slavery is Freedom because if we have consented to submit to it. It must therefore be admitted, that however necessary and advantageous for reasonable Liberty Representation may be, and that each Representative should be elected by the universal Consent of each Individual of the district He represents, yet if such Representative is entrusted to legislate in all Cases without further Reference to his Constituents, they do in fact consent to be governed by Laws to which they have not consented.

In some Instances indeed, the Representatives or Deputies, as in that case they were more properly called, may in particular Cases be restrained from assenting to any chance without recurring to their Constituents as being specially authorized by them what to do on such occasions, as was the case in the late Constitution of the State General of Holland. But there the Constituents were the magistrates of the Provinces and Towns themselves only Representatives and the Inconveniences of such a Government were every Day experienced. But with us our Representatives in Parliament are under no such Restraint or any control from their Constituents. Hopes for a future Election or Regard for the opinion of those by whom He is chosen may influence His Conduct. But once elected has an undoubted Right to vote upon every Question as He may think proper without any Reference, and even contrary to what He may know to be the opinion of his Electors. And such is the true Spirit of our Constitution founded upon two very sound Principles. The first that each representatives tho chosen by the Inhabitants of a particular district is not chosen to represent them only or to attend only to their Concerns, but is elected to be one of those to whom the Interests of the whole nation is confided, and consequently ought not to be led by local or partial opinions. The other, that in the assembly of Representatives, where

He sits and which is to legislate He has the opportunity of hearing the opinions of Persons from all Parts of the Kingdom, & the discussions had thereupon, which He cannot regularly and fully report to his constituents, and without which they cannot be so capable as He is (supposing their Talents equal) to form a right Judgment.

With us therefore every Individual except the King and the Members of the two houses of Parliament does by our Constitution resign His right to be governed only by Laws to which He has himself consented and submits to all those which may be enacted by others. A more or less extended number of voters and frequency of Elections, Qualification and Independence of Representatives may be very proper Guards against the abuse of their Powers, but their Powers are limited only by their own Sense of Right. To say that this absolute will of our Representatives is our own will because we have chosen them is only to deceive ourselves by a fallacy of words, like that of a virtual Representation in those who are not admitted Electors. The Plain Truth is that this the freest country in the universe has of necessity been obliged to give up that Principle that every man has a right to be governed only by Laws to which He has himself consented for consent by His Representative is not as has been shown his but his Representative's consent.

The next point to be considered, is consent by not universal but by a majority. Here also we at once abandon all Pretence that every man has a right to be governed only by Laws to which he himself assented. And this Concession must have been made at the first outset of establishing Society. For supposing even that from the small number that may be conceived to have at first met to form Society, the Consent of every individual was obtained for the Laws and Regulations that were then proposed, it never would be imagined that in future and when that Society grew larger the same universal consent could be obtained on every occasion. It must therefore have been one of the first Rules established that for all future concerns, the opinion of a majority should bind the whole; whether that majority should consist of simply the larger number or be required to be two thirds, three fourths, or any other Proportion is not material, the Principle necessary to be established was, that some Majority should bind the Minority, and this I contend was renouncing in the first instance the Principle that every man should be governed only by his own Consent. For the Instant that I enter into a Society and agree that a Majority shall have a right to Legislate for me, I submit my Life, Liberty Property Reputation and all that is dear to me to the will of others. And yet unless I do, Society could not go on for one Moment. I must therefore run the risks of [?] [that] this arbitrary Power, for such it is, to which I submit, and trust that it will be properly use for my Benefit instead of Detriment. I must take then what care I can, hoping that I may be one of the majority, that it shall lay itself under such Restraints that it shall not abuse its Power, but Power absolute it must have.

NOTE ON SOURCES

ARCHIVAL MATERIALS

The 3rd Duke of Richmond charged his ward, Henriette le Clerc, to destroy his papers. She appears to have succeeded at this, as the 3rd Duke's correspondence does not remain in any single coherent archive. This has always made it more difficult to tell his story than that of other British politicians of the era. At least nine archival categories yielded the material used for this book.

First, the Duke of Richmond's most coherent personal archive exists in the form of marginalia in the books in his library. This book is the first treatment of the Duke of Richmond to have had access to that considerable body of material.

Second, there are materials by and about the 3rd Duke in the broader family archives. These include the Goodwood Papers, housed at the West Sussex Record Office, Chichester, which include his father's letters and the letters to him by James Wolfe; the letter collections of his sisters, Emily, Louisa, and Sarah; and a small set of family correspondence held at the British Library, which importantly includes letters between the 3rd Duke and his brother George (Richmond Family Private Correspondence, Loan MS 57/103–106, British Library). The British Library also houses correspondence with family friend Peter Collinson. Horace Walpole's extensive archive of letters, housed at the Walpole Archive at Yale University and available electronically, also includes substantial material. In addition, a 1911 biography of the 2nd Duke, by the then Earl of March (*A Duke and His Friends: The Life and Letters of the Second Duke of Richmond*, 2 vol.), published family letters, including letters from the children to the 2nd Duke and 2nd Duchess, which are not now otherwise available. These family materials are rich but also have striking absences. Caroline's letters are largely missing. Both the Goodwood Papers and the sisters' letters have gaps between 1769 and 1774.

Third, there is the political correspondence of the 2nd and 3rd Dukes of Richmond. The 2nd Duke's correspondence with Newcastle has been published in Timothy J. McCann, ed., *The Correspondence of the Dukes of Richmond and Newcastle, 1724–1750*, vol. 73 of *Sussex Record Society* (Lewes, UK: Sussex Record Society, 1984). The 3rd Duke's political correspondence is most richly represented in the papers of the dukes of Newcastle, the Marquess of Rockingham, Edmund Burke, and Holland House (which contain the letters of Charles James Fox). Alison Olson has also published a selection of farther flung material in her 1961 study, *The Radical Duke: The Career and Correspondence of Charles Lennox, Third Duke of Richmond*. Finally, some important letters are to be found in the Royal Collections, in the editions of the letters of King George III, and in Historical Manuscript Commission Reports, including the Carlisle and Bathurst MSS.

Fourth, there are memoirs by other political figures in the era, including General James Wolfe, the Marquess of Rockingham, Duke of Grafton, Earl of Shelburne/Marquess of Lansdowne, Sir Philip Francis, Major John Cartwright, Granville Sharp, and Charles James Fox.

Fifth, there are the records of proceedings in the House of Lords in the *Journal of the House of Lords* and William Cobbett, ed., *The Parliamentary History of England from the Norman Conquest in 1066 to the Year 1803*.

Sixth, there are the official documents of Richmond's service in government as ambassador to Paris, secretary of state, and master-general of the ordnance. These are held in the British Library, Public Record Office, William L. Clements Library (University of Michigan), and the Historical Manuscript Commission Report for the Earl of Bathurst.

Seventh, there are the private Junius letters, which are housed in the British Library. While these have all been published in *The Letters of Junius*, edited by John Cannon (Oxford: Clarendon Press, 1978), consulting the original manuscripts is valuable. Some of the letters were sealed with signet rings with distinctive engravings. Also the process of editing the letters for publication included annotations of the texts that in style resemble the 3rd Duke's annotations in the books in his library. While I was ultimately not able to make a close comparative study of these annotations, it would be a job worth doing.

Eighth, newspapers and magazines of the period have been invaluable, including *The Public Advertiser*, *The London Chronicle*, the *Lewes Journal or Sussex Weekly Advertiser*, and *The Gentleman's Magazine*. While most of these materials are available digitally, the *Lewes Journal or Sussex Daily Advertiser* must be consulted at The Keep, the East Sussex Record Office.

Ninth, the Society of Arts is now the Royal Society of Arts and holds archives dating to the 1750s and 1760s. Regrettably this archive was not open to researchers during the final phase of my study when I had recognized its import. Here too there are likely to be materials of interest.

SECONDARY SOURCES

A short list of secondary sources that have been exceptionally useful to my work and are cited frequently in the notes. Accordingly, I abbreviate them throughout and list them here.

Baird: Rosemary Baird. *Goodwood: Art and Architecture, Sport and Family*. London: Frances Lincoln, 2007.

Black: Eugene Charlton Black. *The Association: British Extraparliamentary Political Organization, 1769–1793*. Cambridge, MA: Harvard University Press, 1963.

Burke Correspondence: Edmund Burke. *The Correspondence of Edmund Burke*.
Vol. 1, April 1744–June 1768. Edited by Thomas W. Copeland. Cambridge & Chicago: Cambridge University Press & University of Chicago Press, 1958.
Vol. 2, July 1768–June 1774. Edited by Lucy S. Sutherland. Cambridge & Chicago: Cambridge University Press & University of Chicago Press, 1960.
Vol. 3, July 1774–June 1778. Edited by George H. Guttridge. Cambridge & Chicago: Cambridge University Press & University of Chicago Press, 1961.
Vol. 4, July 1778–June 1782. Edited by John A. Woods. Cambridge & Chicago: Cambridge University Press & University of Chicago Press, 1963.

Cobbett: William Cobbett, ed. *The Parliamentary History of England from the Norman Conquest in 1066 to the Year 1803*, vol. 16. London: T.C. Hansard, 1813.

Collected Paine: Greg Claeys, Carine Lounissi, Scott Cleary, Gary Berton, Marc Belissa, and Yannick Bosc, eds. *The Collected Works of Thomas Paine.* Princeton, NJ: Princeton University Press, 2026.

Junius Letters: *The Letters of Junius*, edited by John Cannon. Oxford: Clarendon Press, 1978.

Leinster Correspondence: Emily, Duchess of Leinster. *Correspondence of Emily, Duchess of Leinster (1731–1814)*, edited by Brian FitzGerald. Vols. 1–4. Dublin: Irish Manuscripts Commission, 1949.

Olson: Alison Gilbert Olson. *The Radical Duke: The Career and Correspondence of*

Charles Lennox, Third Duke of Richmond, 1735–1806. Oxford: Oxford University Press, 1961.

Reese: M. M. Reese. *Goodwood's Oak: The Life and Times of the Third Duke of Richmond, Lennox, and Aubigny*. Chichester: Phillimore, 1987.

Roberts: Andrew Roberts. *The Last King of America: The Misunderstood Reign of George III*. New York: Viking, 2021.

Rockingham Letters: George Thomas Keppel, Earl of Albemarle. *Memoirs of the Marquis of Rockingham and His Contemporaries*, 2 vols. London: Richard Bentley, 1852.

Sarah Lennox: Letters Lady Sarah Lennox Bunbury Napier. *The Life and Letters of Lady Sarah Lennox, 1745–1826: Daughter of Charles, 2nd Duke of Richmond, and Successively the Wife of Sir Thomas Charles Bunbury, and of the Hon. George Napier; Also a Short Political Sketch of the Years 1760 to 1763, by Henry Fox, 1st Lord Holland*, eds. the Countess of Ilchester and Lord Stavordale, 2 vols. London: John Murray, 1902.

Tillyard: Stella Tillyard. *Aristocrats: Caroline, Emily, Louisa, and Sarah Lennox, 1740–1832*. London: Chatto & Windus, 1994.

NOTES

PROLOGUE

xx **"superb eyes" . . . "the great beauty":** John Thomas Smith, *A Book for a Rainy Day: Or Recollections of the Events of the Years 1766–1833*, ed. Wilfred Whitten (London: Methuen & Co., 1905), 146.

xxii **destroyed her letters:** Sarah Lennox Letters, vol. 1, 223.

xxii **Someone destroyed almost all:** Tillyard, xx–xiii. Caroline's papers have many gaps so it is harder to distinguish a specific missing period.

xxii **collection that exceeds Thomas Jefferson's:** Shortly after his death, the Duke's library was calculated to hold some 9,000 volumes, a number that overtops the 6,487 volumes Thomas Jefferson sold to the Library of Congress in 1823. Perhaps a third of Richmond's books had been acquired by his father, the 2nd Duke. The rest were bought in England and on travels abroad by the 3rd Duke and his extended family.

xxiii **new six-volume 2026 edition**: Collected Paine. For discussion of the methodology, see Berton, Gary, Smiljana Petrovic, Lubomir Ivanov, and Robert Schiaffino, "Examining the Thomas Paine Corpus: Automated Computer Authorship Attribution Methodology Applied to Thomas Paine's Writings," in *New Directions in Thomas Paine Studies*, eds. Scott Cleary and Ivy Linton Stabell (Palgrave Macmillan, 2016), 31–50.

xxiv **Our research led:** Danielle Allen and Emily Sneff, "The Sussex Declaration: Dating the Parchment Manuscript of the Declaration of Independence Held at the West Sussex Record Office (Chichester, UK)," *Papers of the Bibliographical Society of America* 112, no. 3 (2018), 357–403. But see John Bidwell, "The Sources of the Sussex Declaration: A Reconsideration," *Studies in Bibliography* 61 (2025), 105–26, published by the Bibliographical Society of the University of Virginia, which argues for a later dating and British provenance. I am currently working on a response to this paper and stand by the findings in our original article. Key details include the fiber displacement and raised burrs of the nail holes, which are strong indicators of hand-wrought nails, and the total absence of Bridgham copies from the UK.

xxiv **appears to have been commissioned:** Danielle Allen and Emily Sneff, "Golden Letters: James Wilson, the Declaration of Independence, and the Sussex Declaration," *Georgetown Journal of Law & Public Policy* 17, no. 1 (2019), 193–230.

xxiv **mode of production makes clear:** Allen and Sneff, "The Sussex Declaration."

xxiv **Paine brought the key back:** W. H. G. Armytage, "Thomas Paine and the Walkers: An Early Episode in Anglo-American Cooperation," *Pennsylvania History: A Journal of Mid-Atlantic Studies* 18, no. 1 (January 1951), 24.

xxiv **Benjamin Franklin had sent:** On November 19, 1783, Lafayette wrote to William Temple Franklin requesting a print copy of the Declaration, that he hoped to have "Engraved in Golden letters" and placed "on the Most Conspicuous part of my Cabinet" (letter is held at the American Philosophical Society). Carl Becker (*The Declaration of Independence: A Study in the History of Political Ideas* [New York: Harcourt, Brace and Company, 1922]) records Lafayette's prominent display of this copy of the Declaration to visitors, citing *Memoires et correspondence du general LaFayette*, III, 197.

xxv **"experience of 26 years":** Duke of Richmond to County Meeting, Whitehall, January 17, 1783, contained within Documents from General Meeting for the County, 1780–83, ESRO reference: L/C/X/1/1, East Sussex Record Office.

xxvi **"one of the prettiest":** Louisa Conolly to Emily, Duchess of Leinster, January 21, 1773, in Leinster Correspondence, vol. 3, 67.

xxvii ***The Juryman's Touchstone*:** The pamphlet is included in Goodwood, Large Library G4, *Tracts: Cartwright (Major John) Take your Choice (on Parliaments) 1776; Rous (G.) Letter to Jurors, 1785; Vindication of Right of Election, 1769; and two others on legal matters. In one volume*, 8 vo., half calf.

xxviii **every Harvard student:** Morton D. Paley, "To Defend the Bible in This Year 1798 Would Cost a Man His Life," *Blake/An Illustrated Quarterly* 32, no. 2 (Fall 1998), 32.

xxviii **"I hope . . . your intention":** Richard Watson, *Apology for the Bible: In a Series of Letters Addressed to Thomas Paine* (London: T. Evans, 1796), 6.

CHAPTER 1. YOUTH

5 **twenty-seven times:** Horace Walpole to Sir Horace Mann, February 25, 1750, *Walpole's Correspondence*, Yale Online Edition, Henry Colburn, London, 1837, vol. 20, 125.

5 **"the loveliest lady":** 2nd Duke of Richmond to Princess Trivulci, [1748], in Earl of March, *A Duke and His Friends: The Life and Letters of the Second Duke of Richmond*, vol. 2 (London: Hutchinson & Co., 1911), 641.

5 **"grown so noisy":** 3rd Earl of Berkeley to 2nd Duke of Richmond, July 15, 1736, ibid., vol. 1, 309.

6 **prince of the blood:** Horace Walpole, *Memoirs of the Reign of King George the Third*, vol. 1, ed. G. F. R. Barker (London: Lawrence and Bullen, 1894), 26.

4 **he signed:** C. March to 2nd Duke, September 3, 1749, and C. March to Henry Fox, June 2, 1750, in Earl of March, *A Duke and His Friends*, vol. 2, 676ff and 707ff.

7 **published correspondence:** Timothy J. McCann, ed., *The Correspondence of the Dukes of Richmond and Newcastle, 1724–1750*, vol. 73 of *Sussex Record Society* (Lewes, UK: Sussex Record Society, 1984).

7 **Caroline and her friends performed:** Baird, 31.

7 **"base-ball":** Roberts, 10, citing Mary Lepel, *Letters of Mary Lepel, Lady Hervey*, 1821, Hathi Trust, 139.

8 **"Comment portez-vous":** Tillyard, 109.

8 **patriotic songs:** Ibid.

8 **godfather:** Baird, 42.

9 **His day started:** Roberts, 12–13.

9 **overnighted on occasion:** At least once to escape smallpox exposure in 2nd Duke of Richmond to Duke of Newcastle, January 7, 1740/1 in McCann, ed., *The Correspondence of the Dukes of Richmond and Newcastle, 1724–1750*, vol. 73 of *Sussex Record Society*, 54–55.

9 **love of animals:** Earl of March, *A Duke and His Friends*, vol. 2, 626–27.

9 **monkey:** Baird, 56, 63.

9 **named Thomas Robinson:** Ibid., 104.

9 **ornate columns:** Ibid., 80.

9 **unwrapping of a mummy:** Ibid., 72.

10 **was first sent to school:** Dates are based on his letters home in Earl of March, *A Duke and His Friends*, vol. 2, 691ff. Earlier biographies have misdated his arrival to 1745.

10 **Cricket arrived at Westminster:** On cricket and the Sackvilles at Westminster, John Sargeaunt, *Annals of Westminster School* (London: Methuen, 1898), 186–87. General information on the school also from this volume.

10 **"Throughout all the history of the School":** Sargeaunt, *Annals of Westminster School*, 175.

10 **take a wife:** Ibid., 170.

10 **John Penn:** Lorett Treese, *The Storm Gathering: The Penn Family and the American Revolution* (University Park, PA: Penn State University Press, 1995), 24.

11 **"I have heard some time ago":** Earl of March to the 2nd Duchess, October 14, 1746, in Earl of March, *A Duke and His Friends*, vol. 2, 692.

11 **"set fire to his master's greasy locks":** Sargeaunt, *Annals of Westminster School*, 173.

12 **expenditure on a victory celebration:** Earl of March, *A Duke and His Friends*, vol. 2, 407.
12 **testifying to the valor:** Ibid., 404ff.
13 **Fox, though, was determined:** The episode described in this paragraph is related in detail in Tillyard, 20–29.
13 **planned a great ball:** Baird, 43.
14 **Isle of Wight:** Peter Collinson to 2nd Duke of Richmond, August 27 [1744], in Earl of March, *A Duke and His Friends*, vol. 2, 441.
14 **colonial venture to Nova Scotia:** 2nd Duke of Richmond to Duke of Newcastle, July 31, 1745, and August 7, 1745, in McCann, ed., *The Correspondence of the Dukes of Richmond and Newcastle, 1724–1750*, vol. 73 of *Sussex Record Society*, 169–71.
15 **write to the Duke at length:** Earl of March, *A Duke and His Friends*, vol. 2, 456–60.
15 **"our cousin":** Tillyard, 41.
15 **prince wrote personally:** Lord John Sackville to 2nd Duke of Richmond, September 14, 1745, Earl of March, *A Duke and His Friends*, vol. 2, 597–98.
16 **"expressed a wish":** Sargeaunt, *Annals of Westminster School*, 168–69.
17 **ran off to the army:** Ibid., 169.
17 **"He was too modest":** Ibid.
18 **John Fletcher . . . whom March met:** Earl of March, *A Duke and His Friends*, vol. 2, 537.
18 **books on fortifications:** M. Coehorn, *Nouvelle Fortification . . . l'Hexagone à la françoise* (The Hague, 1741); L'Abbé Deidier, *Le parfait ingénieur François, ou la fortification* (Paris, 1742); J. Muller, *Treatise Containing the Elementary Part of Fortification* (London, 1746); Baron F. Rothberg, *L'Ingénieur moderne, ou essai de fortification* (The Hague, 1747).
18 **intellectual companionship with her children's tutor:** See Tillyard.
19 **Remember that you promised us:** Montesquieu to Folkes, February 14, 1744, *Correspondance II*; cited in Robert Shackleton, *Montesquieu: A Critical Biography* (Oxford: Oxford University Press, 1961), 175.
20 **miscarriage:** Letters of 2nd Duke of Richmond to Duke of Newcastle, July 30, August 1, 11, and 13, 1740, in McCann, ed., *The Correspondence of the Dukes of Richmond and Newcastle, 1724–1750*, vol. 73 of *Sussex Record Society*, 36–39.
21 **"considerable young Nobleman of Sussex":** Duke of Newcastle to 2nd Duke of Richmond, August 29, 1747, in ibid., 255.
21 **"My eldest boy":** 2nd Duke of Richmond to Princess Trivulci, [1748], in Earl of March, *A Duke and His Friends*, vol. 2, 641.

CHAPTER 2. PURPOSE

23 **"I am very obliged to you":** Earl of March to 2nd Duke of Richmond, August 27, 1749, in Earl of March, *A Duke and His Friends*, vol. 2, 693.
23 **"Dear Papa, I have just":** Earl of March to 2nd Duke of Richmond, September 3, 1749, ibid., vol. 2, 676.
24 **interested only in:** Earl of March to 2nd Duke of Richmond, September 3, 1749, ibid., vol. 2, 676–77; Earl of March to 2nd Duke of Richmond, September 6, 1749, ibid., vol. 2, 599.
24 **"At my return from Oxford":** Earl of March to 2nd Duke of Richmond, September 18, 1749, ibid., vol. 2, 694.
24 **"The pinch":** T. Gibberd to 2nd Duke of Richmond, September 18, 1749, ibid., vol. 2, 696.
24 **"Dear Mama, I have reflected":** Earl of March to 2nd Duchess of Richmond, undated, in ibid., 695–96.
24 **long, spicy, confessional letter:** C. March to Henry Fox, June 2, 1750, in ibid., vol. 2, 707ff.
27 **Boredom drove him to it:** Lady Sarah Lennox to Emily, Duchess of Leinster, Goodwood, February 6, 1779, in Leinster Correspondence, vol. 2, 279. For a full picture of Trembley's pedagogic methods, see James Peill, *Glorious Goodwood: A Biography of England's Greatest Sporting Estate* (London: Constable, 2019), ch. 6.
28 **"the Duke loves dogs prodigiously":** Tillyard, 78.
28 **secure a commission:** His appointment was announced in *London Gazette*, no. 9147, March 7, 1752, 3.

28 **promotion to captain:** The appointment to captain in the 20th Regiment of Foot was announced on June 18, 1753, and reported in *London Gazette,* June 23, 1753.

28 **asking to come home:** Baird, 86.

30 **"As far as my discernment goes":** James Wolfe to his father, December 4, 1752, in Beckles Willson, *The Life and Letters of James Wolfe* (London: William Heinemann, 1909), 193.

30 **"splendour and magnificence":** This and the subsequent quotations are all from James Wolfe to his mother, January 2, 1753 in ibid., 197–98.

30 **"through the fortified towns":** Ibid.

31 **"He made me read":** Lord Edmond Fitzmaurice, *The Life of William, Earl of Shelburne,* vol. 1 (London: Macmillan, 1875), 94–95.

31 **danced at his first ball:** Marie Liechtenstein, *Holland House* (London: Macmillan and Co., 1875), 213.

32 **"the young duke of Richmond":** Peter Collinson to Benjamin Franklin, March 21, 1753, *Founders Online* [Original source: *The Papers of Benjamin Franklin,* vol. 4, *July 1, 1750, through June 30, 1753,* ed. Leonard W. Labaree (New Haven, CT: Yale University Press, 1961), 457–58.]

32 **on their way again:** Baird, 87.

32 **Venetian Lagoon Froze:** A. Trembley to W. Adair, Venice, January 17, 1755, Goodwood Mss., 222–28, West Sussex Record Office.

32 **pitching his tent:** For a thorough review of the Grand Tour as reported in letters held at the West Sussex Record Office, see Baird, 86–87 and Reese, 51–58.

32 **The botany professor:** Ibid. and see also Joan Coutu, *Then and Now: Collecting and Classicism in Eighteenth-Century England* (Montreal: McGill-Queen's University Press, 2015), 106.

33 **"received 'em with a smile":** General James Wolfe to the 3rd Duke of Richmond, January 3, 1755, Goodwood Mss., Folder 223, West Sussex Record Office. This is one among fifteen letters in this folder, dating 1755–1758.

33 **Wolfe urged Richmond:** General James Wolfe to the 3rd Duke of Richmond, Canterbury, December 9, 1755, ibid.

33 **"to stroke her bum and thighs":** Quoted in Baird, 87, and Reese, 53.

36 **concocted a plan:** Coutu, *Then and Now: Collecting and Classicism in Eighteenth-Century England,* 93–126.

36 **"I hope your Grace":** General James Wolfe to the 3rd Duke of Richmond, undated [letter 1], Goodwood Mss. 223, West Sussex Record Office.

38 **"You will find a wide difference":** General James Wolfe to the 3rd Duke of Richmond, December 9, 1755, Goodwood Mss. 223, West Sussex Record Office.

38 **The percentage of the people:** John Brewer, *Party Ideology and Popular Politics at the Accession of George III* (Cambridge: Cambridge University Press, 1976), 6–7.

38 **never had to work again:** Baird, 88.

39 **"I was told tother day":** 3rd Duke of Richmond to Lord George Lennox, January 25, 1757, Richmond Family Private Correspondence, Loan MS 57/103, folio 2568, British Library.

39 **"I do not see why I should":** Ibid.

40 **"country diversions":** This and immediately following quotations are from General James Wolfe to the 3rd Duke of Richmond, January 19, 1757, Goodwood 223, West Sussex Record Office.

40 **"the perfectest match":** Quoted in Reese, 64.

40 **"whenever I have any leisure":** 3rd Duke of Richmond to Lord George Lennox, September 9, 1757, Richmond Family Private Correspondence, Loan MS 57/103, folio 2573, British Library.

40 **"their Graces not being up":** These quotations are from letters between sister Emily and her husband, the Duke of Leinster, May 22, 1757; June 1757, in Leinster Correspondence, vol. 1, 38, 43.

41 **"I would have you fill":** General James Wolfe to the 3rd Duke of Richmond, April 23, 1757, Goodwood 223, West Sussex Record Office.

41 **members of the new Society:** For Franklin's engagement in the society in the 1760s, see Benjamin Franklin to Joseph Galloway, April 14, 1767, *Founders Online* [Original source: *The Papers of Benjamin Franklin,* vol. 14, *January 1 through December 31, 1767,* ed. Leonard W. Labaree (New Haven and London: Yale University Press, 1970), 122–25.]

41 **Franklin quickly embedded himself:** Alison G. Olson, *Anglo-American Politics, 1660–1775: The Relationship Between Parties in England and Colonial America* (Oxford: Clarendon Press, 1973), 145–52.
42 **"To an active mind like yours":** General James Wolfe to the 3rd Duke of Richmond, March 20, 1756, Goodwood 223, West Sussex Record Office.
42 **with his troops:** Reese, 66.
42 **One periodical, *The Monitor*:** This paragraph relies throughout on Marie Peters, "The 'Monitor' on the Constitution, 1755–1765: New Light on the Ideological Origins of English Radicalism," *English Historical Review* 86, no. 339 (1971), 706–27, including for the quotations from *The Monitor.*
43 **"disjointed State":** This and subsequent quotations in this paragraph are from General James Wolfe to the 3rd Duke of Richmond, July 10, 1757, Goodwood 223, West Sussex Record Office.
43 **"England is on its decline":** 3rd Duke of Richmond to Lord George Lennox, September 9, 1757, Richmond Family Private Correspondence, Loan MS 57/103, folio 2573, British Library.
43 **"Tis hard they will not":** Ibid.
44 **"to be of some service to my country":** 3rd Duke of Richmond to Lord George Lennox, February 2, 1758, Richmond Family Private Correspondence, Loan MS 57/103, folio 2598, British Library.
44 **opened their sculpture gallery:** Richmond's account books from February 25, 1758, record three advertisements for the new statue gallery in *London Chronicle.* The opening was covered in the *Chronicle* on February 25, 1758; *Daily Advertiser* on February 28, 1758; and *Gentleman's Magazine,* March 1758. On the opening, generally see Coutu, *Then and Now: Collecting and Classicism in Eighteenth-Century England*, 93–126, 243n.
45 **One survivor wrote:** Quoted in H. C. Wylly, *History of the King's Own Yorkshire Light Infantry*, vol. 1 (London: Percy Lund, Humphries & Co., 1926), 48–49.
47 **Wolfe's corpse left Wilton:** A. McNairn, *Behold the Hero, General Wolfe and the Arts in the Eighteenth Century*, Quebec, 1997, 64.

CHAPTER 3. A NEW KING AND A QUARREL

48 **heart attack:** All details from Roberts, 55.
49 **Frederick had drafted:** This summary of George's education is drawn from Roberts.
49 **between a fifth and a quarter:** Reese, 97; see also Peter D. G. Thomas, *George III: King and Politicians 1760–1770* (Manchester: Manchester University Press, 2002), 13–16.
50 **"Her beauty is not easily described":** Henry Fox Memoir, included in Sarah Lennox Letters, vol. 1, 26–27.
50 **"drawing rooms" . . . "levees":** On these rituals, see Roberts, 14, 80–81, 86.
51 **"What I now lay before you":** George III, *Letters from George III to Lord Bute, 1756–1766*, ed. Romney Sedgwick (London: Macmillan, 1939), 37–38.
52 **charged the ambassador:** Roberts, 65.
52 **"I had not chose to put myself":** 3rd Duke of Richmond to Mr. Wyndham, June 21, 1783, in George Bubb Dodington, *The Diary of the Late George Bubb Dodington*, ed. Henry Penruddocke Wyndham (London: J. Dodsley, 1784), appendix.
53 **"all [Ferdinand's] people":** Ibid.
54 **"It is too bad to be repeated":** Henry Fox Memoir, in Sarah Lennox Letters, vol. 1, 22–23.
54 **"had never been forgotten or forgiven":** This and subsequent quotations in the paragraph are from Horace Walpole, *Memoirs of the Reign of King George the Third*, vol. 1, ed. G. F. R. Barker (London: Lawrence and Bullen, 1894), 27.
55 **"I thought it my duty":** 3rd Duke of Richmond to Mr. Wyndham, June 21, 1783, in Dodington, *The Diary of the Late George Bubb Dodington*, appendix.
55 **"I don't doubt but my Dearest Friend":** George III to Earl of Bute, Monday Dec. 8, 1760, *Letters from George III to Lord Bute, 1756–1766*, Letter 64, 50–51.
55 **"he was sorry the Duke of Richmond":** Walpole, *Memoirs of the Reign of King George the Third*, 28.
56 **"Believe that I have the strongest attachment":** Henry Fox Memoir, included in Sarah Lennox Letters, *Short Political Sketch of the Years 1760 to 1763, by Henry Fox, 1st Lord Holland*, ed. the Countess of Ilchester and Lord Stavordale (London: John Murray, 1902), vol. 1, 49.

56 **"upon urgent & important business":** Ibid., 50.

56 **"In short, his behaviour":** Lady Sarah Lennox to Lady Susan Fox-Strangways, July 7, 1761, in Sarah Lennox Letters, vol. 1, 105.

56 **attended Parliament only four times:** All references to Richmond's attendance in Parliament come from *Journal of the House of Lords Volume 29–39*, (London, 1767–1830), *British History Online.*

56 **controlling both seats:** Reese, 87.

56 **persuaded to serve only one:** Ibid. and also Thomas, *George III: King and Politicians 1760–1770*, 45; Olson, 5–6. See also 3rd Duke of Richmond to Duke of Newcastle 27 and 29 September 1767; Duke of Newcastle to 3rd Duke of Richmond 28 and 30, September 1767, ADD MS 33,985, ff 245, 255, 288, British Library.

57 **wealthiest man:** Baird, 104.

57 **the ranks of his protégés:** On Stubbs, see Reese, 83. On Carleton, see Lande, *The 3rd Duke of Richmond: A Study in Early Canadian History* (Montreal, 1956, reprinted 2021 by Hassell Street Press), 1. On the moose, see Baird, 105.

57 **another then-unknown painter, George Romney:** Author unknown, "The Kendal Town Hall Sketchbook," *The Romney Society*, n.d., 6. See also John Kenworthy-Browne, "The Duke of Richmond's Gallery in Whitehall," *British Art Journal* X/1, 2009.

58 **For that ceremony:** 3rd Duke of Richmond to Peter Collinson, Sep. 3, 1761, ADD MS 28727, f82, British Library.

58 **gone unpaid:** Coutu, *Then and Now: Collecting and Classicism in Eighteenth-Century England*, 118.

58 **800,000 pounds a year:** For King's wealth, see Roberts, 58.

59 **two thousand copies a day, and it would hit five thousand:** Thomas, *George III: King and Politicians 1760–1770*, 16.

59 **King's maiden speech to open Parliament:** King George III in Parliament, Nov 18, 1760, in *Journal of the House of Lords Volume 30, 1760–1764, British History Online.*

60 **clear indication:** Roberts, 70.

61 **"league of Dukes":** George III to Earl of Bute, circa June 14, 1762, *Letters from George III to Lord Bute*, 116. See also the editor's note to the letter for information about the court spy's reporting on the ducal "association."

61 **contemptible:** Ibid.

61 **"The league of the Dukes is a most contemptible one":** D. H. Watson, "The Rise of the Opposition at Wildman's Club," *Bulletin of the Institute of Historical Research* 44, no. 109 (May 1971), 55–77; John Almon, *The History of the Late Minority: Exhibiting the Conduct, Principles, and Views, of That Party, During the Years 1762, 1763, 1764, and 1765* (London: Printed in the year 1765, and reprinted, with some additions, in the year 1766), 297–300.

61 **tennis almost daily:** Baird, 93.

61 **"They play [cards] and sit up":** Lady Caroline Fox to Emily, Marchioness of Kildare, 1762, in Leinster Correspondence, vol. 1. 317–18.

61 **"painted doll":** Lady Louisa Conolly to Emily, Countess of Kildare, April 10, 1759, in Leinster Correspondence, vol. 3, 10. See also Baird, 92.

62 **working through his brother-in-law:** Olson, 18, 189, 195.

62 **this alliance:** On Fox's role, see Roberts, 92–93, 99–100. For voting records in the House of Lords, see *Journal of the House of Lords Volume 29–39*, (London, 1767–1830), *British History Online.*

62 **demanded that all Opposition Whigs:** Roberts, 100.

62 **"dine a fifth Duke":** Henry Fox to Earl of Bute March 27, 1763, Bute MSS. See also Fox memo to Bute, March 11, 1763, in Fitzmaurice, *The Life of William, Earl of Shelburne: From His Birth in 1737 to the Peace of Paris in 1763*, vol. 1, 188.

63 **a grand masked ball:** For newspaper reports, *Public Advertiser*. For general description, Jérôme Lalande, *Diary of a Trip to England 1763*, trans. Richard Watkins (Kingston, Tasmania: Richard Watkins, 2002), June 5, 1763, entry, 32.

63 **Richmond was conspicuously absent:** Watson, "The Rise of the Opposition at Wildman's Club,", 62n3.

63 **"responsible for law and order":** Reese, 87.

64 **vice president of the society:** Henry Trueman Wood, "The Royal Society of Arts. II—The Earliest Lists of Members," *Journal of the Royal Society of Arts* 59, no. 3056 (June 16, 1911), 786.

64 **"natural bent of mind":** Collected Paine, vol. 3, a description of himself.

65 **greatest devotees:** On the society, see Anton Howes, *Arts and Minds: How the Royal Society of Arts Changed a Nation* (Princeton, NJ: Princeton University Press, 2020). Also D. G. C. Allan, "The Society of Arts and Government, 1754–1800: Public Encouragement of Arts, Manufactures, and Commerce in Eighteenth-Century England," *Eighteenth-Century Studies* 7, no. 4 (Summer 1974), 434–52. On Paine's scientific activities in London in the late 1750s and likely connection to Franklin at that time, see Collected Paine, vol. 1, introduction.

65 **met Paine:** Collected Paine, vol. 1, introduction, traces the likely meeting of Paine and Franklin in the 1750s.

65 **entered London's intellectual universe:** Ibid., front matter.

65 **dabble in writing:** Ibid., vol. 1, intro.

65 **shared scientific passion:** See note 153.

66 **Close in age:** Biographical details about Thomas Paine here and throughout are from Collected Paine, vol. 1, unless otherwise indicated.

66 **pursued the office:** For the technicalities of pursuing an excise role, see Paul Myles, *The Rise of Thomas Paine: and The Case of the Officers of Excise* (Lewes, UK: Thomas Paine Society UK, 2018), 16–17. See also Colin Brent, "Thirty Something: Thomas Paine at Bull House in Lewes 1768–74—Six Formative Years," *Sussex Archaeological Collections* 147 (2009), 160.

CHAPTER 4. THE WILKES AFFAIR AND THE ORIGINS OF RADICALISM

72 **the economic precariousness of the cloth industry:** All quotations in this paragraph are from Isaac Ashley, *Bold Defiance: The Spitalfields Silkweavers, London's Luddites?* (London: Past Tense Publications, 2012).

73 **earn him the moniker:** Roberts, 132, quoting Grenville papers ed. Smith, vol. 3, 116.

73 **bipolar affective disorder:** Roberts, 133, 677–80.

74 **raised a ferment:** Augustus Henry FitzRoy, *Autobiography and Political Correspondence of Augustus Henry, Third Duke of Grafton*, ed. Sir William R. Anson (London: John Murray, 1898), 28.

74 **bought and bound:** Goodwood, Small Library, Wilkes (John)]. The North Briton. 2 vols., 12 mo., calf. 1763.

75 **limiting the fortunes of politically prominent colonial leaders:** Roberts, 124.

75 **actively writing for *The North Briton*:** Collected Paine, vol. 1, introduction.

75 **"extend to the Case":** *Journal of the House of Commons*, vol. 28 (1761–64), 674; and November 25, 1763, in *Journal of the House of Lords*, vol. 30 (1760–64), 426.

75 **"a false, scandalous, and seditious libel":** As reported for November 25, 1763, in *Journal of the House of Lords*, vol. 30, 1760–64, *British History Online*.

76 **"decency [was] thus satisfied":** Walpole, *Memoirs of the Reign of King George the Third*, vol. 1, 195.

76 **"the Personal Liberty of every common Subject":** This and all subsequent quotations in the paragraph are from November 29, 1763, in *Journal of the House of Lords*, vol. 30 (1760–64).

76 **furious crowds:** "Today in London's Radical History: Crowd Prevent the Burning of the North Briton, 1763," *Past Tense*, December 3, 2016.

77 **won his lawsuit:** Walpole, *Memoirs of the Reign of King George the Third*, vol. 1, 197.

77 **"the general matter of the propriety and possibility":** Duke of Richmond's political journal, looseleaf inserted in the 1764 journal, Goodwood Mss. 192, West Sussex Record Office. See also Walpole, *Memoirs of the Reign of King George the Third*, 344.

77 **formal lists of members:** Almon, *The History of the Late Minority: Exhibiting the Conduct, Principles, and Views, of That Party, During the Years 1762, 1763, 1764, and 1765*, 297–300.

77 **Not only Wildman's:** On Brooks, see *Memorials of Brooks's: From the Foundation of the Club 1764 to the Close of the Nineteenth Century*, compiled from the records of the club (London: Ballantyne & Co., 1907).

78 **"the boldness of the step":** Walpole, *Memoirs of the Reign of King George the Third*, vol. 1, 408.

78 **"anonymously published a pamphlet":** Most biographers take this to be the anonymous pamphlet *A Counter-Address to the Public, on the Late Dismission of a General Officer* (London:

Printed for W. Nicoll, 1764); see also Walpole, *Memoirs of the Reign of King George the Third*, vol. 1, 406.

79 **"Thoughts on the Dismission of Officers":** The anonymous pamphlet *Thoughts on the Dismission of Officers, Civil or Military, for Their Conduct in Parliament* (London: Printed for John Almon, 1765) is attributed to Adair. In addition, Adair's 1768 pamphlet, *Observations on the Power of Alienation in the Crown before the First of Queen Anne: Supported by Precedents and the Opinions of Many Learned Judges; Together with Some Remarks on the Conduct of Administration Respecting the Case of the Duke of Portland* (London: Printed for J. Almon, 1768) is in the Duke of Richmond's library and includes corrections or marginalia by the Duke on five of the pages. Goodwood, Large Library, G1.

79 **lengthy memorandum in his journal:** Duke of Richmond's political journal, loose leaf inserted in the 1764 journal, Goodwood Mss. 192, West Sussex Record Office.

79 **mundane work:** January through June 1764, *Journal of the House of Lords*, vol. 30 (1760–64).

79 **reviewing the troops:** *Major General His Grace the Duke of Richmond's Review Return*, Autumn 1764, Royal Archives.

79 **budget cuts had reduced:** On the cuts, see Roberts, 103.

79 **wages in lieu of tips:** Reese, 86.

29 **six-volume set:** Montesquieu (Charles de Secondat, Baron de), *Oeuvres*. 6 vols., 12 mo., Amsterdam. 1764. Goodwood, Large Library, N8.

80 **"historical and chronological deduction":** Anderson (A.), *Historical and Chronological Deduction of the Origin of Commerce*, 2 vols., rebacked, folio, calf. 1764. Goodwood, Large Library, T3.

80 **such as the Abbé Baudeau:** Baudeau (l'Abbé), *Idées d'un Citoyen sur les besoins, les droits . . . des vrais pauvres*. 8vo., calf. Amsterdam. 1765. Goodwood, Large Library, N3.

80 **"no taxation without representation":** James Otis Jr., *The Rights of the British Colonies Asserted and Proved* (Boston: Edes and Gill, 1764).

81 **maximum revenue:** Roberts, 140–41 for the details in this and previous sentence.

81 **"tumults and insurrections":** December 17, 1765, in *Journal of the House of Lords*, vol. 31 (1765–67), *British History Online*.

81 **whom George did not like:** Roberts, 144ff.

81 **"late Indisposition":** April 24, 1765, in in *Journal of the House of Lords*, vol. 31 (1765–67), *British History Online*.

82 **yet another affront from the Duke:** For the details of this episode, see April 1765, 21–30 in *Journal of the House of Lords*, vol. 31 (1765–67). *British History Online* and Roberts, 146.

82 **read the Riot Act:** Ashley, *Bold Defiance: The Spitalfields Silkweavers, London's Luddites?*.

82 **calling in one or another military figure:** King George III to [Lord Halifax?], [? May 1765], Letter No. 72 in George III, *The Correspondence of King George the Third from 1760 to December 1783*, vol. 1, ed. Sir John Fortescue (London: Macmillan and Co., 1927), 105.

82 **Duke of Cumberland, kept:** Walpole, *Memoirs of the Reign of King George the Third*, 168–70.

83 **offered the ambassadorship:** Olson, 14–15, 111–12.

84 **Birdsworth fired Paine:** Myles, *The Rise of Thomas Paine: and The Case of the Officers of Excise*, 18–21.

84 **secure a place as a teacher:** Collected Paine, vol. 1, introduction.

CHAPTER 5. RICHMOND FINDS HIS VOICE

85 **"Centre of Taste, Magnificence":** William Cole, *A Journal of My Journey to Paris, 1765*, ed. Francis Griffin Stokes (London: Constable & Company, 1931), 1.

85 **"exorbitant taxes" . . . "Eatables and Drinkables":** Cole, *A Journal of My Journey to Paris, 1765*, 55.

86 **"fine & stately Parcel of Oaks, Elms":** Cole, *A Journal of My Journey to Paris, 1765*, 44, 37.

86 **"squalid and forlorn":** Cole, *A Journal of My Journey to Paris, 1765*, 47.

86 **"as the Duke of Richmond's Pack of Dogs":** Cole, *A Journal of My Journey to Paris, 1765*, 80.

87 **"nothing could be more settled":** Duke of Richmond to General Henry Conway, October 30, 1765, Richmond Family Private Correspondence, Loan MS 57/104, 500, British Library.

87 **Roy's charge was:** Humphrey Welfare, *General William Roy, 1726–1790: Father of the Ordnance Survey* (Edinburgh: Edinburgh University Press, 2022), 54, 87.

87 **Captain Thomas Jones:** Lieutenant Thomas Jones first appears under Lieutenant Colonel Chas. Duke of Richmond for the 33rd Regiment of Foot in The Army List of 1757, p. 12, British Online Archives.

87 **"one of the most puny, thin":** Cole, *A Journal of My Journey to Paris, 1765*, 54.

88 **He introduced the couple:** Reese, 109.

88 **riding school:** Cole, *A Journal of My Journey to Paris, 1765*, 167.

88 **first pieces of Sèvres porcelain:** Baird, 110–12. See also Ghenete Zelleke, "An Embarrassment of Riches: Fifteen Years of European Decorative Arts Acquisitions," *Museum Studies* 17 (1991), 22–89.

88 **Richmond visited him:** John Almon, *The Correspondence of the Late John Wilkes with His Friends*, vol. 2 (London: Printed for the Editor by R. Phillips, 1805), 219; see also Peter D. G. Thomas, *John Wilkes: A Friend to Liberty* (Oxford: Oxford University Press, 1996).

88 **John Horne Tooke:** Thomas, *John Wilkes: A Friend to Liberty*.

89 **preparing his brother:** Duke of Richmond to General Henry Conway, November 30, 1765, Richmond Family Private Correspondence, Loan MS 57/104, 510, British Library.

89 **"to putt the jetties":** Duke of Richmond to General Henry Conway, December 19, 1765, Richmond Family Private Correspondence, Loan MS 57/104, 517, British Library; Le Duc de Choiseul, French order from Versailles concerning the jetties, January 28, 1766, Richmond Family Private Correspondence, Loan MS 57/104, 551, British Library.

89 **first available fishing boat:** Olson, 15. See also Welfare, *General William Roy, 1726–1790: Father of the Ordnance Survey*.

89 **went down within days:** *Lloyd's List*, no. 3142 (February 25, 1766), in *Lloyd's List 1766–1767*, HathiTrust Digital Library.

89 **"children planted":** House of Commons Debate, Committee of Ways and Means: Resolutions for colonial stamp duties, February 6, 1775, excerpted in National Humanities Center, "Parliamentary Debate on the American Stamp Act (1765)," America in Class, online resource.

90 **"oppressions [that] planted them":** Ibid.

90 **"My brother is just awake":** Lady Sarah Bunbury to Lady Susan O'Brien, March 8, 1766, in Sarah Lennox Letters, vol. 1, 191.

90 **"I think the Duke of Richmond":** Edmund Burke to Arthur Blennerhassett, March 11, 1766, in *The Correspondence of Edmund Burke*, vol. 1, July 1744–June 1768, ed. Thomas W. Copeland (Cambridge: Cambridge University Press, 1958), 262, cited in Olson, 9n4.

90 **"[a]t night many coffee houses":** *London Chronicle*, March 20, 1766.

90 **the cider tax was scrapped:** *London Chronicle*, April 22–24, 1766.

91 **"On the 23rd of April":** Rockingham Letters, vol. 1 (London: Richard Bentley, 1852), 320.

91 **"The sovereignty of the Crown":** Benjamin Franklin, *The Works of Benjamin Franklin*, ed. Jared Sparks, vol. 4 (Boston: Hilliard, Gray, and Company, 1840), 207.

92 **"authority, dignity, and extension":** Rockingham Letters, vol. 2 (London: Richard Bentley, 1852), 46.

93 **"that Duke had neither":** King George III to Earl of Bute [?], July 12, 1766, letter 339 in George III, *Letters from George III to Lord Bute, 1756–1766*, ed. Romney Sedgwick (London: Macmillan, 1939), 251. See also Olson, 16; Rockingham Letters, vol. 2, 334–35; Walpole, *Memoirs of the Reign of King George the Third*, vol. 1, 404ff.

93 **Richmond secured the appointment:** Lande, *The 3rd Duke of Richmond: A Study in Early Canadian History*.

94 **"measures, not men":** Michael C. McGee, " 'Not Men, but Measures: The Origins and Import of an Ideological Principle," *Quarterly Journal of Speech*, 64:2 (1978), 141–54.

94 **"men *and* measures":** Charles Watson-Wentworth, 2nd Marquess of Rockingham, Rockingham to the Earl of Scarborough, November 20, 1766, in Rockingham Letters, vol. 2, 24. See also 3rd Duke of Richmond to Charles Watson-Wentworth, 2nd Marquess of Rockingham, May 23, 1766, printed in Olson, 113.

95 **"Ld. Rockingham bounced":** Memorandum is printed in Alison Gilbert Olson, "The Duke of Richmond's Memorandum, 1–7 July 1766," *English Historical Review* 75, no. 296 (1960), 475–88.

96 **"their King and Country":** *Public Advertiser*, July 12, 1766, 2.

96 **"harmony":** *Public Advertiser*, July 14, 1766, 4.

96 **"The time I enjoyed":** Myles, *The Rise of Thomas Paine: and The Case of the Officers of Excise*, 23.
97 **He continued his teaching:** Collected Paine, vol. 1, intro.
97 **spent time preaching:** Myles, *The Rise of Thomas Paine: and The Case of the Officers of Excise*, 25; Commonplace book of William Wisdom of Glynde (born 1757), PAR 347/7/1/1, Entry for 1767, East Sussex Record Office.
97 **Paine was also writing regularly:** Collected Paine, vol. 1, introduction.
97 **Paine had found his voice:** Ibid.
97 **network included:** Ibid.
98 **Richmond finally answered:** Joseph Parkes and Herman Merivale, *Memoirs of Sir Philip Francis, K.C.B.*, vol. 1 (London: Longmans, Green, and Co., 1867), 119.
99 **kept late hours:** Lady Sarah Bunbury to Lady Susan O'Brien, November 6, 1766, in Sarah Lennox Letters, vol. 1, 202.

CHAPTER 6. THE INVENTION OF JUNIUS

101 **"We have now I think no prospect":** 3rd Duke of Richmond to Duke of Newcastle, August 7, 1767, in Olson, 124–26, quotation on 126.
103 **sixty-one candidates:** Junius Letters, 540.
103 **sixty-two Junius letters:** This counts the sixty-one letters from Junius or a Junius ally to someone else the Cannon edition (Junius Letters), and adds the November 1768 letter.
103 **Scholars have occasionally:** Junius Letters, 555ff; Frank Monaghan, "A New Document on the Identity of 'Junius,'" *The Journal of Modern History* 4, no. 1 (March 1932), 69; Anson, William, ed. *Autobiography and Political Correspondence of Augustus Henry, Third Duke of Grafton, K.G.* London: John Murray, 1898, xxxi.
103 **link between Junius and three:** Junius Letters, 442n2.
104 **three writers were routinely:** Identifications of Atticus authorship have been made by Gary Berton, one of the coeditors of Collected Paine. Numbers of letters are from Appendix 3.B in Junius Letters. Identifications were shared with author by email on December 20, 2024.

misc 32	8/10/1768	Lucius	Francis
misc 35	8/29/1768	Lucius	Paine
misc 37	9/1/1768	Lucius	Paine/Francis
misc 39	9/7/1768	Lucius	Francis
misc 41	9/9/1768	Lucius	Francis
misc 42	9/10/1768	Lucius	Paine/Francis/Tooke
misc 43	9/15/1768	Lucius	Paine
misc 44	9/20/1768	Lucius	Francis
misc 33	8/19/1768	Atticus	Burke
misc 45	10/6/1768	Atticus	Paine
misc 48	10/19/1768	Atticus	Francis
misc 50	10/27/1768	Atticus	Paine

104 **Their essays advanced:** Atticus, *Public Advertiser,* September 19, 1766 (by Burgh), and October 25, 1766 (by Wilkes and William Moore), identifications by Gary Berton, communicated to author by email March 15, 2025; *A Collection of the Letters of Atticus, Lucius, Junius, and Others: With Observations and Notes* (London: Printed for J. Almon, 1769).

106 **"the Arts of Peace":** A.Z., *Public Advertiser,* October 31, 1766.

106 **"I am in no business":** September 20, 1766, "To the Printer," *Gazetteer and London Advertiser,* identification by Gary Berton communicated to author by email, March 15, 2025.

106 **"just and patriotic Reflextion":** Atticus, *Public Advertiser,* October 25, 1766.

106 **crowds broke into bakeries:** *The Annual Register, or a View of the History, Politics, and Literature for the Year 1766* (London: J. Dodsley, 1767), 137–40.

107 **Richmond urged:** Olson, 13.

107 **"Nobility will not be browbeaten":** Quoted in Olson, 30.

107 **two men were required to pledge:** December 6, 1766, in *Journal of the House of Lords,* vol. 31, 1765–67, *British History Online.*

107 **principal speaker:** Olson, 30.

109 **Rockingham found it hard:** On the complicated politics of this period, see Olson, 17–25; Rockingham Letters, vol. 2, 59–63. Thomas, *George III: King and Politicians 1760–1770,* 154–70.

109 **"all in extremes":** 3rd Duke of Richmond to Duke of Newcastle, August 7, 1767, in Olson, 126.

109 **"many signs of uneasiness":** Edmund Burke to the Marquess of Rockingham, Parson's Green, August 18, 1767, in Burke Correspondence, vol. 1, 319. See also Olson 125n4.

109 **"faithful and resolute":** Edmund Burke to the Marquess of Rockingham, ibid.

109 **Meanwhile, in Boston:** Pauline Maier, *From Resistance to Revolution: Colonial Radicals and the Development of American Opposition to Britain, 1765–1776* (New York: Norton, 1991).

109 **boycotts on the importation of British goods:** Massachusetts Historical Society, "Non-Consumption and Non-Importation," in *The Coming of the American Revolution: 1764 to 1776,* accessed July 24, 2025, Massachusetts Historical Society, online resource.

111 **object of attention:** Tillyard, 109. Rumors of lovers, a story of an affair with an actor, and a tale of an assignation in Covent Garden circulated in *Town and Country* and *Covent Garden Journal.*

111 **Benjamin Franklin reported on:** Lande, *The 3rd Duke of Richmond: A Study in Early Canadian History,* 120.

111 **he engaged Burgh and Burke:** The following letters are found in Junius Letters, appendix 3. Author identifications by Gary Berton provided to the author by email on March 24, 2025, are as follows:

Anon to Chatham January 2, 1768 - Burgh, some Burke.
C to Grenville February 6, 1768 - Burke, some Burgh, Francis wrote Introduction as C.
C to Grenville September 3, 1768 - Burke alone.
Anon. to Grenville October 20, 1768 - Burke and Francis.
Junius November 21, 1768 - Francis, a little of Paine.
Junius January 21, 1769 - Junius I - Paine, some Burgh.
Junius February 7, 1769 - Burke alone.
Junius August 22, 1769 - Francis with some Shelburne and Burke.
Junius December 19, 1769 - Burke alone.
Junius to Chatham January 14, 1772 - Burke, some Burgh, Francis.
Junius January 21, 1772 - Burke, Lee, Burgh, Paine.

111 **the letter ended:** Texts of these letters by "C" are available in Junius Letters, ibid.

112 **received his next assignment:** Myles, *The Rise of Thomas Paine: and The Case of the Officers of Excise,* 25.

113 **"It is really an extraordinary event":** Franklin, *The Works of Benjamin Franklin,* ed. Jared Sparks, vol. 7, 400.

113 **A volatile crowd:** Roberts, 185.

114 **tearing down Buckingham Palace:** Roberts, 185.

114 **daily newspaper sales:** Thomas, *George III: King and Politicians 1760–1770,* 17.

114 ***The Sussex Advertiser*:** Myles, *The Rise of Thomas Paine: and The Case of the Officers of Excise*, 54–62.

114 **"Connections among persons":** Thomas, *George III: King and Politicians 1760–1770*, 31.

115 **two of Paine's letters:** On fire escapes, *Sussex Weekly Advertiser*, June 1, 1772; on the poor and poor laws, October 9, 1773. See Brent, "Thirty Something: Thomas Paine at Bull House in Lewes 1768–74—Six Formative Years,", 158.

117 **"Dunkirk remains undemolished":** *A Collection of the Letters of Atticus, Lucius, Junius, and Others: With Observations and Notes* (London: Printed for J. Almon, 1769), 9.

117 **Atticus also warned:** Ibid., 13–14.

118 **Atticus offered a justification:** Ibid., 12.

118 **"the reasonable part":** Ibid.,15.

119 **"I trust I shall be forgiven":** 3rd Duke of Richmond to Marquess of Rockingham, March 10, 1771, in Olson, 131.

119 **"as the beautiful Fatima":** Henry B. Wheatley, *Round About Piccadilly and Pall Mall; or, A Ramble from the Haymarket to Hyde Park: Consisting of a Retrospect of the Various Changes That Have Occurred in the Court End of London* (London: Smith, Elder & Co., 1870), 132.

119 **linking eighteenth-century English radicalism:** Cf. Caroline Robbins, *The Eighteenth-Century Commonwealthman: Studies in the Transmission, Development, and Circumstance of English Liberal Thought from the Restoration of Charles II until the War with the Thirteen Colonies* (Cambridge, MA: Harvard University Press, 1959).

120 **"A Man so injured":** All quotations in the section that follows are from Junius Letters, and can be found in that volume by means of the date of the letter.

121 **opened with a condemnation:** All speech excerpts here are from November 8, 1768, *Journal of the House of Lords*, vol. 32, 1768–70, *British History Online*.

121 **four artists:** All quotations in this paragraph are from Roberts, 188–91.

122 **"You disdain sir":** Ibid.

CHAPTER 7. JUNIUS ROCKS THE MONARCHY AND AMERICA TAKES NOTICE

125 **Of sixty-two letters:** Gary Berton, "Junius Summary," communicated by email to author, December 24, 2024.

125 **more or less lived at Holland House:** Parkes and Merivale, *Memoirs of Sir Philip Francis, K.C.B.*, vol. 1, 12.

125 **ran a school:** Ibid., 4.

125 **classmates included Woodfall:** Ibid., 5.

125 **regurgitate one of his memos:** Ibid., 364.

125 **"You know His under-taking":** Quoted in Helen B. Bates, "Some Notes on Thomas Mante (Alias 'Junius'?)," *Journal of Modern History* 4, no. 2 (June 1932), 233–34. See also Monaghan, "A New Document on the Identity of 'Junius,'", 68–71.

125 **Mante considered Richmond:** Ibid., 232.

126 **"If you receive a letter":** Thomas Mante Richmond, March 13, 1778. Add. MSS, 32, 425 fol. 269, British Library. See also Monaghan, "A New Document on the Identity of 'Junius.'"

126 **"most excellent dish":** Lord Edward Fitzgerald to Emily, Duchess of Leinster, January 19, 1777, letter 24 in *The Letters of Emily, Duchess of Leinster*, vol. 2, ed. Brian FitzGerald (Dublin: Stationery Office, 1949), 19.

126 **an active pamphleteer:** Black, 194, n43.

126 **Duke had deserted him:** Thomas Northcote to John Adams, October 23, 1786, *Founders Online*, National Archives.

126 **"that low, intriguing":** Entry for "James Adair," in *The History of Parliament: The House of Commons 1790–1820*, ed. R. Thorne (London: Boydell and Brewer, 1986).

127 **called foolscap:** "You as a Monarchist chose to work upon *Crown* Paper, and found it profitable; while I work'd upon *Pro-patria* (often indeed call'd *Fools-Cap*) with no less advantage," in "From Benjamin Franklin to William Strahan, 19 August 1784," *Founders Online*, National Archives. [Original source: *The Papers of Benjamin Franklin*, vol. 43, *August 16, 1784, through March 15, 1785*, ed. Ellen R. Cohn (New Haven and London: Yale University Press, 2018), 26–31.] See also "To Ben-

jamin Franklin from Peter Timothy, 8 June 1755," *Founders Online*, National Archives. [Original source: *The Papers of Benjamin Franklin*, vol. 6, *April 1, 1755, through September 30, 1756*, ed. Leonard W. Labaree (New Haven and London: Yale University Press, 1963), 68–69.]

127 **containing his "Creed":** Burke Correspondence, vol. 4, 235–36.

127 **encouraged him to write:** Olson, 161.

127 **nearly four thousand, and even to five thousand:** Junius Letters, xv.

128 **"have been invaded":** Junius Letters, ibid., 25–26.

128 **"minister by accident":** Ibid., 27.

128 **"It may be candid":** Ibid., 28.

128 **They all told the same story:** Hearing on Duke of Grafton's Divorce Bill, March 6, 1769, in *Journals of the House of Lords*, vol. 32 (London: HMSO, 1769), 265–89.

129 **"The right of election":** Junius Letters, Letter 11 (April 24, 1769), 63ff.

130 **nearly three thousand signatures:** Myles, *The Rise of Thomas Paine: and The Case of the Officers of Excise*, passim.

131 **"The same discretion":** Ibid.

131 ***Boston Gazette* printed:** Quoted in Pauline Maier, "John Wilkes and American Disillusionment with Britain," *William and Mary Quarterly* 20, no. 3 (July 1963), 389.

131 **somewhere between one quarter:** Ibid., 390.

131 **197 pieces that year:** Myles, *The Rise of Thomas Paine: and The Case of the Officers of Excise*, 54–62.

131 **"there is no other language":** *South Carolina Gazette*, September 14, 1769; quoted in Maier, "John Wilkes and American Disillusionment with Britain,", 390.

132 **"Sir. I have been out of town":** Junius Letters, private letter no. 11 (November 8, 1769), 356.

132 **"I am now meditating":** Ibid., 359.

132 **new computational analysis:** Email from Gary Berton to author, December 20, 2024. Methodology is described in detail in Collected Paine, vol. 1, intro.

132 **"without the least disguise":** Burke Correspondence, vol. 2, 115.

133 **"It may be a matter of curious SPECULATION":** Junius Letters, letter 35 (December 19, 1769), 159–73.

136 **Woodfall was charged with seditious libel:** Ibid., 362.

136 **snow falling and black frost:** Weather reference is from Lady Louisa Conolly to Emily, Duchess of Leinster, January 7, 1770, in Leinster Correspondence, vol. 3, 72.

136 **"Nothing," wrote Horace Walpole:** Quoted in Junius Letters, 173.

137 **"Finding sedition ascendant":** Samuel Johnson, "Thoughts on the Late Transactions Respecting Falkland's Islands (1771)," quoted in *The Works of Samuel Johnson, LL.D.*, vol. 4 (London: F. C. and J. Rivington, 1825), 315–16.

138 **three dozen servants:** Baird, 130.

138 **purchase of such a seal:** Account Books, Michelmas 1775, Goodwood Mss. 240–41, West Sussex Record Office.

138 **"I now give you my word":** Edmund Burke speech in the House of Commons (November 27, 1770), quoted in *The Parliamentary History of England: Vol. XVI* (Hansard, 1813), columns 1154–55; also quoted in Junius Letters, 539.

139 **regular excise officer:** Moncure Daniel Conway, *The Life of Thomas Paine*, vol. 1 (New York: G. P. Putnam's Sons, 1892), 232.

139 **"anxious to see it":** Samuel Rogers, journal entry, July 15, 1789, in P. W. Clayden, *The Early Life of Samuel Rogers* (London: Smith, Elder & Co., 1887), 94–95.

139 **"extremely tall and handsome":** Fanny Burney, *The Early Journals and Letters of Fanny Burney*, vol. 3, eds. Lars E. Troide and Stewart J. Cooke (Oxford: Clarendon Press, 1994), 429.

140 **"Savil, Richmond, Camden, Rockingham, and Chatham":** Junius, Letter 59 (October 5, 1771), 291ff.

140 **circulated the story:** Collected Paine, vol. 1, intro.

CHAPTER 8. SPEAKER FOR THE OPPOSITION

142 **"the treachery and tyranny":** Arthur Lee, *The Political Detection; or, the Treachery and Tyranny of Administration, Both at Home and Abroad; Displayed in a Series of Letters, Signed Junius Americanus* (London: J. and W. Oliver, 1770).

143 **Richmond led the drafting:** The details and quotations in this paragraph are from William Cobbett, ed., *The Parliamentary History of England from the Norman Conquest in 1066 to the Year 1803*, vol. 16 (London: T. C. Hansard, 1813), 826.

144 **They worked in sync:** This becomes visible when you compare Richmond's contributions in the House of Lords in Cobbett's *Parliamentary History* with the Junius Letters. Compare the protest above, for instance, to Letter 36 from February 14, 1770, where Junius laments that the King had not responded to the petitions of the English nation: "The English people will not tamely submit to this unworthy treatment;— they had a right to be heard." Grafton has rendered the King "contemptible" and members of the government could not be "insensible of its approaching dissolution."

144 **fresh petitions to the King:** Junius Letters, editor's note, 182.

144 **"Now is the crisis":** Junius Letters, private letters, 363-64. Note that Cannon's dating of these letters appears to be off by a week because they were written before the meeting with the King which was on March 14.

145 **elegant edifice:** Thomas Hosmer Shepherd (artist) and John Le Keux (engraver), "Thatched House Club: Society Dinner," in *London Interiors*, published by Joseph Mead, 1841, engraving, 25 × 20 cm, London Picture Archive, record no. 309711.

145 **In attendance were the dukes:** Walter Evelyn Manners, *Some Account of the Military, Political and Social Life of John Manners, Marquis of Granby* (London: Macmillan, 1899), 384. On the weather, see Lady Louisa Conolly to Emily, Duchess of Leinster, March 19, 1770, in *The Correspondence of Emily, Duchess of Leinster (1731–1814)*, vol. 3, ed. Brian FitzGerald (Dublin: Stationery Office for the Irish Manuscripts Commission, 1957), 55.

145 **did not go as expected:** Details from this and preceding paragraph can be found in Thomas, *John Wilkes: A Friend to Liberty*, 109–24.

145 **subjects were "misled":** John Noorthouck, book 1, ch. 25: 1769–1770, 450–85, in *A New History of London Including Westminster and Southwark* (London, 1773), *British History Online.*

145 **John Horne Tooke, published this account:** Recorded in John A. Graham, *Memoirs of John Horne Tooke, together with his valuable speeches and writings: also, containing proofs identifying him as the author of the celebrated letters of Junius* (New York: A. Gould and L. Jacobus, 1828), 157–58. See also Maier, "John Wilkes and American Disillusionment with Britain," 373–95.

146 **"The time is come":** Junius Letters, no. 37 (March 19, 1770), 182–83.

146 **"Their speech is rude, but intelligible":** Junius Letters, no. 38 (April 3, 1770), 193.

146 **"wholehearted cooperation":** Black, 25.

147 **"bod[ies] of men united":** Edmund Burke, *Thoughts on the Present Discontents* (London: J. Dodsley, 1770), 74.

147 **bells pealed across the country:** Details on bell-ringing are from Central Council of Church Bell Ringers, "Oxford Diocesan Guild Combined Annual Reports 1770–1779," available online. The specifics on Lewes are from Brent, "Thirty Something: Thomas Paine at Bull House in Lewes 1768–74—Six Formative Years," 160.

149 **"the state of the British empire":** Cobbett, ed., *The Parliamentary History of England from the Norman Conquest in 1066 to the Year 1803*, vol. 16, 1010–23.

150 **"Secluded from the world":** Junius Letters, no. 39 (May 28, 1770), 193–203.

150 **Five other publishers:** Junius Letters, xvi, n5.

151 **Mansfield declared a mistrial:** Ibid.

151 **"Our language has no term":** Ibid., no. 41 (November 14, 1770), 207, 212.

152 **Richmond also weighed in:** Paine's authorship of this text is identified both by a dedication from the author to the Duke of Richmond in his hand and by Automated Computer Authorship Attribution Methodology applied by Gary Berton. Berton's identification also found Franklin as a significant coauthor and Richmond as a minor author. Sent by email March 17, 2025. On file with author.

152 **attributed to him several years later:** On the pseudonym "Censor-General," see Letter in the *Pennsylvania Journal*, signed "Common Sense," February 3, 1779. In addition, the 1776 Pennsylvania Constitution, in which Paine had a hand in drafting, included a Council of Censors.

152 **Censor-General turned to the subject of Lord Mansfield:** Thomas Paine, *The Juryman's Touchstone* (London: T. Evans, 1771), sec. 7.

154 **wasn't willing to give up:** One version of the story is available in Walpole, *Memoirs of the Reign of King George the Third*, , vol. 4, 179. See also Reese, 183.

155 **"as possibly it might":** Duke of Richmond to King George III, October 21, 1770, Georgian Papers Online.

155 **"Pray do not communicate":** Rockingham Letters, vol. 2, 188–89.

156 **schedule of a party leader:** The House of Lords Journals provide the record of Richmond's attendance there. He reports his private meetings in a letter to Rockingham from February 12, 1771, printed in Olson, 132–45.

157 **"Adieu my Dear Lord":** 3rd Duke of Richmond to Marquess of Rockingham, February 12, 1771, printed in Olson, 132–145.

158 **King was hissed at in the streets:** Roberts, 214–16.

158 **"become as contemptible":** Cobbett, ed., *The Parliamentary History of England from the Norman Conquest in 1066 to the Year 1803*, vol. 17, 214–19.

159 **law established election procedures:** 1771: 11 George 3 c. 55: New Shoreham Election Corruption.

159 **"Farmer Short's Dog Porter":** Thomas Paine, "Farmer Short's Dog Porter: A Tale," *Pennsylvania Magazine*, July 1775, reprinted in *The Writings of Thomas Paine*, ed. Moncure Daniel Conway, vol. 1 (New York: G. P. Putnam's Sons, 1894).

160 **center on Wilkes's causes specifically:** Junius Letters, 253n1.

160 **burned an effigy of Horne Tooke:** "Tooke, John Horne," in *Oxford Dictionary of National Biography*, edited by H. C. G. Matthew and Brian Harrison (Oxford: Oxford University Press, 2004).

161 **Wilkes *had* accepted bribes:** Junius Letters, no. 53 (July 31, 1771), 267.

161 **truly reflect the people's will:** Junius Letters, appendix 2.

161 **approvingly cited Burke's arguments:** Junius Letters, private letter no. 67, Junius to John Wilkes, September 7, 1771, 404–14.

162 **"When a man who stands forth":** Junius Letters, no. 59 (October 5, 1771), 298.

163 **"that really to inform":** Junius Letters, Extract from Letter to John Wilkes, 345.

163 **reported him to be severely ill:** All quotations in this paragraph from Lady Louisa Conolly to Emily, Duchess of Leinster, April 10, 1772, in Leinster Correspondence, vol. 3, 59–61.

164 **bride was Elizabeth Ollive:** All details and quotations in this paragraph are from Brent, "Thirty Something: Thomas Paine at Bull House in Lewes 1768–74—Six Formative Years," 154–56.

164 **After their nearly two years of commercial partnership:** All details and quotations in this paragraph are from Brent, ibid.

165 **Lee, the printer of *The Sussex Advertiser*:** Myles, *The Rise of Thomas Paine: and The Case of the Officers of Excise*, passim.

165 **From this poverty, he argued:** Ibid.

165 **applied for a job:** Myles, *The Rise of Thomas Paine: and The Case of the Officers of Excise*; Brent, "Thirty Something: Thomas Paine at Bull House in Lewes 1768–74—Six Formative Years." On the job application at the Society of Arts, this detail is in the minutes of the Society of Arts, now called the Royal Society of Arts, from 1773. Unfortunately, these archives were closed to visitors at the point that this detail came to my attention. Other scholars report: "After a bit of hunting I managed to find the reference. It was in Dr Allan's review in the RSA Journal for January of 1974 of Audrey William's biography of Paine. It was actually for the post of Register and there was a Thomas Paine who competed unsuccessfully on 4th February 1773 with seven others for the position." Susan Bennett and Paul Myles, email communication of December 7, 2024, on file with author.

CHAPTER 9. ROMANCE AND A BRIEF RESPITE FROM RADICALISM

173 **"Dr. Price presents his compliments":** Goodwood, Small Library, Q5, Price (Richard), *Observations on Reversionary Payments, . . . Annuities, etc.*) 8 vol., calf. 1773.

173 **"Though it is right to have":** Edmund Burke to Duke of Richmond, Nov. 17, 1772, Burke Correspondence, vol. 2, 374. Junius had made a similar observation about another politician: "Struck

with the principal figure, we do not sufficiently mark in what manner the canvass is filled up." Junius Letters, 30 (Oct. 17, 1769), 143.

173 **when he opened Parliament:** *Journal of the House of Lords*, vol. 33, 1770–73, *British History Online*.

174 **worked to organize networks of activists:** For a general overview of his work on the East India Company, see Olson, 38–40; Reese, 167–71.

174 **Francis was put out:** Joseph Parkes, *Memoirs of Sir Philip Francis, K.C.B.: With Correspondence and Journals*, ed. Herman Merivale, vol. 1 (London: Longmans, Green, and Company, 1867), 367–68.

174 **"the Triumphs or Amusements":** Ibid., 364.

174 **Stephen Popham, a Wilkes supporter:** As Wilkes supporter, see Walpole, *Memoirs of the Reign of King George the Third*, vol. 4, 409.

174 **Richmond presented a divorce bill:** May 1774, 1–10, in *Journal of the House of Lords* vol. 34, 1774–1776 (London, 1767–1830), *British History Online*.

174 **The two men worked together:** James Adair was in the Bill of Rights Society and a regular correspondent of Richmond. See for instance a letter from the 3rd Duke of Richmond to James Adair concerning the East India Company business of December 1, 1773, in Olson, *The Radical Duke: The Career and Correspondence of Charles Lennox, Third Duke of Richmond, 1735–1806* 159ff.

175 **"that System of Government":** The Duke of Richmond to Marquess of Rockingham, September 10, 1773, in Olson, 155.

175 **"over-fatigued" if he went out hunting:** Lady Louisa Conolly to Emily, Duchess of Leinster, January 21, 1773, in Leinster Correspondence, vol. 3 (Dublin: Irish Manuscripts Commission, 1949), 66.

176 **His racehorses were exercised:** Baird, passim.

176 **"tall and full of dignity":** Quoted in Roberts, 229.

176 **"I hope he [the Duke] will":** Lady Mary Coke, *The Letters and Journals of Lady Mary Coke*, ed. James Archibald Home, vol. 4 (Edinburgh: David Douglas, 1889), 187.

177 **"showed blackness":** George III to Lord North, June 12, 1773, Corr. Geor III ii 504, quoted in Olson, 4.

177 **"Madame de Cambis":** Lady Ailesbury to Horace Walpole, Paris, November 23, 1774, in *The Yale Edition of Horace Walpole's Correspondence*, vol. 39, 218.

178 **"very ridiculous":** Lady Sarah Lennox to Lady Susan O'Brien, November 20, 1777, in Sarah Lennox Letters, vol 1, 260. See also Lady Sarah Lennox to Emily, Dowager Duchess of Leinster, January 2, 1777, in Leinster Correspondence. Edited by Brian FitzGerald, vol. 2, 213.

178 **"I am afraid poor Mary":** Edward Gibbon to Horace Walpole, June 16, 1777, quoted in Baird, 116. More generally, Baird, offers the most complete account of Richmond's romantic liaisons.

178 **"As to my brother's flirting":** Lady Louisa Conolly to Emily, Dowager Duchess of Leinster, August 23, 1776, in *Correspondence of Emily, Duchess of Leinster (1731–1814)*, ed. Brian FitzGerald, vol. 3 (Dublin: Irish Manuscripts Commission, 1957), 216.

179 **"that it was *his* child":** Ibid., 222.

179 **"fort affligé":** Madame du Deffand to Horace Walpole, August 26, 1776, in *The Yale Edition of Horace Walpole's Correspondence*, ed. W. S. Lewis et al., vol. 6, 352.

180 **in accord with the naturalistic principles:** On Emily's relationship to Ogilvie, see Tillyard, 215–23, 266–94.

180 **married in October 1774:** Ibid.

181 **hired a tutor for him:** Baird, 129.

182 **supervision of the family tutor:** Emily, Duchess of Leinster, Leinster Correspondence, vol. 2, x, 236, 264, 283; vol. 3, p. 235, 276–80.

182 **"My brother is as earnest":** Lady Sarah Lennox to Lady Susan O'Brien, August 17, 1778, in Sarah Lennox Letters, vol. 1, 274.

182 **"We have had most heavenly":** Lady Louisa Conolly to Emily, Dowager Duchess of Leinster, April 6, 1778, in Emily, Duchess of Leinster, *Correspondence of Emily, Duchess of Leinster*, 38, 43.

182 **"Captain Jones' little girl,":** For instance, Sarah Lennox to Emily, Dowager Duchess of Leinster, July 13, 1778, in Leinster Correspondence, vol. 2, 234.

182 **amid family portraits:** D. Jacques, *A Visit to Goodwood: Near Chichester, the Seat of His Grace the Duke of Richmond, with an Appendix Descriptive of an Ancient Painting* (Chichester: Published by the author, North Street; and by Messrs. Lackington, Hughes & Co., London; printed by W. Mason, 1822), 37, 41. On Henriette, see generally Baird, 117–18, though Baird, does accept the received view that Henriette was Richmond's natural daughter.

182 **Henriette was not Richmond's natural daughter:** The sources for this assessment are the letters of Madame du Deffand to Horace Walpole (especially April 22, 1772, through December 19, 1773) in *The Yale Edition of Horace Walpole's Correspondence*, ed. W. S. Lewis, vols. 4 and 5; Biron, A. de Gontaut, Rutherford, G., Scott-Moncrieff, C. K. (Charles Kenneth) (1928). *Memoirs of the Duc de Lauzun* (New York: Brentano's., 27–31; and Maugras, G. (1895), *Le duc de Lauzun et la cour de Marie-Antoinette.* 5. éd. (Paris: Plon-Nourrit et cie, 121).

183 **"so easy and all *right* for me":** Lady Louisa Conolly to Emily, Dowager Duchess of Leinster, April 6, 1778, in Leinster Correspondence, vol. 2, 266.

183 **she asked Emily to pass:** Lady Louisa Conolly to Emily, Dowager Duchess of Leinster, April 21, 1778, in Leinster Correspondence, vol. 2, 274.

184 **"renew his acquaintance":** Edmund Burke to Walker King, April 4, 1774, Morgan Library collection, Record ID 372812, Accession number MA 693.4 See also Bertelsen, Lance, "Richmond's Rhetoric and Chatham's Collapse: A Media History," *Eighteenth-Century Life* 36, no. 3 (2012), 16, quoting Edmund Burke to Walker King, April 4, 1774, in *The Correspondence of Edmund Burke*, ed. Thomas W. Copeland, et al., vol. 2, 525 (Cambridge: Cambridge University, 1958–78).

184 **"Such an acquaintance":** Ibid.

184 **They "never feel thoroughly":** Morgan Library, series of letters from Edmund Burke to Walker King, June 21, 1774, MA 693.5; August 29, 177[?] MA 693.7; September 15, 1774 MA 0693.

CHAPTER 10. FRIEND OF AMERICA, FRIEND OF REFORM

187 **correspondence with Burke and Rockingham trailed off:** For a good overview of the changes in Richmond's patterns of correspondence with Burke and Rockingham, and of his generally increasing distance from them, see Olson, 31–47.

188 **When Gage landed:** The details in this paragraph come from Roberts, 231–32.

189 **always deferring to the King:** Ibid.

189 **Scholars have recently identified:** Collected Paine.

190 **"as containing the soundest":** Cobbett, ed., *The Parliamentary History of England from the Norman Conquest in 1066 to the Year 1803*, vol. 17, 1350–53. Both the pamphlet and the sermon are bound in the same volume of tracts housed at Y3 in the Small Library. The catalog entry misattributes Considerations to Matthew Robinson, Lord Rokeby.

190 **did not take this defeat:** Duke of Richmond to Marquess of Rockingham, June 12, 1780, in Rockingham Letters, vol. 1, 419–20.

190 **Richmond worried that the bill:** Cobbett, ed., *The Parliamentary History of England from the Norman Conquest in 1066 to the Year 1803*, vol. 17, 1350–53.

191 **"I really think":** Lady Louisa Conolly to Emily, Dowager Duchess of Leinster, June 12, 1776, in Leinster Correspondence, vol. 3, 205.

191 **"splendid reputation":** Edmund Burke to Duke of Richmond, September 26, 1774, Burke Correspondence, vol. 3, 40.

191 **"the studied and expensive Respect":** John Adams to Abigail Adams, September 18 , 1774, *Founders Online,* National Archives. [Original source: *The Adams Papers*, Adams Family Correspondence, vol. 1, *December 1761—May 1776*, ed. Lyman H. Butterfield (Cambridge, MA: Harvard University Press, 1963), 158–59.]

191 **thirty-four toasts were drunk:** *Dunlap's Pennsylvania Packet or, the General Advertiser* (Philadelphia), September 19, 1774.

192 **"high-flown ideas of right":** Lady Sarah Lennox to Emily, Dowager Duchess of Leinster, January 20, 1775, in Leinster Correspondence, vol. 2, 144.

192 **he was harassed:** Roberts, 239.

192 **The Quebec Act, Richmond argued:** Cobbett, ed., *The Parliamentary History of England from the Norman Conquest in 1066 to the Year 1803*, vol. 18, 655–76.

193 **"The more I live":** Duke of Richmond to Edmund Burke, September 26, 1774, in Burke Correspondence, vol. 3, 37.

194 **"Your birth will not suffer":** Edmund Burke to Duke of Richmond, September 26, 1774, Burke Correspondence, vol. 3, 38ff.

195 **"exhort[ed] the King":** Cobbett, ed., *The Parliamentary History of England from the Norman Conquest in 1066 to the Year 1803*, vol. 18, 36–37.

195 **"I think the Americans are a rebellious":** *The Diary and Letters of His Excellency Thomas Hutchinson*, ed. P. O. Hutchinson (2 vols., London, 1886), vol. 1, 316–37.

195 **buying military supplies:** Roberts, 255.

195 **Burke spent a sleepless:** Edmund Burke to Marquess of Rockingham, January 24, 1775, Burke Correspondence, vol. 3, 107.

196 **"the whole dominion":** "Franklin's Notes for a Conversation with Lord Chatham," January 31, 1775, *Founders Online,* National Archives. [Original source: *The Papers of Benjamin Franklin,* vol. 21, *January 1, 1774, through March 22, 1775*, ed. William B. Willcox (New Haven and London: Yale University Press, 1978), 459–62.]

197 **"the desperate temerity":** Duke of Richmond to Earl of Chatham, February 1, 1775; Olson, 45.

197 **"a Ballad offered by a drunken Porter":** Benjamin Franklin to Charles Thomson, February 5, 1775, *Founders Online,* National Archives. [Original source: *The Papers of Benjamin Franklin,* vol. 21, *January 1, 1774, through March 22, 1775*, ed. William B. Willcox (New Haven and London: Yale University Press, 1978), 475–79.]

198 **Richmond passionately:** Cobbett, ed., *The Parliamentary History of England from the Norman Conquest in 1066 to the Year 1803*, vol. 18, 265–98.

200 **"Senate appointed ambassadors":** G. Stahlberg, *History of the Late Revolution in Sweden*, 1772. 8 vo., calf. Edinburgh. 1776 in Goodwood, Small Library, Q6.

200 **"particular friends":** Rev. John Romney, *Memoirs of the Life and Works of George Romney . . . also some particulars of the life of Peter Romney, his Brother*, 1830, 135; see also 72–73.

202 **News of the rout at Bunker Hill:** Roberts, 268.

202 **Privy Council published:** Ibid., 275.

203 **"[i]n 1780, the government payroll":** Ibid., 374.

203 **"The anxiety of his mind":** Quoted in ibid., 335.

204 **at the center of decision-making:** Cobbett, ed., *The Parliamentary History of England from the Norman Conquest in 1066 to the Year 1803*, vol. 18, 895–936.

205 **He warned that trade embargoes:** Cobbett, ed., *The Parliamentary History of England from the Norman Conquest in 1066 to the Year 1803*, vol. 18, 1073–4, 1076.

205 **"at different times disputed with everyone":** Quoted in Roberts, 287.

205 **personal to-do list:** John Adams, diary, 25: 6–7, [February?] 1776, Adams Family Papers, Massachusetts Historical Society.

206 **renewed gossip about Sarah:** Lady Louisa Conolly to Emily Ogilvie, April 23, 1776, in Leinster Correspondence, vol. 3, 197–98.

206 **"sensible and attentive":** Lady Louisa Conolly to Emily Ogilvie, May 17, 1776, in Leinster Correspondence, vol. 3, 201.

206 **"much to his taste":** quoted in Baird, 116; Madame du Deffand to Horace Walpole, Paris, June 18, 1776, in *The Yale Edition of Horace Walpole's Correspondence*, ed. W. S. Lewis, vol. 7 (New Haven: Yale University Press, 1939), 331.

206 **"Love, you know":** Lady Sarah Lennox to Emily Ogilvie, January 22, 1777, in Leinster Correspondence, vol. 2, 213.

207: **"Who knows that":** Ibid., Duke of Richmond to Edmund Burke, August 26, 1776, in Edmund Burke, *The Works and Correspondence of Edmund Burke*, vol. 1 (London: F. & J. Rivington, 1852), Kindle edition, Location 6662–6697.

207 **"What these fundamental maxims":** Ibid., Location 6662.

208 **One of the serving dishes:** Ibid.

CHAPTER 11. A TOTAL CHANGE OF SYSTEM

210 **"the strongest Hopes":** *Journal of the House of Lords*, vol. *35, 1776–1779* (London, 1767–1830), *British History Online.*

210 **"the most deplorable Calamities":** Cobbett, ed., *The Parliamentary History of England from the Norman Conquest in 1066 to the Year 1803*, vol. 18, 1368–95.

212 **began to circulate:** Olson, 53.

212 **"care not that [their country]":** Ibid.

213 **"the offensive page":** John Cartwright and Frances Dorothy Cartwright, *The Life and Correspondence of Major Cartwright*, vol. 1 (London: H. Colburn, 1826), 99.

213 **"obliged to consult the good":** Duke of Richmond to Marquess of Rockingham, September 10, 1773, printed in Olson, 155.

213 **"peculiar view":** Reese, 142.

214 **with Sharp:** Prince Hoare, *Memoirs of Granville Sharp, Esq.*, vol. 1 (London: Henry Colburn, 1828), 264, 291.

215 **"extreme degeneracy":** Cobbett, ed., *The Parliamentary History of England from the Norman Conquest in 1066 to the Year 1803*, vol. 18, 1368–95.

216 **Duchess Mary stayed home:** Baird, 117.

216 **led to rumors:** Lady Sarah Lennox to Lady Susan O'Brien, November 20, 1777, in Sarah Lennox Letters, vol. 1, 260.

217 **way of the French:** All details in this paragraph are from Baird, 116.

217 **"Give the ministers no respite":** This and subsequent quotations from Horace Walpole to Richmond, October 27, 1775, in *The Yale Edition of Horace Walpole's Correspondence*, vol. 41, ed. W. S. Lewis (New Haven, CT: Yale University Press, 1981), 310–17.

217 **"England will not much":** Duke of Richmond to Edmund Burke, June 16, 1775, in Burke Correspondence, vol. 3, 170.

219 **Washington cunningly sent Burgoyne:** For details in this paragraph, Roberts, 327.

219 **"I am not much pleased":** Lady Sarah Lennox to Lady Susan O'Brien, November 20, 1777, in Sarah Lennox Letters, vol. 1, 259.

219 **"America *cannot*":** Lady Sarah Lennox to Lady Susan O'Brien, April 21, 1779, in Sarah Lennox Letters, vol. 1, 295.

219 **"The sincere wish":** Cobbett, ed., *The Parliamentary History of England from the Norman Conquest in 1066 to the Year 1803*, vol. 19, 472–85.

220 **"fell into agonies":** Roberts, 328.

220 **"unleashed a furore":** Roberts, 328.

220 **summers of 1776 and 1777:** Details in this paragraph are from Baird, passim.

221 **sustained series of victories:** February 6–11, 1778, in Cobbett, ed., *The Parliamentary History of England from the Norman Conquest in 1066 to the Year 1803*, vol. 19, 708–18.

222 **starting to crack:** Cobbett, ed., *The Parliamentary History of England from the Norman Conquest in 1066 to the Year 1803*, vol. 19, 745–58.

222 **"called upon some of the King's servants":** Cobbett, ed., *The Parliamentary History of England from the Norman Conquest in 1066 to the Year 1803*, vol. 19, 834–67.

222 **Richmond was skeptical:** Ibid.

223 **objected to the language in the Declaration:** Ibid.

223 **"It has been the government's object":** Ibid., 839–42.

224 **became the first member:** Cobbett, ed., *The Parliamentary History of England from the Norman Conquest in 1066 to the Year 1803*, vol. 19, 914–26.

224 **"to procure an accommodation":** Hoare, *Memoirs of Granville Sharp, Esq.*, 180.

225 **"fell back upon his seat":** Quoted in Roberts, 345.

226 **Shelburne had come round:** Olson, 46.

228 **letting the French get away:** Ibid., 355.

228 **"The Year 1779":** Roberts, 366.

228 **"My dear brother":** Lady Sarah Lennox to Lady Susan O'Brien, July 30, 1778, in Sarah Lennox Letters, vol. 1, 266–69.

229 **"a total destroyer":** Lady Sarah Lennox to Emily, Dowager Duchess of Leinster, July 13, 1783, in Leinster Correspondence, vol. 2, 233.

229 **single most annotated book:** *Addresses from the Court of Common Council to the King (on the City of London.)* 8 vo., calf. 1770. Goodwood, Small Library X3. (The date on the catalog entry captures only the date of the first document in the volume. The final document is dated 1778.)

232 **laid down its foundational principles:** His pamphleteer, James Burgh, and intellectual partner, John Cartwright, had been working on the same puzzle. Burgh, in *Political Disquisitions* (1775), had proposed suffrage for all tax-paying men, and divided the British population into equally sized groups of householders.

233 **"what they call spasms":** Lady Sarah Lennox to Emily, Dowager Duchess of Leinster, December 15, 1778, in Sarah Lennox Letters, vol. 2, 126.

233 **"No system was proposed":** Duke of Richmond to Charles James Fox, February 7, 1779, Add. Mss. 47568, fols. 71–75, British Library.

234 **"His noble friend [Shelburne]":** Cobbett, ed., *The Parliamentary History of England from the Norman Conquest in 1066 to the Year 1803*, vol. 20, 635–57.

234 **"total change of that system":** Cobbett, ed., *The Parliamentary History of England from the Norman Conquest in 1066 to the Year 1803*, vol. 20, 876–95.

CHAPTER 12. A BRITISH LAFAYETTE

236 **"cannot be looked upon as Commands":** Resolutions "in a meeting of the High Sheriff, Grand Jury Lord Lieutenant and other Lords and Gentleman of the County of Sussex, assembled at the Assizes held at Lewes on Friday the 30th Day of July 1779," ESRO reference: SAS/A741/2-15, Doc 4, East Sussex Record Office.

236 **"I have had the honour":** General Amherst to Duke of Richmond, August 5, 1779, ESRO reference: SAS/A741/2-15, Doc 8, East Sussex Record Office.

236 **"What may be the intentions":** John Robinson to Lord Pelham, August 24, 1779, ESRO reference: SAS/A741/2-15, Doc 12, East Sussex Record Office.

237 **Richmond was empowered:** Minutes from a meeting of the subscribers for carrying out execution of the plan for raising twenty-four volunteer companies associate of the Defense of the County of Sussex held at the White Hart Inn at Lewes on Friday Nov. 19, 1779, ESRO reference: SAS/A741/2-15, Doc 15, East Sussex Record Office.

238 **"There is such a million":** On the details of the Duke's departure, Lady Sarah Lennox to Lady Susan O'Brien, August 27, 1779, Sarah Lennox Letters, vol. 1, 300. On the broader military details, see Roberts, 366.

239 **"founded on unyielding opposition":** The magazine clipping is housed in the Richmond family papers and is quoted in Reese, 165.

239 **"fairest of any I know":** F. D. Cartwright, *The Life and Correspondence of Major Cartwright* (London: Henry Colburn, 1826), 128–29.

239 **"I have constantly":** Ibid.

241 **"leave it in the possession":** This quote and all those above from Walker King are from Walker King to Edmund Burke, Burke Correspondence, vol. 4, 165–68.

242 **monthly meeting:** Black, 36–37.

242 **Rockingham moved a defiant Amendment:** *Journal of the House of Lords*, vol. 36, *1779–1783* (London, 1767–1830), *British History Online*.

243 **He planned to use:** Black, 33.

244 **two issues were intimately connected:** Black, 37.

244 **"general indignation":** A letter of December 7, 1779, quoted in Edmond George Petty-Fitzmaurice, *Life of William, Earl of Shelburne, Afterwards First Marquess of Lansdowne*, vol. 2 (London: Macmillan, 1912), 46.

245 **one hundred more:** Black, 40–42.

246 **The resolution also added:** Ibid., 43–45.

246 **spread the reform message like wildfire:** Ibid., 46.

247 **Crown registered the growing movement:** Ibid., 48.

247 **Richmond paid for advertisements:** Documents from General Meeting for the County, 1780–1783, ESRO reference: L/C/X/1/1, East Sussex Record Office.

248 **The Sussex gentlemen printed:** "General Meeting 20 Jan 1780," ESRO reference: L/C/X/1/1; Committee Meeting, ESRO reference: L/1/8/1/2, East Sussex Record Office. See also Fanny Burney, journal entry for May 25, 1780, in *The Early Journals and Letters of Fanny Burney: The Streatham Years, Part II, 1780–1781*, ed. Betty Rizzo (Oxford: Clarendon Press; Kingston and Montreal: McGill-Queen's University Press, 2003).

249 **"a plan of association":** This quotation and the details in the preceding paragraph are from the Resolution taken at the February 24th meeting, which is reported in Documents from General Meeting for the County, 1780–1783, ESRO reference: L/C/X/1/1, East Sussex Record Office.

249 **Richmond had good reason:** Black, 46–61.

250 **Westminster Committee formally recommended:** *Report of the Sub-Committee of Westminster, Appointed April 12, 1780, to Take into Consideration All Such Matters, Relative to the Election of Members of Parliament, as May Promote the Purposes of the Present Association* (London: Society for Constitutional Information, 1780).

251 **"One would think":** John Adams to the President of the Congress, No. 10, February 27, 1780, *Founders Online*, National Archives.

213 **As one scholar has put it:** Black.

253 **"to find a safe harbor":** Quoted in Black, 148.

254 **"run all hazards with him":** Black, 154.

254 **a week of rioting:** Good accounts of the Gordon Riots can be found in both Black and Roberts.

254 **"a hardened criminal element":** Ibid., 162.

255 **"evident loss of their own liberty":** Duke of Richmond to Marquess of Rockingham, June 12, 1780, Rockingham Memoirs, vol. 2, 420.

256 **100-pound rewards:** Black, 167.

256 **"noxious Humours":** Quoted in ibid.

CHAPTER 13. RECONCILIATION WITH THE KING

263 **"the main object of all their government":** Duke of Richmond to Earl of Shelburne, June 16, 1780, quoted in Petty-Fitzmaurice, *Life of William, Earl of Shelburne, Afterwards First Marquess of Lansdowne*, vol. 2, 57–58.

263 **branded both men as:** Petty-Fitzmaurice, *Life of William, Earl of Shelburne, Afterwards First Marquess of Lansdowne*, vol. 2, 66–67.

264 **He drove out from London:** Olson, 181.

265 **"the smallest Inclination":** Duke of Richmond to Marquess of Rockingham, July 11, 1780, in Olson, 181ff.

266 **"My Belief":** Ibid.

266 **saving monthly:** Roberts, 387.

268 **Any member could attend:** On the society, see Black, 174–212.

269 **"a radical reform":** *The Trial of John Horne Tooke for High Treason: At the Sessions House in the Old Bailey, on Monday the Seventeenth . . . [through] Saturday the Twenty-second of November, 1794*, vol. 2 (London: M. Gurney, 1795), 239.

269 **"had had many conversations":** Ibid., 392; Black, 175.

269 **an additional ten thousand:** Black, 182, 183n17.

269 **annual meeting:** Olson, 187, editorial note.

270 **younger generation of reformers:** Ibid.

270 **neither Rockingham nor Shelburne:** Petty-Fitzmaurice, *Life of William, Earl of Shelburne, Afterwards First Marquess of Lansdowne*, vol. 2, 66–67.

270 **"Every Day produces":** Duke Richmond to Lord Mahon, March 12, 1781, in Olson, 187–88.

270 **"split into miserable":** Duke of Richmond to Marquess of Rockingham, January 18, 1781, in Rockingham Memoirs, vol. 2, 429.

270 **Gordon might be guilty:** Thomas Erskine, *Mr. Erskine's Speech at the Trial of Lord George Gordon, in the Court of King's Bench, On Monday, February 5, 1781* (London: Printed for J. Stockdale, 1781).

271 **speech arguing for the moderate electoral:** Roberts, 426.

271 **Parliamentary reform was fizzling:** Black, 167.
271 **advocating for better treatment of American prisoners:** Olson, 65.
272 **Paine solicited Richmond's assistance:** Edmund Jenings to John Adams, November 28, 1781, *Founders Online,* National Archives; Isaac Collins to John Adams, March 1782, *Founders Online,* National Archives.
273 **six mutinies:** Roberts, 392.
273 **marrying a veteran:** The story of Sarah Lennox's marriage to George Napier is told in many places, including Tillyard and Baird.
274 **"made me like this world":** Quoted in Tillyard, 300.
274 **"This is my birthday":** Lady Sarah Napier to Lady Susan O'Brien, February 25, 1783, Sarah Lennox Letters, vol. 2, 32.
275 **the permanence of his principles:** Roberts, 400.
275 **regretted that his "assiduous endeavours":** November 27, 1781, *Journal of the House of Lords,* vol. 27, *1746–1752* (London, 1767–1830), *British History Online.*
275 **"Our losses have been singularly calamitous":** Parliamentary Debate, December 11, 1781, Hansard's Parliamentary History, vol. 22, col. 1094.
275 **"I cannot put on the face":** Horace Walpole to Horace Mann, November 29, 1781; see also Walpole to Mann, November 26, 1781. Both in *The Yale Edition of Horace Walpole's Correspondence,* ed. W. S. Lewis et al., vol. 9, 210, 208.
276 **consequences of Yorktown unfolded:** Roberts, passim.
277 **he found the demands "so strange"::** Roberts, 409–10.
277 **"His Majesty, during the twenty years":** Ibid.
278 **any disinclination to serve:** Duke of Richmond to Marquess of Rockingham, April 19, 1782, in Rockingham Memoirs, vol. 2, 467.
279 **King was "civil":** G. Selwyn to Lord Carlilse, 28 March 1782, H.M.C. Carlisle, 608–9.
280 **already hard at work:** *Public Advertiser,* April 2, 1782.
281 **raised wages to drive out tips:** Olson, 74.
281 **didn't want those:** Edmund Jenings to John Adams, March 31, 1782, *Founders Online,* National Archives.
282 **"most indefatigable Man":** *Public Advertiser,* April 3, 1782.
282 **"many persons of high rank":** Roberts, 421.
282 **corral people into shared strategy:** John M. Norris, *Shelburne and Reform* (London: Macmillan, 1963), 163; Rockingham Memoirs, vol. 2, 481; Charles James Fox, *The Correspondence of Charles James Fox,* vol. 1, ed. George Otto Trevelyan (London: Richard Bentley and Son, 1883), 344.
283 **"My Dear Lord":** Rockingham Memoirs, vol. 2, 481.
236 **Richmond called a meeting:** Charles Lennox, *A Letter from His Grace the Duke of Richmond to Lieutenant Colonel Sharman, Chairman of the Committee of Correspondence Appointed by the Delegates of Forty-five Corps of Volunteers Assembled at Lisburn in Ireland: With Notes by a Member of the Society for Constitutional Information* (London: J. Johnson, 1792), 6. Black, 84, but Black gets the date wrong by two days.
283 **"The Quintuple Alliance":** Black, 85.
284 **Pitt kept the minutes:** Black, 84.
284 **"*neither the liberty*":** Lennox, *A Letter from His Grace the Duke of Richmond to Lieutenant Colonel Sharman, Chairman of the Committee of Correspondence Appointed by the Delegates of Forty-five Corps of Volunteers Assembled at Lisburn in Ireland: With Notes by a Member of the Society for Constitutional Information,* 6. Emphasis in the original.
285 **"*so general* an illness":** Lady Sarah Napier to Lady Susan O'Brien, May 29, 1782, Sarah Lennox Letters, vol. 2, 16.
286 **persistently advocating:** Olson, 68.
287 **"extreme unpopularity":** Fox, *The Correspondence of Charles James Fox,* vol. 1, 344.
287 **"its utter impracticability":** Charles James Fox to Lord Holland, Dec. 12, 1804, in Charles James Fox, *Memorials and Correspondence of Charles James Fox,* vol. 4, ed. Lord John Russell (London: Richard Bentley, 1853), 66.

288 **"that where your Grace leads":** John Cartwright, *The Life and Correspondence of Major Cartwright*, ed. Frances Dorothy Cartwright, vol. 1 (London: H. Colburn, 1826), 142.

289 **"I intreated both":** Fox, *Memorials and Correspondence of Charles James Fox*, ed. John Russell, vol. 1, 346.

289 **"so pressed and stung":** Lord Carlisle to Lord Gower, July 8, 1782, Historical Manuscripts Commission, *The Manuscripts of the Earl of Carlisle, Preserved at Castle Howard*, 4th Report, vol. 1 (London: Her Majesty's Stationery Office, 1874), 632.

289 **life-size white marble statue:** Coutu, *Then and Now: Collecting and Classicism in Eighteenth-Century England*, 49.

290 **"To-morrow it is expected":** Duke Richmond to Lord George Lennox, July 8, 1782, Historical Manuscripts Commission, *The Manuscripts of the Earl Bathurst, Preserved at Cirencester Park* (London: Her Majesty's Stationery Office, 1923), 698–99.

290 **"concerted Measure":** Edmund Jenings to John Adams, July 24, 1782, *Founders Online*, National Archives.

290 **"great principles" of the Shelburne ministry:** Cobbett, ed., *The Parliamentary History of England from the Norman Conquest in 1066 to the Year 1803*, vol. 23, 152–201.

CHAPTER 14. RICHMOND SAVES THE KING

292 **Richmond would have been largely pleased:** Olson, 192–95.

292 **Shelburne passed:** For the letter to Shelburne, Thomas Paine, *A Letter to the Earl of Shelburne, Now Marquis of Lansdowne, on His Speech, July 10, 1782, Respecting the Acknowledgement of American Independence* (Dublin: Printed for G. Burnet, P. Byrne, P. Wogan, W. Sleater, A. Grueber [and others], 1791), 1. The pamphlet is inscribed "Office for Foreign Affairs" on the title page and is housed at Goodwood in a bound volume of tracts catalogued as "Thomas Paine, *Letter to the Abbé Raynal on the Affairs of North America. Philadelphia,* (with) Stennet (S.) 1782; *Sermon on Death of John Howard*, 1790; and another (theological). In one volume, 8 vo., quarter calf. 1782–90, Goodwood, Large Library, K10.

292 **"one man in Administration":** Edmond Fitzmaurice, *The Life of William, Earl of Shelburne: From His Birth in 1737 to His Death in 1805*, vol. 2 (London: Macmillan, 1876), 224.

292 **Richmond refused to help:** Tillyard, 303–4, 324–26.

293 **could not get the Prime Minister's attention:** Olson, 70, 72, 192–93.

293 **work closely with the Society:** Black, 102, 186, 196.

293 **"a bird of his own feather":** Jeremy Bentham to Jeremiah Bentham, October 5, 1782, in *Electronic Enlightenment Scholarly Edition of Correspondence*, ed. Robert McNamee et al. (University of Oxford).

293 **the White Hart in Lewes in January:** "General Meeting 20 Jan 1780," ESRO Reference L/C/X/1/1, East Sussex Record Office. Despite the title, this file records the proceedings of several meetings January 20, 1780; April 13, 1780; and January 18, 1783.

294 **ten thousand copies of Cartwright's:** Black, 192.

294 **expressed exasperation:** Lady Sarah Napier to Lady Susan O'Brien, March 25, 1783, in Sarah Lennox Letters, vol. 2, 33.

294 **"As to the chaos":** Lady Sarah Napier to Lady Susan O'Brien, February 19, 1783, in Sarah Lennox Letters, vol. 2, 28–31.

295 **appears to have weighed:** Roberts, 434–41.

295 **hoped to win 400,000 pounds:** Olson, 74.

296 **Parliament voted Richmond's budget:** Olson, 74.

296 **"the power to prevent":** Duke of Richmond, to Bishop of Exeter, February 25, 1783, in Olson, 195–97.

297 **conditioned the offer:** Roberts, 451.

297 **"frisk for a month":** Lady Sarah Napier to Lady Susan O'Brien, July 4, 1783, in Sarah Lennox Letters, vol. 2, 36–37.

297 **"to consider further regulations":** June 3, 1783, in *Journal of the House of Lords Volume 36, 1779–1783* (London, 1767–1830), *British History Online*. See also Olson, 197.

297 **fell even further short:** Roberts, 447; Black, 105–7.

299 **letter to Scotch reformers:** Richmond's and Wyvill's answers were published in the *Scots Magazine*, 46 (December 1784), 696.
299 **still only partway to Richmond's goal:** Black, 210.
300 **endorse Quaker petitions:** Ibid., 200.
301 **paper glumly predicted:** *London Chronicle*, December 18, 1783–December 20, 1783, issue: 4234, 8.
301 **undertook desperate measures:** Roberts, 458–63.
302 **"last, mad thing":** *London Chronicle*, December 18, 1783–December 20, 1783, issue: 4234, 8.
302 **Richmond's strong standing:** Olson, 71.
302 **more contested seats:** Roberts, 469.
302 **worked to bring the Quintuple Alliance radicals:** Black, 113–14.
303 **elected a president of the Society for Constitutional Information:** Ibid., 186.
303 **"there was no man in his dominions":** Charles James Fox, *Memorials and Correspondence of Charles James Fox*, ed. John Russell, vol. 1 (London: Richard Bentley, 1853), 351.
303 **"the fullest support of the people":** Duke of Richmond to Duke of Rutland, April 25, 1784, quoted in Black, 117.

CHAPTER 15. HURRICANE SEASON

307 **"all go *harum-scarum*":** Lord Edward Fitzgerald to William Ogilvie, June 20, 1786, in Leinster Correspondence, vol. 2, ed. Brian FitzGerald (Dublin: Irish University Press, 1972), 47.
307 **sponsored the first hot-air balloon trials:** James Glenie, *A Reply to the Answer to A Short Essay on the Modes of Defence Best Adapted to the Situation and Circumstances of This Island, &c. In a Letter to His Grace the Duke of Richmond* (London: G. G. and J. Robinson, 1794), 127. The text was originally published by another publisher in 1785.
307 **technical improvements in firearms:** Reese, 204.
307 **born the Ordnance Survey:** Reese, 197; Baird, 87; also Welfare, *General William Roy, 1726–1790: Father of the Ordnance Survey*, 54, 87.
309 **Pitt also planned:** Reese, 188.
309 **"only member of cabinet":** Olson, 79.
310 **"his support 'for the legal prerogative of the Crown'":** Roberts, 468.
310 **"reverence the constitution":** From the debate on Mr. Flood's parliamentary reform motion (March 4, 1790), quoted in Sean Lang, *Parliamentary Reform 1785–1928* (London: Routledge, 1999), 19.
311 **rejected in May:** Details in this paragraph are from Black, 121–22.
311 **"keeping government cheap":** Black, 129.
311 **Toryism was born:** P. Kelly, "British Parliamentary Politics, 1784–1786," *Historical Journal* 17, no. 4 (1974), 733–53.
312 **assisted in its first publication:** The book in question is a collection of revolutionary era pamphlets that reflect the core principles of Paine and his network of associates. The first pamphlet, ostensibly by Demophilus, is called *The Genuine Principles of the Ancient Saxon, or English Constitution.* It is likely to have been a collaborative work in which Paine may have had a hand. The book was published by Robert Bell, publisher of *Common Sense.* For a full account of it, and of Paine's role in the assemblage of the book, see Collected Paine, introduction. In addition to the Declaration, the other pamphlets included an updated edition of *Common Sense* with new appendices; Paine's *Considerations on the Measures Carrying on with respect to the British Colonies in North America*; Cartwright's *American Independence the Interest and Glory of Great Britain; containing Arguments which prove, that not only in Taxation, but in Trade, Manufactures, and Government, the Colonies are entitled to an entire Independency of the British Legislature*; Richard Price, *Observations on the Nature of Civil Liberty, the Principles of Government, and the Justice and Policy of the War with America. To which is added, An Appendix, containing, A State of the National Debt*; and Joseph Tucker, *The True Interest of Britain, set forth in Regard to the Colonies; and the only Means of Living in Peace and Harmony with them. . . . To which is Added by the Printer, A few more Words, on the Freedom of the Press in America.*

John Dunlap published his broadside of the Declaration on July 5. *The Pennsylvania Evening Post* published an unauthorized version on July 6. Both Dunlap's newspaper printing and

Bell's printing came out on July 8. Given punctuation (a long dash after happiness) in the Bell that follows Dunlap, it would appear that Bell was working from the Dunlap broadside produced at the request of Congress on July 4 and 5. This suggests close proximity for the publishing team to the congressional process around the Declaration. Certainly, the Bell team was among the first to have access to the text outside of Congress.

313 **he revealed some secret:** On this point, and the other biographical details in this and subsequent paragraphs, see Collected Paine, vol. 1, intro.

313 **renewal of the bank's charter:** On March 7, 1787, Paine writes his final piece on the Bank of North America; on March 17, 1787, passage of its charter is secured. See Alfred Owen Aldridge, "Why Did Thomas Paine Write on the Bank?" *Proceedings of the American Philosophical Society* 93, no. 4 (1949), 309–15.

314 **copies of the Declaration:** Allen and Sneff, "Golden Letters: James Wilson, the Declaration of Independence, and the Sussex Declaration,", 193–230.

315 **wrote a letter to the Marquess of Lansdowne:** Collected Paine, vol. 2, part 1.

315 **Burke invited Paine:** This account of Paine's activities for his bridge project is drawn from Armytage, "Thomas Paine and the Walkers: An Early Episode in Anglo-American Cooperation,", 16–30. The political details about the individuals he connected with are drawn from Black.

315 **listed as "the author of *Common Sense*":** Black, 208.

315 **attended on December 4:** For Paine, Armytage, "Thomas Paine and the Walkers: An Early Episode in Anglo-American Cooperation,", 16–30. For Richmond, *Journal of the House of Lords*, vol. 38, 1787–1790 (London, 1767–1830), *British History Online.*

316 **cricket club made Paine:** John Keane, *Tom Paine: A Political Life* (London: Bloomsbury, 2007), 604–5, n. 117.

318 **Something had happened:** As John Bidwell ("Sources of the Sussex Declaration," 2025) puts it about the folded-up parchment, "If it was owned by Richmond, then it must have fallen out of favor in a bad way to end up in that ignominious condition." Exactly!

319 **"Spit on such Patriotism":** Thomas Paine to Thomas Walker, Esqr. February 26, 1789, in Collected Paine, vol. 4.

319 **Critics of Richmond:** Olson, 65.

319 **King's insanity:** Thomas Paine to Thomas Jefferson, February 26, 1789, in Collected Paine. See also Keane, *Tom Paine: A Political Life*, 287.

319 **House of Lords had to go:** Thomas Paine to Thomas Jefferson, February 26, 1789, in Collected Paine, vol. 4.

319 **worked aggressively with Pitt:** Olson, 77–79, 99, 211.

322 **to maintain order:** A. J. Ayer, *Thomas Paine* (New York: Athenaeum, 1988), 75.

322 **Also with them:** Kirsty Carpenter, *Refugees of the French Revolution: Émigrés in London, 1789–1802* (New York: St. Martin's Press, 1999), 19.

323 **"more like an hospital":** Ibid.

323 **an annuity:** Baird, 141.

323 **visited the Opposition bookseller:** Paine to [Jefferson?] London, April 16, 1790, in Collected Paine, vol. 4.

323 **"Have I the pleasure":** Ibid.

323 **dinner with two radicals:** Ibid.

324 **"My friend Paine":** Edward Fitzgerald to Emily Ogilvie, December 15, 1791, in Leinster Correspondence, vol. 2, 62.

324 **planned to attend an anniversary celebration:** Ayer, *Thomas Paine*, 114.

324 **refused admittance to the dinner guests:** Ibid.

324 **society took the occasion:** Ibid.

325 **Paine had described himself:** Keane, *Tom Paine: A Political Life*, 284.

325 **"the Duke of Richmond, Dr Price":** John Adams to James Madison, 17 June 1817, *Founders Online,* National Archives.

325 **Paine named only one example:** Thomas Paine, *Rights of Man*, Part I (1792), chap. 4, in *The Rights of Man and Other Political Writings*, ed. Mark Philp (Oxford: Oxford University Press, 1995), 69n.

325 **"maintain two thousand poor":** Ibid., ch. 5, p. 106.

325 **"iniquitously and wantonly applied":** Ibid., ch. 5, p. 135.

326 **"band of parasites":** Ibid., ch. 4, p. 69.

326 **"outworks to protect the citadel":** Ibid.

326 **"Humanity dictates":** Ibid., 69n.

326 **"no personal dislike":** Ibid.

327 **disappointed to learn:** Ayer, *Thomas Paine*, 116.

327 **painted Paine's portrait:** Romney had seen Paine at a dinner, which led to the project. He made note of the dinner engagement in his sitter's book, although mistakenly recording the dinner as taking place on July 4. Paine was still in Paris on that date but did host a dinner in London on July 14, 1791, to celebrate Bastille Day. My thanks to Alex Kidson for that detail, and for details about Romney's relationship to Richmond. Kidson confirms that Romney was a sloppy recorder of dates. See also Humphry Ward and W. Roberts, *George Romney: A Biographical and Critical Essay* (London: Thomas Agnew and Sons, 1904), 126.

328 **his books circulated widely:** Black, 227–30.

328 **200,000 copies:** Ayer, *Thomas Paine*, 116.

328 **refuse the gift:** Black, 230.

328 **in June republished:** Other societies also followed suit. For instance, Charles Lennox, Duke of Richmond, *A Letter from His Grace the Duke of Richmond to Lieutenant Colonel Sharman, Chairman of the Committee of the Volunteers of Ireland. With Notes by a Member of the Society for Constitutional Information* (Sheffield: Sheffield Constitutional Society, 1792).

329 **"repairing our house":** MP Charles Grey in Parliament, 1793, quoted in Sean Lang, *Parliamentary Reform 1785–1928* (Questions and Analysis in History) (London: Taylor and Francis, 2005), 21.

329 **agitate reform:** Cobbett, ed., *The Parliamentary History of England from the Norman Conquest in 1066 to the Year 1803*, vol. 29, 1522.

329 **"It was impossible":** Sean Lang, *Parliamentary Reform 1785–1928* (Questions and Analysis in History) (London: Taylor and Francis, 2005), 21. See also Linda Colley, *Britons: Forging the Nation, 1707–1837* (New Haven, CT: Yale University Press, 1992), 248–50.

330 **Lauderdale was obliged:** Cobbett, ed., *The Parliamentary History of England from the Norman Conquest in 1066 to the Year 1803*, vol. 29, 1518.

330 **Paine advised the destruction:** Ibid., 1522.

330 **"called for by the people":** Ibid., 1521.

331 **"Tom Paine, a sower":** quoted in H. T. Dickson, "Tom Paine and His Critic," *Enlightenment and Dissent* 27 (2011), 52.

332 **he implored them:** Thomas Paine, "to the SHERIFF OF THE COUNTY OF SUSSEX or, the gentleman who shall preside at the meeting to be held at Lewes, July 4," in *The Writings of Thomas Paine, Collected and Edited by Moncure Daniel Conway* (New York: G.P. Putnam's Sons, 1894). Vol. 3. Also in Collected Paine, vol. 2.

333 **as lord lieutenant:** Paine addressed the role of lord lieutenants and of the Duke of Richmond specifically in *The Address to the Addressors*, a published response to the Surrey County meeting. Quoting the lord lieutenant of Surrey he wrote: " 'I do not come here,' said Onslow, at the Surrey County meeting, 'as the Lord Lieutenant and Custos Rotulorum of the county, but I come here as a plain country gentleman.' The fact is, that he came there as what he was, and as no other, and consequently he came as one of the beings I have been describing. If it be the character of a gentleman to be fed by the public, as a pauper is by the parish, Onslow has a fair claim to the title; and the same description will suit the Duke of Richmond, who led the Address at the Sussex meeting. He also may set up for a gentleman." Collected Paine, vol. 2.

333 **Paine's friends—hissed:** *Sussex Weekly Advertiser*, 9 July 1792; see also Frank O'Gorman, "The Paine Burnings of 1792–1793." *Past & Present*, no. 193 (2006), 111–55.

333 **an address of thanks to the King:** Also, on the King's proclamation, see W. A. Speck, *A Political Biography of Thomas Paine* (Routledge, 2013), 118.

334 **"dead man":** Ayer, *Thomas Paine*, 116.

334 **condemned to the guillotine:** Ayer, *Thomas Paine* , 130.

CHAPTER 16. WITNESS FOR THE DEFENSE

337 **settled the Duchesse in a home:** Baird, 141–42.
337 **"demanding the immediate":** Roberts, 548.
337 **circle of Paine supporters:** Thomas Clio Rickman, quoted in Ayer, *Thomas Paine*, 126.
338 **"Edward Fitzgerald has acted a romance":** Lady Sarah Napier to Lady Susan O'Brien, January 6, 1793, in Sarah Lennox Letters, vol. 2, 90.
338 **dressed in mourning:** Roberts, 552.
338 **Eddy was his translator:** Ayer, *Thomas Paine*, 118. For Fitzgerald reference, John Epps, *The Life of John Walker, M.D.* (London: Whittaker, Treacher, and Co., 1831), 140–41.
338 **to invite French forces:** Reese, 228.
338 **"a strong inclination":** Lady Sarah Napier to Lady Susan O'Brien, February 25, 1793, in Sarah Lennox Letters, vol. 2, 92.
338 **duty to answer their call:** Add. Mss. 30990, British Library.
339 **refuge at Goodwood:** Tillyard, 109, passim.
339 **justified in more absenteeism:** Olson, 77, 93, 214–21.
339 **Richmond's only true home:** For the details in this paragraph, Baird, 136–42.
340 **"ministers [who] have sacrificed":** Olson, 97.
341 **family doctor advised:** Lady Louisa Conolly to Emily, Dowager Duchess of Leinster, April 12, 1794, in Leinster Correspondence, vol. 3, 422–23.
341 **"family affection":** Lady Sarah Napier to Lady Susan O'Brien, July 30, 1792, in Sarah Lennox Letters, vol. 2, 83–86.
341 **political dynamic reversed course:** Black, 228.
342 **the lower-middle and working-class populace:** Black, 225–26; on corresponding societies generally, see Roberts, 545–76.
342 **a thousand people:** Black, 226.
342 **"a public clamour":** Roberts, 545.
342 **the government interpreted this as a sign:** Ibid.
342 **famously whipping a dagger:** Black, 167 and 167n45.
342 **local chapters in every region:** Ibid., 237.
343 **"a great Body of the People":** Black, 252–56, 289–92.
344 **beautifully simple defense:** *The Trial of John Horne Tooke, on a Charge of High Treason: Containing the Whole of the Proceedings of Each Day at the Old-Bailey, Including the Examinations of Lord Camden, Duke of Richmond, Lord Fred. Campbell . . . &c. &c., with Chief Justice Eyre's Charge, and Mr. Tooke's Address to the Jury* (London: Printed for Allen and West, 1794).
344 **"The progress of Jacobinism":** William Fox, *On Jacobinism* (London, 1794), 16. See also William Fox, *A Defence of the War Against France* (London, 1794), 8.
344 **"It was the abuses pointed out":** Harold M. Wheeler, *Lord Erskine's Defence of Thomas Paine: On the Occasion of His [1792] Trial at Guildhall, London, for a Libel Upon the Constitution* (London: T. Fisher Unwin, 1900), 182.
344 **"adhered strictly to":** *The Trial of John Horne Tooke, on a Charge of High Treason* (London: Printed for Allen and West, 1794), 221.
345 **"Never":** Ibid., 247–48.
345 **eight minutes:** Nancy E. Johnson, "Fashioning the Legal Subject: Narratives from the London Treason Trials of 1794," *Eighteenth-Century Fiction* 21, no. 3 (Spring 2009), 422.
346 **proposing to resume:** Duke of Richmond to William Pitt, December 15, 1794, in *Report on the Manuscripts of the Earl Bathurst, Preserved at Cirencester Park*, Historical Manuscripts Commission, vol. 76 (London: His Majesty's Stationery Office, 1923), 706.
346 **"I see that your resuming":** William Pitt to Duke of Richmond, January 26, 1795, in *Report on the Manuscripts of the Earl Bathurst, Preserved at Cirencester Park*, Historical Manuscripts Commission, vol. 76 (London: His Majesty's Stationery Office, 1923), 711.
347 **"in the most shuffling manner":** Duke of Richmond to Charles Lennox, June 6, 1804, in Olson, 221–25.
348 **"I do want some":** Baird, 143.

348 **"inward consciousness":** Lady Sarah Napier to Emily, Dowager Duchess of Leinster, January 20, 1775, Stoke, in Leinster Correspondence, vol. 2, 144–45.

348 **"more steady":** Walpole to Lady Ossory, November 13, 1796, in *The Yale Edition of Horace Walpole's Correspondence*, ed. W. S. Lewis et al., vol. 34, 221–22.

349 **folded into the extended family:** Baird, 143–44, 153–55.

349 **perpetual motion machine:** Description inspired by Linda Colley's description of Cartwright in *Britons: Forging the Nation, 1707–1837* (New Haven, CT: Yale University Press, 1992), 499.

349 **"one in whom the knowledge":** John Cartwright, *England's Aegis: or, The Military Energies of the Constitution* (London: J. Johnson, 1806), 119.

350 **"attachment to the constitution":** Cartwright, *The Life and Correspondence of Major Cartwright*, vol. 2, 320.

350 **sold the family's coal duty back:** Olson, 3 and 3n1; Reese, 233–35.

351 **"Indeed unattainable as perfect Happiness":** Untitled Memo [Thoughts on Representation], 1804, Goodwood Mss. 1622, West Sussex Record Office.

352 **ambition only leads:** Duke of Richmond to Charles Lennox, June 5, 1806, Goodwood Mss. 224, West Sussex Record Office.

353 **"private and inexpensive manner":** Quoted in Reese, 256. Other details also from this source.

353 **"limited mental abilities":** Olson, 64.

354 **"to march side by side":** Cartwright, *The Life and Correspondence of Major Cartwright*, vol. 2, 121–22.

LIST OF ILLUSTRATIONS

Photographic acknowledgements are found in parentheses.

INDEX

Page numbers in italics indicate figures.

ABOUT THE AUTHOR

Danielle Allen is James Bryant Conant University Professor at Harvard University and Director of the Allen Lab for Democracy Renovation at Harvard's Kennedy School. She is the author most recently of *Justice by Means of Democracy* and publishes *The Renovator* substack.